Korean

2nd Edition

by EunYoung Won and Jeongyi Lee, PhD

A Wiley Brand

Korean For Dummies®, 2nd Edition

Published by: **John Wiley & Sons, Inc.**, 111 River Street, Hoboken, NJ 07030-5774, www.wiley.com

Copyright © 2025 by John Wiley & Sons, Inc. All rights reserved, including rights for text and data mining and training of artificial technologies or similar technologies.

Media and software compilation copyright © 2025 by John Wiley & Sons, Inc. All rights reserved, including rights for text and data mining and training of artificial technologies or similar technologies.

Published simultaneously in Canada

For general information on our other products and services, please contact our Customer Care Department within the U.S. at 877-762-2974, outside the U.S. at 317-572-3993, or fax 317-572-4002. For technical support, please visit https://hub.wiley.com/community/support/dummies.

Wiley publishes in a variety of print and electronic formats and by print-on-demand. Some material included with standard print versions of this book may not be included in e-books or in print-on-demand. If this book refers to media that is not included in the version you purchased, you may download this material at http://booksupport.wiley.com. For more information about Wiley products, visit www.wiley.com.

Library of Congress Control Number: 2024946903

ISBN 978-1-119-93273-4 (pbk); ISBN 978-1-119-93274-1 (ebk); ISBN 978-1-119-93275-8 (ebk)

SKY10086551_100224

Korean

for dummies®
A Wiley Brand

Contents at a Glance

Table of Contents

Introduction

Acquiring a new language is so much more than memorizing words and phrases. It's like stepping into a whole new mindset and wrapping your arms around the wide, wonderful world of diversity. There's this famous quote that nails it: "Learning a new language is like gaining a new soul." This idea comes to life as you immerse yourself in the culture and daily life of a place.

Now imagine yourself wandering Korea's vibrant streets, chatting with locals, ordering tasty dishes in Korean, and expressing your appreciation to the chefs. You're swapping your map app for real-life interactions, asking for what you need with words instead of pointing. These little moments? They're just some of the things that make you feel connected with the culture around you. And you don't even have to travel to start your journey. Korean culture is as accessible as downloading a language exchange app or finding a local community. Every effort to speak in the language is golden for meaningful friendships that endure.

Guess what? You might already have a head start with Korean. Ever used a Korean smartphone, driven a Korean car, or binged on a Korean drama series? Maybe savored Korean cuisine, jammed to K-pop, or indulged in their skincare? If not, that's perfectly okay! Whether you're eyeing a trip, aiming to study, planning to clinch business deals in Korea, or simply snagged this book from sheer curiosity, *Korean For Dummies* is a crash course in the Korean language and culture.

This book is brimming with cultural gems and savvy tips to help you nail the basics of Korean. So, ready to jumpstart this adventure with us? As Koreans cheer, 화이팅! (hwah-ee-teeng!), which means "Go for it! You've got this! Good luck!" (Literally, "fighting.") Let's dive in and make it unforgettable!

About This Book

Good news! This isn't an old-school language textbook loaded with mind-boggling grammar rules. It's a reference guide designed to help you to converse in Korean with little effort. Packed with phrases for real-life situations like shopping, dining out, or making reservations, it also offers cultural insights to deepen your grasp of the language. You're the captain of your learning ship! Pick any chapter that interests you, and off you go! You can even read the chapters backward — no judgment here!

Each chapter's got the lowdown: background info, words and phrases, grammar tips, and dialogue that's spot-on for the theme. Here's what you'll find in each chapter:

>> **Talkin' the Talk dialogue:** Engage in conversations that offers context with Korean phrases, pronunciation, and translations. Don't forget to check out the audio versions on our website (www.dummies.com/go/Korean). Spot the Play icon? Tune in and join the fun!

>> **Words to Know:** Mastering vocab is key when learning a new language. Keep an eye out for our vocab boxes where you find words and phrases from the Talkin' the Talk dialogues.

>> **Fun & Games:** Finished a chapter? Time for some brain teasers! Don't worry; the exercises cover the essentials of the topic and are not overly challenging at all. The answers are in Appendix C, ready to give you a high-five for a job well done.

Foolish Assumptions

To write this book, we imagined what our potential readers are like. Here are a few foolish assumptions that we made about you. Do these descriptions sound like you?

>> You don't know much Korean aside from a phrase or two you picked up from a movie or elsewhere.

>> You're not planning to take a proficiency test any time soon, nor are you trying to start translating literature or interpreting. You just want to be able to communicate basic information in Korean and gain familiarity with Korean culture.

>> You don't want to wake up in a cold sweat after memorizing tables upon tables of grammatical rules and conjugations.

>> You want to have fun while learning Korean at the same time.

Icons Used in This Book

Here are some icons that draw attention to important information:

TIP

This icon indicates a go-to spot for some tidbits that highlight linguistic aspects or cultural tips. These little tidbits can be super helpful, helping you save time and avoid frustration.

REMEMBER

This icon appears when you come across important info that is repeated and should be remembered.

CULTURAL WISDOM

These snippets provide a sneak peek into a wide range of Korean culture and give you valuable insights.

GRAMMATICALLY SPEAKING

This icon flags instances where we go a little more in-depth about grammar rules.

PLAY

The online audio files give you a chance to listen to native speakers of Korean reading the Talkin' the Talk dialogue. This icon marks the "Talkin' the Talk" sections available online at www.dummies.com/go/Korean.

Notes on the Korean Romanization

Because Korean has its own script, romanization is provided for our readers who don't know Korean. There're different romanization systems used in Korea, and each has its own strengths and shortcomings. For this book, we crafted a new system that demonstrates as accurately as possible how Korean is pronounced, considering the needs of readers who are familiar with American English. Here's our system of romanization for Korean: (Visit our website to listen to audio files for each vowel and consonant sound.)

Vowels

ㅏ	ㅑ	ㅓ	ㅕ	ㅗ	ㅛ	ㅜ	ㅠ	ㅡ	ㅣ	ㅢ
ah	yah	uh	yuh	oh	yoh	oo	yoo	eu	ee	eui

ㅐ	ㅔ	ㅒ	ㅖ	ㅚ	ㅙ	ㅞ	ㅘ	ㅝ	ㅟ
ae	eh	yae	yeh	wae	wae	weh	wah	wuh	wee

Vowels grouped together in a box have merged into the same sounds in modern Korean.

Consonants

	ㄱ	ㄴ	ㄷ	ㄹ	ㅁ	ㅂ	ㅅ	ㅇ	ㅈ	ㅊ
At start of syllable	g	n	d	r	m	b	s/sh	silent	j	ch
At end of syllable	k	n	t	l	m	p	t	ng	t	t

	ㅋ	ㅌ	ㅍ	ㅎ	ㄲ	ㄸ	ㅃ	ㅆ	ㅉ
At start of syllable	k	t	p	h	kk	tt	pp	ss	jj
At end of syllable	k	t	p	t	k			t	

The consonants ㄸ, ㅃ, and ㅉ are not used as final consonants. The consonant chart shows sounds at syllable ends that are not released, meaning they are not followed by another syllable (for example, 국 [gook], 밥 [bahp]).

Exploring this chart, you'll notice some intriguing aspects of our romanization approach:

>> The letter "h" is added to some vowels to aid English speakers with pronunciation (for example, "ㅏ" is romanized as "ah" to resemble the sound in "father"). Accordingly, 삼성 (Samsung), for instance, is romanized as "sahm-suhng," to prevent confusion with the varying sounds of "a" in English, like in *Sam, same, narrate*, and *mall*. Remember, the "h" is silent.

>> We don't differentiate long or short vowels. The vowel "ㅣ" is romanized as "ee," not "i," to avoid the multiple sounds that "i" can represent in English, like in *sit* versus *site*.

>> Although vowels like ㅐ (ae) and ㅔ (eh), as well as ㅒ (yae) and ㅖ (yeh) merge into the same sounds in contemporary Korean, they are still romanized differently to reflect their distinct spellings. For example, the Korean words

for "dog" and "crab" are homophones, which means they sound alike but have different spellings; "dog" uses ㅐ, and "crab" uses ㅔ.

>> Our romanization focuses on the actual pronunciation of words or phrases, not a direct letter-by-letter transcription. For instance, 한국어 (Korean Language) is romanized as "hahn-goo-guh," not "hahn-gook-uh," illustrating Korean's liaison where sounds blend smoothly, similar to the English phrase "an apple" where the "n" connects with the vowel sound at the start of "apple."

For a deeper dive into pronunciation rules and tips, check out Chapter 2, and also explore our Cheat Sheet, detailed in the following section.

Beyond the Book

In addition to what you're reading right now, this product also comes with a free, access-anywhere Cheat Sheet. To get this Cheat Sheet, simply go to www.dummies.com and type **Korean For Dummies Cheat Sheet** in the Search box. And as mentioned earlier, you can find the audio files for a selection of "Talkin' the Talk" dialogues at www.dummies.com/go/Korean.

Where to Go from Here

Now that you've got a good grasp of the layout of *Korean For Dummies*, 2nd Edition, you're ready to embark on your Korean learning journey from any chapter of the book. Simply glance at the Table of Contents, choose a topic that catches your eye, flip to that chapter, and start honing your Korean skills!

Not sure where to begin? You can start from Chapter 1 and work your way through sequentially. Or, jump right into Chapter 2 to uncover the magic of Hangeul, the Korean alphabet. It's like unlocking the key to a hidden garden of language proficiency, and once unlocked, you're on your way to mastering Korean!

Curious about Korean grammar intricacies? Chapter 3 is your sidekick, ready to unravel the mysteries. Think of us as your expert navigator, guiding you through the grammar maze with ease.

But if you're itching to start conversing in Korean pronto, feel free to skip ahead to your favorite section and find a treasure trove of handy phrases. This book is designed to turn you into a Korean conversational wizard faster than you might expect.

Planning a trip to Korea? Consider this book your travel companion, your ticket to a linguistic adventure! With us by your side, you'll be chatting up locals and ordering bibimbap like a pro, along with so many more, in no time. Bon voyage! Enjoy your journey into the Korean language and culture! 화이팅!

1
Getting Started with Korean

IN THIS CHAPTER

» Introducing the Korean alphabet

» Looking at grammar in a new perspective

» Getting started with useful words and expressions

» Putting Korean to use in common social situations

» Taking Korean on the road

Chapter **1**

Korean in a Nutshell

Welcome to the exciting world of *Korean For Dummies*! Whether you're a die-hard fan of K-pop and K-dramas or completely new to Korean culture, you're now taking the first step towards acquiring a new 언어 (uh-nuh) (*language*). Learning a 외국어 (wae-goo-guh) (*foreign language*) is intellectually challenging, but the rewards it brings are boundless. It unlocks pathways to forging new connections with people, cultures, and communities in ways you've never imagined. As you delve deeper into the language, you'll uncover the intricate relationship between language and culture, further enhancing your understanding and appreciation of both.

In this "nutshell" chapter, we offer you a sneak peek into what lies ahead in the rest of this book. Prepare to immerse yourself in the beauty of 한국어 (hahn-goo-guh) (*Korean language*) and 문화 (moon-hwah) (*culture*). So, ready to dive in and give it your all? Let's go!

Unraveling the Depths of Korean

When first dipping your toes into the Korean language, it's a good idea to start by familiarizing yourself with 한글 (hahn-geul) (*Hangeul*), the Korean alphabet, and its pronunciation. Understanding grammar is another crucial part when learning any 외국어 (wae-goo-guh) (*foreign language*). Along with these fundamentals, you'll also enjoy learning a selection of simple yet engaging Korean phrases that you can begin using immediately.

Discovering Korean script and sounds

Ever wondered how 한국어 (hahn-goo-guh) (*Korean language*) and 영어 (yuhng-uh) (*English*) share a similarity in their script? Just like English, 한글 (hahn-geul) (*Hangeul*), the Korean alphabet, notates both vowels and consonants. With 40 letters in total, 21 represent 모음 (moh-eum) (*vowels*) and 19 stand for 자음 (jah-eum) (*consonants*), each with a direct 1:1 sound match. Learning 한글 is a wise first step if you want to learn 한국어 quickly. It will open doors to a wealth of information, accelerating your journey to fluency.

For those curious about the nitty-gritty details, Chapter 2 awaits. There, we meticulously introduce each letter and its sound, unveiling the art behind constructing the syllable blocks that form words.

Getting a grip on basic grammar

문법 (moon-ppuhp) (*grammar*) is often thought of as a "glue" that holds words together. The order in which you "glue" your words together can create sentences with totally different meanings.

A BRIEF JOURNEY TO HANGEUL HISTORY

한글 (hahn-geul) (*Hangeul*), the Korean alphabet, was developed in 1443 by King 세종 (seh-johng) (*Sejong*), who is revered as Korea's most respected king, pretty much an icon in Korean history. His motivation behind creating 한글 was to devise a written system that the commoners could easily master.

한글 stands out globally as one of the rare languages with its creation story on record — who made it, for whom, why, and how. Pretty unique! Fast forward to today, 한글 is basically the backbone of all written communication in Korea, boosting the country to one of the top spots for literacy worldwide. Thanks to King 세종, 한글 has woven itself into the fabric of Korean culture and identity, becoming something people hold dear every single day. (For more on the story behind 한글, check out Chapter 2.)

Korean 문법 is *different* (not *difficult*, mind you) from English. Most distinctively, word order is different. The natural order of an English sentence is subject–verb–object, and, unlike Korean, English is much stricter in the word order. For example, in the popular TV drama "Friends," Rachel and Ross argued about who was the "dump-er" and who was the "dump-ee" in their breakup. To them, the sentences "Ross dumped Rachel" and "Rachel dumped Ross" would each garner a very different response, even though all we did was switch two words. As another example, think about the sentence "The dog bit the thief" versus "The thief bit the dog." The order of the words makes a big difference in the meaning of each sentence.

However, even if you switch places for Rachel and Ross, or the dog and the thief, in these sentences, the meaning can still remain the same in Korean. "Impossible!" you may think. But it *is* possible, thanks to a small tag-like element called a "particle" that marks the grammatical role of the words in the sentence. The concept of grammar particles may be new to you, but don't let the new parts of Korean grammar intimidate you.

For more details and an introduction to simple Korean grammar, from the basic parts of speech to how to form sentences, read Chapter 3.

Starting a simple conversation

When meeting someone new, your conversation becomes much more engaging and welcoming if you can greet them in their language. Here are a few of the easiest and shortest phrases:

» 네 (neh) (*Yes*)

» 아니요 (ah-nee-yoh) (*No*)

» 안녕하세요 (ahn-nyuhng-hah-seh-yoh) (*Hello*)

» 고맙습니다 (goh-mahp-sseum-nee-dah) (*Thank you*)

» 저기요 (juh-gee-yoh) (*Excuse me; hey*) This is an attention getter. Use it when you need to catch someone's eye, like in a restaurant to call over the waiter, when a passerby drops their wallet in front of you, or even when someone cuts in line.

Chapter 4 shows numerous basic Korean expressions that enable you to start speaking Korean immediately (and politely).

Counting in Korean

숫자 (soot-jjah) (*numbers*) are everywhere in life. Countless activities involve numbers — telling 시간 (shee-gahn) (*time*) and 나이 (nah-ee) (*age*), counting 돈 (dohn) (*money*), calculating 가격 (gah-gyuhk) (*price*), discussing 가족 (gah-johk) (*family*), and countless more.

Korean has two 숫자 sets of cardinal numbers: native-Korean and Sino-Korean. Native Korean numbers are used for counting "how many," and Sino numbers are used for other purposes, like money, math, and labeling. Don't be intimidated by 숫자! With the guidance in Chapter 5, you'll get a handle on numbers in Korean and will be up to speed on all these tasks.

Speaking Korean around the house

집 (jeep) (*house*) is where most of your days begin and end, making it crucial to know the words used around your 집. As you move through your 집 or enter a 방 (bahng) (*room*), try to recall the Korean words for various areas, such as 거실 (guh-sheel) (*living room*), 부엌 (boo-uhk) (*kitchen*), or 화장실 (hwah-jahng-sheel) (*restroom*).

Chapter 6 acquaints you with homey words for common rooms, household items, and regular everyday activities you do at home such as eating, drinking, sleeping, and doing chores that are essential for daily life at home.

Using Korean in Social Scenarios

Learning a 외국어 (wae-goo-guh) (*foreign language*) is all about connecting with people and communities outside of your comfort zone. Part 2 comes in handy in a lot of life scenarios: making small talk with new acquaintances; handling banking and payment, eating out, acquainting yourself with the diverse array of 한국 음식 (hahn-gook eum-sheek) (*Korean foods*), mastering the art of shopping, and exploring the town, communicating effectively at 직장 (jeek-jjahng) (*work*) and 학교 (hahk-kkyoh) (*school*), and more.

When learning a 외국어, one thing that gets you speaking it early on is conversational phrases. Instead of focusing on grammar points and speculating about why the language works the way it does, we'll jump right in to show you how it works firsthand. The following chapters highlight everyday words and phrases in Korean social settings.

Building connections

You'll find it easier to connect with the world around you when you make an effort to speak the language of your new 친구 (cheen-goo) (*friends*) or 동료 (dohng-nyoh) (*colleagues, business associates*).

Chapter 7 guides you through initiating conversations with folks in Korean. You'll learn key words and phrases that you can use during quick chats, impressing those around you as you discuss topics like 고향 (goh-hyahng) (*hometown*), 직업 (jee-guhp) (*jobs*), 가족 (gah-johk) (*family*), and more.

TIP

When meeting someone from Korea, don't be surprised if they ask about your 나이 (nah-ee) (*age*). As you may know, 한국어 (hahn-goo-guh) (*the Korean language*) is an honorific language and 나이 is an important factor in determining how to address people. But, don't worry! Chapter 7 has some alternative ways to respond to age-related questions without giving away your exact age.

Making cents of money

돈 (dohn) (*money*) is a must-have for various aspects of life, including 여행 (yuh-haeng) (*traveling*), 쇼핑 (shyoh-peeng) (*shopping*), 외식 (wae-sheek) (*eating out*), and countless other activities. This is particularly true when journeying through a 외국 (wae-gook) (*foreign country*), where familiarity with handling foreign currency is vital. Korean currency is called 원 (wuhn), and it's denoted by the symbol ₩.

Chapter 8 highlights more about 한국 돈 (hahn-gook dohn) (*Korean money*) and how 환전 (hwahn-juhn) (*exchanging money*) works. You can also discover words and phrases to use at the bank and while making payments. It pays you to be prepared!

Going out for an eating adventure

Dining out at a 식당 (sheek-ttahng) (*restaurant*) can be a lot of fun (and satisfying!). Indeed, indulging in authentic cuisine and dining alongside locals is a great way to learn about a new language and culture. Here are some basic words and phrases for Korean dishes:

>> 밥 (bahp) (*rice, meal*)

>> 국 (gook) (*soup*)

>> 김치 (geem-chee) (*kimchi*)

>> 반찬 (bahn-chahn) (*side dishes*)

>> 맛있어요! (mah-shee-ssuh-yoh) (*delicious!*)

In Chapter 9, we take you on a culinary journey through Korean cuisine, introducing a delectable array of 음식 (eum-sheek) (*foods*) vocabulary and phrases.

Making shopping easy and fun

쇼핑 (shyoh-peeng) (*shopping*) is another fun way to put your language skills to good use. Korea is a shopper's mecca and you'll find great buys almost everywhere you go. One of Korea's biggest attractions is 전통 시장 (juhn-tohng-shee-jahng) (*traditional markets*), and among them, 남대문 시장 (nahm-dae-moon shee-jahng) (*South Gate Market*) in Seoul is the largest. 백화점 (bae-kwah-juhm) (*department stores*) or 가게 (gah-geh) (*small stores*) are other places for 쇼핑.

If you don't like the hustle and bustle, then don't forget to check out 온라인 쇼핑 (ohn-nah-een shyoh-peeng) (*online shopping*). Some of the popular online shopping malls in Korea are *Coupang* and *G-market*. For second-hand As Korea is ranked as one of the largest e-commerce markets, you'll be amazed how convenient 온라인 쇼핑 is there.

In Chapter 10, you can explore important words, phrases, and tips to help you shop 'til you drop. Discover basic shopping lingo, where to go to buy what, when and how to negotiate prices, and more!

Going around the town

Korea is a vibrant country, and its major cities are bustling with exciting activities around the clock. Whether it's day or night, get ready to explore the town with essential vocabulary to immerse yourself in fun places and cultural activities such as 민속촌 (mee-sohk-chohn) (*folk village*), 박물관 (bahng-mool-gwahn) (*museums*), 극장(geuk-jjahng) (*theaters*), pop-culture spots, and more! And don't forget to check out Korea's unique "방 문화" (bahng moon-hwah) ("*room culture*") as well:

>> 노래방 (noh-rae-bahng) (*Korean style karaoke room*)

>> 찜질방 (jjeem-jeel-bahng) (*Korean bathhouses; sauna rooms*)

>> PC방 (pee-ssee-bahng) (*computer rooms*)

>> 만화방 (mahn-hwah-bahng) (*cartoon room*)

For further guideline, consult Chapter 11 for help navigating all these places and activities in Korean.

Getting connected using technology

South Korea is known for having one of the fastest 인터넷 (een-tuh-neht) (*Internet*) speeds in the world. The country is blanketed in free Wi-Fi. Public areas like cafés and malls — as well as public transit like busses and subways — are well equipped with 와이파이 (wah-ee-pah-ee) (*Wi-Fi*). You'll be well connected with your friends and family at home even while on the other side of the hemisphere.

Chapter 12 introduces you to the handy terms and phrases for using 전화 (juhn-hwah) (*phones*), 휴대전화 (hyoo-dae-juhn-hwah) (*cellphones*), 편지 (pyuhn-jee) (*letters*), 소포 (soh-poh) (*packages*), and 이메일 (ee-meh-eel) (*emails*).

Speaking Korean at work and school settings

Planning to work in Korea? Starting a new job in a foreign country can be a bit daunting, but no worries. We've got you covered. Knowing the right terms and phrases for your new workplace can make your work life much easier. Equipping yourself with the necessary terms and phrases for your new 직장 (jeek-jjahng) (*workplace*) will come in handy and make your 직장 생활 (jeek-jjahng saeng-hwahl) (*work life*) much easier.

If you envision a future working for a 회사 (*company*) or teaching at a 학교 (hahk-kkyoh) (*school*) in Korea, Chapter 13 is indispensable! It is packed with useful info on job searching and application, complemented by handy phrases and cultural notes to help you land the job as well as thrive in your new 직장.

Tackling Tasks on the Move

Now that you've honed your Korean skills in various social settings, it's time to consider traveling to Korea if you haven't yet! Rember the Korean saying, "아는 만큼 보인다" (ah-neun-mahn-keum boh-een-dah). (*You can see as much as you know.*) The more prepared you are, the more enjoyable your trip will be. The upcoming chapters in Part 3 give you plenty of 여행 안내 (yuh-haeng ahn-nae) (*travel guidance*) to help you with everything from making plans to finding accommodations to handling emergencies.

Preparing for a trip

A major milestone for any learner of 외국어 (wae-goo-guh) (*foreign language*) is being able to navigate 여행 (yuh-haeng) (*travel*) through a different country!

Chapter 14 helps you make the most of your 한국 여행 (hahn-gook yuh-haeng) (*travel to Korea*). We bring out essential words and phrases necessary for sorting out the logistics of your trip, such as 언제 (uhn-jeh) (*when*), 어디로 (uh-dee-roh) (*to where*), what to bring, and more.

Searching for a place to stay

If you're a first-time visitor to Korea, it may be challenging to find the right 숙소 (sook-ssoh) (*accommodation*) for you. But no worries! Korea has an incredible variety of places to stay, including 한옥 게스트 하우스 (hah-nok geh-seu-teu hah-woo-sseu) (*Hanok guest house*) and 템플 스테이 (tehm-peul seu-teh-ee) (*temple stay*). 한옥 refers to a traditional Korean house, and staying at one during your trip can be an unforgettable experience.

Chapter 15 provides information about the types of 숙소, and how to make 예약 (yeh-yahk) (*reservations*), 체크인 (cheh-keu-een) (*check in*) and 체크아웃 (cheh-keu-ah-oot) (*check out*), and more.

Getting around with transportation

Navigating Korea is a breeze, thanks to its awesome 대중교통 (dae-joong-gyoh-tohng) (*public transport*) system. However, exploring the cities might initially seem daunting, especially if you don't know your way around. Even with good 대중교통, dealing with transportation can be a bit of a hassle if you're not fluent in the local language. Don't get panicky — just turn to Chapter 16. We help you make your way around using different modes of transportation: 비행기 (bee-haeng-gee) (*plane*), 지하철 (jee-hah-chuhl) (*subway*), 버스 (buh-sseu) (*bus*), 택시 (taek-ssee) (*taxi*), and 렌트카 (lehn-teu-kah) (*rental car*).

Asking for directions

While having 지도앱 (jee-doh-aep) (*map apps*) on your phone is undoubtedly convenient, mastering the art of asking for directions remains a vital skill when traveling a 외국 (weh-gook) (*foreign country*). Your phone battery might run out, or locals might offer inside shortcuts. Chapter 17 provides details on how to give directions, ensuring you navigate with confidence and ease wherever your travels take you.

Taking action in an emergency

Although the chances of something majorly bad happening during your trip to Korea are rather slim, you always run the chance of needing to call the 경찰서 (gyung-chahl-ssuh) (*police*) or ending up in a 병원 (byuhng-wuhn) (*hospital*). You can best manage emergencies when you are prepared. Chapter 18 helps you with words and phrases to know when dealing with life's unexpected (not-so-fun) adventures.

Chapter **2**

The Korean Alphabet and Pronunciation

We bring good news: It's very easy to learn how to read and write in Korean, thanks to the simple Korean alphabet called 한글 (hahn-geul) (*one writing, the great writing, Hangeul*). Now you may be wondering how easy it really is. There's a famous saying from one of the scholars during King Sejong's time: "A wise man can learn the alphabet in one morning; even if you're a fool, it will only take you ten days." This centuries-old quote reflects the remarkable simplicity and accessibility King Sejong aimed for with his invention. It has been proven by many learners of Korean worldwide.

We'd like to share the spirits of the Korean alphabet and its cultural and linguistic significance with you, followed by a brief introduction of vowel and consonant letters of the Korean alphabet, along with their sound values. You'll also learn how to form a syllable and a word with individual letters. Then, we'll share some key points and tips to hone your pronunciation skills.

Hangeul, the Alphabet for the People

Writing has come a long, long way from just pictographs in a cave. Believe it or not, of about six thousand languages spoken around the world, only 1 percent have their own writing.

Do you know who invented the Roman alphabet, that English uses, and when? Who invented Chinese characters and when? Who invented the Japanese Kana and when? No one knows for sure. But who invented the Korean alphabet and when? This we do know.

Here's the story behind the birth of the Korean alphabet. Cue the curtains!

Enter King Sejong

Once upon a time, before they had their own writing system, Koreans adopted classical Chinese characters to write Korean. But here's the snag: Korean and Chinese are two different languages. Imagine the hassle of trying to express their thoughts and ideas with characters that didn't match the sounds of their own language — talk about a square peg in a round hole! Not surprisingly, this method was far from popular, making literacy a privilege of the elite and leaving most ordinary people in the dust. Not cool.

Placing himself in the shoes of his people, 세종대왕 (seh-johng-dae-wahng) (*King Sejong the Great*) took on the challenge of creating a native writing system. After spending decades studying the sound system of Korean, in 1443, he introduced an entirely new writing system designed to represent the sounds of spoken Korean. Most importantly, as 세종대왕 planned, 한글 (hahn-geul) was much more efficient and easier to learn than Chinese characters, a true breakthrough promoting universal literacy!

세종대왕 detailed his motives in the preface of 훈민정음 (hoon-meen-juhng-eum) (*Hunminjeongeum*, "*Proper Sounds to Instruct the People*"), the book he published to provide guidelines for learning 한글:

> Because our spoken language is completely different from that of China, it cannot be well expressed in Chinese characters. Some of my people cannot properly express what they think in writing, I feel sorry for this, so I have created 28 new letters myself. My people shall be able to learn them quickly and to use them every day.

Thanks to King Sejong's pragmatism and his determination to empower the people, Korean readers and writers have a readily learnable language. What a king! With its new writing system, Korea started flourishing culturally and intellectually, achieving higher levels of literacy and education. 한글 is one of the youngest alphabets created in the world, and one of the few widely used alphabets whose development is historically documented, down to the details of how it was invented. 한글 is indeed the centerpiece of Korea's history and culture, and the foundation of Korean identity.

With this historical background story of 한글, we're ready for you to explore the individual letters and their sounds.

Consonants and Vowels

한글 (hahn-geul) is recognized by linguists around the world as one of the most scientific writing systems and the growing global popularity of Korean culture, including K-Pop music and Korean dramas, contribute to a strong interest in learning 한글. So, you're about to dive into the "one great writing" system, which will open up a vast, rich array of opportunities for you to explore the underlying cultural, academic, economic, and strategic significance of the Korean language.

One of the reasons so many linguists admire the Korean alphabet lies in the logical structure of the consonants and vowels. 한글 is simple and straightforward. Similar to English, it consists of vowels and consonants. However, unlike English, where letters can have shifting pronunciations – like the "i" in "bike" versus "miss" – 한글 is a highly phonetic writing system where, for the most part, each letter corresponds to one sound.

Let's take a look at the 21 vowel letters and 19 consonant letters of 한글 in Table 2-1.

TABLE 2-1

Korean Vowels and Consonants

Vowels	Simple	ㅏ ㅑ ㅓ ㅕ ㅗ ㅛ ㅜ ㅠ ㅡ ㅣ ㅐ ㅔ
	Complex	ㅒ ㅖ ㅘ ㅙ ㅚ ㅝ ㅞ ㅟ ㅢ
Consonants	Simple	ㄱ ㄴ ㄷ ㄹ ㅁ ㅂ ㅅ ㅇ ㅈ ㅊ ㅋ ㅌ ㅍ ㅎ
	Double	ㄲ ㄸ ㅃ ㅆ ㅉ

Vowels

Before we continue with the sound of each vowel letter, let's explore the fascinating mechanics behind the creation of the 한글 vowel letters by King Sejong.

He developed the basic vowel letters based on three fundamental elements of the universe, as understood in many East Asian philosophies: the sky or the sun, represented as a round dot (•), the earth depicted as a horizontal line (—), and humankind represented by a vertical line (I). All the vowel letters in 한글 are made using one or more of these three components. (For a detailed look at how these principles are applied to the actual letter forms, see the examples in Table 2-2.)

TABLE 2-2 **Eight Basic Vowels**

Basic Vowel Letters	Pronunciation Tips
ㅣ • = ㅏ	f<u>a</u>ther, sp<u>a</u>
• ㅣ = ㅓ	b<u>u</u>t, <u>a</u>wake
⁛ = ㅗ	h<u>o</u>pe, <u>o</u>pen
̵ = ㅜ	m<u>oo</u>d
─	b<u>oo</u>k or p<u>e</u>tit in French
ㅣ	h<u>ee</u>d, s<u>ee</u>
ㅣ • + ㅣ = ㅐ	h<u>ea</u>d, b<u>a</u>d
• ㅣ + ㅣ = ㅔ	s<u>e</u>t, b<u>e</u>d

It's also crucial to remember the proper stroke order when writing 한글 letters: from left to right and top to bottom. This ensures that each character maintains its balance and form.

Let's start with eight basic vowel letters in Table 2-2. Each letter is presented first with how it looked historically, followed by how it is currently written. Pronunciation tips follow the nearest counterparts in American English.

Each of these vowels is produced without any gliding of the jaw. Since these vowels form the foundation of all other vowels of Korean, practice with the audio files available with this book and with your native speaker friends if possible.

Learning new vowels isn't always easy, especially if they don't exist in your first language. But try linking them to similar English sounds, as in the Table 2-2.

Sounding off: ─

This vowel doesn't have a good equivalent in American English. But here's a tip: try saying the vowel sound in *book*, while flatten your lips by pulling the corners back instead of rounding them- you'll get pretty close! Alternatively, if you're familiar with the French, it's similar to the vowel *petit*. Just remember to spread your lips to the sides as you say it. And there you go! You got it!

Sounding off: ㅐ and ㅔ

Notice anything odd in Table 2-2? Bingo! Yes, ㅐ is the combination of ㅏ and ㅣ, and ㅔ is the combination of ㅓ and ㅣ; these are a bit different from the rest of the basic vowel letters. These combinations were used because these letters originally represented diphthongs, a sequence of two vowel sounds. Over the course of history, however, they have eventually evolved into simple vowel sounds and now these letters represent single vowel sounds.

Unlike the clear distinction between *bad* and *bed* in English, the distinction between ㅐ and ㅔ isn't as clearcut. In casual, fast speech, they sound the same way. You can pronounce both ㅐ and ㅔ like the vowel in *bed*. But you still need to distinguish them in spelling.

Table 2-3 shows the next group of vowels, all of which include the sound "y". These are derived from the basic vowel letters (ㅏ, ㅓ, ㅗ, ㅜ, ㅐ, and ㅔ) by addition one short graphic stroke to them. This table shows how they were created, how they are pronounced, and is another example of how brilliant King Sejong was.

TABLE 2-3

Six y-Diphthong Vowels

y-Diphthong Letters	Pronunciation Tips
ㅣ + ㅏ = ㅑ	yacht
ㅣ + ㅓ = ㅕ	young
ㅣ + ㅗ = ㅛ	yo-yo
ㅣ + ㅜ = ㅠ	you
ㅣ + ㅐ = ㅒ	yam
ㅣ + ㅔ = ㅖ	yes

Sounding off: ㅒ and ㅖ

Much like the subtle difference in the pronunciations between yeah and yes, the vowels ㅒ and ㅖ are very similar. As with their simple vowel counterparts (ㅐ, ㅔ), these two vowels (ㅒ, ㅖ) are generally both pronounced like the "ye" in yes. Just remember, although they have merged to produce the same sound, they differ in spelling.

To wrap up the vowel letters, Table 2-4 shows the remaining vowels, which are also diphthongs.

TABLE 2-4
Seven Other Diphthong Vowels

Other Diphthong Vowel Letters	Pronunciation Tips
ㅗ + ㅏ = ㅘ	<u>wa</u>tch
ㅗ + ㅐ = ㅙ	<u>wa</u>cky
ㅗ + ㅣ = ㅚ	<u>wea</u>ther
ㅜ + ㅓ = ㅝ	<u>wa</u>s
ㅜ + ㅔ = ㅞ	(1) <u>wea</u>ther; (2) <u>wai</u>ter (without i-gliding)
ㅜ + ㅣ = ㅟ	<u>wea</u>ver
ㅡ + ㅣ = ㅢ	(1) h<u>oo</u>k + b<u>e</u>; (2) b<u>e</u>; (3) h<u>ea</u>d

Sounding off: ㅢ

The last vowel in Table 2-4, ㅢ, combines ㅡ and ㅣ, in both its shape formation and pronunciation. You start off with the ㅡ sound and then quickly shift into the ㅣ 'y' sound. The diphthong ㅢ has three different pronunciations, ㅢ, ㅣ, or ㅔ, depending on where it occurs in a word:

>> It is pronounced like its combined letters when it's in word-initial position (for example, 의자).

>> It is pronounced like the vowel in *be* after a consonant in initial position (for example, 흰).

>> It is pronounced like its combined letters or like the vowel in *be* when it appears in non-initial position (for example, 대의, 한의원).

>> It is pronounced like its combined letters or like the vowel in *head* when it's used as the possessive particle (for example, 나의 [*my*]). There's more info about particles in Chapter 3.

Just perk up your ears and practice reading various words aloud.

Sounding off: ㅙ, ㅚ, and ㅞ

Confused with the approximated English vowels for ㅙ and ㅚ in Table 2-4? The letter ㅚ used to be pronounced similar to the French word *hors d'oeuvres* with that unfamiliar vowel produced with your lips sticking out and rounded. Did King Sejong have some French instinct? Don't worry if you don't; not everyone can pull off a beret! It's now pronounced identically as ㅙ. So simple, right?

Also, because of difficulties in differentiating those simple vowels involved in ㅙ and ㅞ, more specifically between ㅐ and ㅔ and between ㅗ and ㅜ, the distinction between ㅙ and ㅞ is weakened or lost.

In practice, in modern Korean, ㅚ, ㅙ, and ㅞ are identical to each other as in the English equivalent word _weather_ due to the merger of ㅐ and ㅔ, even though all three have to be used in spelling Korean words.

Consonants

Things tend to come in pairs: pairs of animals on Noah's ark, day and night, peanut butter and jelly, Jack and Jill, needle and thread, salt and pepper, hide and seek, and Tom and Jerry! The list of pairs goes on and on. Anything to pair vowels with? Of course, consonants!

King Sejong created the five basic consonant letters ㄱ, ㄴ, ㅁ, ㅅ, and ㅇ inspired by the five elements of nature — tree, fire, soil, metal, and water, respectively — and based on the shape of the mouth — tongue, lips, teeth, and throat — when pronouncing them. Then, nine more consonant letters were made by adding extra strokes to these five basic consonant letters. So a compound consonant letter(s) derived from a basic consonant letter is produced at the same place of articulation as the initial consonant letter.

Take a look at the five basic consonant letters ㄱ, ㄴ, ㅁ, ㅅ, and ㅇ and the nine consonant letters derived from them along with their respective places of vocal articulation for making those sounds in Table 2-5.

TABLE 2-5   **The Five Basic Consonants**

Place of Articulation	Basic Consonant	Derived Consonant		
Tongue back (touching the soft palate)	ㄱ /g/	ㅋ /k/		
Tongue tip (touching the gum ridge)	ㄴ /n/	ㄷ /d/	ㅌ /t/	ㄹ /l, r/

(continued)

TABLE 2-5 *(continued)*

Place of Articulation	Basic Consonant		Derived Consonant	
Lip	ㅁ /m/		ㅂ /b/	ㅍ /p/
Teeth (with the tongue tip touching the lower teeth)	ㅅ /s/		ㅈ /j/	ㅊ /ch/
Throat	ㅇ /ng/		ㅎ /h/	

Now it's time to learn how to pronounce the Korean consonant letters. Table 2-6 displays the 14 simple consonant letters with pronunciation tips in the order they appear in most Korean dictionaries.

First, try going over the corresponding English sounds listed in Table 2-6. Don't worry if you have trouble figuring out how to pronounce some of the sounds. We go over how to distinguish and pronounce some of the trickier ones.

TABLE 2-6

Fourteen Simple Consonants

Simple Consonant Letters	Pronunciation Tips
ㄱ	<u>big</u>ger or mu<u>g</u>; soft *k*
ㄴ	<u>n</u>oise or su<u>n</u>
ㄷ	un<u>d</u>o or car<u>d</u>; soft *t*
ㄹ	<u>cr</u>oss or <u>l</u>ife
ㅁ	<u>m</u>outh or tea<u>m</u>

Simple Consonant Letters	Pronunciation Tips
ㅂ	rabbit or tab; soft p
ㅅ	Sweden or smile
ㅇ	long or morning
ㅈ	unjust or ginger; soft ch
ㅊ	chair or teach
ㅋ	king or stomach
ㅌ	twin or retain
ㅍ	power or sleepy
ㅎ	hope or head

Of these 14 consonant letters, the sounds of ㄴ, ㅁ, ㅇ, and ㅎ are exactly the same as English, n, m, ng, and h, respectively. Good start to learning the consonant letters! And here are some key pronunciation points for the rest of the consonants.

Sounding off: ㄱ, ㄷ, ㅂ, and ㅈ

When each of these plain, lax consonants come in the middle of a word, their sounds are pretty much the same as the English letters g, d, b, and j as in bigger, undo, rabbit, and unjust. But when these letters begin a word, they sound more like the English letters k, t, p, and ch, as in kid, tail, piano, and chair.

No matter what they sound like, make sure to have no puff of air when pronouncing these plain consonant letters. You got this!

Sounding off: ㄹ

Pronouncing this consonant letter is not as simple as it looks because its sound is very different from that of either the English l or r. Don't panic. We'll do a walk-through so you can get a better sense of the sound.

When the ㄹ sound comes between vowels or at the beginning of a word, it is pronounced as a so-called flap r like the Spanish r as in the Spanish word pero. Don't know Spanish? No worries. The ㄹ consonant in the same positions sounds very much like the American English t or d in words such as water, letter, or ladder. Sounds familiar?

REMEMBER

Unlike English, in which pronunciation rules depend on what speech sounds like in a word, not how it is spelled, spelling/letters are consistent and relevant to all sound-pattern rules in Korean.

When the ㄹ letter comes elsewhere, it is pronounced as the so-called English light *l* in words like *flow, lip*.

On a related side note, the so-called English dark *l* in words like *ball, milk*, and *real* doesn't exist in Korean. The ㄹ sound is produced with the tip of your tongue toward the front of your mouth with no change in the tongue positioning, but the English dark *l* is made by pulling the tongue back into the mouth toward the throat. That's why Koreans have difficulty pronouncing English words with a dark *l*. Since you have a light *l*, which is similar to the ㄹ sound, it would be easier for English speakers to make the ㄹ sound correctly, so bear with Koreans not being able to produce the correct sound of the American dark *l*.

Sounding off: ㅅ

The Korean ㅅ sound is similar to the *s* sound in English words like *stay, spring*, and *skim*, where *s* is followed by a consonant with a low pitch and sounding very soft. It is pronounced more like *sh* before vowels ㅣ /ee/ and ㅟ /wee/ and before the *y*-vowels like ㅑ /yah/, ㅕ /yuh/, ㅛ /yoh/, and ㅠ /yoo/. For the *sh* sound in Korean, you shouldn't round your lips or stick them out with a low pitch, and you should sound very soft. Then, your ㅅ will be *stunning* and *spectacular*.

Sounding off: ㅋ, ㅌ, ㅍ, and ㅊ

Korean pronunciation relies heavily on how much air you let out when you pronounce consonants. These four "aspirated" consonant letters are produced with a strong burst of air (aspiration) as in the initial sounds of the English words, *king, toy, port* and *chain*, respectively. Try it! Put your hand in front of your mouth when pronouncing these sounds; you'll feel a strong breath of air.

Usually, English speakers have no problem in pronouncing these aspirated consonants as English has the consonants corresponding exactly to these. Fair enough!

Double the fun, right? Let's double five of the simple consonant letters and see what's happening in Table 2-7.

The formation of these double consonant letters is very simple and systematic, spelled by doubling the corresponding plain letters, and just like any letter of 한글 (hahn-geul), they are pronounced as one sound. But, these are the sounds that English speakers have difficulty producing most. Life's not fair!

TABLE 2-7

Five Double Consonants

Double Consonant Letters	Pronunciation Tips
ㄲ	ski
ㄸ	stay
ㅃ	spill
ㅆ	cinema or psychology
ㅉ	pizza

To make this matter less complex, remember the two game changers for pronouncing these double consonant letters correctly: the amount of air coming out of your mouth and the use of the throat.

Sounding off: ㄲ, ㄸ, ㅃ, and ㅉ

When you are saying ㅋ, ㅌ, ㅍ, and ㅊ, you allow a strong puff of air to flow out through the mouth. Contrastingly, try saying them while letting no burst of air (aspiration) out of your mouth with a slight popping of air. That's how you can make their counterpart tense sounds, ㄲ, ㄸ, ㅃ and ㅉ.

So, basically, pronounce them in the same way as ㄱ, ㄷ, ㅂ, and ㅈ with the same amount (no or at least not a strong burst) of air. But the difference between the plain consonants and these tense consonants comes from what's happening with the throat. With no burst of air, you should feel strong tension in your throat and emit a very loud, high pitch when making these tense sounds. You may even feel like these sounds are made in the throat, not in the mouth, no matter what other parts of your mouth work together to make each sound.

To make the matter simpler, here's a cheat sheet for you. Here are some English words that are pronounced in a similar way to these double tense consonants ㄲ, ㄸ, ㅃ and ㅉ: ski, stay, spill, and pizza (but with an Italian accent; using their signature hand gesture is encouraged). It might help if you exaggerate the tension in your throat and make your pitch as loud and high as you can. Your efforts will pay off!

Sounding off: ㅆ

Again, the game changers in pronouncing the ㅆ sound are airflow and the tension in your throat. However, the defining characteristic of this double consonant that is different from the other double consonants is that it involves a hissing sound, just like its corresponding plain consonant ㅅ.

Try saying *expensive*, *cinema*, and *psychology* with more tension and a harsher hissing sound. Don't forget the familiar raised pitch of double consonants. You got the ㅆ sound!

To sum up, Table 2-8 displays the distinction between the three members of a series of the plain, aspirated, and tense consonants.

TABLE 2-8

Plain, Aspirated, and Tense Consonants

Plain Consonant	Aspirated Consonant	Tense Consonant
ㄱ	ㅋ	ㄲ
ㄷ	ㅌ	ㄸ
ㅂ	ㅍ	ㅃ
ㅅ		ㅆ
ㅈ	ㅊ	ㅉ

Before we move onto the next section where you learn how to write those letters you just mastered, take a moment to feel proud of yourself. You deserve a pat on the back for making it this far. Hats off to you!

Forming Syllables and Words

This section guides you in how to write those individual 한글 (hahn-geul) letters in a word or a sentence.

Most writing systems construct words by simply placing the letters next to one another. Boring? Here's another fun part of the 한글. The phonetic consonant and vowel letters of 한글 are combined to create a syllable in a block. The consonant and vowel letters are written side-by-side or top-to-bottom within that block according to their shapes, and every syllable gets separated out into own block, like this:

$$한국$$

The first syllable block 한 is comprised of the three letters ㅎ, ㅏ, and ㄴ to be pronounced as */hahn/*. Similarly, the three letters ㄱ, ㅜ, and ㄱ combine and form the second syllable block, pronounced as */gook/*. These two syllable blocks together are the word meaning *Korea*, the common name of the country.

Here are some key points you need to remember to write letters into a syllable. One at a time!

Every syllable requires a vowel. In other words, a consonant letter alone can't form a syllable. In addition, two consonant sounds cannot occur in a row at either the beginning or end of a syllable. So English words like _clean_ or _pans_ are not possible in Korean, let alone even more complicated sequences of consonants sounds as in _twelfths_.

One vowel sound can form a syllable, just like the English word _a_. The difference between English and Korean is that English words consisting entirely of vowels are rare, whereas there are many Korean words with vowels only, just like the word _eau_ in _eau de perfume_.

Vertical-shaped vowel letters such as ㅣ, ㅏ, ㅓ, ㅐ, ㅔ, ㅑ, ㅕ, ㅒ, and ㅖ go to the right of the first consonant, and the horizontal shaped ones such as ㅡ, ㅗ, ㅜ, ㅛ, ㅠ, and ㅠ go below the first consonant. And the other compound vowels such as ㅘ, ㅙ, ㅚ, ㅝ, ㅞ, ㅟ, and ㅢ surround the first consonant.

To help you visualize a syllable, take a look at the following graphics for possible syllable blocks:

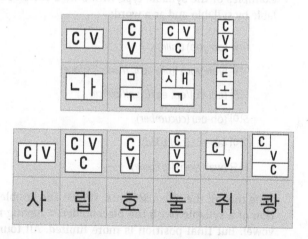

You might be scratching your head wondering what a syllable only with a vowel or a syllable that begins with a vowel would look like. King Sejong has a solution for it!

When a syllable begins with a vowel, we can't leave the space empty, and a placeholder consonant fills the space before the vowel in the block: the letter ㅇ. So, when the letter ㅇ comes before a vowel in a syllable, it doesn't have any sound value (like silent letters in English words). Take a close look at your very first Korean sentence.

관용은 뜻이 뭐예요?

This sentence is comprised of three words: The first word has three syllables (관, 용, and 은); the second word has two syllables (뜻 and 이); and the third word has three syllables (뭐, 예, and 요).

Focus on the syllables that begin with a vowel in this sentence. The first syllable, 용 (yohng), combines the vowel ㅛ and the final consonant ㅇ, with the placeholder ㅇ before the vowel. Similarly, 은 (eun) combines the vowel and the final consonant ㄴ, with the placeholder ㅇ before the vowel. The third syllable, 이 (ee), consists of just the vowel ㅣ, but it is written with the placeholder ㅇ in the syllable block. The same is true for the fourth syllable 예 and the last syllable 요 with one vowel, ㅖ and ㅛ, respectively. Again, the place of the placeholder either on top of the vowel or to the left of the vowel depends on the shape of the following vowel.

We mentioned that many Korean words consist entirely of vowels. Here are some examples of the syllable type with only a vowel. Practice pronouncing them syllable by syllable and as a word:

우유 (oo-yoo) (*milk*)

여유 (yuh-yoo) ([*physical, mental*] *space*)

의의 (eui-eui/eui-ee) (*significance*)

오이 (oh-ee) (*cucumber*)

아이 (ah-ee) (*child, kid*)

와요 (wah-yoh) (*to come*)

Note that all the 19 consonants, simple and double, can occur in the initial position of a syllable (with the placeholder ㅇ having no sound value) followed by a vowel. But final position is more limited. All fourteen single consonant letters can occur in final position, but only two of the double letters, ㄲ and ㅆ can do so. In addition, there are eleven combinations of two different consonant letters that can occur as final consonants. (We'll refer to them as "two-single-letter consonants" here.) ㄳ, ㄵ, ㄶ, ㄺ, ㄻ, ㄼ, ㄽ, ㄾ, ㄿ, ㅀ, ㅄ. But wait! Didn't we just say that Korean doesn't have sequences of consonant sounds like in English *pans*? It's true. But these aren't sounds, they are letters. In the next section we will talk about how they are actually pronounced.

Some example words with the two double final consonants and the eleven two-single letter final consonants follow. Note that the mismatch in these examples between spelled letters and pronounced sounds is explained in the next section.

>> 값 (gahp) (*price*)

>> 깎다 (kkahk-ttah) (*to cut, peel*)

>> 있다 (eet-ttah) (*to exist, have*)

>> 읽다 (eek-ttah) (*to read*)

>> 여덟 (yuh-duhl) (*eight*)

>> 외곬수 (wae-gohl-ssoo) (*a stubborn person*)

>> 젊다 (juhm-ttah) (*to be young*)

>> 흙 (heuk) (*soil*)

TIP

Whether you're old school or tech savvy, handwriting is a must. These days, typing on a computer or a hand-held device is also necessary. There are many online resources to learn Korean typing. From there, you can practice forming 한글 letters into syllables and words and increase your typing speed.

Sounding Fluent

After you have a grasp of the basic Korean sounds, mimicking the cadence of a Korean native speaker should take just a little more work. But this doesn't mean that the path to mastery of Korean pronunciation is one without hiccups. As always, hard doesn't mean impossible.

In this section, we provide a few tips for mastering Korean pronunciation and making your Korean sound even more natural. These don't capture all the phonetic details, of course, but it is nonetheless helpful. For more extensive pronunciation rules, go to www.dummies.com and type Korean for Dummies Cheat Sheet in the search box.

Liaison

In French, to pronounce the words "petit ami," the second *t* is pronounced with the second word "ami" as in /tami/. This joining of one to the following syllable is called *liaison* and is supposed to help the fluidity of the spoken language. The same phenomenon occurs in Korean when a consonant in a final position is followed by a vowel in the initial position of the following syllable. Take a close look at the following examples, paying special attention to where the consonant sounds appear:

국이 /구기/ (goo-gee) (*soup*) 국이 너무 짜요. (goo-gee nuh-moo jjah-yoh) (*The soup is too salty.*)

달은 /다른/ (dah-reun) (*moon*) 달은 지구를 공전해요. (dah-reun jee-goo-reul gohng-juhn-haeh-yoh) (*The moon orbits the Earth.*)

받아 /바다/ (bah-dah) (*to receive*) 제 반지를 받아 주세요. (jeh bahn-jee-reul bah-dah joo-seh-yoh) (*Please receive my ring.*)

It could be a trap! The underlined words in the preceding sentences are pronounced exactly the same way as 구기, 다른, and 바다, which mean *ball games/sports*, *different*, *sea*, respectively. Although spelled differently, when spoken aloud only the context of the sentence will reveal the meaning.

There are some variations of this liaison rule. (It's like adding spice to your life.)

We briefly introduced two double final consonants and a limited set of two-single letter final consonants. What happens when they are followed by a vowel is very interesting.

>> 갔어요/가써요/(gah-ssuh-yoh) (*went*)

>> 깎아/까까/(kkah-kkah) (*cut, peel*)

>> 맑아요/말가요/(mahl-gah-yoh) (*clear, sunny*)

>> 있어요/이써요/(ee-ssuh-yoh) (*exist, have*)

>> 젊은/절믄/(juhl-meun) (*young*)

So what's happening? Those two double final consonants (that is, ㄲ, ㅆ) before a vowel go together as an individual consonant and are carried over to the initial position of the following syllable.

The set of 11 combination letters looks rather arbitrary. In fact, the reason only these combinations exist has to do with old spellings and historical changes that happened to Korean pronunciation over hundreds of years. It's a bit like the arbitrary-seeming *k* at the beginning of English *knee* and *knight*, which was pronounced like it's spelled hundreds of years ago.

Unlike the double final consonants (ㄲ, ㅆ), which never separate, when followed by a vowel, the combination letters get separate into two pronounced sounds, one at the end of one syllable and the other at the start of the next syllable. In other words, they're easily broken apart, as shown in the previous examples.

Nasalization

Just like English *m*, *n*, and *ng*, Korean consonants ㄴ, ㅁ, and ㅇ are classified as nasal. There are instances where nonnasal consonants become nasalized in some conditions.

[ㄷ, ㅌ, ㅅ, ㅆ, ㅈ, ㅊ, ㅎ] + ㄴ or ㅁ → [ㄴ]

The final consonants ㄷ, ㅌ, ㅅ, ㅆ, ㅈ, ㅊ, and ㅎ change into ㄴ, when ㄴ or ㅁ is the initial consonant of the next syllable.

꽃말 [꼰말] (kkohn-mahl) (*language of flowers; floriography*)

좋네요 [존네요] (john-neh-yoh) (*to be good*)

[ㅂ, ㅍ] + ㄴ, ㄹ, ㅁ → [ㅁ]

The final consonants ㅂ and ㅍ change into ㅁ, when ㄴ, ㄹ, or ㅁ is the initial consonant of the next syllable.

돕는 [돔는] (dohm-neun) (*to help*)

[ㄱ, ㅁ, ㅂ, ㅇ] + ㄹ → [ㄴ]

When the initial consonant ㄹ follows the final consonants ㄱ, ㅁ, ㅂ, or ㅇ, the ㄹ sound changes into a ㄴ sound.

동료 [동뇨] (dohng-nyoh) (*colleague*)

[ㄱ, ㅋ, ㄲ] + ㄴ, ㄹ, ㅁ → [ㅇ]

The final consonants ㄱ, ㅋ, and ㄲ change into ㅇ, when ㄴ, ㄹ, or ㅁ is the initial consonant of the next syllable.

한국말 [한궁말] (hahn-goong-mahl) (*Korean language*)

Tensification

In Korean, there's a phonological process by which a consonant becomes tense. Here are the phonological situations where tensification of the subsequent consonant occurs.

[ㄱ, ㄷ, ㅂ] + ㄱ, ㄷ, ㅂ, ㅅ, ㅈ → [ㄲ, ㄸ, ㅃ, ㅆ, ㅉ]

The plain consonant sounds ㄱ, ㄷ, ㅂ, ㅅ, and ㅈ change to their respective tense counterparts ㄲ, ㄸ, ㅃ, ㅆ, and ㅉ, when they appear after ㄱ, ㄷ or ㅂ sounds.

몇 시 [면씨] (myut-ssee) (*what time*)

식당 [식땅] (sheek-ttahng) (*restaurant*)

ㄹ + [ㄷ, ㅅ, ㅈ] → [ㄸ, ㅆ, ㅉ]

The plain consonant sounds ㄷ, ㅅ, and ㅈ become their respective tense counterparts ㄸ, ㅆ, and ㅉ, after ㄹ.

열심히 [열씸히] (yuhl-sseem-hee) (*diligently*)

The seven representatives

Continuing to discuss the matter of consonant letters in the final position of a syllable or word, the consonant sounds in the final position, when they stand alone, are actually pronounced as only seven representative consonants: ㄴ, ㅁ, ㅇ, ㄹ, ㄱ, ㄷ, and ㅂ. Table 2-9 lists the final consonants that are pronounced as one of the seven representative letters in Korean.

REMEMBER

This representative rule applies only when a syllable or word ends in consonants. If any of the consonants including double-consonants in the final position is followed by a vowel, the liaison rule overrules: They are spilled over to the initial position of the following syllable and pronounced as they are written. Related to this, when a syllable or word ends in two single-letter consonants, such as 닭 (*chicken*), 삶 (*life*), or 몫 (*portion*), only one of the two consonants is pronounced. It might seem tricky at first, but here's a rule of thumb to remember: for ㄺ, ㄻ, and ㄿ, the second consonant is typically pronounced as the final consonant, as in 닭 (/닥/ dahk) and 삶 (/삼/ sahm). For other combinations, the first consonant is pronounced, as in 몫 (/목/ mohk) or 값 (/갑/ gahp). Of course, there are a few exceptions, as with any language, but don't worry too much. You'll encounter some combinations more frequently than others, and as you gain more exposure to these words, you'll improve.

TABLE 2-9

The Seven Representative Consonants

The Representative	The Represented	Examples
ㄱ	ㄱ ㅋ ㄲ	박 /박/, 부엌 /부억/, 밖 /박/
ㄷ	ㄷ ㅅ ㅆ ㅈ ㅊ ㅌ ㅎ	곧 /곧/, 곳 /곧/, 있고 /읻꼬/, 곶 /곧/, 꽃 /꼳/, 밭 /받/, 히읗 /히읃/
ㅂ	ㅂ ㅍ	입 /입/, 잎 /입/
ㄴ	ㄴ	눈 /눈/
ㄹ	ㄹ	꿀 /꿀/
ㅁ	ㅁ	꿈 /꿈/
ㅇ	ㅇ	강 /강/

Loan words

Approximately five percent of the Korean vocabulary are loan words, borrowed mainly from English in the last 150 years or so. As technology has constantly evolved, more loan words are entered into Korean dictionaries, and people use them on a daily basis. A few of them sound similar to the original English words, but for others you might have to use your imagination. Most of these words should be easy to memorize and help you better understand Korean pronunciation.

Try reading the following examples of words borrowed from English that are conventionally spelled in Korean and guess their meanings. Answers are found below. No peeking!

텍사스	조지아	워싱턴	플로리다	시애틀
뉴욕	시드니	파리	두바이	런던
스페인	프랑스	베트남	캐나다	브라질
웹사이트	프린터	라디오	와이파이	인터넷
스키	골프	마라톤	스케이트	펜싱
샌드위치	콜라	핫도그	아이스크림	파인애플

One last tip: Although it may be tempting to read each syllable quickly, if you enunciate each syllable clearly, it'll be easier for you to pronounce words accurately and easier for Koreans to understand you. Remember to speak like an Australian or British person, such as pronouncing ㅏ as *ah*. Time to pull out your David Attenborogh or Bear Grylls impersonation!

Here are the answers:

Texas	Georgia	Washington	Florida	Seattle
New York	Sydney	Paris	Dubai	London
Spain	France	Vietnam	Canada	Brazil
Website	Printer	Radio	Wi-fi	Internet
Ski	Golf	Marathon	Skate	Fencing
Sandwich	Cola	Hot dog	Ice cream	Pineapple

FUN & GAMES

A. Combine the following 한글 consonant and vowel letters into a syllable. Don't forget the placeholder ㅇ before the vowel. See Appendix C for correct answers.

1. ㅖ _____

2. ㅃ ㅡ ㄴ _____

3. ㅑ ㅇ _____

4. ㅁ ㅏ ㄹ _____

5. ㅡ ㄹ _____

6. ㅅ ㅏ _____

7. ㅑ _____

8. ㄷ ㅙ _____

9. ㅛ _____

B. Put all the syllables in order to make a sensible sentence.

— .

C. Try reading the following words borrowed from English that might sound familiar to you. Guess the meaning of those words.

1. 인터넷 _____

2. 햄버거 _____

3. 커피 _____

4. 이메일 _____

5. 카메라 _____

6. 스타벅스 _____

7. 컴퓨터 _____

8. 멕시코 _____

9. 텔레비전 _____

10. 드라마 _____

Chapter **3**

The Nitty-Gritty: Basic Korean Grammar

I magine you're in the kitchen, all set to cook up a new dish. You start by gathering the flour, butter, and other 재료 (jae-ryoh) (*ingredients*). Have you ever wondered how these 재료 combine to create a variety of dishes? The 재료 themselves and the 순서 (soon-suh) (*order*) in which you add them play a huge role because every little change can positively or negatively affect the final outcome.

The same principle applies to learning a new 언어 (uh-nuh) (*language*). You don't need to master all the intricate details from the start. Just like how flour, butter, and eggs can help you bake a cake, basic 단어 (dah-nuh) (*words*) and 표현 (pyoh-hyuhn) (*expressions*) can help you communicate.

But just like how binding agents, garnishes, and cooking methods bring everything together in a dish, 문법 (moon-ppuhb) (*grammar*) brings together the words and adds a touch of character to your sentences. As you come across more complex situations, you will find moments when you wish you knew more 문법 — *the world beyond vocabulary* — to structure your thoughts and communicate them effectively. Although it may take some 시행 착오 (shee-haeng chah-goh) (*trial and error*) to discover better ways to form a 문장 (moon-jahng) (*sentence*), the end result is sure to be amazing.

Roll up your sleeves and get ready to whip up something new. Your first "cooking" journey is on Korean speech styles. At first, things might feel a little bland, but it's important to push through, because soon enough, you'll get the hang of it!

Using Appropriate Speech Styles

Korean has an intricate system of speech levels that change based on who you're talking to or about. This means, when speaking Korean, the focus is more on the addressee or referent, not yourself. A key way to express different levels of politeness and formality is by changing the verb endings (a.k.a., verb conjugation).

For instance, when asking "Are you okay?" you say it differently depending on who you're addressing. When talking to someone in a higher social position (including people older than you), like your boss or grandparents, you use polite speech with an honorific suffix (세요) and say 괜찮으세요? (gwaen-chah-neu-seh-yoh?). To people you have a non-casual relationship with, like your colleagues in a similar rank, use the polite speech style and say 괜찮아요? (gwaen-chah-nah-yoh?). To someone who you are very close with, like your siblings, close friends, or your kids, use informal, casual speech — 괜찮아? (gwaen-chah-nah?)

Did you notice that the Korean phrases become shorter the more you move down the hierarchy? All these different speech styles are embedded in the suffixes attached to the verb.

Linguists say there are seven speech levels in Korean. Some of them have almost been faded out; you'll only hear them in historical dramas. (Phew!)

Two of the most common speech styles

In daily life settings, such as 집 (jeep) (*home*), 학교 (hahk-kkyoh) (*school*), and 직장 (jeek-jjahng) (*work place*), the following two speech styles are most commonly used: *informal polite* speech (verbs ending in -아요/어요) and *intimate* speech (verbs ending in -아/어).

>> **The *informal polite* speech:** -아요/어요 is a type of 존댓말 (john-daen-mahl) (*polite speech*). 존대 (john-dae) means *to treat with respect* and 말 (mahl) means *speech/language*. This 존댓말 is a polite and ordinary speech style used in most kinds of social situations by all kinds of people. It's polite enough so that you never sound rude, and it's informal enough so that it can be used in a variety of situations. So, for new learners of Korean like you, it's a great catch-all! For those reasons, we focus on this style throughout this book.

>> **The *intimate* speech:** -아/어 is a 반말 (bahn-mahl). 반 (bahn) means *half* and 반말 literally means *half talk/speech*. How can you "half-talk"? If you leave the -요 suffix out in the *informal polite* form (that is, 아요/어요), it becomes 반말. When 요 is taken off, the speech becomes shorter, which means the distance in the relationship is closer, or "cut in half." It indicates that the speaker and the listener are in an *intimate* relationship. Now you can see why *intimate* speech is called 반말, right?

Table 3-1 shows some examples of simple phrases for these two speech styles. You'll learn how to conjugate verbs in later sections of this chapter.

TABLE 3-1   Speech Styles: Informal Polite (아요/어요) vs. Intimate (아/어)

Meaning	Informal Polite (아요/어요)	Intimate (아/어)
It's good/great!	좋아요 (joh-ah-yoh)	좋아 (joh-ah)
It's fun!	재미있어요 (jae-mee-ee-ssuh-yoh)	재미있어 (jae-mee-ee-ssuh)
Thank you.	고마워요 (goh-mah-wuh-yoh)	고마워 (goh-mah-wuh)
I'm sorry.	미안해요 (mee-ahn-hae-yoh)	미안해 (mee-ahn-hae)
Nice to meet you.	반가워요 (bahn-gah-wuh-yoh)	반가워 (bahn-gah-wuh)

Formal polite speech style

Are you wondering if Koreans ever use formal speech? They certainly do! In more rigid formal settings like the military, business conferences, TV news broadcast, or public presentations, you may hear *formal polite* speech (verbs ending in -니다 (nee-dah) for statements, -니까? (nee-kkah) for questions, -시오 (see-oh) for commands). Some basic expressions are often used in their *formal polite* form. Read on:

고맙습니다 (goh-mahp-sseum-nee-dah.) (*Thank you.*)

반갑습니다 (bahn-gahp-sseum-nee-dah.) (*Nice to meet you.*)

안녕하십니까? (ahn-nyuhng-hah-sheem-nee-kkah?) (*Hello.*)

안녕히 가십시오 (ahn-nyung-hee gah-sheep-ssee-oh.) (*Good bye.*)

Table 3-2 summarizes general guidelines about when to use different speech styles in Korean.

TABLE 3-2 **Speech Styles: Whom to Use Them With**

Speech styles	Settings/Used With
Formal Polite (-니다, -니까?)	Military officers, business customers, companies with a rigid hierarchy, judges, in official public speeches, TV news broadcasts, conference presentations
Informal Polite (-아요/어요)	Your colleagues, teachers, neighbors, acquaintances, shopkeepers, friend's parents, people you don't know (people you meet on the street, bus, train, and park) and in everyday situations in which politeness is expected, to someone who you want to show some respect to
Intimate (-아/어)	People with very close relationships to you such as close friends, siblings, classmates, children, and family members

"SHALL WE LET GO OF THE POLITE SPEECH?"

When Koreans think you're close enough friends that you don't need to keep up the formalities, they may say 우리, 말 놓아요 (놔요 in shortened form). (oo-ree mahl noh-ah-yoh) (*Let's let go of our polite speech.*) 말 (mahl) means *speech*, and 놓다 (noh-tah) means to *let go/put (down).* 말 놓다 as a phrase means to *let go of the polite speech* (that is, use 반말/the intimate speech style). If you want your Korean friend's parents to speak 반말 to you, you can say to them 말씀 놓으세요 (mahl-sseum noh-eu-seh-yoh) (*Please put down your polite speech*) or 말씀 편하게 하세요. (mahl-sseum pyuhn-hah-geh hah-seh-yoh) (*Please speak casually/comfortably.*) Speaking 반말 with people of your age in casual situations may help break the ice.

Getting into Nouns and Pronouns

You may know the elements that make up 영어 문장 (yuhng-uh moon-jahng) (*English sentences*) like nouns, verbs, adjectives, and adverbs. Don't worry if these grammar terms are unfamiliar; we do a quick review in this chapter. 한국어 문장 (hahn-goo-guh moon-jahng) (*Korean sentences*) are also mostly made up of these same parts, with one more important element called 조사 (joh-sah) (*particles*). English doesn't have these. (Bummer.) Reviewing basic grammar terms can't hurt. Let's start with nouns and pronouns.

Nouns

명사 (myuhng-sah) (*Nouns*) are 이름 (ee-reum) (*names*): 이름 of an object, person, place, or even an abstract thing. The name of the city you live in, say 시드니 (see-deu-nee) (*Sydney*), is a proper noun. A name like 조이 (joh-ee) (*Zoe*) is also a proper noun. You may be a 친구 (cheen-goo) (*friend*) to one, but a 동료 (dohng-nyoh) (*colleague*) to another; these words are *common nouns*. You must be full of 열정 (yuhl-jjuhng) (*passion*) and 용기 (yohng-gee) (*courage*) to learn new languages; these abstract things are also nouns.

In Korea, there are some politer versions of common nouns as follows:

>> **Age:** 연세 (yuhn-seh) instead of 나이 (nah-ee)

>> **Birthday:** 생신 (saeng-sheen) instead of 생일 (saeng-eel)

>> **Home:** 댁 (daek) instead of 집 (jeep)

>> **Meal:** 진지 (jeen-jee) instead of 밥 (bahp)

>> **Name:** 성함 (suhng-hahm) instead of 이름(ee-reum)

>> **Speech/talk:** 말씀 (mahl-sseum) instead of 말 (mahl)

You can use the politer form when speaking to people who are elderly or of a higher social status than you. However, in casual situations, you can get by without them. When we get to a situation in which you should use the honorific form of the noun, we'll bring it to your attention again.

Here are a few more cool things about Korean nouns:

>> There's no need to distinguish between singular and plural nouns. For instance, in Korean, "a person" and "people" are both called 사람 (sah-rahm). There *is* a plural particle, 들 (deul), to add after noun if you want to emphasize the plurality of a noun. However, you can still convey the meaning even

without it. Both of the following Korean sentences have the same English translation: "There are many people." (Literally, "people are many.")

- 사람이 많아요. (sah-rah-mee mah-nah-yoh.)
- 사람들이 많아요. (sah-rahm-deu-ree mah-nah-yoh.)

>> Korean doesn't have masculine or feminine parts of speech. So, no need to worry about memorizing the genders of the nouns.

Pronouns

A pronoun is a noun you use to avoid repeating yourself over and over. Check out some subcategories of pronouns.

Personal pronouns

There are two first-person singular pronouns in Korean: 나 (nah), the plain form, and 저 (juh), the polite version. 저 is used in polite speech. Table 3-3 shows more Korean personal pronouns.

TABLE 3-3   **Personal Pronouns**

	Pronouns	Polite/Humble Form	English
1st person	나 (nah)	저 (juh)	I, me
	* 내 (nae) (나 + 의)	* 제 (jeh) (저 + 의)	my
	우리 (oo-ree)	저희 (juh-hee)	we, us
2nd person	너 (nuh)	당신 (dahng-sheen)	you (singular)
		그대 (geu-dae)	
	* 네 (neh) (너 + 의)	당신의, 그대의	your (singular)
	너희 (nuh-hee)	여러분 (yuh-ruh-boon)	you (plural)
3rd person	그 (geu)	그분 (geu-boon)	he, him
	그녀 (geu-nyuh)		she, he
	그들 (geu-deul)	그분들 (geu-boon-deul)	they, them
	그녀들 (geu-nyuh-deul)		

* Only 내, 제, and 네 have shortened forms for possessive pronouns; all other pronouns use [pronoun]+의 without any abbreviations.

REMEMBER

Pronouns are rarely used in Korean. How do you know who did something or who is being talked about? No worries. You'll understand from the context. For example, to say "I love you" in Korean, you can simply say 사랑해(요) (sah-rahng-hae-(yoh)) (literally, *love*). The pronoun *I* and *you* are left out. Here are more examples:

Q: 제니 알아요? (jeh-nee ah-rah-yoh) (*Do you know Jenny?*) (Literally, *Jenny know?*)

A: 네, 알아요. (neh, ah-rah-yoh) (*Yes, I know (her).*) (Literally, *Yes, know.*)

GRAMMATICALLY SPEAKING

When you address someone in English, you sometimes use *personal pronouns* or their *first name*. In Korean, however, avoid calling people by their first names, if the relationship is formal or work-related. Instead, use job titles, like 매니저님 (mae-nee-juh-neem) (*manager*), 선생님 (suhn-saeng-neem) (*instructor*), or 사장님 (sah-jahng-neem) (*CEO*). You can also use -씨 (*Ms./Mr.*) after the first name or full name, to someone of similar social rank or lower at your workplace. Koreans also often use kinship terms in more informal, non-work-related settings, even if they're not biologically related. Interesting, right? Look at the examples and see how "you" is expressed in different situations:

매니저님 언제 오셨어요? (mae-nee-juh-neem uhn-jeh oh-shuh-ssuh-yoh) (*When did you come, Manager Choi?*)

최 선생님은요? (chweh suhn-saeng-nee-meun-nyoh) (*How about you, Intructor/Ms. Choi?*)

해나 씨, 뭐 좋아해요? (hae-nah-ssee, mwuh joh-ah-hae-yoh) (*Hannah, what do you like?*)

언니, 어디에서 만날래? (uhn-nee, uh-dee-eh-suh mahn-nahl-lae) (*Where would you like to meet?*) (언니: *older sister* for female.)

Possessive pronouns

Just like in English, the possessor comes before the possessed, like this: *possessor* + (의) + *possessed*. Note that, 의, the possessive particle, is pronounced '에' /eh/.

If you want to make the fact that this 책 (chaek) (*book*) belongs to you, add 의 (eui/eh) (*~'s*) particle after the pronoun — 나의 책 (nah-eh chaek) (*my book*) or, in the polite/humble form, 저의 책 (juh-eh chaek).

REMEMBER

For *my*, then, the shortened forms — 내 (nae) and 제 (jeh) — are used more frequently than 나의 and 저의 — for example, 내 친구 (nae cheen-goo) (*my friend*), 제 이름 (jeh ee-reum) (*my name*). For other pronouns, add 의 in between the pronoun and the possessed. (See Table 3-3 for more on the pronouns.)

"MY" HUSBAND OR "OUR" HUSBAND?

In Korean, people tend to use 우리 (oo-ree) (*we/us*) or 저희 (juh-hee) (*we/us*, polite form) a lot more than 내 (nae) (*my*) or 제 (jeh) (*my*, polite form) when talking about things they own, especially if they are talking about something or someone they "have" communally with other people, such as family members or co-workers. They refer to them as 우리 가족 (oo-ree gah-johk) (*our family*), 우리 학교 (oo-ree hahk-kkyoh) (*our school*), or 저희 선생님 (juh-hee suhn-sehng-neem) (*our teacher*). Even if you are the only one who lives in your house, you still say 우리 집 (oo-ree jeep) instead of 내 집 (nae jeep) (*my house*). And, yes, they even use the term 우리 남편 (oo-ree nahm-pyuhn) (*our husband*) and 우리 아내 (oo-ree ah-nae) (*our wife*) when referring to their own spouses. Just because a Korean uses the word 우리 (oo-ree) (*our*), don't get any wrong ideas!

REMEMBER

Then, keep in mind that Koreans often omit the possessive particle, 의, in casual speech. For example, they'll say 우리 회사 (oo-ree hwae-sah) (*our company*) instead of 우리의 회사, and 수지 엄마 (soo-jee uhm-mah) (*Suzie's mom*) instead of 수지의 엄마.

Demonstrative pronouns

In 영어 (yuhng-uh) (*English*), the difference between *this* and *that* as well as *here* and *there* has to do with the relative location of a thing to the speaker. *This* is closer to the speaker than *that*, and *here* is closer than *there*.

In 한국어 (hahn-goo-guh) (*Korean*), the word for *this* is 이 (ee), but there are two options for the word *that*. It depends on the proximity of an item relative to the speaker and the listener. If an item, 것 (guht) in Korean, is close to the listener but far from the speaker, use 그 (geu) and say 그것 (or 그거 in casual speech) to refer to *that thing*. 그 can also refer to something previously mentioned or understood in context, so 그것 can translate to "it." If it's far from both the speaker and the listener, use 저 (juh) and say 저것 (or 저거 for casual speech) to refer to *that thing over there*. The same concept applies to people, place, and other nouns, as shown in Table 3-4:

TABLE 3-4   Demonstrative Pronouns

Pronoun	이 (ee) (this)	그 (geu) (that)	저 (juh) (that over there)
Meaning	Things close to the speaker	Things close to the listener, far from speaker	Things far from both speaker and listener
thing/object	이거 (ee-guh) (this one)	그거 (geu-guh) (that one; it)	저거 (juh-guh) (that one over there)
direction	이쪽 (ee-jjohk) (this side)	그쪽 (geu-jjohk) (that side)	저쪽 (juh-jjohk) (that side over there)
person	이 사람 (ee-sah-rahm) (this person)	그 사람 (geu-sah-rahm) (that person; already mentioned person)	저 사람 (juh-sah-rahm) (that person over there)
place	여기 (yuh-gee) (here)	거기 (guh-gee) (there; already mentioned place)	저기 (juh-gee) (over there)

Working with Verbs

Finally, on to 한국어 동사 (hahn-goo-guh dohng-sah) (*Korean verbs*), the heart of the sentence! One interesting fact about 한국어 동사 is that there is no such a thing as subject-verb agreement found in 영어 (yuhng-uh) (*English*), where verbs conjugate according to person, number, or tense (e.g., *I am, we are, it was. . .*). In Korean, verbs like "to be" or "to have" are the same for her and them and you and me.

Sadly, this doesn't mean that 한국어 동사 are a one-size-fits-all kind of deal. In fact, 동사 can express all sorts of info in your sentences by attaching different suffixes to the verb stems (a.k.a., verb conjugation). They have multiple purposes beyond just indicating the sentence type (whether it's a statement, question, command, or suggestion) or tense and aspect (whether an event has happened, will happen, or is happening). They can also express the level of formality, modesty, and politeness (speech style) that you want to convey to the person you're talking to or about. What's more, 동사 can even convey your mood or emotion during speech. This is why the verbs are the most important parts of Korean sentences.

Whether you aim to ace a job interview, impress your in-laws, address new acquaintances politely, or assertively confront an adversary, all of these scenarios demand a grasp of Korean verb conjugation. By the end of this chapter, you'll feel unstoppable!

Now, let's begin with the basics of verb forms.

Understanding basic verb forms

Korean verbs are always made up of two pieces: a verb stem and an ending suffix (either a sentence-ending or clause-ending suffix). To conjugate a verb, you take the verb stem and attach one or more ending suffixes. See the following discussion on two important terms:

>> **Verb stem:** The verb stem is the bare form of the verb without any ending suffix. It's a "root" part that contains the meaning. Examples of some verb stems are 먹 (muhk) (*eat*), 만나 (mahn-nah) (*meet*), and 있 (eet) (*have/exist*).

>> **Dictionary form:** The dictionary form of a verb is what you find in a dictionary. Alone, they behave like English infinitives such as *to see* and *to go*. They are made up of the verb stem and 다 (dah) (*the suffix for the dictionary form*).

For example, if you combine the verb stem 먹 (*eat*) and 다 (*dictionary form suffix*), you get the dictionary form, 먹다 (muhk-ttah) (*to eat*). More dictionary forms: 만나다 (mahn-nah-dah) (*to meet*), 있다 (eet-ttah) (*to have, to exist*). To conjugate the verbs into different tenses and speech styles, you must drop the 다 first and then apply the various endings to the stem.

Two types of verbs

Before digging into conjugation rules, let's have a look at what's special about 한국어 동사 (hahn-goo-guh dohng-sah) (*Korean verbs*) and 형용사 (hyuhng-yohng-sah) (*adjectives*).

You know that a verb expresses an action. Words like 사다 (sah-dah) (*to buy*), 말하다 (mahl-hah-dah) (*to speak*), 생각하다 (saeng-gah-kah-dah) (*to think*), 좋아하다 (joh-ah-hah-dah) (*to like*) are categorized as verbs. If you've got that down, you're definitely on the right track.

In English, words like *colorful, funny, genuine,* and *immaculate,* are categorized as *adjectives,* as they describe something or someone. They don't change their forms regardless of their roles in a sentence. For instance, in the sentences, *It's a good book* and *The book is good,* the *good* remains the same, with no change in its form.

But in Korean, adjectives are considered a type of verb and are alternatively referred to as *descriptive verbs.* Why? Because they can do verb stuff like having infinitive forms and conjugating like action verbs.

For example, 좋다 (joh-tah) is the dictionary form of a descriptive verb, meaning *to be good*. To express *good book*, you change 좋다 to its noun-modifying form, 좋은 (joh-eun). As a result, you have 좋은 책 (joh-eun chaek) (*good book*). To say *The book is good*, you conjugate 좋다 to its sentence ending form, 좋아요 (joh-ah-yoh) (*is good*). Then, you have 책이 좋아요 (chae-gee joh-ah-yoh).

Here are some examples of Korean adjectives, that is, descriptive verbs: 친절하다 (cheen-juhl-hah-dah) (*to be kind*), 행복하다 (haeng-boh-khah-dah) (*to be happy*), 바쁘다 (bah-ppeu-dah) (*to be busy*), *spicy* (맵다) (maep-ttah), 달다 (dahl-dah) (*to be sweet*), and more.

Conjugations: Informal polite

Now, let's dive into conjugation for the most commonly used speech style, *informal polite*. Informal polite uses the verb-ending suffix -아요 or -어요. It may be confusing at first figuring out if a verb should take the -아요 or the -어요 ending, but don't worry! There is a method to the madness.

TIP

The key here lies in the *final vowel of the stem* — the vowel the stem ends in. For example, in the following dictionary form of the verbs, 알다 (ahl-dah) (*to know*), 먹다 (muhk-ttah) (*to eat*), and 믿다 (meet-ttah) (*to believe*), the stems are 알, 먹, and 믿. Got it so far? Then the game's nearly over! Take the following steps to finish the conjugation:

1. Check whether the last vowel of the stem is ㅏ (ah) or ㅗ (oh). If it's one of those two vowels, add 아요 (ah-yoh) to the verb stem.

2. If the last vowel of the stem *is not* ㅏ (ah) or ㅗ (oh), add 어요 (uh-yoh).

Taking the examples from the verbs above, the LAST vowel of the stems in 알, 먹, and 믿 are ㅏ, ㅓ, and ㅣ, respectively. The first verb calls for the suffix -아요, and the last two call for -어요.

Hence, the informal polite forms are 알아요 (ah-rah-yoh), 먹어요 (muh-guh-yoh), and 믿어요 (mee-duh-yoh). Remember, the LAST vowel in the stem determines the right match. Table 3-5 has some more examples.

TABLE 3-5 Consonant-ending Stem Conjugation for Informal Polite 아요/어요

Meaning	Dictionary Form	Stem + 아 or 어	Conjugated Form	Example Sentences
to hang out	놀다	놀 + 아	놀아요 (noh-rah-yoh)	친구하고 놀아요. (cheen-goo-hah-goh noh-rah-yoh) (*I hang out with a friend.*)
to sit	앉다	앉 + 아	앉아요 (ahn-jah-yoh)	소파에 앉아요. (ssoh-pah-eh ahn-jah-yoh) (*I sit on the sofa.*)
to wipe, clean	닦다	닦 + 아	닦아요 (dah-kkah-yoh)	이를 닦아요. (ee-reul dah-kkah-yoh) (*I brush my teeth.*)
to receive	받다	받 + 아	받아요 (bah-dah-yoh)	선물을 받아요. (suhn-moo-reul bah-dah-yoh) (*I receive a gift.*)
to be good	좋다	좋 + 아	좋아요 (joh-ah-yoh)	날씨가 좋아요. (nahl-ssee-gah joh-ah-yoh.) (*The weather is good.*)
to take (photos)	찍다	찍 + 어	찍어요 (jjee-guh-yoh)	사진을 찍어요. (sah-jee-neul jjee-guh-yoh.) (*I take photos.*)
to read	읽다	읽 + 어	읽어요 (eel-guh-yoh)	책을 읽어요. (chae-geul eel-guh-yoh.) (*I read a book.*)
to make	만들다	만들 + 어	만들어요 (mahn-deu-ruh-yoh)	피자를 만들어요. (pee-jah-reul mahn-deu-ruh-yoh.) (*I make pizza.*)
to exist, possess	있다	있 + 어	있어요 (ee-ssuh-yoh)	숙제가 있어요. (sook-jjeh-gah ee-ssuh-yoh.) (*I have homework.*)
to be fun	재미있다	재미있 + 어	재미있어요 (jae-mee-ee-ssuh-yoh)	드라마가 재미있어요. (deu-rah-mah-gah jae-mee-ee-ssuh-yoh.) (*The drama is fun.*)
to be tasteless	맛없다	맛없 + 어	맛없어요 (mah-duhp-ssuh-yoh)	파스타가 맛없어요. (pah-seu-tah-gah mah-dup-ssuh-yoh.) (*The pasta is tasteless.*)

When the stem ends in a vowel without a final consonant, such as 가 in 가다 (gah-dah) (*to go*) and 보 in 보다 (boh-dah) (*to see*), vowels are contracted. Check out the rules in Table 3-6.

TABLE 3-6 **Vowel-Ending Stem Conjugation**

Stem vowel + 아 or 어요	Vowel Contraction Rules	Examples in Dictionary Form	Ending Suffix	Conjugated Form
ㅏ + 아요	Drop one 아	가다 (gah-dah) (*to go*)	가 + 아요	가요 (gah-yoh)
ㅗ + 아요	Merge the vowels	오다 (oh-dah) (*to come*)	오 + 아요	와요 (wah-yoh)
ㅓ + 어요	Drop one 어	서다 (suh-dah) (*to stand, stop*)	서 + 어요	서요 (suh-yoh)
ㅜ + 어요	Merge the vowels	주다 (joo-dah) (*to give*)	주 + 어요	줘요 (jwuh-yoh)
ㅣ + 어요	ㅣ + ㅓ → ㅕ	치다 (chee-dah) (*to hit, beat*)	치 + 어요	쳐요 (chyuh-yoh)
― + 어요	1. Drop ― 2. Add 아요 if the preceding vowel ends in ㅏ or ㅗ.	바쁘다 (bah-ppeu-dah) (*to be busy*)	바빠 + 아요	바빠요 (bah-ppah-yoh)
	1. Drop ― 2. Add 어요 if there's no preceding vowel or if it's not ㅏ or ㅗ.	크다 (keu-dah) (*to be big*)	ㅋ + 어요	커요 (kuh-yoh)
		예쁘다 (yeh-ppeu-dah) (*to be pretty*)	예뻐 + 어요	예뻐요 (yeh-ppuh-yoh)
ㅐ, ㅔ + 어요	Can drop 어	내다 (nae-dah) (*to submit*)	내 + 어요	내어요/내요 (nae-uh-yoh/nae-yoh)
		베다 (beh-dah) (*to cut/mow*)	베 + 어요	베어요/베요 (beh-uh-yoh/beh-yoh)
Complex vowels (ㅚ,ㅟ,ㅞ) + 어요	Add 어요 (for ㅚ verbs, merge the vowels into ㅙ)	쉬다 (shwee-dah) (*to rest*)	쉬 + 어요	쉬어요 (shwee-uh-yoh)
		되다 (dwae-dah) (*to become*)	되 + 어요	되어요 (= 돼요) (dwae-yoh)

COLORS OF VOWELS AND VOWEL HARMONY

Did you know that vowels have colors? The sound they make in your mouth determines whether they are "bright," "dark," or "neutral." Bright vowels sound "light/bright," like 아 (ah) and 오 (oh), while dark vowels sound "heavy/dark," like 어 (uh) and 우 (oo).

King Sejong was well aware of this difference between vowel sounds, and he incorporated the concept of "bright" and "dark" vowels into 한글 (Hangeul) when it was made in the 15th century. 아, 야, 오 and 요 (hereafter *bright vowels*) carry a "light," "bright," and "small" nuance. 어, 여, 우, and 유 (hereafter *dark vowels*) carry a "heavy," "dark," and "big" nuance. 이 are neutral. We're a bit too late to ask King Sejong his thoughts on bright and dark vowels, but it's no coincidence that the bright vowels are the ones that have "sun" (ㆍ) on top of the earth (ㅗ) or facing the east (ㅏ) where the sun rises.

Bright vowels tend to be paired with bright vowels, and dark vowels tend to be paired with dark vowels. This is called vowel harmony, and understanding it will help you learn Korean better. Here are some examples of vowel harmony:

- **Complex vowels:** You've already seen this vowel harmony in Chapter 2: Hangeul. For complex vowels, the bright vowels (ㅏ, ㅗ) are combined with other bright vowels or neutral vowels, resulting in the combinations ㅘ (ㅗ + ㅏ) and ㅚ (ㅗ + ㅣ). Bright and dark vowels don't mix! That's why you don't see complex vowels that combine ㅗ and ㅓ or ㅜ and ㅏ together.

- **Verb conjugation:** When conjugating to -아요/어요 (informal polite speech) form in this chapter, you discover that having a bright vowel (ㅏ or ㅗ) in the end of the verb stem leads to a bright 아요 conjugation, as in 좋다 (joh-tah) (*to be good*) becoming 좋아요 (joh-ah-yoh) (*it's good*).

- **Onomatopoeia:** The most widespread use of bright and dark vowels in Korean is 의성어 (eui-suhng-uh) (*onomatopoeia*) and 의태어 (eui-tae-uh) (*mimetic words*). The bright vowel 의성어 and 의태어 have a *lighter, smaller* nuance; the dark vowels give *heavier and bigger* vibes. Try reading aloud these words and feeling the color of the vowels.

  Sparkling: 반짝 (bahn-jjahk) versus 번쩍 (buhn-jjuhk)

  Water splashing: 퐁당 (pohng-dahng) versus 풍덩 (poong-duhng)

  Soft, chewy: 말랑 (mahl-lahng) versus 물렁 (mool-luhng)

Forming the past tense

Making the past tense of the 아요/어요 is super simple. You just add ㅆ어요 in the place of 요 in the present tense 아요/어요 form. For instance, to create the past tense for 알아요 (ah-rah-yoh) (*I know*), replace 요 with ㅆ어요. Then voilà! You got the past tense form — 알았어요 (ah-rah-ssuh-yoh) (*I knew*) (알아+ㅆ어요). Read on for more examples of verbs in their dictionary form, 아요/어요 present and past tense:

가다 (*to go*) — 가요 — 갔어요 (gah-ssuh-yoh)

보다 (*to watch, see*) — 봐요 — 봤어요 (bwah-ssuh-yoh)

먹다 (*to eat*) — 먹어요 — 먹었어요 (muh-guh-ssuh-yoh)

쉬다 (*to rest*) — 쉬어요 — 쉬었어요 (shwee-uh-ssuh-yoh)

배우다 (*to learn*) — 배워요 — 배웠어요 (bae-wuh-ssuh-yoh)

바쁘다 (*to be busy*) — 바빠요 — 바빴어요 (bah-ppah-ssuh-yoh)

읽다 (*to read*) — 읽어요 — 읽었어요 (eel-guh-ssuh-yoh)

주다 (*to give*) — 줘요 — 줬어요 (jwuh-ssuh-yoh)

되다 (*to become*) — 돼요 (되어요) — 됐어요 (dwae-ssuh-yoh)

재미있다 (*to be fun*) — 재미있어요 — 재미있었어요 (jae-mee-ee-ssuh-ssuh-yoh)

Conjugation exceptions

As with any language, a few Korean verbs conjugate irregularly. In Korean, they are the copular verbs 이다 (ee-dah) (*to be*), 아니다 (ah-nee-dah) (*to not be*), and the action verb 하다 (hah-dah) (*to do*). See Table 3-7 for - 아요/어요 (*informal polite speech*), and -아/어 (*intimate speech style*) in their present and past tense form.

Forming the future tense

In Korean, the present tense can express future events, often with future time adverbs like 내일 (nae-eel) (*tomorrow*) and 내년 (nae-nyuhn) (*next year*). Hence, you can say 내일 도착해요 (nae-eel doh-chah-kae-yoh) (*I'll be arriving tomorrow.*) without having to worry about conjugating the verb. In this case, the future event is more certain and definite.

TABLE 3-7   Irregular

Dictionary Form	Speech Style	Present Tense	Past Tense	Example Sentences: Present – Past Tense
이다 (ee-dah) (to be)	Informal polite	C+이에요 * C: Consonant-ending noun	C+이었어요	수지는 학생이에요. (soo-jee-neun hahk-ssaeng-ee-yeh-yoh.) (Susie is a student.) 수지는 학생이었어요. (soo-jee-neun hahk-ssaeng-ee-uh-ssuh-yoh.) (Susie was a student.)
		V+예요 * V: Vowel-ending noun	V+였어요	수지는 가수예요. (soo-jee-neun gah-soo-yeh-yoh.) (Susie is a singer.) 수지는 가수였어요. (soo-jee-neun gah-soo-yuh-ssuh-yoh.) (Susie was a singer.)
	Intimate speech	C+이야	C+이었어	수지는 학생이야. (soo-jee-neun hahk-ssaeng-ee-yah.) (Susie is a student.) 수지는 학생이었어. (soo-jee-neun hahk-ssaeng-ee-uh-ssuh.) (Susie was a student.)
		V+야	V+였어	수지는 가수야. (soo-jee-neun gah-soo-yah.) (Susie is a singer.) 수지는 가수였어. (soo-jee-neun gah-soo-yuh-ssuh.) (Susie was a singer.)
아니다 (ah-nee-dah) (to not be)	Informal polite	아니에요	아니었어요	저는 학생이 아니에요. (juh-neun hahk-ssaeng-ee ah-nee-eh-yoh.) (I am not a student.) 저는 학생이 아니었어요. (juh-neun hahk-ssaeng-ee ah-nee-uh-ssuh-yoh.) (I was not a student.)
	Intimate speech	아니야	아니었어	나는 가수가 아니야. (nah-neun gah-soo-gah ah-nee-yah.) (I am not a singer.) 나는 가수가 아니었어. (nah-neun gah-soo-gah ah-nee-uh-ssuh.) (I was not a singer.)

Dictionary Form	Speech Style	Present Tense	Past Tense	Example Sentences: Present – Past Tense
하다(hah-dah) (to do)	Informal polite	해요	했어요	저는 매일 운동해요. (juh-neun mae-eel oon-dohng-hae-yoh.) (I work out every day.)
				저는 매일 운동했어요. (juh-neun mae-eel oon-dohng-hae-ssuh-yoh.) (I worked out everyday.)
	Intimate speech	해	했어	이번 주말에 뭐 해? (ee-buhn joo-mah-reh mwuh-hae?) (What do you do this weekend?)
				지난 주말에 뭐 했어? (jee-nahn joo-mah-reh mwuh-hae-ssuh?) (What did you do last weekend?)

When you want to express *I'm going to go to a concert tonight* (that is, your intention), *I'll do it later* (immediate plans), or *It's going to rain tomorrow* (probability), as expressed with *be going to* in English, you can use –(으)ㄹ 것이다. In spoken Korean, a shortened form, (으)ㄹ 거다, is used. Here is how you can conjugate (으)ㄹ 거다 in different speech style:

	Verb	아요/어요 (Informal polite)	아/어 (Intimate)
Vowel-ending stem+ ㄹ 거다	가다	갈 거예요 (gahl kkuh-yeh-yoh)	갈 거야 (gahl kkuh-yah)
Consonant-ending stem+ 을 거다	먹다	먹을 거예요 (muh-geul kkuh-yeh-yoh)	먹을 거야 (muh-geul kkuh-yah)

Table 3-8 presents more examples.

TABLE 3-8 Conjugating into the Future Form –(으)ㄹ 거예요

Meaning in English	Dictionary Form	Stem +(으)ㄹ 거예요	Conjugated Form
to do	하다 (hah-dah)	하 + ㄹ 거예요	할 거예요 (hahl kkuh-yeh-yoh)
to learn	배우다 (bae-woo-dah)	배우 + ㄹ 거예요	배울 거예요 (bae-wool kkuh-yeh-yoh)
to teach	가르치다 (gah-reu-chee-dah)	가르치 + ㄹ 거예요	가르칠 거예요 (gah-reu-cheel kkuh-yeh-yoh)
to eat	먹다 (muhk-ttah)	먹 + 을 거예요	먹을 거예요 (muhl-geul kkuh-yeh-yoh)
to read	읽다 (eek-ttah)	읽 + 을 거예요	읽을 거예요 (eel-geul kkuh-yeh-yoh)
to be fun	재미있다 (jae-mee-eet-ttah)	재미있 + 을 거예요	재미있을 거예요 (jae-mee-ee-sseul kkuh-yeh-yoh)

Adverbs: Handy additionals to verbs

An adverb is a word that you "*add to a verb*" to spice it up and give more details about how, when, where, how often, or to what extent an action is performed. 한국어 부사 (hahn-goo-guh boo-sah) (*Korean adverb*) work pretty similarly to English 부사. No need to worry about tinkering around with stems — 한국어 부사 don't conjugate!

Although 부사 can be placed almost anywhere within a sentence, the safest way to use them is to place them immediately before the word they modify. For example, 비가 와요 (bee-gah wah-yoh) means *It rains* (literally, *The rain comes.*). To express *It rains a lot*, you can put the adverb 많이 (mah-nee) (*a lot*) right before the word it modifies — the verb 와요 (wah-yoh) (*comes*) in this case. Therefore, you say 비가 많이 와요 (bee-gah mah-nee wah-yoh).

GRAMMATICALLY
SPEAKING

In English, adjectives can be transformed into adverbs by adding the suffix -*ly* to the adjective (for example, *kind* becomes *kindly*). This is also the case in Korean. Some Korean adverbs are formed by adding suffixes like -게, -히, or -이 to adjectives.

크다 (keu-dah) (*to be big*) — 크게 (keu-geh) (*greatly, loudly*)

많다 (mahn-ttah) (*to be many*) — 많이 (mah-nee) (*a lot, many*)

솔직하다 (sohl-jjee-kah-dah) (*to be honest*) — 솔직히 (sohl-jjee-kee) (*honestly, frankly*)

Table 3-9 displays some of the common adverbs and how they can be used in a sentence.

GRAMMATICALLY
SPEAKING

There are also conjunctive adverbs that hold sentences together. This helps you connect ideas, show contrast, or give explanations. Some examples include 그리고 (geu-ree-goh) (*and, and then*), 그런데/근데 (geu-ruhn-deh/geun-deh) (*but, by the way*), 그래서 (geu-rae-suh) (*so, therefore*), 그럼 (geu-ruhm) (*then, if that's the case*), 그러니까 (geu-ruh-nee-kkah) (*for that reason, so*). They work like English conjunctions, but they go at the beginning of a sentence. See the examples:

주말에 보통 영화 봐요. **그리고** 친구 만나요. (joo-mah-reh boh-tohng yuhng-hwah bwah-yoh. geu-ree-goh cheen-goo mahn-nah-yoh.) (*I usually watch movies and meet friends over the weekend.*)

커피를 좋아해요. **그런데** 차는 안 좋아해요. (kuh-pee-reul joh-ah-hae-yoh. geu-ruhn-deh chah-neun ahn joh-ah-hae-yoh.) (*I like coffee, but I don't like tea.*)

드라마를 정말 좋아해요. **그래서** 자주 봐요. (deu-rah-mah-reul joh-ah-hae-yoh. geu-rae-suh jah-joo bwah-yoh.) (*I really like dramas, so I watch them often.*)

TABLE 3-9 **Examples of Korean Adverbs**

Types	Korean Adverbs	English	Examples
degree	많이 (mah-nee)	many, a lot	어제 많이 잤어요. (uh-jeh mah-nee jah-ssuh-yoh.) (*I slept a lot yesterday.*)
	조금 (joh-geum)	a little bit	조금 알아요. (joh-geum ah-rah-yoh.) (*I know a little.*)
	더 (duh)	more	조금 더 주세요. (joh-geum duh joo-seh-yoh.) (*Give (me) a little more please!*)
	덜 (duhl)	less	오늘은 덜 추워요. (oh-neu-reun duhl choo-wuh-yoh.) (*Today is less cold.*)
	너무 (nuh-moo)	too	너무 바빠요. (nuh-moo bah-ppah-yoh.) (*I'm too busy.*)
	제일 / 가장 (jeh-eel / gah-jahng)	most	봄을 제일 좋아해요. (boh-meul jeh-eel joh-ah-hae-yoh.) (*I like spring the most.*)
	정말 (juhng-mahl)	really	정말 잘했어요. (juhng-mahl jahl-hae-ssuh-yoh.) (*You did really good.*)
manner	열심히 (yuhl-sseem-hee)	diligently, hard	열심히 했어요. (yuhl-sseem-hee hae-ssuh-yoh.) (*I worked hard.*)
	크게 (keu-geh)	bigly, loudly	크게 말해 주세요. (keu-geh mahl-hae joo-seh-yoh.) (*Please speak loudly.*)
	솔직히 (sohl-jjeek-kee)	honestly, frankly	솔직히 말해. (sohl-jjee-kee mahl-hae.) (*Tell me the truth* - intimate speech)
	갑자기 (gahp-jjah-gee)	suddenly	갑자기 비가 왔어요. (gahp-jjah-gee bee-gah wah-ssuh-yoh.) (*Suddenly, it rained.*)
	같이 (gah-chee)	together	같이 가요! (gah-chee gah-yoh!) (*Let's go together!*)
	빨리 (ppahl-lee)	hurry, fast	빨리 와! (ppahl-lee wah!) (*Come quickly!*)
frequency / time	곧 (goht)	soon, instantly	곧 도착해요. (goht doh-chah-kae-yoh.) (*It arrives soon.*)
	자주 (jah-joo)	often	영화 자주 안 봐요. (yuhng-hwah jah-joo ahn bwah-yoh.) (*I don't watch movies often.*)
	가끔 (gah-kkeum)	occasionally	가끔 외식해요. (gah-kkeum wae-shee-kae-yoh.) (*I eat out occasionally.*)
	보통 (boh-tohng)	usually, normally	주말에 보통 등산해요. (joo-mah-reh boh-tohng deung-sahn-hae-yoh.) (*I usually hike on the weekend.*)
	나중에 (nah-joong-eh)	later	나중에 봐요. (nah-joong-eh bwah-yoh.) (*See you later.*)

Negation adverbs

Sometimes things just don't go the way we expect them to. For simple negation denoting something doesn't/didn't happen, use 안 (ahn) (*not*) before the verb: 눈이 안 왔어요 (noo-nee ahn wah-ssuh-yoh) (*It didn't snow*), 학교에 안 갔어요 (hahk-kkyoh-eh ahn gah-ssuh-yoh) (*I didn't go to school.*).

If you can't / couldn't do something, use 못 (moht) (*can't*): 못 가요 (moht kkah-yoh) (*can't*), 못 했어요 (moh tae-ssuh-yoh) (*couldn't do it*), and 못 먹었어요 (mohn muh-guh-ssuh-yoh) (*couldn't eat*).

Note the pronunciation of 못. When 못 is followed by ㅎ as in 못 해 (*can't do*), it makes an aspirated sound ㅌ. So, you pronounce 못 해 as /모태/, and /모태써요/ for 못 했어요.

If the verb is "[noun]+하다" verb, put 안 or 못 between the noun and 하다: 공부 안 해요 (gohng-boo ahn hae-yoh) (*I don't study.*), 운동 못 했어요 (oon-dohng moh tae-ssuh-yoh) (*couldn't work out.*). For all the other 하다 ending verbs or adjectives, like 깨끗하다, 복잡하다, and 좋아하다, put 안 in front of the verb: 안 깨끗해요 (ahn kkae-kkeu-tae-yoh) (*it's not clean*), 안 복잡해요 (ahn bohk-jjah-pae-yoh) (*it's not crowded/ complicated*), and 안 좋아해요 (ahn joh-ah-hae-yoh) (*I don't like*).

Three verbs don't use 안 or 못 when negated and instead have special negative counterparts. Check out Table 3-10.

TABLE 3-10   Special Negative Form

Positive	Negative form	Example sentences
이다 (ee-dah) (*to be*)	아니다 (ah-nee-dah) (*to not be*)	리사는 미국 사람이 아니에요. (Lisa-neun mee-gook ssah-rah-mee ah-nee-eh-yoh.) (*Lisa is not American.*)
있다 (eet-ttah) (*to exist, possess*)	없다 (uhp-ttah) (*to not have, not exist*)	요즘 너무 바빠서 시간이 없어요. (yoh-jeum nuh-moo bah-ppah-suh shee-gah-nee uhp-ssuh-yoh.) (*I'm too busy lately so have no time.*)
알다 (ahl-dah) (*to know*)	모르다 (moh-reu-dah) (*to not know*)	스페인어(를) 몰라요. 그런데 배우고 싶어요. (seu-peh-ee-nuh(-reul) mohl-lah-yoh. geu-ruhn-deh bae-oo-goh shee-puh-yoh.) (*I don't know Spanish. But I want to learn.*)

Talkin' the Talk

PLAY

Chris is chatting with his colleague, Jennifer, during coffee break on a Monday morning.

Chris: 제니퍼 씨, 주말에 뭐 했어요?
jeh-nee-puh ssee, joo-mah-reh mwuh hae-ssuh-yoh?
Jennifer, what did you do on the weekend?

Jennifer: 집에서 쉬었어요. 크리스 씨는요?
jee-beh-suh shwee-uh-ssuh-yoh. keu-ree-sseu-ssee-neun-nyoh?
I just took a rest at home. How about you, Chris?

Chris: 한국 영화 봤어요.
hahn-gook yuhng-hwah bwah-ssuh-yoh.
I watched a Korean movie.

Jennifer: 그래요? 뭐 봤어요?
geu-rae-yoh? mwuh bwah-ssuh-yoh?
Did you? What did you watch?

Christ: JSA (Join Security Area) 알아요?
JSA ah-rah-yoh?
Do you know JSA?

Jennifer: 아니요, 몰라요.
ah-nee-yoh, mohl-lah-yoh.
No, I don't know.

Chris: 정말 재미있어요. 나중에 꼭 보세요.
juhng-mahl jae-mee-ee-ssuh-yoh. nah-joong-eh kkohk boh-seh-yoh.
It's really fun. You should watch it later.

WORDS TO KNOW

주말	joo-mahl	weekend
뭐 했어요 (뭐 하다)	mwuh hae-ssuh-yoh	what did (you) do?
쉬었어요 (쉬다)	shwee-uh-ssuh-yoh	rested
영화	yuhng-hwah	movie
봤어요/보세요 (보다)	bwah-ssuh-yoh/ boh-seh-yoh	watched/ please watch
그래요? (그렇다)	geu-rae-yoh?	is that so? / really?
알아요 (알다)	ah-rah-yoh	I know
몰라요 (모르다)	mohl-lah-yoh	I don't know
나중에	nah-joong-eh	later

Forming Sentences

So far we've talked about what makes up a sentence. You're now well-versed in how each part of speech works, especially the verbs. Now let's look at how to put those different pieces together to form a sentence.

Getting the word order right

One major difference between 한국어 문장 (hahn-goo-guh moon-jahng) (*Korean sentences*) and 영어 문장 (yuhng-uh moon-jahng) (*English sentences*) is the word order. English goes subject-verb-object, and Korean goes subject-object-verb. In the sentence *I drink coffee*, *I* is the subject (the action performer), *coffee* is the object (action receiver), and *drink* is the verb. The Korean equivalent for this English sentence is 저는 커피를 마셔요. (juh-neun kuh-pee-reul mah-shuh-yoh) (*literally, I coffee drink*).

Always remember that the VERB goes at the END in Korean. Instead of saying *I learn Korean*, you say *I Korean learn*. (저는 한국어를 배워요; juh-neun hahn-goo-guh-reul bae-wuh-yoh). Instead of *I bought Kimchi*, you say *I Kimchi bought*. (저는 김치를 샀어요; juh-neun geem-chee-reul sah-ssuh-yoh). See the pattern?

It may feel like you're impersonating Yoda at first, but subject-object-verb is the correct word order for Korean. Now you the Korean standard word order know!

Marking nouns with particles

Now that you know the verb goes at the end no matter what the situation is, how about the other elements of a sentence? Is there any specific order you have to put them in? Good question! As long as the verb goes at the end, the positions of the other elements are rather flexible. Then, how do you know who did what to whom?

Korean gets around such possible confusions by adding a short suffix called 조사 (joh-sah) (*particles*) at the end of each noun phrase. The 조사 tell you what role a word plays within the sentence (what's the *subject* and what's the *object*).

The particle for the action performer (the subject) is 이 or 가 (hence, the subject particle), and the particle for the action receiver (the object) is 을 or 를 (hence, the object particle). You can see that both of the following sentences have the same basic meaning:

엘라가 러스를 초대했어요. (ehl-lah-gah luh-sseu-reul choh-dae-hae-ssuh-yoh.)
(*Ella invited Ross.*) (literally, *Ella Ross invited*.)

러스를 엘라가 초대했어요. (luh-sseu-reul ehl-lah-gah choh-dae-hae-ssuh-yoh.)
(*Ella invited Ross.*) (literally, *Ross Ella invited*.)

You can add more to the sentence at the beginning or middle, like the details about when or where: *Yesterday Ella Ross invited* or *Ella yesterday Ross invited*. No need to memorize the word order. You'll get more comfortable with Korean word order with more exposure to Korean sentences. Just make sure to keep the verb at the end.

Some particles have more rigid English translations such as *also, only, with, or, to, from,* and *until.* Other particles are multi-functional and context-dependent, for which there is no "all-purpose" English translation. So, it's better to know the particles in terms of their general functions, not their English translations. Table 3-11 shows some of the important Korean particles with their general functions and example sentences.

TABLE 3-11   Particles and Example Sentences

Particles	General Functions	Example Sentences
- 이 (ee) (after **C (c**onsonant-ending noun)	marks the subject of the sentence	에릭이 왔어요. (eh-ree-gee wah-ssuh-yoh.) *(Eric came yesterday.)*
- 가 (gah) (after **V (v**owel-ending noun)	(No English equivalent)	그 드라마가 재미있어요. (geu deu-rah-mah-gah jae-mee-ee-ssuh-yoh.) *(The drama is fun.)*
- 을 (eul) (after C)	marks the object of the sentence	비빔밥을 먹었어요. (bee-beem-ppah-beul muh-guh-ssuh-yoh.) *(I ate bibimbap.)*
- 를 (reul) (after V)	(No English equivalent)	영화를 좋아해요? (yuhng-hwah-reul joh-ah-hae-yoh?) *(Do you like movies?)*
- 은 (eun) (after C)	marks the topic of the sentence;	서울은 재미있는 도시예요. (suh-oo-reun jae-mee-een-neun doh-shee-yeh-yoh.) *(Speaking of Seoul, it's a fun city.)*
- 는 (neun) (after V)	marks contrast (No English equivalent)	저는 햄버거를 좋아해요. 피자는 안 좋아해요. (juh-neun haem-buh-guh-reul joh-ah-hae-yoh. pee-jah-neun ahn joh-ah-hae-yoh.) *(I like hamburgers (but) I don't like pizza.)*
- 도 (doh)	also	피터는 머리가 좋아요. 성격도 좋아요. (pee-tuh-neun muh-ree-gah joh-ah-yoh. suhng-kkyuhk-ttoh joh-ah-yoh.) *(Peter is smart. His personality is also good. / He's also a good person.)*
- 만 (mahn)	only	아침에 커피만 마셨어요. 그래서 배고파요. (ah-chee-meh kuh-pee-mahn mah-shyuh-ssuh-yoh.) *(I only drank coffee for breakfast, so I am hungry.)*
- 에 (eh)	at/in (place), on (time), to (destination)	명동은 서울에 있어요. (myuhng-dong-eun suh-oo-reh ee-ssuh-yoh.) *(Myungdong is in Seoul.)* 토요일에 명동에 가요. (toh-yoh-ee-reh myuhng-dohng-eh gah-yoh.) *(I go to Myungdong on Saturday.)*
- 에서 (eh-suh)	from, at	우리 커피숍에서 만나요. (oo-ree kuh-pee-shoh-beh-suh mahn-nah-yoh.) *(Let's meet at the coffee shop.)*
- 한테 (hahn-teh)	to (someone)	친구가 저한테 선물 줬어요. (cheen-goo-gah juh-hahn-teh suhn-mool jwuh-ssuh-yoh.) *(My friend gave me a gift.)*
- 하고	and	나는 커피하고 차 다 좋아해. (nah-neun kuh-pee-hah-goh chah dah joh-ah-hae.) *(I like both coffee and tea.)*
	with	친구하고 어디에 갔어요? (cheen-goo-hah-goh uh-dee-eh gah-ssuh-yoh?) *(Where did you go with your friend?)*

Particles	General Functions	Example Sentences
- (으)로	toward;	이쪽으로 오세요. (ee-jjoh-geu-roh oh-seh-yoh.) (*Please come this way.*)
(after C + 으로)	by means of	한국어로 말하세요. (hahn-goo-guh-roh mahl-hah-seh-yoh.) (*Please speak in Korean.*)
(after V, ㄹ-ending noun + 로)		명동에 지하철로 갔어요. (myuhng-dong-eh jee-hah-chuhl-loh gah-ssuh-yoh.) (*I went Myeong-dong by subway.*)
- (이)나	or	물이나 차 주세요. (moo-ree-nah chah joo-seh-yoh.) (*Water or tea, please.*)
(after C + 이나) (after V + 나)		저는 우유나 주스를 마실 거예요. (juh-neun oo-yoo-nah joo-seu-reul mah-sheel kkuh-yeh-yoh.) (*I'm going to drink milk or tea.*)

Giving a heads-up: Telling the topic

The concept of *topic* in Korean is probably new to you. The *topic* tells you what the sentence is *about*. It's marked with the topic particle 은 (eun) or 는 (neun): 은 after consonant-ending nouns and 는 after vowel-ending nouns.

Topics typically come at the beginning of a statement and serve as a heads-up for what you're about to say. You can think of a topic as the equivalent of "As for [topic]," "Speaking of [topic]," or "What I'm going to talk about now is [topic]" in English.

Say you are going to talk about your plan tomorrow. You can start with the word for **tomorrow** (내일; nae-eel), and add the topic particle 은 (eun) to signal the listener that *tomorrow* is your topic and that you're going to say something about it in the rest of the sentence. Any noun can be the topic, whether it's the subject or the object.

See the following statements that differ in what the speaker is talking about. The topic can be about *I*, about *tomorrow*, or about *Jini*, depending on what's marked by 은/는. All three share the same translation in English — *I meet Jini tomorrow.*

저는 내일 지니를 만나요. (juh-neun nae-eel jee-nee-reul mahn-nah-yoh.) (*As for me, I meet Jini tomorrow.*)

내일은 지니를 만나요. (nae-ee-reun jee-nee-reul mahn-nah-yoh.) (*Speaking of tomorrow, I'm meeting Jini.*)

지니는 내일 만나요. (jee-nee-neun nae-eel mahn-nah-yoh.) (*Speaking of Jini, I'm meeting her tomorrow.*)

Topic vs. subject particles

You might be scratching your head wondering what to use between 은/는 (topic particle) and 이/가 (subject particle) when the topic is also the subject of the sentence. Here's the deal: 이/가 is used when the subject carries the key info and needs to be emphasized. But, if the predicate (verb and adjectives) carries the key info and is more important, you use 은/는. To recap:

	Subject	Predicates
이/가	* key info	
은/는		* key info

See the following two sentences:

> 리사가 춤을 잘 춰요. (Lisa-gah choo-meul jahl chwuh-yoh.) (*It's **Lisa** that dances well (not someone else).*)

> 리사는 춤을 잘 춰요. (Lisa-neun choo-meul jahl chwuh-yoh.) (*Lisa **dances well**.*)

In the preceding two sentences, when you use 이/가, it's **Lisa** that is the key info and is being focused on, as if you're responding to the question, *Who dances well? It's Lisa who dances well.* When you use 은/는, the important information is 춤을 잘 춰요 (*dances well*) as if you are talking about what Lisa is good at.

Then, if your friend asks you 여기 뭐가 맛있어요? (yuh-gee mwuh-gah mah-shee-ssuh-yoh) (*What is delicious here?*) what particle would you use? (Say, their pasta is the most delicious and popular dish in this restaurant.) Would you say 파스타가 맛있어요 or 파스타는 맛있어요? Yes, you want to use 이/가 here: 파스타가 맛있어요 because 파스타 carries the key info in this context.

Let's chill for a bit on the 은/는 and 이/가 particles. Particles are contextual and it can be a whole new chapter just to talk about the different contexts. Switching particles between 은/는 and 이/가 won't be incorrect; it's a matter of sounding more natural. And in casual situations, particles are often dropped. So, don't get too stressed and just enjoy creating sentences. The following section on dropping assumed elements will also be useful.

Dropping understood words

In spoken English, you often shorten sentences by dropping words. For instance, "I love you" can become "Love you" and "Are you done with your homework for today?" can become "Done?" You can drop huge portions of a sentence without a breakdown in communication. Of course, you may only do so when the context of the conversation is clear.

Koreans do the same thing, though they do it more frequently and systematically, as Korean is more a situation-based language than English. Contextually understood elements are often dropped. Pronouns are dropped most frequently, but other words can also be dropped to pare down sentences. Sentences without a subject, an object, and other phrases work perfectly fine. Have a look at these examples:

재미있어요. (jae-mee-ee-ssuh-yoh) (*It's fun.*) (literally, *fun*)

보고 싶어요. (boh-goh-shee-puh-yoh.) (*I miss you/I want to see.*) (literally, *want to see*)

일요일에 만났어요. (ee-ryo-ee-reh mahn-nah-ssuh-yoh.) (*I met (her/him/them) on Sunday.*) (literally, *on Sunday met*)

REMEMBER

These examples might make you wonder if Koreans spend most of their days trying to figure out what the other person just said. Although it's fun to imagine someone completely misinterpreting the context of these short sentences, the truth is that this happens less often than you would expect. If it ever does, though, Koreans are quick to ask about what they just missed, so don't be afraid to ask questions. Stay tuned for how to form questions.

Asking Questions: It's a Cinch!

Forming a 질문 (jeel-moon) (*question*) in Korean is incredibly simple! Unlike 영어 (yuhng-uh) (*English*), you don't need to invert the subject and the verb or add a helping verb like the *do* verb when you ask a question in Korean.

Let's look at how to make Yes/no questions (questions that expects *yes* or *no* as an answer) and Wh- questions (questions with question words like who, when, what, why, where, how, and so on).

Yes/no questions

Questions like "Is it fun?" and "Have you seen it?" are 네/아니요 질문 (neh/ah-nee-yoh jeel-moon) (*yes/no questions*). In Korean, all you have to do is raise the intonation at the end of the sentence. In written Korean, just add a question mark at the end.

For example, "Korean is fun!" in Korean is 한국어가 재미있어요 (hahn-goo-guh-gah jae-mee-ee-ssuh-yoh). To ask "is Korean fun?", you simply use a rising intonation to say 한국어가 재미있어요?

Remember that personal pronouns are rarely used in Korean, and no need to worry about pronouns in the question form. "I'm an actor" is (저는) 배우예요

((juh-neun) bae-oo-yeh-yoh). To ask if someone is an actor, you simply drop the pronoun "저" (juh) (*I*) and say "배우예요?" "I am busy" in Korean is 바빠요 (bah-ppah-yoh). How would you ask if someone is busy? That's right! 바빠요? (with a rising intonation).

TIP

Need to specify who you're asking the question to? Just put their name or job title, or any other address terms in front of the question as in "리사 씨, 지금 바빠요?" (*Lisa, are you busy now?*) (You can also check the pronouns section in this chapter to review how to address people.)

Now, can you change the following statements to 네/아니요 질문?

케이팝 좋아해요. (keh-ee-pahp joh-ah-hae-yoh). ((I) *like K-pop.*)

감기 걸렸어요. (gahm-gee guhl-lyuht-ssuh-yoh.) ((I) *got a cold.*)

그거 인터넷에서 샀어요. (geu-guh een-tuh-neh-seh-suh sah-ssuh-yoh.) ((I) *bought it on the Internet.*)

You got it! All you have to do is just raise the intonation at the end. It's that simple!

Wh- questions

To ask questions for specific info such as who, what, when, and so on, use a question word. Korean question words include 누구 (noo-goo) (*who*), 뭐 (mwuh) (*what*), 언제 (uhn-jeh) (*when*), 어디 (uh-dee) (*where*), 어떻게 (uh-ttuh-keh) (*how*), 왜 (wae) (*why*), and more.

TIP

Just like Yes/no questions, forming Wh- questions is also simple. No need to alter the word order with auxiliary verbs like *do*. Just place the question word for the information you are seeking. For instance, if you're discussing movies with a colleague and are curious about what he watched over the weekend, take the question word 뭐 (mwuh) (*what*) and combine it with the past tense verb 봤어요 (bwah-ssuh-yoh) (*watched*), to create the question "뭐 봤어요?" To specify "*over the weekend*" (= 주말에 (joo-mah-reh)), simply prepend it to your question, forming "주말에 뭐 봤어요?" (*What did you watch over the weekend?*)

Should your curiosity extend to *where* he watched the movie, use 어디 (uh-dee) (*where*) alongside the location particle 에서, indicating the place of the action. This yields "어디에서 봤어요?" (uh-dee-eh-suh bwah-ssuh-yoh).

If you're ever wondering who he watched it with, just combine 누구 (noo-goo) (*who*) and the particle 하고 (hah-goh) (*with*). That gives you "누구하고 봤어요?" (noo-goo-hah-goh bwah-ssuh-yoh) (*Who did you watch (it) with?*). The questions can just keep coming, much like a detective embarking on a quest for clues, without having to worrying about changing the word order!

If you want to ask "*how*" questions like *how to do something*, utilize 어떻게 (uh-ttuh-keh) (*how*). Place whatever you're asking about in front of it.

어떻게 해요? (uh-ttuh-keh hae-yoh?) (*How do I/you do it?*)

김치, 어떻게 만들어요? (geem-chee, uh-ttuh-keh mahn-deu-ruh-yoh?) (*How do you make Kimchi?*)

To ask questions like *Who is it?*, *What is it?*, or *When is it?*, you use the verb 이다 (ee-dah) (*to be*) which conjugates to 예요 after a vowel-ending noun: 누구예요? (noo-goo-yeh-yoh?) (*Who is it?*), 뭐예요? (mwuh-yeh-yoh?) (*What is it?*), or 언제예요? (uhn-jeh-yeh-yoh?) (*When is it?*). You can put whatever you want to know in front of the question.

이 사람, 누구예요? (ee-sah-rahm, noo-goo-yeh-yoh?) (*Who is this person?*)

그거, 뭐예요? (geu-guh, mwuh-yeh-yoh?) (*What is that?*)

생일, 언제예요? (saeng-eel, uhn-jeh-yeh-yoh?) (*When is your birthday?*)

화장실, 어디예요? (hwah-jahng-sheel, uh-dee-yeh-yoh?) (*Where is the restroom?*)

TIP

Some interrogative pronouns such as 어느 (uh-neu) (*which (of these)*), 무슨 (moo-seun) (*what (kind of)*), and 몇 (myuht) (*how many*) can't stand alone and must be followed by a noun.

어느 학교에 다녀요? (uh-neu hahk-kkyoh-eh dah-nyuh-yoh?) (*Which/what school do you go?*)

무슨 음악을 좋아해요? (moo-seun eu-mah-geul joh-ah-hae-yoh?) (*What kinds of music do you like?*)

몇 시예요? (myuht ssee-yeh-yoh?) (*What time is it?*)

Making Proposals: Let's Do It!

When inviting your colleague to do something together, like "Let's + verb" form in English, the informal polite -아요/어요 ending itself can do the job. You can sometimes add 우리 (oo-ree) (*we*) and/or 같이 (gah-chee) (*together*) in front to make it clearer.

같이 해요. (gah-chee hae-yo.) (*Let's do it together.*)

우리 택시 타요. (oo-ree taek-ssee tah-yoh.) (*Let's take a taxi.*)

우리 같이 가요. (oo-ree gah-chee gah-yoh.) (*Let's go together.*)

The 반말 (bahn-mahl) (*intimate speech*) version is [**verb stem +**] 자. For example, to express "Let's go" to your close friend, take the verb stem 가 from 가다 (gah-dah) (*to go*) and add the ending 자, making 가자 (gah-jah) (*Let's go*). To add a destination like *Busan*, you add the 에 (*to*) particle after the place, making 부산에 (boo-sah-neh) (*to Busan*). Put this phrase in front of the verb, and now you have 부산에 가자 (boo-sah-neh gah-jah)!

Now, you can change the following phrases to -자 invitations to use them to your close friends.

점심 먹다 (juhm-sheem muhk-ttah) (*to eat lunch*)

영화 보다 (yuhng-hwah boh-dah) (*to watch a movie*)

내일 만나다 (nae-eel mahn-nah-dah) (*to meet tomorrow*)

All you have to do is drop 다 from the dictionary form and replace it with the 자 suffix! You then have 점심 먹자! 영화 보자! and 내일 만나자! Piece of cake, huh? (Fun fact, an equivalent phrase for "Piece of cake" in Korean is 식은 죽 먹기 (shee-geun jook muhk-kkee) (*eating cooled porridge*)!)

Just remember that the -자 ending form is a 반말, so only use it to people you're in an intimate or casual relationship with, like siblings or friends in your age group. If you use it to your boss, you may be met with a puzzled look!.

Commanding Politely

There are three common endings used for commands/requests. -(으)세요 is the most polite, then – 아요/어요, and – 아/어 is the most casual.

Polite requests using honorific suffix

When making polite requests to the elderly, your boss, or your customers, use the –(으)세요 (eu-seh-yoh) ending. It's a combination of the honorific suffix (으)시 and the informal polite 아요/어요 ending. For a consonant-ending verb stem, add 으세요 (for exemple, 받다 – 받으세요). For a vowel-ending verb stem, add 세요 (for exemple, 오다 – 오세요). Table 3-12 displays more examples.

TABLE 3-12 ## Polite Commands/Requests with -(으)세요

Dictionary Form	Conjugated Form: (으)세요	Example Sentences
읽다 (eek-ttah) (to read)	읽으세요	신문을 읽으세요. (sheen-moo-neul eel-geu-seh-yoh) (Please read the newspaper.)
받다 (baht-ttah) (to receive)	받으세요	이거 받으세요. (ee guh bah-deu-seh-yoh) (Please take this.)
앉다 (ahn-ttah) (to sit)	앉으세요	여기 앉으세요. (yuh-gee ahn-jeu-seh-yoh) (Please sit here.)
운동하다 (oon-dohng-hah-dah) (to work out)	운동하세요	매일 운동하세요. (mae-eel oon-dohng-hah-seh-yoh.) (Please exercise every day.)
기다리다 (gee-dah-lee-dah) (to wait)	기다리세요	잠시만 / 잠깐 기다리세요. (jahm-shee-mahn/jahm-kkahn gee-dah-ree-seh-yoh.) (Please wait a moment.)
가다 (gah-dah) (to go)	가세요	저쪽으로 가세요. (juh-jjoh-geu-roh gah-seh-yoh.) (Please go that way.)
오다 (oh-dah) (to come)	오세요	이쪽으로 오세요. (ee-jjoh-geu-roh oh-seh-yoh.) (Please come this way.)
타다 (tah-dah) (to get on/in, ride)	타세요	지하철 타세요. (jee-hah-chuhl tah-seh-yoh.) (Please take the subway.)

A handful of verbs have special –(으)세요 honorific form as follows:

to eat: 드세요 (deu-seh-yoh) instead of 먹어요 (먹다)

맛있게 드세요. (mah-shee-kkeh deu-seh-yoh.) (Please enjoy the food.)

to drink: 드세요 (deu-seh-yoh) instead of 마셔요 (마시다)

따뜻한 차 드세요. (ttah-tteu-tahn chah deu-seh-yoh.) (Please drink warm tea.)

to sleep: 주무세요 (joo-moo-seh-yoh) instead of 자요 (자다)

안녕히 주무세요. (ahn-nyuhng-hee joo-moo-seh-yoh.) (Good night.)

to speak: 말씀하세요 instead of 말해요 (말하다)

먼저 말씀하세요. (muhn-juh mahl-sseum-hah-seh-yoh.) (Please speak first = Please go ahead.)

to be at (location): 계세요 (gyeh-seh-yoh) instead of 있어요 (있다)

안녕히 계세요. (ahn-nyuhng-hee gyeh-seh-yoh.) (Goodbye to a person who's staying) (Literally, Stay peacefully.)

TIP

The honorific suffix –시 is not just used when talking to the elderly or seniors, but when talking *about* them as well. For example, if you want to tell your colleague about your active grandmother who hikes every day, you can say 우리 할머니는 매일 등산하세요. (oo-ree hahl-muh-nee-neun mae-eel deung-sahn-hah-seh-yoh) (*My grandmother hikes everyday.*) Don't sweat it. In casual situations, you can manage without them. We'll tackle things that need your attention when they arise.

Polite requests using 아요/어요

When making polite commands to someone of similar social rank at your workplace, you can just use the informal polite –아요/어요 form. For example;

수잔 씨, 이 차 마셔요. (su-jahn-ssee, ee chah mah-shuh-yoh.) (*Susan, please drink this tea.*)

지민 씨, 빨리 와요. (jee-meen-ssee, ppahl-lee wah-yoh.) (*Jimin, please come quickly.*)

Casual requests using 아/어

How about when you need to tell close friends what to do? You can use the 아/어 반말 (bahn-mahl) (*intimate speech*) ending. All you have to do is leave out 요 from the 아요/어요 ending. For example:

수잔, 이거 마셔. (su-jahn, ee-guh mah-shuh.) (*Susan, drink this.*)

지민, 빨리 와. (jee-meen, ppahl-lee wah.) (*Jimin, come quickly.*)

전화해. (juhn-hwa-hae.) (*call me.*)

Now you've got an idea of how the degree of politeness in commands changes as you move from (으)세요 to 아요/어요 to 아/어. "Happy new year" in Korean is 새해 복 많이 받으세요 (sae-hae bohk mah-nee bah-deu-seh-yoh). (Literally, *receive many new year blessings*). You can change the ending of the verb 받다 (to receive) depending on who you're talking to: 받으세요 (bah-deu-seh-yoh) – 받아요 (bah-dah-yoh) – 받아 (bah-dah).

Negative commands

Inevitably, you sometimes want to tell someone *not* to do something. The suffix for negative command form is **[verb stem +]** 지 말다 (jee mahl-dah) (*not do*). It conjugates to 지 마세요 (jee mah-seh-yoh) (*Please do not* + verb) for polite negative commands. Read on for examples:

하다 (*to do*):

하지 마세요. (hah-jee mah-seh-yoh.) (*Please don't do it.*)

마시다 (*to drink*):

많이 마시지 마세요. (mah-nee mah-shee-jee mah-seh-yoh.) (*Please don't drink a lot.*)

전화하다 (*to make a call*):

운전하면서 전화하지 마세요. (oon-juhn-hah-myuhn-suh juhn-hwah-hah-jee mah-seh-yoh.) (*Please don't call while driving.*)

TIP

The 반말 (bahn-mahl) (*intimate speech style*) version is –지 마. For example, *to fight* is 싸우다 (ssah-oo-dah) in Korean. To say "Don't fight," you take the stem 싸우 and attach the –지 마 ending to it. You have "싸우지 마!" and now you know what to say when you see your close friends or kids are fighting!

Talkin' the Talk

PLAY

Lisa was invited to her Korean friend's house for dinner. She talks to her friend's mother, Ms. Park, over the food.

Lisa: 어머니, 초대 감사합니다.
uh-muh-nee, choh-dae gahm-sah-hahm-nee-dah.
Mother, thank you for the invitation.

Ms. Park: 어서 와요. 반가워요. 여기 앉아요.
uh-suh wah-yoh. bahn-gah-wuh-yoh. yuh-gee ahn-jah-yoh.
Please come in! Nice to meet you. Please sit here.

Lisa: 와... 음식이 진짜 많네요.
wah. . . eum-shee-gee jeen-jjah mahn-neh-yoh.
Wow, there's a lot of food.

Ms. Park: 매운 음식 좋아해요?
mae-oon eum-sheek, joh-ah-hae-yoh?
Do you like spicy food?

Lisa: 네, 좋아해요. 그런데 많이 못 먹어요.
neh, joh-ah-hae-yoh. geu-ruhn-deh mah-nee mohn-muh-guh-yoh.
Yes, I do. But I can't eat a lot.

Ms. Park: 불고기는 안 매워요. 맛있게 먹어요.
bool-goh-gee-neun ahn mae-wuh-yoh. mah-shee-kkeh muh-guh-yoh.
Bulgogi is not spicy. Enjoy the food.

Lisa:	어머니, 이거는 뭐예요?
	uh-muh-nee, ee-guh-neun mwuh-yeh-yoh?
	Mother (Ms. Park), what's this?
Ms. Park:	잡채예요. 이것도 안 매워요.
	jahp-chae-yeh-yoh. ee-guht-ttoh ahn mae-wuh-yoh.
	It's Korean glass noodle stir fry. This is also not spicy.
Lisa:	음식이 다 맛있어요. 그런데 어머니, 말씀 놓으세요.
	eum-shee-gee dah mah-shee-ssuh-yoh. geu-ruhn-deh uh-muh-nee, mahl-sseum noh-eu-seh-yoh.
	The food is all delicious! By the way, please use bahn-mahl. (Literally, Let go of your polite speech.)
Ms. Park:	그래. 많이 먹어.
	geu-rae. mahn-nee muh-guh.
	Sure. Enjoy the food. (Literally, eat a lot.)

WORDS TO KNOW

초대	choh-dae	invitation
어서 와요 (어서 오다)	uh-suh wah-yoh	come in quickly, come on in = welcome
매운 음식	mae-woon eum-sheek	spicy food
좋아해요 (좋아하다)	joh-ah-hae-yoh	(I) like (it)
매워요 (맵다)	mae-wuh-yoh	it's spicy

FUN & GAMES

A. You're talking to your Korean classmates. Change the following statements to Yes/No questions. Turn to Appendix C for the answers.

[Example] 한국 드라마 봐요. (hahn-gook deu-rah-mah bwah-yoh.) ((*I*) *watch Korean dramas.*): 한국 드라마 봐요? (*Do you watch Korean dramas?*)

1. K-pop 들어요. (K-pop deu-ruh-yoh.) ((*I*) *listen to K-pop.*)

2. 불고기 좋아해요. (bool-goh-gee joh-ah-hae-yoh.) ((*I*) *like bulgogi.*)

3. 한국어가 재미있어요. (hahn-goo-guh-gah jae-mee-ee-ssuh-yoh.) (*Korean is fun.*)

4. 한국 친구가 있어요. (hahn-gook cheen-goo-gah ee-ssuh-yoh.) ((*I*) *have a Korean friend.*)

B. You are at a Korean restaurant. Change the following verbs to (으)세요 for polite requests that the waitstaff or you say. (Hint: Consonant stem+으세요, Vowel stem+세요.)

[Example] 이쪽으로 오다 (*to come this way*): 이쪽으로 오세요.

1. 여기 앉다 (to sit here): 여기 앉_____

2. 메뉴 주다 (to give menu): 메뉴 주_____

3. 잠시 기다리다 (to wait a moment): 잠시 기다리_____

4. 안녕히 가다 (to go peacefully): 안녕히 가_____

C. Change the following 존댓말 (*polite speech*) to 반말 (*intimate speech*).

[Example] 뭐 해요? (*What do you do?*): 뭐 해?

1. 뭐 먹어요? (What do you eat?):

2. 어디 가요? (Where do you go?):

Chapter **4**

Getting Started with Basic Expressions

안녕하세요! (ahn-nyuhng-hah-seh-yoh) (*Hello; Hi!*) Greeting someone warmly along with a thoughtful introduction is more than a mere formality. It's an excellent tool for meaningful engagement in any setting. These initial moments are a great opportunity to show your genuine enthusiasm not only for the person you're talking to but also for embracing a new language and culture.

In this chapter, we guide you through simple but essential Korean expressions, from greetings and farewells to expressions of gratitude and some ice-breakers. Get ready to turn your 대화 (dae-hwah) (*conversation*) into opportunities to enchant and connect — no magic wand required.

Starting and Ending Conversations

Whether for business or socializing, networking is essential to make connections. The following sections provide you the Korean words and phrases for effective and appropriate communication across various contexts.

Mastering greetings

When meeting someone new, whether through a friend or a potential business partner, introductions begin with a simple 인사 (een-sah) (*greeting*), like saying *hello*. Here is a quick guide to common Korean greetings:

» **안녕하세요?** (ahn-nyuhng-hah-seh-yoh) (*hello/how are you*): Initially a question about well-being, "*Are you well?*", this phrase has evolved as a polite greeting used any time of the day.

» **처음 뵙겠습니다.** (chuh-eum bwaep-kkeht-sseum-nee-dah) (*It's my first time to meet you; How do you do?*): Great for first-time meeting in formal contexts.

» **(만나서) 반갑습니다.** ((mahn-nah-suh) bahn-gahp-sseum-nee-dah) (*It's nice to meet you.*): For a slightly more casual tone, use 반가워요 (bahn-gah-wuh-yoh). Just repeat the phrase to respond.

Greetings for catching up with friends

If you're reconnecting with a friend you haven't seen recently, take a look at the phrases in Table 4-1.

TABLE 4-1   **Greetings for Catching Up**

Meaning	Informal polite	Honorific	Examples
How are you doing?	어떻게 지내요? (uh-ttuh-keh jee-nae-yoh)	어떻게 지내세요? (uh-ttuh-keh jee-nae-seh-yoh)	A: 어떻게 지내요? B: 잘 지내요. 어떻게 지내세요?
How have you been?	어떻게 지냈어요? (uh-ttuh-keh jee-nae-ssuh-yoh)	어떻게 지내셨어요? (uh-ttuh-keh jee-nae-shyuh-ssuh-yoh)	A: 어떻게 지내셨어요? B: 좀 바빴어요. (johm bah-ppah-ssuh-yoh) (*I've been a little busy.*)
Are you doing well?	잘 지내요? (jahl jee-nae-yoh)	잘 지내세요? (jahl jee-nae-seh-yoh)	A: 잘 지내? B: 응 (eung) (*yes*), 잘 지내.
Have you been doing well?	잘 지냈어요? (jahl jee-nae-ssuh-yoh)	잘 지내셨어요? (jahl jee-nae-shyuh-ssuh-yoh)	A: 잘 지냈어? B: 어 (uh) (*yes*), 잘 지냈어.

REMEMBER

In English, "how are you?" works for anyone, even if you just met them yesterday. However, in Korean, phrases like, 어떻게 지내요? Or 잘 지내요?, both commonly translated as "How are you?", are used only if you haven't seen someone recently or for a while. These phrases are reserved for catching up after some time has passed.

Removing 요 from the informal polite forms convert them into 반말 (bahn-mahl) (*intimate speech*), suitable for very close friends. For instance, 지내요 becomes 지내, and 지냈어요 becomes 지냈어. When responding affirmatively in 반말, replace 네 (neh) (*yes*) with either 응 (eung) or 어 (uh), both of which are used interchangeably in 반말.

Greetings for Daily Acquaintances and Family

For casual interactions with acquaintances, a simple 안녕하세요? usually suffices. For family members you see daily, you can greet them in the morning with the honorific phrase, 안녕히 주무셨어요? (ahn-nyung-hee joo-moo-shyuh-ssuh-yoh) or, in a more casual tone, 잘 잤어(요)? (jah jah-ssuh(-yoh)), depending on who you're talking to. Both phrases ask, "Did you have a good sleep?"

Saying goodbye

In Korean, the way you say goodbye can depend on whether you or the other person is leaving or staying. You wish "go well" to someone who is leaving, and "stay well" to someone who stays behind. Table 4-2 displays the specific expressions to use to non-family members:

TABLE 4-2 **Expressions for Goodbye**

Meaning	Informal Polite (Honorific)	Polite (casual: to peers/juniors)
"Goodbye" to someone who is leaving	안녕히 가세요 (ahn-nyuhng-hee gah-seh-yoh) (Literally, *go peacefully*)	잘 가(요) (jahl gah-yoh) (Literally, *go well*)
"Goodbye" to someone who is staying	안녕히 계세요 (ahn-nyuhng-hee gyeh-seh-yoh) (Literally, *stay peacefully*)	잘 있어(요) (jahl ee-ssuh-yoh) (Literally, *stay well*)
"See you next time"	다음에 봬요 (dah-eu-meh bwae-yoh) * 봬요 (shortened form of 뵈어요)	다음에 봐(요) (dah-eu-meh bwah-yoh) (*See you next time*)

For "다음에 봬요," feel free to replace "다음에" with other time adverbs like 내일 (nae-eel) (*tomorrow*), 다음 주에 (dah-eum jjoo-eh) (*next week*), 일요일에 (ee-ryoh-ee-reh) (*on Sunday*), 나중에 (nah-joong-eh) (*later*), or 이따가 (ee-ttah-gah) (*later today*) depending on when you plan to meet again. 봬요 is from the verb 뵈다, a polite version of 보다.

In Korean, there's a specific phrase serving as a "goodbye" when you plan to return soon: "다녀오겠습니다" (dah-nyuh-oh-geht-sseum-nee-dah), or in a more casual tone, "다녀올게요" (dah-nyuh-ohl-kkeh-yoh) (*I will attend/go and come back*). This phrase is ideal for departures to school, work, errands, or simply stepping away from your desk. You can use it any time you leave for a short while and expect to return soon. To indicate where you're going, simply add the location in front of the phrase:

» 심부름 (sheem-boo-reum) (*errand*)

» 학교 (hahk-kkyoh) (*school*)

» 회사 (hwae-sah) (*workplace, company*)

» 회의/미팅 (hwae-ee/mee-teeng) (*meeting*)

Upon your return, use the greeting 다녀왔습니다 (dah-nyuh-waht-sseum-nee-dah) (Literally, *I went and have come back*), to let others know you're back.

Talkin' the Talk

PLAY

Christina runs into her upper class friend, Seojun, on campus.

Christina: 서준 선배님, 안녕하세요.
suh-joon suhn-bae-neem, ahn-nyuhng-hah-seh-yoh.
Hello, Mr. Seojun.

Seojun: 크리스티나, 오랜만이야. 잘 지냈어?
keu-ree-seu-tee-nah, oh-raen-mah-nee-yah. jahl jee-nae-ssuh?
Christina, it's been a long time. Are you doing well?

Christina: 네. 선배님도 잘 지내셨어요?
neh. suhn-bae-neem-doh jahl jee-nae-shyuh-ssuh-yoh?
Yes. Are you doing well too?

Seojun: 응. 밥 먹었어?
eung. bahm muh-guh-ssuh?
Yes. Have you eaten?

Christina: 네. 전 수업이 있어서 . . . . 선배님, 다음에 또 봬요.
neh. juhn soo-uh-bee ee-ssuh-suh . . . . suhn-bae-neem, dah-eu-meh ttoh bwae-yoh.
Yes. I have a class, so I'll see you again later.

Seojun: 그래. 다음에 보자. 잘 가.
geu-rae. dah-eu-meh boh-jah. jahl gah.
Okay. See you later. Bye.

WORDS TO KNOW

선배님	suhn-bae-neem	friends in higher grade
오랜만이야 (오랜만이다)	oh-raen-mah-nee-yah	It's been a long time
잘 지냈어 (잘 지내다)	jahl jee-nae-ssuh	have been well; get along
밥 먹었어 (먹다)	bahm muh-guh-ssuh	had a meal
봬요 (뵈다)	bwae-yoh	see (polite form of 보다)
다음에	dah-eu-meh	next time

Making Introductions

In English, introductions usually start with the person's 이름 (ee-reum) (*name*) and may include details like their job. In Korean, it's common to mention specific details about the person, like their organization or their relationship to you (such as a friend or family), before stating their name. The following guide walk you through the basics of introducing yourself and others in Korean, starting with how to ask for someone's 이름.

Asking people for their names

When meeting someone new, the first piece of information you typically seek is their name. Here are some common phrases for asking, "What is your name?" with details on when to use each:

>> **성함이 어떻게 되세요?** (suhng-hah-mee uh-ttuh-keh dwae-seh-yoh): Highly respectful, used with elders, higher-ups, or strangers. Uses the honorific noun, 성함.

>> **이름이 어떻게 되세요?** (ee-reu-mee uh-ttuh-keh dwae-seh-yoh): Honorific but less formal; suitable among young adults in casual settings.

>> **이름이 뭐예요?** (ee-reu-mee mwuh-yeh-yoh): Informal yet polite; common in daily converations among peers or with younger people.

>> **이름이 뭐야?** (ee-reu-mee mwuh-yah): * 반말 (*Intimate speech*); Most casual form, appropriate among close peers or toward younger individuals.

Introducing your name

To introduce your name formally, use one of these common phrases:

» 저는 [name]입니다. (juh-neun [name] eem-nee-dah) (*I am [name].*)

» 저는 [name](이)라고 합니다. ((juh-neun) [name](ee-)rah-goh hahm-nee-dah)
(*I'm [name].*) (Literally, *I'm called [name].*)

These formal and polite introductions are ideal in new or formal settings. Note that the pronoun 저는 can be omitted. Depending on the last sound of your name:

» If your name ends in a consonant, use "이라고 합니다"

Example: 마이클이라고 합니다 (*Michael*)

» If your name ends in a vowel sound, use "라고 합니다"

Example: 크리스라고 합니다 (*Chris*)

In informal contexts, you might use:

» [name]이에요/예요 (ee-eh-yoh/yeh-yoh) * *Informal polite*

Example: 톰이에요 (toh-mee-eh-yoh) (*I'm Tom*). 수예요 (soo-yeh-yoh) (*I'm Sue*).

» [name]이야/야 (ee-yah/yah) * 반말 (*Intimate speech*)

Example: 톰이야 (*I'm Tom*). 수야 (*I'm Sue*).

(For more explanation on informal speech style and verb conjugation, please refer to Chapter 3.)

TIP

Feeling at ease when introducing yourself for the first time is important. A common Korean expression to foster a friendly and welcoming atmosphere is 잘 부탁합니다/부탁해요 (jahl boo-tah-kahm-nee-dah/boo-tah-kae-yoh), or in a more humble tone, 잘 부탁드립니다 (jahl boo-tahk-deu-reem-nee-dah). These phrases roughly translate to "I look forward to working with you" and are used to ask for kindness and cooperation in new settings.

Introducing others

Sometimes you might be in a position to lead introductions, whether at a casual meet-up or at work. Here's how you can do it:

제 [친구] 소개할게요. (je [cheen-goo] soh-gae-hahl-kkeh-yoh) (*Let me introduce my [friend]*.)

You can replace 친구 (cheen-goo) (*friend*) with 동료 (dohng-nyoh) (*co-worker*) or 가족 (gah-johk) (*family*) based on the situation.

To introduce someone, start with 이 사람은 (ee sah-rah-meun) (*this person, "as for this person"*) followed by their name, and possibly role if needed. For a more casual touch in less formal contexts, use 이쪽 (ee-jjohk) (*this side*) or 여기 (yuh-gee) (*here*). To add a layer of respect, especially with acquaintances or less familiar people, opt for 이분은 (ee boo-neun), which uses 분 (boon), an honorific form for "person."

Example introductions:

이 사람은/이쪽은 [사라] 씨예요. (ee sah-rah-meun/ee-jjoh-geun sah-rah ssee-yeh-yoh) (*This is [Ms. Sarah]*.)

여기는 제 [동생] 존이에요. (yuh-gee-neun jeh dohng-saeng joh-nee-eh-yoh) (*Here is my [younger brother], John.*)

이분은 우리 [선생님]입니다. (ee boo-neun oo-ree suhn-saeng-nee-meem-nee-dah) (*This is our [teacher]*.)

이분은 힐튼 [변호사님]입니다. (ee boo-neun heel-teun byuhn-hoh-sah-nee-meem-nee-dah) (*This is the [lawyer], Hilton.*)

You can swap out the words in the brackets with other names, job titles, or relationships. Here are some popular terms you might use when introducing others. For a more extensive list of terms for family and professional roles, check Chapter 7.

- ≫ 동료 (dohng-nyoh) (*colleague, co-worker*)
- ≫ (여자/남자)친구 ([yuh-jah/nahm-jah-]cheen-goo) (*[girl/boy]friend*)
- ≫ 룸메이트 (room-meh-ee-teu) (*roommate*)
- ≫ 선배(님) (suhn-bae[-neem]) (*friends in higher grade, senior colleagues*)
- ≫ 후배 (hoo-bae) (*friends in lower grade, junior colleagues*)
- ≫ 상사 (sahng-sah) (*[in business] boss, supervisor*)
- ≫ 선생님 (suhn-saeng-neem) (*teacher; also used as a respectful address for anyone*)

When introducing someone with their affiliation, mention the organization first, followed by the name and the position:

삼성전자 최선회 과장님 (sahm-suhng-juhn-jah chwae-suhn-hee gwah-jahng-neem) (*Manager Kim, Sunhee, Samsung Electronics*)

서울대학교 김현식 교수님 (suh-ool-dae-hahk-kkyoh geem-hyuhn-sheek gyoh-soo-neem) (*Professor Kim, Hyunsik, Seoul National University*)

Talkin' the Talk

PLAY

Jiyoung wants to introduce her boyfriend, Eric, to her mother, Mrs. Park.

Jiyoung: 엄마, 여기는 내 남자 친구 에릭이에요.
uhm-mah, yuh-gee-neun, nae nahm-jah cheen-goo
eh-lee-gee-eh-yoh.
Mom, here's my boyfriend, Eric.

Mrs. Park: 반가워요, 에릭 씨.
bahn-gah-wuh-yoh, eh-reek ssee.
Nice to meet you, Mr. Eric.

Eric: 안녕하세요, 어머니? 처음 뵙겠습니다.
ahn-nyuhng-hah-seh-yoh, uh-muh-nee. chuh-eum
bwaep-kkeht-sseum-nee-dah.
Hello, Mrs. Park. It's a pleasure to meet you.

Jiyoung: 에릭은 학원 영어 선생님이에요.
eh-ree-geun hah-gwuhn yuhng-uh
suhn-saeng-nee-mee-eh-yoh.
Eric is an English teacher at a tutoring institute.

Eric: 어머님, 잘 부탁드립니다.
uh-muh-neem, jahl boo-tahk-deu-reem-nee-dah.
Mrs. Park, I look forward to your support and guidance.

Mrs. Park: 자주 놀러 와요.
jah-joo nohl-luh wah-yoh.
Come over often.

WORDS TO KNOW

여기	yuh-gee	here
남자 친구	nahm-jah cheen-goo	boyfriend
반가워요 (반갑다)	bahn-gah-wuh-yoh	nice to meet you
영어 학원	yuhng-uh hah-gwuhn	English tutoring institute
선생님	suhn-saeng-neem	teacher
부탁드립니다 (부탁하다)	boo-tahk-deu-reem-nee-dah	request a favor
놀러 와요 (놀러 오다)	nohl-luh wah-yoh	come hangout

Breaking the Ice

Koreans often start conversations with a "just checking in" approach, whether it's with a work colleague or a dear friend. This friendly gesture not only opens up dialogue, but also shows genuine interest and helps strengthen community bonds. By asking about someone's 안부 (ahn-boo) (*well-being*), you can make the interaction more personal and relaxed.

Here are some commonly used Korean phrases for these casual check-ins and as icebreakers:

» **오랜만이에요!** (oh-raen-mah-nee-eh-yoh) (*Long time no see!; It's been a long time!*): A friendly conversation opener, it's typically followed by check-in greetings like 어떻게 지냈어요? (uh-ttuh-keh jee-nae-ssuh-yoh) (*How have you been?*)

» **안녕하셨어요?** (ahn-nyuhng-hah-shyuh-ssuh-yoh) (*Were you well?; Have you been well?*): An honorific way to ask someone about their well-bing since you last met. It's the past tense of "안녕하세요?" A common reply to this might be " 네, 잘 지냈어요" (neh, jahl jee-nae-ssuh-yoh) (*Yes, I've been doing well.*)

» **별일 없지요/없으시지요?** (byuhl-leel uhp-jjee-yoh/ uhp-sseu-shee-jee-yoh) (*Is everything all right?*): Literally translates to "*Nothing bad happened, right?*" You can respond with "별일 없어요, 잘 지내요" if all is well.

» **요즘 많이 바빠요/바쁘세요?** (yoh-jeum mah-nee bah-ppah-yoh/bah-ppeu-seh-yoh) (*Are you very busy lately?*) A good way to touch base on their current activities and can help to kickstart further conversation.

>> 식사했어요?/식사하셨어요? (sheek-ssah-hae-ssuh-yoh/sheek-ssah-hah-shyuh-ssuh-yoh) (*Have you eaten?*): Often used around meal times to express concern, this phrase is more of a social check-in rather than an actual meal invitation.

These phrases, along with earlier mentioned greetings like 어떻게 지내요? or 잘 지내요?, are excellent conversation starters.

Offering a friendly compliment

Who doesn't appreciate a kind word about their skills or a thoughtful 칭찬 (cheeng-chahn) (*compliment*)? Effective communication often involves expressing genuine interest and positivity towards others. By complimenting someone, you not only brighten their day but also help break the ice and build interpersonal connections.

Wondering how to give compliments in Korean? Here are some universally appreciated phrases. Swap out the words in the brackets with appropriate nouns to suit the context.

>> [가방] 멋있어요. ([gah-bahng] muh-shee-ssuh-yoh) (*[Your bag] looks cool.*): Ideal for complimenting someone's fashion accessory.

>> [모자] 잘 어울려요. ([moh-jah] jahl uh-ool-lyuh-yoh) (*You look good in [the hat].*) Great for a casual yet flattering comment on someone's attire.

>> [영어] 잘하네요/하시네요. ([yuhng-uh] jahl hah-neh-yoh/hah-shee-neh-yoh) (*You're good at speaking [English].*) This can be adapted for any skills, like speaking 한국말 (hahn-goong-mahl) (*Korean language*), 요리 (yoh-ree) (*cooking*), or 노래 (noh-rae) (*singing*), by replacing 영어 with other appropriate noun.

>> 잘 했어요/하셨어요. (jahl hae-ssuh-yoh/hah-shyuh-ssuh-yoh) (*You did a good job.*) Useful for acknowledging someone's effort on a task.

>> [목소리] 좋네요/좋으시네요. (mohk-ssoh-ree john-neh-yoh/joh-eu-shee-neh-yoh) (*Your voice is nice.*) A way to compliment someone's voice, whether singing or speaking.

When delivering compliments in Korean, using the -네요 (neh-yoh) ending can add a touch of surprise or admiration, enhancing the sincerity of your words. Also, incorporating the honorific -시 (shee) suffix show respect, especially when speaking to someone older or in a formal context.

Talking about the weather

Chatting about the 날씨 (nahl-ssee) (*weather*) might sound cliché, but it's another popular conversation starter worldwide. Whether it's sunny, snowy, or anything in between, weather talk is a great way to break the ice. Here are some essential Korean phrases to seamlessly weave into your small talk:

>> 여름 날씨 어때요? (yuh reum nahl-ssee uh-ttae-yoh) (*How's the summer weather?*)

>> 맑아요. (mahl-gah-yoh) (*It's clear, sunny.*)

>> 흐려요. (heu-ryuh-yoh) (*It's cloudy.*)

>> 추워요. (choo-wuh-yoh) (*It's cold.*)

>> 더워요. (duh-wuh-yoh) (*It's hot.*)

>> 따뜻해요. (ttah-tteu-tae-yoh) (*It's warm.*)

>> (안) 좋아요. ((ahn) joh-ah-yoh) (*It's (not) good.*)

>> 비가 와요. (bee-gah wah-yoh) (*It's raining.*)

>> 눈이 와요. (noo-nee wah-yoh) (*It's snowing.*)

>> 바람이 불어요. (bah-rah-mee boo-ruh-yoh) (*Wind is blowing.*)

>> 시원해요. (shee-wuhn-hae-yoh) (*It's cool.*)

To add more detail to your weather description, add adverbs like 너무 (nuh-moo) (*too*), 정말 (juhng-mahl) (*really*), or 조금/좀 (joh-geum/johm) (*a little*) before the verbs (for example, 너무 더워요 (*It's too hot*), 비가 많이 와요 (*It rains a lot*)). These can help convey a clearer picture of atmosphere and make your chat more engaging.

Talkin' the Talk

PLAY

Joonsoo and Sarah are roommates. Joonsoo just woke up when Sarah came back home from her workout.

Sarah: 잘 잤어요, 준수 씨.
jahl jah-ssuh-yoh, joon-soo ssee.
Good morning, Joonsoo.

Joonsoo: 네. 사라 씨, 운동 열심히 하시네요!
neh. sah-rah ssee, oon-dohng yuhl-sseem-hee hah-shee-neh-yoh!
Yes. Sarah, you are exercising hard!

Sarah:	아니에요. 오늘은 30분만 했어요.
	ah-nee-eh-yoh. oh-neu-reun sahm-sheep-ppoon-mahn hae-ssuh-yoh.
	Don't mention it! I did it only 30 minutes today.
Joonsoo:	오늘 날씨 어때요?
	oh-neul nahl-ssee uh-ttae-yoh.
	How's the weather today?
Sarah:	좀 추워요.
	johm choo-wuh-yoh.
	It's a little bit cold.

WORDS TO KNOW

잤어요 (자다)	jah-ssuh-yoh	slept
운동	oon-dohng	work out, exercise
열심히	yuhl-sseem-hee	diligently
아니에요 (아니다)	ah-nee-eh-yoh	not at all
날씨	nahl-ssee	weather
어때요 (어떻다)	uh-ttae-yoh	how is it?
추워요 (춥다)	choo-wuh-yoh	is cold

Expressing Gratitude and Regret

A 미소 (mee-soh) (*smile*), a word of 감사 (gahm-sah) (*thanks*), and a heartfelt 사과 (sah-gwah) (*apology*) can greatly impact your interactions across various cultures. Here are essential Korean phrases that can help:

Showing gratitude

Gratitude isn't just for Thanksgiving — it's a vital part of daily life! Here's how to say "thank you" in Korean, anywhere you go:

>> **고맙습니다/고마워요.** (goh-mahp-sseum-nee-dah/goh-mah-wuh-yoh) (*Thank you*): This native Korean word is perfect for everyday use. Use 고맙습니다 in formal settings or when addressing elders, and 고마워요 for friends and peers in more relaxed settings.

>> **감사합니다/감사해요.** (gahm-sah-hahm-nee-dah/gahm-sah-hae-yoh) (*Thank you*): This Sino-Korean phrase is often used interchangeably with 고맙습니다. 감사합니다 is more formal than 감사해요.

For a casual and friendly tone with close friends and family, use 고마워, the 반말 (bahn-mahl) (*intimate speech*) form.

Handling compliments

In Korea, gracefully dodging 칭찬 (cheeng-chahn) (*compliment*) is almost an essential skill.

>> 아니에요 (ah-nee-eh-yoh) (*No, not at all*): Humble and modest, use this phrase, perhaps with a gentle hand wave, to decline a compliments. Always follow up with 고맙습니다 or 감사합니다 (*Thank you*) to show gratitude.

>> It's also completely fine to simply accept a compliment with 고맙습니다 or 감사합니다. Or you can playfully respond with 정말이요? (juhng-mah-ree-yoh) (*Really?*) as a light-hearted preliminary before accepting the praise.

Apologizing

Mistakes happen! And when they do, nothing can replace a sincere apology. Knowing the right words to say is crucial, so here are the key Korean phrases for apologizing.

>> **죄송합니다/죄송해요.** (jwae-sohng-hahm-nee-dah/jwae-sohng-hae-yoh) (*I'm sorry.*): The go-to for formal apologies, perfect for professional settings or among acquaintances, or when addressing strangers.

>> **미안합니다/미안해(요).** (mee-ahn-hahm-nee-dah/mee-ahn-hae-yoh) (*I'm sorry.*): A bit less formal than 죄송합니다, but still respectful. Use 미안해 among friends and siblings.

>> **실례합니다/실례했습니다.** (sheel-lyeh-hahm-nee-dah/sheel-lyeh-haet-sseum-nee-dah) (*Excuse me/I caused you a trouble.*): Typically reserved for minor disturbances or inconveniences, this is used less frequently. Unlike the multi-purpose English "Excuse me," 실례합니다 is used in limited contexts, like when asking a stranger for directions, or navigating through a crowd.

BOWING AND NODDING

Bowing is more than just a gesture in Korea; it's an integral part of daily etiquette used for apologies, greetings, and expressing gratitude. A slight nod about 15 degrees is common for casual greetings, while a deeper bow of around 45 degrees conveys greater respect. Just be cautious not to overdo it; going too deep might make it look like you're gearing up for a martial arts match!

Nodding in Korea is similar to elsewhere, primarily indicating agreement or attentiveness. It's like silently saying "yes." To avoid mixed signals, make sure you don't say 아니요 (ah-nee-yoh) (*no*) while nodding. Stick with 네 (neh) (*yes*) for full clarity. You can enhance your nods with these phrases to fully engage in conversations: 그래요? (geu-rae-yoh) (*Is that right?*), 맞아요 (mah-jah-yoh) (*That's correct*), 그렇군요 (geu-ruh-koon-yoh) (*I see*), 알겠습니다 (ahl-geh-sseum-nee-dah) (*I got it*).

Talkin' the Talk

PLAY

Megan is at the front desk of an English tutoring institute looking for her friend who is a teacher in the institute.

Megan: 실례합니다.
sheel-lyeh-hahm-nee-dah.
Excuse me.

Mr. Chang: 네. 누구 찾으세요?
neh, noo-goo chah-jeu-seh-yoh?
Yes. Who are you looking for?

Megan: 죄송한데요. 김수호 선생님 계세요?
jwae-sohng-hahn-deh-yoh. geem-soo-hoh suhn-saeng-neem gyeh-seh-yoh?
I'm sorry, but is Teacher Kim, Sooho in?

Mr. Chang: 실례지만 성함이 어떻게 되세요?
sheel-lyeh-jee-mahn suhng-hah-mee uh-ttuh-keh dwae-seh-yoh?
I'm sorry but what's your name?

Megan: 저는 메간 윌슨이라고 합니다.
juh-neun meh-gahn weel-sseu-nee-rah-goh hahm-nee-dah.
I am Megan Wilson.

Mr. Chang: 잠깐 기다리세요.
jahm-kkahn gee-dah-ree-seh-yoh.
Please wait a moment.

Megan: 네. 감사합니다.
neh, gahm-sah-hahm-nee-dah.
Sure. Thank you.

- -

WORDS TO KNOW

실례합니다 (실례하다)	sheel-lyeh-hahm-nee-dah	Excuse me
누구	noo-goo	who
찾으세요 (찾다)	chah-jeu-seh-yoh	find, look for
죄송한데요 (죄송하다)	jwae-sohng-hahm-deh-yoh	I am sorry but. . .
계세요 (계시다)	gyeh-seh-yoh	exist, stay (honorific)
성함	suhng-hahm	name (honorific)
기다리세요 (기다리다)	gee-dah-ree-seh-yoh	wait
감사합니다 (감사하다)	gahm-sah-hahm-nee-dah	Thank you

FUN & GAMES

Analyze the following situations and the Korean expressions below. Match each situation with the most appropriate Korean expression that *you* would use. See the answers in Appendix C.

1. You're leaving the professor's room after a meeting when he stays behind.

2. You're about to leave home for school.

3. Your neighbor visited your house and is about to leave, while you're staying.

4. You stayed at your friend's parents' house and see them coming out of their room in the morning.

5. Your colleague held the door open for you.

6. You accidentally stepped on someone's foot in the subway.

7. You need to ask a passerby for directions.

8. You ran into a friend whom you haven't seen in a while.

9. Your colleague complimented your Korean speaking skills.

a. 실례합니다. (sheel-lyeh-hahm-nee-dah)

b. 죄송합니다. (jwae-sohng-hahm-nee-dah)

c. 감사합니다. (gahm-sah-hahm-nee-dah)

d. 아니에요. (ah-nee-eh-yoh)

e. 안녕히 가세요. (ahn-nyuhng-hee gah-seh-yoh)

f. 다녀오겠습니다. (dah-nyuh-oh-geht-sseum-nee-dah)

g. 안녕히 계세요. (ahn-nyuhng-hee gyeh-seh-yoh)

h. 안녕히 주무셨어요? (ahn-nyuhng-hee joo-moo-shyuh-ssuh-yoh)

i. 잘 지냈어요? (jahl jee-nae-ssuh-yoh)

Chapter **5**

Getting Your Numbers, Times, and Measurements Straight

Have you ever found yourself pondering how many 컵 (kuhp) (*cups*) of sugar goes into a can of soda? Maybe you've stayed up late on New Year's Eve to count down to the 새해 (sae-hae) (*new year*), or hit the snooze button on your 알람 (ahl-lahm) (*alarm*) to catch a few more precious minutes? Whether you realize it or not, you deal with tons and tons of 숫자 (soot-jjah) (*numbers*) all the time. From ordering food to setting appointments or cooking with 레시피 (leh-shee-pee) (*recipes*) — you name it, the whole world is full of 숫자.

Needless to say, 숫자 are an essential part of learning a new language. The good news is that Korean 숫자 are decimal-based, which means you don't need to memorize separate words for each "teen" number. If you've studied a vigesimal-based language, you'll find Korean 숫자 to be a bit of relief.

In this chapter, you learn all about Korean 숫자, how to count in Korean and perform essential tasks like telling the 시간 (shee-gahn) (*time*), and using 날짜 (nahl-jjah) (*dates*) and measurements. 숫자 in a new language may sound a bit wonky or overwhelming at first. However, learning numbers in Korean will open up an infinite number of possibilities for understanding and using the language.

Now, let's dive in!

Two Sets of Korean Numbers: Native Versus Sino-Korean

The first thing to know is that there are two distinct counting systems in 한국어 (hahn-goo-guh) (*Korean*). One is of Korean origin, *native Korean numbers*, and the other is of Chinese origin, *Sino-Korean numbers*. These two systems are used for different things.

Hold up — let's rewind. Two number systems? Why? Well, when you think of 영어 (yuhng-uh) (*English*), you can get a sense why some languages have two or more number sets. In 영어, you have *one, two, three . . .* but you also have Latin and Greek roots like *mono/solo, duo/duet, trio, quad, quint . . .* or *I, II, III, IV, V . . .* and these are all used for different purposes.

In the case of 한국어 숫자, both the native and Sino-Korean number sets are actively used for different situations. Native Korean numbers are used when counting quantities (that is, how many times you can jump rope, how many bowls of rice you had), and Sino-Korean numbers are used to read or label numbers, including math and money (that is, Chapter 5, No. 235, $100).

Let's start off with some native Korean number exercises. Ready? 하나 (hah-nah) (*one*), 둘 (dool) (*two*), 셋 (seht) (*three*), 시작 (shee-jahk) (*start/go*)!

Hah-nah, dool: Native Korean numbers

TIP

A good general rule of thumb is that native Korean numbers are used for counting *how many*. You can use them to count, for example, how many pushups and kicks you do in your 태권도 (*Taekwondo*) lesson, how many cups of coffee you drank (watch the caffeine), and how many friends you're inviting to your party. All of these are counted using native Korean numbers. Table 5-1 shows a list of the native Korean numbers from 1 to 99.

TABLE 5-1 Native Korean Numbers

Number	Korean	Pronunciation	Number	Korean	Pronunciation
1	하나	hah-nah	11	열하나	yuhl-hah-nah
2	둘	dool	20	스물	seu-mool
3	셋	seht	30	서른	suh-reun
4	넷	neht	40	마흔	mah-heun
5	다섯	dah-suht	50	쉰	shween
6	여섯	yuh-suht	60	예순	yeh-soon
7	일곱	eel-gohp	70	일흔	eel-heun
8	여덟	yuh-duhl	80	여든	yuh-deun
9	아홉	ah-hohp	90	아흔	ah-heun
10	열	yuhl	99	아흔아홉	ah-heun-ah-hohp

REMEMBER

In modern Korean, native Korean numbers are only used for counting from 1 to 99. There used to be native Korean words like 온 (ohn) (*100*), 즈믄 (jeu-meun) (*1000*), 골 (gohl) (*10000*), and 잘 (jahl) (*100 million*) . . . but they aren't used as numbers anymore but just used to express *all*, *whole*, or *innumerable*. What do people do for numbers beyond 99, you may ask? Just switch to Sino-Korean numbers! (In many counting situations, it's also common for Koreans to switch to Sino-Korean numbers for larger numbers, around 40 or 50.)

Native Korean numbers from 11 to 99

To count any number larger than 10 using the native Korean numbers, you just combine the numbers using the formula: tens digit + ones digit. So, numbers 11 through 19 go like 열 (10) + *X*. *Eleven* is 열하나 (yuhl-hah-nah), the combination of 10 (열) and 1 (하나). *Fourteen?* Same thing. It's 열넷 (yuhl-neht). *Eighteen* is 열여덟 (yuhl-yuh-duhl).

The same logic applies to numbers 21 through 29, which are 스물 (20) + *X*. *Twenty-two* is 스물둘 (seu-mool-dool). *Twenty-eight?* Yes, it's 스물여덟 (seu-mool yuh-duhl). How about 34? Right, it's 서른넷 (suh-reun-neht). You can use this pattern to count up to 아흔아홉 (ah-heun-ah-hohp) (99). Let's look at the example conversation:

몇 살이에요? (myuht ssah-ree-eh-yoh?) *(How old are you?)*

서른둘이에요. (suh-reun-doo-ree-eh-yoh.) *(I'm thirty-two.)*

스물하나예요. (seu-mool-hah-nah-yeh-yoh.) *(I'm twenty-one.)*

Eel-ee-sahm: Sino-Korean numbers

Sino-Korean numbers are used for naming or labeling things like *Room No. 235* or *Page 119*. They are also used in math, addresses, phone numbers, currency, measurements, and time expressions such as years, months, dates, minutes, and seconds (but NOT hours)! Table 5-2 lists Sino-Korean numbers 0 through 99.

TABLE 5-2   Sino-Korean Numbers

Number	Korean	Pronunciation	Number	Korean	Pronunciation
0	공 / 영	gohng / yuhng	10	십	sheep
1	일	eel	11	십일	shee-beel
2	이	ee	20	이십	ee-sheep
3	삼	sahm	30	삼십	sahm-sheep
4	사	sah	40	사십	sah-sheep
5	오	oh	50	오십	oh-sheep
6	육	yook	60	육십	yook-sheep
7	칠	cheel	70	칠십	cheel-sheep
8	팔	pahl	80	팔십	pahl-sheep
9	구	goo	99	구십구	goo-sheep-goo

Sino-Korean numbers from 11 to 99

Sino-Korean numbers use the same logic as the native Korean numbers. For numbers 11 through 19, you use the formula 10 + X. For example, *eleven* is 십일 (shee-beel), which is the combination of 십 (10) and 일 (1). *Fifteen* is 십오 (shee-boh).

Twenty is two sets of ten, so you say "two-tens," 이십 (ee-sheep). You can think of it as being 2 times 10. Thirty is "three-tens," 삼십 (sahm-sheep). Fifty is "five-tens," 오십 (oh-sheep).

How about 51? Right, it's 오십일 (oh-shee-beel). You simply add the ones digit at the end. Read on for more examples:

> 25 = 이십오 (ee-shee-boh)
>
> 63 = 육십삼 (yook-sheep-sahm)
>
> 84 = 팔십사 (pahl-sheep-sah)
>
> 97 = 구십칠 (goo-sheep-cheel)

Sino-Korean numbers from 100 to 9,999

Numbers beyond 100 aren't too difficult, either. One hundred is 백 (baek), and 200 is "two hundreds" — 이백 (ee-baek). One thousand is 천 (chuhn), so 2,000 is 이천 (ee-chuhn). If there's 0 in a number, just skip the digit, as in 이천이십팔 (ee-chuhn-ee-sheep-pahl) (2,028). Here are more examples:

124 = 백이십사 (baek-ee-sheep-sah)

365 = 삼백육십오 (sahm-baek-yook-shee-boh)

2025 = 이천이십오 (ee-chuhn-ee-shee-boh)

8,730 = 팔천칠백삼십 (pahl-chuhn-cheel-baek-sahm-sheep)

Now, want to try 9,999? Yes, it's 구천구백구십구 (goo-chuhn-goo-baek-goo-sheep-goo).

GRAMMATICALLY SPEAKING

When using Sino-Korean numbers, you don't add "one" (일, eel) in front of numbers like you do in English with *one hundred* or *one thousand*. Just say 십 (sheep) (*ten*), 백 (baek) (*hundred*), 천 (chuhn) (*thousand*), and 만 (mahn) (*ten thousand*) instead of 일십, 일백, 일천, or 일만. For example, 11,111 is 만천백십일 (mahn chuhn-baek-shee-beel), not 일만일천일백일십일.

Whew! It may feel more like math class than Korean class right now, but with practice, you'll get the hang of how to combine numbers, and it'll become second-nature. We're almost there — check out Table 5-3 for a look at the digits for large numbers from 100 and beyond.

TABLE 5-3   Large Sino-Korean Numbers

Number	Korean	English	Number	Korean	English
100	백 (baek)	hundred	100,000,000	억 (uhk)	hundred million
1000	천 (chuhn)	thousand	1,000,000,000	십억 (sheep-buhk)	billion
10,000	만 (mahn)	ten thousand	10,000,000,000	백억 (bae-guhk)	ten billion
100,000	십만 (sheem-mahn)	hundred thousand	100,000,000,000	천억 (chuh-nuhk)	hundred billion
1,000,000	백만 (baeng-mahn)	million	1,000,000,000,000	조 (joh)	trillion
10,000,000	천만 (chuhn-mahn)	ten million	10,000,000,000,000	십조 (sheep-jjoh)	ten trillion

Sino-Korean numbers from 10,000 to 99,999

In English, large numbers are calculated in increments of thousands. But in Korean, they are calculated in increments of *ten thousand*, which is 만 (mahn) in Korean. So, 30,000 is NOT 삼십천, but 삼만 (sahm-mahn) which is 3 × 10,000. Here are more examples:

21,000 = 이만 천 (ee-mahn chuhn)

60,500 = 육만 오백 (yoong-mahn oh-baek)

12,087 = 만 이천팔십칠 (mahn ee-chuhn pahl-sheep-cheel)

Now, can't wait to say 99,999? Yes, it's 구만 구천구백구십구. (goo-mahn goo-chun-goo-baek-goo-sheep-goo)

Sino-Korean numbers greater than 100,000

Korean numbers don't have a "millions digit." *One million* is 백만 (baeng-mahn), which is the combination of 100 (백) × 10,000 (만). Korean does have a special digit name for 100 million, which is 억 (uhk). 200 million is "two 100 millions," or 이억 (ee-uhk).

Now, want to try 999,999,999 in Korean? Yes, it's 구억 구천구백구십구만 구천구백구십구 (goo-uhk goo-chuhn-goo-baek-goo-sheep-goo-mahn goo-chuhn-goo-baek-goo-sheep-goo).

Expressing quantity with counters

When talking about Korean numbers, another important concept to know is *counters*, which are "tags" that follow numbers. Counters identify what types of things you're counting. Whether it's objects, people, or animals, each requires its own counter. The concept of counters isn't new to English speakers. English words like *bowl*, *piece*, *flock*, and *sheet* (as in five *bowls* of rice, two *pieces* of cake, a *flock* of geese, two *sheets* of paper) are counters, too. While 영어 counters are mostly used for non-countable nouns, 한국어 counters are used for almost any nouns.

Counters with native Korean numbers

As the core function of native Korean numbers is counting "how many," native numbers can appear with a variety of counters. Table 5-4 lists some common native Korean counters.

TABLE 5-4 **Counters That Use Native Korean Numbers**

Counter	Use	Examples
개 (gae)	inanimate items/ things/ objects	펜 (pehn) (*pens*), 사과 (sah-gwah) (*apples*), 가구 (gah-goo) (*furniture*)
권 (kwuhn)	books	책 (chaek) (*books*), 잡지 (jahp-jjee) (*magazines*)
대 (dae)	machines/vehicles/ instruments	냉장고 (naeng-jahng-goh) (*refrigerators*), 컴퓨터 (kuhm-pyoo-tuh) (*computer*), 차 (chah) (*car*), 자전거 (jah-juhn-guh) (*bike*), 피아노 (pee-ah-noh) (*piano*)
명 (myuhng)	people	학생 (hahk-ssehng) (*students*), 친구 (cheen-goo) (*friends*)
마리 (mah-ree)	animals	강아지 (gahng-ah-jee) (*dogs*), 고양이 (goh-yahng-ee) (*cats*), 생선 (saeng-suhn) (*fish*)
그릇 (geu-reut)	bowls	밥 (bahp) (*rice*), 국 (gook) (*soup*), 국수 (gook-ssoo) (*noodles*)
장 (jahng)	flat paper-like objects	종이 (johng-ee) (*paper*), 사진 (sah-jeen) (*photos*), 표 (pyoh) (*tickets*)
병 (byuhng)	bottles	물 (mool) (*water*), 맥주 (maek-jjoo) (*beer*), 술 (sool) (*alcoholic drink*)

GRAMMATICALLY SPEAKING

To specify the quantity of a noun in Korean, you start with the noun, followed by the number and a counter. For instance, to indicate "10 books," you'd take 책 (chaek) for "book," and add 열 (yuhl) for "10," then the counter 권 (gwuhn) for books, resulting in "책 열 권" (chaek yuhl kkwuhn).

Constructing a sentence is straightforward. For example, to say "I bought ten books," simply append the verb 샀어요 (sah-ssuh-yoh) (*bought*), to make 책 열 권 샀어요. If you're a book lover and wish to express "I read ten books," replace the verb with 읽었어요 (eel-guh-ssuh-yoh) (*read — past tense*), to make "책 열 권 읽었어요." See more example sentences:

어제 커피 다섯 잔 마셨어요 (uh-jeh kuh-pee dah-suh jjahn mah-shyuh-ssuh-yoh) (*I drank five cups of coffee yesterday.*)

Q: 학생 몇 명 있어요? (hahk-ssaeng myuhn-myuhng ee-ssuh-yoh) (*How many students are there?*)

A: 열다섯 명 있어요. (yuhl-ttah-suhn myuhng ee-ssuh-yoh) (*There're fifteen.*)

Note that five native Korean numbers — 하나 (hah-nah) (*1*), 둘 (dool) (*2*), 셋 (seht) (*3*), 넷 (neht) (*4*), and 스물 (seu-mool) (*20*) — change their forms to 한 (hahn), 두 (doo), 세 (seh), 네 (neh), and 스무 (seu-moo) when you combine them with counters. For example, to express *one bottle*, you say 한 병 (hahn-byuhng). *Two bottles?* Yup, it's 두 병 (doo-byuhng). More examples:

>> **three cookies:** 쿠키 세 개 (koo-kee seh gae)

>> **four cats:** 고양이 네 마리 (goh-yahng-ee neh mah-ree)

>> **twenty computers:** 컴퓨터 스무 대 (kuhm-pyoo-tuh seu-moo-dae)

TIP

When ordering a small number of food or drinks, you can drop the counter and just say the numbers only. For example, at a coffee shop, you can say 라떼 하나 주세요 (lah-tteh hah-nah joo-seh-yoh) (*one latte, please*) instead of 라떼 한 잔 주세요 (lah-tteh hahn jahn joo-seh-yoh) (*one cup of latte, please*). At a 식당 (sheek-ttahng) (*restaurant*), you may say 여기요, 비빔밥 둘 주세요 (yuh-gee-yoh, bee-beem-ppahp dool joo-seh-yoh.) (*Excuse me, two bibimbaps, please.*) without the counter 그릇 (geu-reut) for *bowls*. It's the same in English, right? You can order "one soup" instead of "one bowl of soup" and still be understood. English and Korean aren't so different, after all!

Counters with Sino-Korean numbers

Western measurements and scientific units for length, temperature, distance, and weight/mass, as well as money, years, minutes, and seconds use Sino-Korean numbers with Sino-Korean counters. Table 5-5 gives you some common Sino-Korean counters.

TABLE 5-5 **Counters That Use Sino-Korean Numbers**

English	Korean	Pronunciation	English	Korean	Pronunciation
Korean currency	원	wuhn	minutes	분	boon
dollars	달러	dahl-luh	days	일	eel
miles	마일	mah-eel	months	(개)월	(gae-)wuhl
kilo(gram)	킬로(그램)	keel-loh(geu-raem)	years	년	nyuhn
floors	층	cheung	school years	학년	hahng-nyuhn

Read on for dialogue examples:

Q: 몇 층에 살아요? (myuht cheung-eh sah-rah-yoh) (*What floor do you live on?*)

A: 일 층에 살아요. (eel cheung-eh sah-rah-yoh) (*I live on the 1st floor.*)

Q: 몇 학년이에요? (myuht tahng-nyuh-nee-eh-yoh) (*What school year are you?*)

A: 삼 학년이에요. (sahm hahng-nyuh-nee-eh-yoh) (*I'm a junior/in the third grade.*)

Q: 한국에 몇 년 살았어요? (hahn-goo-geh myuhn nyuhn sah-rah-ssuh-yoh) (*How many years did you live in Korea?*)

A: 육 개월 살았어요. (yook kkae-wuhl sah-rah-ssuh-yoh) (*I lived (there) for six months.*)

Pinpointing with ordinal numbers

Ordinal numbers like *first* and *second* come in handy when pinpointing a position or a rank. To form an ordinal number in Korean, you add 째 (jjae) after a native Korean number. Note that number one has a special form, 첫 (chuht). You may identify the eldest kid as 첫째 (chut-jjae) (*the first*) and say 우리 첫째 아이예요 (oo-ree chuht-jjae ah-ee-yeh-yoh.) (*This is my first kid*), or you can even shorten it to 첫째예요 (chuht-jjae-yeh-yoh.) (*This is the first*). If you want to ask someone what their "birth order" is, you can ask "몇째예요?" (myuht-jjae-yeh-yoh?) (*"What number are you?"*) See more examples:

둘째 딸이에요. (dool-jjae ttah-ree-eh-yoh.) (*I'm the second daughter.*)

셋째 주 목요일에 만나요. (seht-jjae-jjoo moh-gyoh-ee-reh mahn-nah-yoh.) (*We meet on the third Thursday of the month.*)

Table 5-6 lays out the ordinal number from 1st to 10th.

TABLE 5-6   **Ordinal Numbers**

Korean	Pronunciation	English	Korean	Pronunciation	English
첫째	chut-jjae	first	여섯째	yuh-suht-jjae	sixth
둘째	dool-jjae	second	일곱째	eel-gohp-jjae	seventh
셋째	seht-jjae	third	여덟째	yuh-duhl-jjae	eighth
넷째	neht-jjae	fourth	아홉째	ah-hohp-jjae	ninth
다섯째	dah-suht-jjae	fifth	열째	yuhl-jjae	tenth

When you talk about *first time, second time, third time* use 번째.

두 번째 여행 (doo-buhn-jjae yuh-haeng) (*the second/second-time travel*)

세 번째 시험 (seh-buhn-jjae shee-huhm) (*the third/third-time exam*)

Talkin' the Talk

PLAY

Ian and Maree are talking about their pets. Ian asks Maree about the pet salon.

Ian: 마리 씨, 강아지 있어요?
mah-ree-ssee, gahng-ah-jee ee-ssuh-yoh?
Maree, you have a dog?

Maree: 네, 두 마리 있어요.
neh, doo-mah-ree ee-ssuh-yoh.
Yes, I have two.

Ian: 몇 살이에요?
myuht-ssah-ree-eh-yoh?
How old are they?

Maree: 토비는 열한 살이고 주니는 세 살이에요.
Toby-neun yuhl-hahn-sah-ree-goh Juni-neun seh-sah-ree-eh-yoh.
Toby is eleven, and Juni is three.

Ian: 애견샵 어디 다녀요? 저도 얼마 전에 강아지 한 마리 샀어요.
ae-gyuhn-shop uh-dee dah-nyuh-yoh? juh-doh uhl-mah-juh-neh gahng-ah-jee hahn-mah-ree sah-ssuh-yoh.
What pet salon do you go to? I recently bought a puppy, too.

Maree: "주주 애견샵"이에요. 가까워요.
joojoo ae-gyuhn-shyah-bee-eh-yo. gah-kkah-wuh-yoh.
It's called Joojoo Pet Salon. It's nearby.

Ian: 전화번호가 뭐예요?
juhn-hwah-buhn-hoh-gah mwuh-yeh-yoh?
What's their phone number?

Maree: 201-837-6458이에요.
ee-gohng-eel pahl-sahm-cheel yook-sah-oh-pah-ree-eh-yoh.
It's 201-837-6458.

WORDS TO KNOW

강아지	gahng-ah-jee	puppy
몇 살	myuht ssahl	what age
다녀요 (다니다)	dah-nyuh-yoh	go/attend regularly
얼마 전에	uhl-mah-juh-neh	lately, not long ago
샀어요 (사다)	sah-ssuh-yoh (sah-dah)	bought (to buy)
가까워요 (가깝다)	gah-kkah-wuh-yoh (gah-kkahp-dah)	is nearby/close by (to be close)
전화번호	juhn-hwah-buhn-hoh	phone number
뭐예요?	mwuh-yeh-yoh?	what is. . .?

The Clock's Ticking: Telling Time

The phrase "시간은 돈이다" (shee-gah-neun doh-nee-dah) (*time is money*) may feel even more real when you travel. Often, we just don't have enough time to do everything we want to during a trip. In this section, you'll discover how to state 시간 (shee-gahn) (*time*) in Korean.

Noting hours and minutes

If someone asks you 몇 시예요? (myuht ssee-yeh-yoh?), they are asking "*what time is it?*" To state time, you need to use both the Sino-Korean and the native Korean number systems. (This is the only occasion that you need both systems.) The hour, 시 (shee), is told using native Korean numbers. Minutes, 분 (boon), and seconds, 초 (choh), are read using Sino-Korean numbers. In Korean, 10:25 is read as 열 시 이십오 분 (yuhl ssee ee-shee-boh boon). To keep you on track and on time, just check out Table 5-7.

TABLE 5-7   Stating the Hour and Minutes

Time Expression	Pronunciation	Meaning	Time Expression	Pronunciation	Meaning
1시 (한 시)	hahn shee	1:00	1분 (일 분)	eel boon	1 minute
2시 (두 시)	doo shee	2:00	2분 (이 분)	ee boon	2 minutes
3시 (세 시)	seh shee	3:00	3분 (삼 분)	sahm boon	3 minutes
4시 (네 시)	neh shee	4:00	4분 (사 분)	sah boon	4 minutes
5시 (다섯 시)	dah-suht ssee	5:00	5분 (오 분)	oh boon	5 minutes
6시 (여섯 시)	yuh-suht ssee	6:00	6분 (육 분)	yuk ppoon	6 minutes
7시 (일곱 시)	eel-gohp ssee	7:00	7분 (칠 분)	cheel boon	7 minutes
8시 (여덟 시)	yuh-duhl ssee	8:00	8분 (팔 분)	pahl boon	8 minutes
9시 (아홉 시)	ah-hohp ssee	9:00	9분 (구 분)	goo boon	9 minutes
10시 (열 시)	yuhl ssee	10:00	10분 (십 분)	sheep ppoon	10 minutes
11시 (열한 시)	yuhl-hahn shee	11:00	20분 (이십 분)	ee-sheep ppoon	20 minutes
12시 (열두 시)	yuhl-ttoo shee	12:00	30분 (삼십 분)	sahm-sheep ppoon	30 minutes

To express *half an hour* or *30 minutes*, you can use the handy word 반 (bahn) (*half*). 1:30 is 한 시 반 or 한 시 삼십 분. There is no phrase for *a quarter of an hour* in Korean. So, if you want to say *a quarter past 2:00*, you just say 두 시 십오 분 (doo-shee shee-boh-boon) (2:15). How about *a quarter to 2:00?* You can use the word 전 (juhn) (*before*) and say 두 시 십오 분 전 (doo-shee shee-boh-boon juhn) (literally, *15 minutes before 2:00*). Or just say 한 시 사십오 분 (hahn shee sah-shee-boh boon) (1:45). Check out the conversation below on asking and telling time:

지금 몇 시예요? (jee-geum myuh ssee-yeh-yoh?) (*What time is it now?*)

네 시 십 분이에요. (neh shee sheep ppoo-nee-yeh-yoh.) (*It's 4:10.*)

지금 한국은 밤 열한 시예요. (jee-geum hahn-goo-geun bahm yuhl-hahn shee-yeh-yoh.) (*It's 11:00 at night in Korea now.*)

TIP

It is also helpful to know 오전 (oh-juhn) (*a.m.*) and 오후 (oh-hoo) (*p.m.*). If you have an important meeting at 오전 아홉 시 (oh-juhn ah-hop-ssee), then you know the meeting starts at 9:00 a.m. An appointment at 오후 두 시 반 (oh-hoo doo-shee bahn) starts at 2:30 p.m. Note that 오전 and 오후 go *in front of* the time, not *after* the time.

You may also hear more specific time expressions when telling time:

새벽 (sae-byuhk) (*pre-dawn/dawn/late night; around 1 a.m.–5 a.m.*)

아침 (ah-cheem) (*morning/breakfast time; around 6 a.m.–9 a.m.*)

오전 (oh-juhn) (*late morning/before noon; around 10 a.m.–11 a.m.*)

오후 (oh-hoo) (*afternoon; around 12 p.m.–5 p.m.*)

저녁 (juh-nyuhk) (*evening/dinner time; around 6 p.m.–8 p.m.*)

밤 (bahm) (*night; sleeping time*)

For example, 3 a.m. is more often said as 새벽 세 시 instead of 오전 세 시. 10 p.m. is said as 밤 열 시 instead of 오후 열 시. Midnight? Yes, it's 밤 열두 시 (bahm yuhl-ttoo shee). Remember that these time expressions go BEFORE the time and not after, as the Korean language orders words by starting with the largest measurement and ending with the smallest.

Talking about time

To express *at* what time, *from* what time, *until* what time, or *by* what time, you use the following particles: 에 (eh) (*at*), 부터 (boo-tuh) (*from*), and 까지 (kkah-jee) (*until, by*). (For the lowdown on using particles, check out Chapter 3.) See these example sentences:

Q: 비행기, 몇 시에 도착해요? (bee-haeng-gee myuht-ssee-eh doh-chah-kae-yoh?) (*What time does the flight arrive?*)

A: 밤 열한 시에 도착해요. (bahm yuhl-hahn shee-eh doh-chah-kae-yoh.) (*It arrives at 11 p.m.*)

Q: 영화, 몇 시에 시작해요? (yuhng-hwah myuht-ssee-eh shee-jah-kae-yoh?) (*What time does the movie start?*)

A: 한 시 반에 시작해요. (hahn-shee bah-neh shee-jah-kae-yoh.) (*It starts at 1:30.*)

Q: 회의, 몇 시까지 해요? (hweh-ee myuht-ssee-kkah-jee hae-yoh?) (*Until what time do you have the meeting?*)

A: 열 시부터 열두 시까지 해요. (yuhl-ssee-boo-tuh yuhl-ttoo-shee-kkah-jee hae-yoh.) (*I have it from 10 to 12.*)

Save the Date: Delving into Dates

여행 갈 거예요? (yuh-haeng gahl kkuh-yeh-yoh?) (*Are you going to travel?*) If so, one of the first things to decide on would be 언제 가요? (uhn-jeh gah-yoh?) (*When do you leave?*). In the following sections, you discover how to name dates, months, years, and days of the week. You also learn how to express time in relation to the present.

Asking for the dates

When you live a busy life, you often forget what the date is. "What date is it today?" is 오늘, 며칠이에요? (oh-neul, myuht-chee-lee-yeh-yoh?). If you want to know what specific date someone's 생일 (saeng-eel) (*birthday*) is, you put 생일 in front and say, 생일, 며칠이에요? You can also use a more general question, 언제예요? (uhn-jeh-yeh-yoh?) (*When is . . .?*) and say, 생일, 언제예요?

Here are more events you may want to check out the dates. All you need to do is add 며칠이에요? or 언제예요?, after the event you don't want to miss.

>> 생일 파티 (saeng-eel pah-tee) (*birthday party*)

>> 졸업식 (joh-ruhp-sseek) (*graduation ceremony*)

>> 콘서트 (kohn-ssuh-teu) (*concert*)

>> 할머니 생신 (hahl-muh-nee saeng-sheen) (*grandmother's birthday*)

Naming the months and dates

To express the month and date, you need two counters — 월 (wuhl) (*counter for month*) and 일 (eel) (*counter for date*). For 크리스마스 (*Chistmas*), you say 십이월 이십오일 (shee-bee-wuhl ee-shee-boh-eel). 발렌타인 데이 (*Valentine's Day*)? 이월 십사 일 (ee-wuhl sheep-ssah-eel). Check out Tables 5-8 and 5-9 to stay on track with months and dates.

TABLE 5-8

Months

Korean	Pronunciation	English
일월	ee-rwuhl	January
이월	ee-wuhl	February
삼월	sah-mwuhl	March
사월	sah-wuhl	April
오월	oh-wuhl	May
유월 *	yoo-wuhl	June
칠월	chee-rwuhl	July
팔월	pah-rwuhl	August
구월	goo-wuhl	September
시월 *	shee-wuhl	October
십일월	shee-bee-rwuhl	November
십이월	shee-bee-wuhl	December

TABLE 5-9

Dates

Korean	Pronunciation	Meaning
십 일	shee-beel	10th
십삼 일	sheep-ssah-meel	13th
십육 일	sheem-nyoo-geel	16th
십구 일	sheep-kkoo-eel	19th
이십 일	ee-shee-beel	20th
이십일 일	ee-shee-bee-reel	21st
이십이 일	ee-shee-bee-eel	22nd
이십오 일	ee-shee-boh-eel	25th
이십육 일	ee-sheem-nyoo-geel	26th
이십칠 일	ee-sheep-chee-reel	27th
삼십 일	sahm-shee-beel	30th
삼십일 일	sahm-shee-bee-reel	31st

Note that *June* and *October* have special forms made by dropping their final consonants — 유월 instead of 육월, and 시월 instead of 십월.

제 생일은 유월 십육 일이에요. (jeh saeng-ee-reun yoo-wuhl sheem-nyoo-gee-lee-eh-yoh.) (*My birthday is June 16th.*)

시월 십 일에 여행 가요. (shee-wuhl shee-bee-reh yuh-haeng-gah-yoh.) (*I'm on a trip on October 16th.*)

Saying years

To express years in Korean, you need the "year" counter, 년 (nyuhn). Do you remember the digit nouns for 1000, 100, and 10? Right, they're 천 (chuhn), 백 (baek), and 십 (sheep) respectively. The year 1443 is 천사백사십삼 년 (chuhn-sah-baek-sah-sheep-sahm nyuhn) which is the year the Hangeul was created. Here are some more examples:

>> **Year 1945: 천구백사십오 년** (chuhn-goo-baek-sah-shee-boh nyuhn)

>> **Year 2024: 이천이십사 년** (ee-chuhn-ee-sheep-sah nyuhn)

>> **Year 2111: 이천백십일 년** (ee-chuhn-baek-shee-beel nyuhn)

When Koreans introduce themselves, they may say 저는 구팔 년생이에요. (juh-neun goo-pahl-nyuhn-saeng-ee-eh-yo.) (*I'm a year 1998 born.*) "생이에요" means "I was born in." Instead of saying the entire year of 천구백십팔 년 (*Year 1998*), they take the last two digits and just read the numbers one by one to express what year they were born in. If someone says "공삼 년생이에요" (gong-sahm-nyuhn-saeng-ee-eh-yoh), it means they were born in 2003. Read on for example conversation:

Q: 몇 년생이에요?" (myuhn-nyuhn-saeng-ee-eh-yoh?) (*What year were you born?*)

A: 공공 년생이에요. (gong-gohng-nyuhn-saeng-ee-eh-yoh.) (*I'm a year 2000 born.*)

Remember that, if someone asks you, 몇 년생이에요? just a few minutes after meeting you, it's not because they think your references are outdated. They just want to know your age to help them choose the appropriate speech level when speaking to you. But don't worry, not everyone feels the urgency to know this info, and many of them may instead use polite speech until you get to know each other better. So, if someone doesn't ask, it's all good!

THE DATES ARE BACKWARDS!

Korea is a so-called "macro to micro" language, which means that larger entities are placed first. For example, when Koreans say their names, they say their 성 (suhng) (*last name*) first. If your name is *John Doe*, you say 저는 Doe John 입니다 (*I am John Doe*.). Korean addresses are written from largest to smallest, too. That is, the country, province, city, street, house number or apartment name, and number. It's similar for stating time. Korean goes year, month, date, day of the week, a.m./*p.m.*, hour and minute. For example, if you were born on February 10, 2010, on Wednesday at 5 p.m., Koreans would say that you were born on 2010 년 2월 10일 수요일 오후 5시. (ee-chuhn-sheem-nyuhn ee-wuhl-shee-beel soo-yoh-eel oh-hoo dah-suh-ssee)

Talking about the days of the week

The Korean word for *day of the week* is 요일 (yoh-eel). Each day of the week is expressed by the combination of prefix + 요일. The prefix determines which day of the week it is, as follows:

>> 월요일 (wuh-ryoh-eel) (*Monday*)

>> 화요일 (hwah-yoh-eel) (*Tuesday*)

>> 수요일 (soo-yoh-eel) (*Wednesday*)

>> 목요일 (moh-gyoh-eel) (*Thursday*)

>> 금요일 (geu-myoh-eel) (*Friday*)

>> 토요일 (toh-yoh-eel) (*Saturday*)

>> 일요일 (ee-ryoh-eel) (*Sunday*)

When referring to several days of the week, you can sometimes use only the first letters, as in 월수금 (Mon, Wed, Fri), and 화목 (Tue, Thu). 월화수목금 are 주중 (joo-joong) or 평일 (pyuhng-eel) (*weekday*), and 토일 are 주말 (joo-mahl) (*weekend*).

TIP

"What day is it?" in Korean is 무슨 요일이에요? (moo-seun nyoh-ee-ree-eh-yoh?). If you want to ask "what day is it today?" you just put 오늘 (oh-neul) (*today*) in front of the question sentence and say 오늘 무슨 요일이에요? To answer is simple: [day of the week]+이에요. If its Monday, you say 월요일이에요. (wuh-ryoh-ee-ree-eh-yoh.)

GRAMMATICALLY SPEAKING

To decide on what day or what time to meet up with your friend, use the particle 에 which is like *on* or *at* in English. *Meet on Saturday* is 토요일에 만나요. (toh-yoh-ee-reh mahn-nah-yoh.) To add what time to meet, use 에 once at the end of the time, as in 토요일 한 시에 만나요. (toh-yoh-eel hahn-shee-eh mahn-nah-yoh.) (*Let's meet on Sunday at 1 o'clock.*) Read on for more examples. Feel free to replace the words in brackets with different days of the week.

Q: 무슨 요일에 일해요? (moo-seun nyoh-ee-reh eel-hae-yoh?) (*What day of the week do you work?*)

A: [월요일]하고 [수요일]에 일해요. (wuh-ryoh-eel-hah-goh soo-yoh-ee-reh eel-hae-yoh.) (*I work on Monday and Wednesday.*)

Q: [금요일]에 뭐 해요? (geu-myoh-ee-reh mwuh-hae-yoh?) (*What do you do on Friday?*)

A: 그냥 집에서 쉬어요. (geu-nyahng jee-beh-suh shwee-uh-yoh.) (*I just take a rest at home.*)

Telling time in relation to the present

Just as in English, Korean has lots of phrases to talk about a certain time in the past or future in relation to the present moment. Some time-related words that you may hear or say often in Korean can be found in Table 5-10.

TABLE 5-10   **Relative Time Expressions**

Previous	Current	Future
어제 (uh-jeh) (*yesterday*)	오늘 (oh-neul) (*today*)	내일 (nae-eel) (*tomorrow*)
지난주 (jee-nahn-joo) (*last week*)	이번 주 (ee-buhn-jjoo) (*this week*)	다음 주 (dah-eum-jjoo) (*next week*)
지난달 (jee-nahn-dahl) (*last month*)	이번 달 (ee-buhn-ttahl) (*this month*)	다음 달 (dah-eum-ttahl) (*next month*)
작년 (jahng-nyuhn) (*last year*)	올해 (ohl-hae) (*this year*)	내년 (nae-nyuhn) (*next year*)

Talkin' the Talk

PLAY

Lia is planning to throw a party for her birthday so she is inviting Dan to the party.

Lia: 10월 15일에 시간 있어요?
shee-wuhl shee-boh-ee-reh shee-gahn ee-ssuh-yoh?
Do you have time on October 15th?

Dan: 무슨 요일이에요?
moo-seun nyoh-ee-ree-eh-yoh?
What day of the week is that?

Lia: 토요일이에요.
toh-yoh-ee-ree-eh-yoh.
It's a Saturday.

Dan: 네, 시간 있어요. 그런데 왜요?
neh, shee-gahn ee-ssuh-yoh. geu-ruhn-deh wae-yoh?
Yes, I have time. Why?

Lia: 토요일에 우리집에서 제 생일 파티해요.
toh-yoh-ee-reh oo-ree-jee-beh-suh jeh saeng-eel pah-tee-hae-yoh.
I'm throwing my birthday party at my place on Saturday.

Dan: 생일 축하해요! 파티가 몇 시예요?
saeng-eel choo-kah-hae-yoh. pah-tee-gah myuht-ssee-yeh-yoh?
Happy birthday! What time is the party?

Lia: 오후 4시요.
oh-hoo neh-shee-yoh.
4 p.m.

Dan: 좋아요! 4시까지 갈게요. 초대 고마워요!
joh-ah-yoh! neh-shee-kkah-jee gahl-kkeh-yoh. choh-dae goh-mah-wuh-yoh!
Good! I'll be there by 4. Thank you for the invite!

WORDS TO KNOW

시간	shee-gahn	time, hour
있어요 (있다)	ee-ssuh-yoh	to have / exist
무슨 요일	moo-seun nyoh-eel	what day of the week
축하해요 (축하하다)	choo-kah-hae-yoh	congratulation
몇 시	myuht-ssee	what time
초대	choh-dae	invitation

Size Matters: Measuring in Korean

Korea uses 미터법 (mee-tuh-ppuhp) (*metric system*), just like most other countries in the world. If you're traveling to 한국 (hahn-gook) (*Korea*) from 미국 (mee-gook) (*the United States*) or one of the other two countries in the world that uses the imperial system, familiarizing yourself with the 미터법 will come in handy.

Instead of 인치 (een-chee) (*inches*) and 피트 (pee-teu) (*feet*), your 키 (kee) (*height*) and 몸무게 (mohm-moo-geh) (*body weight*) are referenced in 센티미터 (ssehn-tee-mee-tuh) (*centimeters*), 미터 (mee-tuh) (*meters*), and 킬로그램 (keel-loh-geu-raem) (*kilograms*) (or 킬로 (*kilo*) as a shortened form).

The speed-per-hour signs are in 킬로미터 (keel-loh-mee-tuh) (*kilometers*), not 마일 (mah-eel) (*miles*). So when you see a speed limit sign with the number 100 circled in red on the 고속도로 (goh-sohk-doh-roh) (*freeway*) in Korea and step on the gas, you'll soon get to test out your language skills with the Korean police. The speed limit of 100 on the sign refers to 100 kilometers per hour, which equates to 62 miles per hour. Table 5-11 lays out 미터법 and the equivalents of the U.S. Customary System (USCS).

Also, remember that Korea uses Celsius, in which 0도 (yuhng-doh) (*o degree*) is 32도 (sahm-shee-bee-doh) (*32 degrees*) in Fahrenheit. If you're setting your hotel room temperature in Korea to be 68 degrees — a nice, comfortable indoor temperature in Fahrenheit — you'll soon feel the heat. 68도 in Celsius is around 154도 in Fahrenheit. 68도 in Fahrenheit is around 21도 in Celsius.

TABLE 5-11 Conversion of Measurements: Metric to USCS

Measurement	Korean Term (Metric system)	Meaning	USCS
distance	킬로미터 (keel-loh-mee-tuh)	kilometer	1 km = 0.62 miles
length	센티미터 (ssehn-tee-mee-tuh)	centimeter	1 cm = 0.4 inches
	미터 (mee-tuh)	meter	1 m = 3.28 feet
temperature	도 (doh)	degree	1° (C) = 33.8 ° (F)
volume	리터 (lee-tuh)	liter	1 L = 1.06 quarts
weight/mass	킬로 (keel-loh)	kilogram	1 Kg = 2.2 pounds

When asking about measurements, the question word 몇 (myuht) will come in handy. Here are some example questions and responses:

Q: 오늘 몇 도예요? (oh-neul myuht-ttoh-yeh-yoh?) (*How many degrees is it today?*)

A: 삼십 팔도예요. 너무 더워요! (sahm-sheep pahl-ttoh-yeh-yoh. nuh-moo duh-wuh-yoh!) (*It's 38 degrees. Too hot!*)

Q: 키가 몇이에요? (kee-gah myuht-chee-eh-yoh?) (*How tall are you?*)

A: 163이에요. (baeng-yook-sheep-sahm-ee-eh-yoh?) (*I'm 163 (cm).*)

Q: 제한 속도가 몇이에요? (jeh-hah-sohk-ttoh-gah myuht-chee-eh-yoh?) (*What is the speed limit?*)

A: 시속 100 킬로예요. (shee-sohk baek-keel-loh-yeh-yoh.) (*It's 100 kilometers per hour (km/h).*)

FUN & GAMES

Match the illustrations with the correct Korean phrases. Turn to Appendix C for the answers.

1.

2.

3.

4.

5.

a. 여덟 시 이십 분
b. 여섯 시 사십오 분
c. 세 시 십오 분
d. 열두 시 삼십 분
e. 열한 시

Chapter 6

Speaking Korean at Home

N o matter which 집 (jeep) (*home, house*) you find yourself in, you'll want to know your way around it. Knowing home-related words will greatly enhance your experience as a guest.

Settle in! You're about to learn vital vocabulary for visiting a Korean home. You'll learn to identify various areas in a house and 가정용품 (gah-juhng-yohng-poom) (*household items*), and understand terms for daily activities like cooking, sleeping, and even figuring out who does the dishes. We've also included cultural tips to help you move around your surroundings with ease. Get ready to feel right at home in your friend's house, knowing exactly where the extra 수건 (soo-guhn) (*towels*) — and maybe even the snacks — are!

Visiting a Korean Home

When you're a 손님 (sohn-neem) (*guest*) in a Korean home, expect nothing less than genuine hospitality. While the hosts may humbly downplay their efforts, their warmth and welcoming nature are usually very apparent. Coming up, you'll find essential phrases and cultural tips for when you're invited over, ensuring your visit is as smooth and enjoyable as possible.

Inviting friends over

Whether it's for special 초대 (choh-dae) (*invitations*) like a 생일 파티 (saeng-eel pah-tee) (*birthday party*), a 집들이 (jeep-tteu-ree) (*housewarming*), or just casual hangouts, the first step is usually checking the availability of the invitees. When someone invites you over, you might hear these phrases:

> [주말에] 시간 있어요? ([joo-mah-reh] shee-gahn ee-ssuh-yoh) (*Do you have time [on the weekend]?*)

> 우리 집에 놀러 오세요. (woo-ree-jee-beh nohl-luh oh-seh-yoh) (*Please come over to my house to hang out.*)

TIP

You can replace [주말에] with different time expressions, like 내일 (nae-eel) (*tomorrow*), 오늘 저녁에 (oh-neul juh-nyuh-geh) (*this evening*), or specific dates or days of the week, like 7월 9일에 (chee-rwuhl goo-ee-reh) (*July 9th*) or 토요일에 (toh-yoh-ee-reh) (*on Saturday*).

CULTURAL WISDOM

In Korean, using 우리/저희 (oo-ree/juh-hee) (*our*), instead of 내/제 (nae/jeh) (*my*), reflects a community-oriented perspective. For instance, even if living alone, one would describe their home as 우리집 (oo-ree jeep) or more humbly, 저희 집 (juh-hee jeep) (*our house*), instead of 내 집 or 제 집 for "my house." (For more info on this, see Chapter 3.)

TIP

To express the purpose of going somewhere, use the pattern "(으)러 가다/오다" ((eu)-ruh gah-dah/oh-dah): 으러 after a consonant-ending verb stem, and 러 after a vowel-ending verb stem. (For more usage examples, see Chapter 7.)

> 내일 저녁 먹으러 오세요. (nae-eel juh-nyuhk muh-geu-ruh oh-seh-yoh) (*Please come over for dinner tomorrow.*)

> 일요일에 영화 보러 갈래요? (ee-ryoh-ee-reh yuhng-hwah boh-ruh gahl-lae-yoh) (*Would you like to go see a movie on Sunday?*)

> 우유 사러 슈퍼에 가요. (oo-yoo sah-ruh soo-puh-eh gah-yoh) (*I'm going to the supermarket to buy milk.*)

Preparing for a visit

초대 받았어요! (choh-dae bah-dah-ssuh-yoh) (*You've received an invitation!*). Are you excited to visit your friend's house? You can show your appreciation by bringing a small 선물 (suhn-mool) (*gift*) when you go over. Popular choices include 과일 (gwah-eel) (*fruit*), 음료수 (eum-nyoh-soo) (*beverage*), 빵 (ppahng) (*bread*) or 케이크 (keh-ee-keu) (*cake*), or any homemade dish. Here're some useful phrases in preparation for your visit.

뭐 사 갈까요? (mwuh sah gahl-kkah-yoh) (*What should I bring?*)

뭐 좋아해요? (mwuh joh-ah-hae-yoh) (*What do you like?*)

[어머님]이 뭐 좋아하세요? ([uh-muh-neem]ee mwuh joh-ah-hah-seh-yoh) (*What does your [mom] like?*)

몇 시까지 가면 돼요? (myuht ssee-kkah-jee gah-myuhn dwae-yoh) (*By what time do I need to be there?*)

CULTURAL WISDOM

There's a term 빈손 (been-sohn) whose literal meaning is "empty hand." When visiting someone's home, it's usually recommended not to go with 빈손, although you may have been told, "그냥 오세요" (geu-nyahng oh-seh-yoh) (*Just come/just bring yourself*). For more about this cultural aspect, see Chapter 20.

Taking a Tour around the House

CULTURAL WISDOM

When you arrive at a Korean house, forget about the traditional lock and key setup. Most homes in Korea are equipped with digital 도어락 (doh-uh-rahk) (*door lock*). Residents simply punch in a code, tap their finger, smile for a facial scan, or sync their smartphone for entry. Just like that, you're in!

Types of Housing

Table 6-1 shows a quick overview of common Korean housing types. In Korea, residential spaces are commonly referred to as 집 (jeep) (*home, house*), with 아파트 (ah-pah-teu) (*apartment*) being the most prevalent type. Knowing these terms will come in handy if you're considering a long-term stay in Korea.

TABLE 6-1 **Housing Types**

Korean Word	Pronunciation	Meaning
아파트	ah-pah-teu	apartment (most common form of housing in urban Korea)
단독주택	dahn-dohk-joo-taek	single-family house/detached house
연립주택	yuhl-leep-joo-taek	condominium, townhome
원룸	wuhn-noom	studio (popular among students or young professionals)
오피스텔	oh-pee-seu-tehl	"officetel" (office + hotel) — studio building designed for both commercial and residential use
기숙사	gee-sook-ssah	dormitory
고시원	goh-shee-wuhn	one-room rental unit for study, minimal space with shared amenities

If you find yourself discussing living arrangements, here're some handy phrases to know:

어디에서 살아요? 저는 [원룸]에서 살아요. (uh-dee-eh-suh sah-rah-yoh? juh-neun [wuhn-noom]-eh-suh sah-rah-yoh) (*Where do you live? I live in a [studio].*)

[기숙사]에서 살아요. 룸메이트가 있어요. ([gee-sook-ssah]-eh-suh sah-rah-yoh. room-meh-ee-teu-gah ee-ssuh-yoh) (*I live in a [dorm]. I have a roommate.*)

You can replace the words in brackets with the type of housing you reside in as needed.

Inside the house

Once you step into a Korean home, you'll first spot an array of shoes neatly arranged at the front door, which is a cue for you to remove yours. You might also be offered some 실내화 (sheel-lae-hwah) (*indoor slippers*) to wear inside, though it's not guaranteed.

CULTURAL WISDOM

In Korea, homes are always shoe-free zones. Keeping floors clean is crucial in Korean households. (For more on this cultural practice, see Chapter 20.) The following is a list of words for various parts of a house and items found around each part:

>> 현관 (hyuhn-gwahn) (*entry*): 문 (moon) (*door*), 대문 (dae-moon) (*gate*), 도어락 (doh-uh-rahk) (*door lock*), 비밀번호 (bee-meel buhn-hoh) (*password*), 열쇠

(yuhl-sswae) (*key*), 신발장 (sheen-bahl-jjahng) (*shoe rack*), 실내화 (sheel-lae-hwah) (*indoor slippers*)

» 거실 (guh-sheel) (*living room*): 마루 (mah-roo) (*wooden floor*), 소파 (soh-pah) (*sofa*), 탁자 (tahk-jjah) (*table*), 상 (sahng) (*portable dining table*), 방석 (bahng-suhk) (*seating cushion*), TV (tee-bee) (*TV*)

» 벽 (byuhk) (*wall*): 그림 (geu-reem) (*painting*), 사진 (sah-jeen) (*photo*), 시계 (shee-gyeh) (*clock*), 창문 (chahng-moon) (*window*)

» 부엌 (boo-uhk) (*kitchen*): 냉장고 (naeng-jahng-goh) (*refrigerator*), 싱크대 (sseeng-keu-dae) (*sink*), 식탁 (sheek-tahk) (*dining table*), 레인지 (reh-een-jee) (*range*), 오븐 (oh-beun) (*oven*), 식기세척기 (sheek-kkee-seh-chuhk-kkee) (*dishwasher*), 그릇 (geu-reut) (*dishes*), 냄비 (naem-bee) (*pot*), 칼 (kahl) (*knife*), 도마 (doh-mah) (*cutting board*), 전기 밥솥 (juhn-gee bahp-ssoht) (*electric rice cooker*)

» 침실/방 (cheem-sheel/bahng) (*bedroom*): 침대 (cheem-dae) (*bed*), 스탠드 (seu-taen-deu) (*night stand*), 이불 (ee-bool) (*blanket*), 베개 (beh-gae) (*pillow*), 옷장 (oht-jjahng) (*wardrobe*)

» 서재 (suh-jae) (*home office, library*): 책상 (chaek-ssahng) (*desk*), 책장 (chaek-jjahng) (*bookshelf*), 의자 (eui-jah) (*chair*), 컴퓨터 (kuhm-pyoo-tuh) (*computer*), 전등 (juhn-deung) (*light*)

» 화장실/욕실 (hwah-jahng-sheel/yohk-sseel) (*bathroom*): 세면대 (seh-myuhn-dae) (*sink*), 욕조 (yohk-jjoh) (*bathtub*), 샤워기 (shyah-wuh-gee) (*shower head*), 변기 (byuhn-gee) (*toilet*), 거울 (guh-ool) (*mirror*), 샴푸 (shahm-poo) (*shampoo*), 비누 (bee-noo) (*soap*), 칫솔 (cheet-ssohl) (*toothbrush*), 치약 (chee-yahk) (*toothpaste*), 수건 (soo-guhn) (*towel*), 화장지 (hwah-jahng-jee) (*toilet paper*)

» 다용도실 (dah-yohng-doh-sheel) (*multi-purpose room*): 세탁기 (seh-tahk-kkee) (*washing machine*), 건조기 (guhn-joh-gee) (*dryer*), 세제 (seh-jeh) (*detergent*)

» 베란다 (beh-rahn-dah) (*veranda, porch*): 화분 (hwah-boon) (*plant pot*), 건조대 (guhn-joh-dae) (*laundry rack*)

When your 친구 (cheen-goo) (*friend*) is showing you around their house, the following phrases may come in handy:

집 구경할 수 있어요? (jeep goo-gyuhg-hahl ssoo ee-ssuh-yoh) (*Can we/I tour the house?*)

방 볼 수 있어요? (bahng bohl ssoo ee-ssuh-yoh) (*Can we/I see your room?*)

[화장실] 어디에 있어요? ([hwah-jahng-sheel] uh-dee-eh ee-ssuh-yoh) (*Where is/are the [bathroom]?*)

GRAMMATICALLY SPEAKING

"Verb stem+ 을/ㄹ 수 있어요" functions like "can" in English, allowing you to express ability, possibility, or permission. For verb stems ending in a vowel, add "ㄹ 수 있어요" (e.g., 하다 (*to do*): 할 수 있어요 (hahl ssoo ee-ssuh-yoh) (*can do*). For verb stems ending in a consonant, use 을 수 있어요 (e.g., 먹다 (*to eat*): 먹을 수 있어요 (muh-geul ssoo ee-ssuh-yoh) (*can eat*)).

To ask politely if you can tour the house, use the verb stem "구경하" from 구경하다 (goo-gyuhng-hah-dah) (*to tour*) and say "구경할 수 있어요?" (*Can I tour?*). Similarly, to ask if someone can eat 매운 음식 (*spicy food*), you'd say "매운 음식 먹을 수 있어요?" (mae-oon eum-sheek muh-geul ssoo ee-ssuh-yoh) (*Can you eat spicy foods?*).

Responses can be straightforward, like "네" (neh) (*Yes*) or "아니요" (ah-nee-yoh) (*No*). They can also be more detailed based on whether the question relates to permission or ability:

Q: 집 구경할 수 있어요?

A: 네, 그럼요 (neh, geu-ruhm-yoh) (*Yes, of course.*)

아니요, 지금 안 돼요. (ahn-nee-yoh, jee-geum ahn dwae-yoh) (*No, not right now.*) (Literally, *it's not possible/available now.*)

Q: 매운 음식 먹을 수 있어요?

A: 네, 잘 먹어요. (neh, jahl muh-guh-yoh) (*Yes, I eat it well.*)

아니요, (잘) 못 먹어요. (ah-nee-yoh, (jahl) mohn muh-guh-yoh) (*No, I can't eat it (well).*)

CULTURAL WISDOM

The primary bedroom in Korean is called 안방 (ahn-ppahng), literally meaning "*inner room.*" In modern apartments, the 안방 usually comes with its own 화장실 (hwah-jahng-shee) (*bathroom*) with a 샤워실 (shyah-wuh-sheel) (*shower stall*), similar to those in other countries. Korean 화장실 feature 배수구 (bae-soo-goo) (*floor drainage*) and waterproof tiles, making them fully water-resistant. Instead of shower curtains, they have glass walls for shower stalls, and 욕조 (yohk-jjoh) (*bathtubs*) are curtain-free, so no worries about splashing water around! This design allows you to easily wash down the entire bathroom thoroughly. Remember to slip on special bathroom 실내화 (sheel-lae-hwah) (*slippers*) when you enter!

Cooking and Eating

It's all fun and games in the 부엌 (boo-uhk) (*kitchen*)! While ordering takeout is convenient, there's a special joy in cooking at home. Particularly, cooking with friends is a wonderful way to socialize and bond. Here're some phrases for when you want to help out in the 부엌:

뭐 만들어요? (mwuh mahn-deu-ruh-yoh) (*What are you making?*)

뭐 도와줄까요?/도와드릴까요? (mwuh doh-wah-jool-kkah-yoh/doh-wah deu-reel-kkah-yoh) (*What should I do to help?*) (* 도와드릴까요? is politer than 도와줄까요?)

For more exploration of cooking-specific vocabulary, see the following list. You can also find additional food-related terms in Chapter 9.

>> **요리 (yoh-ree) (*cooking*):** 굽다 (goop-ttah) (*to grill*), 끓이다 (kkeu-ree-dah) (*to boil [liquid]*), 삶다 (sahm-ttah) (*to boil [hard objects]*), 볶다 (bohk-ttah) (*to stir fry*), 찌다 (jjee-dah) (*to steam*), 튀기다 (twee-gee-dah) (*to deep fry*)

>> **음식 (bahp) (*dishes/food*):** 밥 (bahp) (*cooked rice/meal*), 국 (gook) (*soup*), 반찬 (bahn-chahn) (*side dish*), 김 (geem) (*dried seaweed*), 김치 (geem-chee) (*kimchi*), 찌개 (jjee-gae) (*stew*), 구이 (goo-ee) (*grilled dish*), 찜 (jjeem) (*steamed dish*), 볶음 (boh-kkeum) (*stir-fried dish*), 튀김 (twee-geem) (*fried dish*), 전 (juhn) (*Korean pancake with fish/vegetable/meat*), 생선 (saeng-suhn) (*fish*), 간식 (gahn-sheek) (*snack between meals*)

TIP

Read on for conversational phrases. Feel free to experiment by replacing the bracketed words with other terms from the list above.

[밥] 있어요? ([bahp] ee-ssuh-yoh) (*Do you have [cooked rice]?*)

[생선 구이] 좋아해요? (saeng-suhn-goo-ee joh-ah-hae-yoh) (*Do you like [grilled fish]?*)

무슨 [찌개] 끓여요? (moo-seun [jjee-gae] kkeu-ryuh-yoh) (*What kind of [stew] are you cooking?*)

[김치전]도 만들까요? ([geem-chee-juhn]-doh mahn-deul-kkah-yoh) (*Should we make [kimchi panckakes], too?*)

[점심]에 [감자 튀김] 먹어요. ([juhm-sheem-]eh [gahm-jah twee-geem] muh-guh-yoh) (*Let's have [potato fries] for [lunch].*)

몇 시쯤 [저녁] 먹어요? (myuht ssee-jjeum [juh-nyuhk] muh-guh-yoh) (*Around what time are we having [dinner]?*)

Talkin' the Talk

PLAY

Doug is hanging out at Juyoung's place. Later in the evening, Doug feels a little hungry and wants to have a snack.

Doug: 주영 씨, 배고픈데 혹시 간식 있어요?
joo-yuhng ssee, bae-goh-peun-deh hohk-ssee gahn-sheek ee-ssuh-yoh?
Juyoung, I'm hungry, and do you by any chance have some snacks?

Juyoung: 식탁에 김밥 있어요. 드실래요?
sheek-tah-geh geem-bahp ee-ssuh-yoh. deu-sheel-lae-yoh?
There's some kimbap on the dining table. Would you like to eat some?

Doug: 김밥 좋지요. 맥주도 있어요?
geem-bahp joh-chee-yoh. maek-jjoo-doh ee-ssuh-yoh?
Kimbap sounds good. Do you have beer, too?

Juyoung: 맥주는 냉장고에 있어요.
maek-jjoo-neun naeng-jahng-goh-eh ee-ssuh-yoh.
Beer is in the refrigerator.

Doug: 같이 드실래요?
gah-chee deu-sheel-lae-yoh?
Would you like to eat with me?

Juyoung: 아니요, 저는 됐어요.
ah-nee-yoh, juh-neun dwae-ssuh-yoh.
No, I'm good.

WORDS TO KNOW

배고픈데 (배고프다)	bae-goh-peun-deh	I'm hungry. . .
혹시	hohk-ssee	by any chance
식탁	sheek-tahk	dining table
김밥	geem-bahp	kimbap (rolled rice)
드실래요 (드시다)	deu-sheel-lae-yoh	Would you like to eat? (honorific)
냉장고	naeng-jahng-goh	refrigerator
됐어요 (되다)	dwae-ssuh-yoh	I'm good

Discussing Daily Activities

In the following section, we explore essential vocabulary for daily activities around the house, from relaxing to tackling household chores.

Chatting about daily routines

Whether you're sharing your own routines or curious about what your friends do at their home, these phrases will come in handy:

집에서 뭐 해요? (jee-beh-suh mwuh hae-yoh) (*What do you do at home?*)

음악 들어요. (eu-mahk deu-ruh-yoh) (*I listen to music.*)

영화/TV 봐요. (yuhng-hwah/tee-bee bwah-yoh) (*I watch a movie/ TV.*)

책 읽어요. (chaek eel-guh-yoh) (*I read a book.*)

차 마셔요. (chah mah-shyuh-yoh) (*I drink tea.*)

비디오게임 해요. (bee-dee-oh-geh-eem hae-yoh) (*I play video games.*)

요리해요. (yoh-ree-hae-yoh) (*I cook.*)

운동해요. (oon-dohng-hae-yoh) (*I work out.*)

가족하고 얘기해요. (gah-joh-kah-goh yeh-gee-hae-yoh) (*I talk with my family.*)

목욕해요. (moh-gyohk-kae-yoh) (*I take a bath.*)

쉬어요. (shwee-uh-yoh) (*I rest.*)

자요. (jah-yoh) (*I sleep.*)

(집)정리해요. ((jeep) juhng-nee-hae-yoh) (*I organize (the house).*)

(집)청소해요. ((jeep) chuhng-soh-hae-yoh) (*I clean (the house).*)

빨래해요. (ppahl-lae-hae-yoh) (*I do laundry.*)

GRAMMATICALLY
SPEAKING

Frequency adverbs are handy when talking about your regular activities. Check out the following adverbs and try slipping them into your conversation in Korean.

>> 가끔 (gah-kkeum) (*occasionally, sometimes*)

>> 자주 (jah-joo) (*frequently*)

>> 주로 (joo-roh) (*mainly, primarily, usually*)

>> 보통 (boh-tohng) (*normally, generally, usually*)

>> 항상 (hahng-sahng) (*always*)

» 매일/날마다 (mae-eel/nahl-mah-dah) (*every day*)

» 매주 (mae-joo) (*every week*)

» 주말마다 (joo-mahl-mah-dah) (*every weekend*)

» 일주일에 한 번 (eel-jjoo-ee-reh hanh buhn) (*once a week*)

» 한 달에 한 번 (hahn dah-reh hanh buhn) (*once a month*)

» 일 년에 두 번 (eel lyuh-neh doo buhn) (*twice a year*)

When forming a sentence, place the adverbs before the verbs:

Q: 자주 요리해요? (jah-joo yoh-ree-hae-yoh) (*Do you cook **often?***)

A: 네, 매일 해요 (neh, mae-eel hae-yoh) (*Yes, I do/cook **every day.***)

Q: 주말에 보통 뭐 해요? (joo-mah-reh boh-tohng mwuh hae-yoh) (*What do you **usually** do on the weekend?*)

A: 집에서 그냥 쉬어요. 그리고 가끔 산책해요. (jee-beh-suh geu-nyahng shwee-uh-yoh. geu-ree-goh gah-kkeum sahn-chaek-hae-yoh) (*I **just** rest at home. And I go on a walk **every now and then**.*)

Talking about household chores

If you're staying at someone's house for more than a night or just for a meal, you may want to offer the nice gesture of helping around the house. You can ask where the 청소기 (chuhng–soh–gee) (*vacummn cleaner*) is; maybe help 설거지 (suhl–guh–jee) (*do the dishes*). Here are some common cleaning supplies.

» 고무장갑 (goh-moo-jahng-gahp) (*rubber gloves*)

» 걸레 (guhl-leh) (*cleaning rag*)

» 주방세제 (joo-bahng-seh-jeh) (*dish soap*)

» 쓰레기(통) (sseu-reh-gee[-tohng]) (*trash, garbage [can]*)

» 분리수거함 (bool-lee-soo-guh-hahm) (*recycling bin*)

» 빗자루 (beet-jjah-roo) (*broom*)

» 청소기 (chuhng-soh-gee) (*vacuum cleaner*)

» 행주 (haeng-joo) (*kitchen towel*)

MANAGING WASTE IN KOREA

The Korean government enforces strict policies on 쓰레기 (sseu-reh-gee) (*trash*). Every household must buy special 쓰레기 봉투 (sseu-reh-gee bohng-too) (*trash bags*) from stores. As a result, most Koreans recycle everything they can.

When disposing of trash, make sure to separate paper, plastic, cans, and food waste. 음식물 쓰레기 (eum-sheeng-mool sseu-reh-gee) (*food waste*) is charged by weight. If you double-wrap a trash bag, ensure the municipal government-issued trash bag is visible to avoid breaking the law. (For more, see Chapter 20.)

You might want to try these useful phrases:

제가 [설거지]할게요. (jeh-gah [suhl-guh-jee] hahl-kkeh-yoh) (*I'll do [the dishes].*)

제가 [청소] 도와 드릴게요. (jeh-gah [chuhng-soh] doh-wah deu-reel-kkeh-yoh) (*I'll help you [with cleaning].*)

[분리수거함] 어디 있어요? ([bool-lee-soo-guh-hahm] uh-dee ee-ssuh-yoh) (*Where are the [recycling bins]?*)

Talkin' the Talk

PLAY

Bill is visiting Haesoo in Seoul, and they are hanging out at Haesoo's place.

Bill: 해수 씨는 아침에 몇 시에 일어나요?
hae-soo see-neun ah-chee-meh myuht see-eh ee-ruh-nah-yoh?
Haesoo, what time do you wake up in the morning?

Haesoo: 보통 여섯 시에 일어나요.
boh-tohng yuh-suht see-eh ee-ruh-nah-yoh.
I normally wake up at 6.

Bill: 아침으로 주로 뭐 먹어요?
ah-chee-meu-roh joo-roh mwuh muh-guh-yoh?
What do you usually eat for breakfast?

Haesoo: 아침으로 주로 빵 먹어요.
ah-chee-meu-roh joo-roh ppahng muh-guh-yoh.
I usually eat bread for breakfast.

Bill: 집에서 주로 뭐 해요?

jee-beh-suh joo-roh mwuh hae-yoh?

What do you usually do at home?

Haesoo: 집에서 주로 요리해요.

jee-beh-suh joo-roh yoh-ree-hae-yoh.

I usually cook at home.

Bill: 일주일에 몇 번 청소해요?

eel-jjoo-ee-reh myuht ppuhn chuhng-soh-hae-yoh?

How many times a week do you clean the house?

Haesoo: 일주일에 한 번 청소해요. 오늘이 청소하는 날이에요.

eel-jjoo-ee-reh hahn buhn chuhng-soh-hae-yoh. oh-neu-ree chuhng-soh-hah-neun nah-ree-eh-yoh.

I clean the house once a week. Today is the day to clean the house.

Bill: 그래요? 내가 청소 도와줄게요.

geu-rae-yoh? nae-gah chuhng-soh doh-wah-jool-kkeh-yoh.

Really? I'll help you with cleaning.

Haesoo: 청소 끝나고 요리도 같이 할까요?

chuhng-soh kkeun-nah-goh yoh-ree-doh gah-chee hahl-kkah-yoh?

After cleaning, shall we cook together?

Bill: 좋아요. 저 요리 잘 해요.

joh-ah-yoh. juh yoh-ree jahl hae-yoh.

Sure. I'm good at cooking.

. . . .

WORDS TO KNOW		
아침	ah-cheem	morning, breakfast
일어나요 (일어나다)	ee-ruh-nah-yoh	I wake up
보통	boh-tohng	normally, usually
주로	joo-roh	mainly, usually

요리해요 (요리하다)	yoh-ree-hae-yoh	I cook
일주일	eel-jjoo-eel	one week
청소해요 (청소하다)	chuhng-soh-hae-yoh	I clean
도와줄게요 (도와주다)	doh-wah-jool-kkeh-yoh	I will help
끝나고 (끝나다)	kkeun-nah-goh	after finishing
같이	gah-chee	together

Staying Over

If you happen to sleep over at someone's house in Korea, these phrases may help:

어느 방에서 자요? (uh-neu bahng-eh-suh jah-yoh) (*Which room should I sleep in?*)

[수건] 어디 있어요? (soo-guhn uh-dee ee-ssuh-yoh) (*Where are the [towels]?*)

샤워해도 돼요? (shyah-wuh-hae-doh dwae-yoh) (*May I take a shower?*)

이 [샴푸] 써도 돼요? (ee [shahm-poo] ssuh-doh dwae-yoh) (*May I use this [shampoo]?*)

REMEMBER

All day–activities are wrapped up, and it's time to go to bed. The phrases below may come in handy:

안녕히 주무세요. (ahn-nyuhng-hee joo-moo-seh-yoh) (*Sleep well/Good night.*): Use it for people with seniority.

잘 자(요). (jahl jah-yoh) (*Sleep well/Good night.*): Use it for anyone besides person with seniority.

내일 뭐 할까요? (nae-eel mwuh hahl-kkah-yoh) (*What should we do tomorrow?*)

FUN & GAMES

Match corresponding activities or rooms in a house with the associated household items. See Appendix C for the answers.

1. 청소 (chuhng-soh): _____

2. 부엌 (boo-uhk): _____

3. 화장실 (hwah-jahng-sheel): _____

4. 빨래 (ppahl-rae): _____

5. 침실 (cheem-sheel): _____

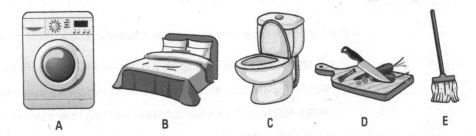

A   B   C   D   E

© John Wiley & Sons, Inc.

2

Korean in Action

Get to know the people you communicate with.

Deal with money.

Go out to eat and drink.

Make purchases.

Get around town.

Get connected using technology.

Speak Korean at work and school.

Chapter 7

Getting to Know You

S triking up a conversation in a 외국어 (wae-goo-guh) (*foreign language*) may seem a little nerve-wracking, especially if you're in a 외국 (wae-gook) (*foreign country*). But it can be an awesome chance to make new friends, gain new perspectives, or feel more at ease in unfamiliar surroundings.

Indeed, chatting with someone and engaging in small talk is a vital skill to have. After all, a perk of learning 외국어 is connecting with people from diverse backgrounds. Common topics of conversation usually revolve around your country of origin, travel purposes, language learning experience, and place of residence. If you're comfortable, you can share more personal info like 직업 (jee-guhp) (*occupation*), 가족 (gah-johk) (*family*), and more!

This chapter shows you how to keep your 대화 (dae-hwah) (*conversation*) going once you've broken the ice. (Flip to Chapter 4 for basic expressions.) Remember that we use the *informal polite speech* (아요/어요) in this book. Get ready to boost your confidence and have some fun conversing in Korean!

Making Small Talk: Posing Simple Introductory Questions

Imagine you're on a 비행기 (bee-haeng-gee) (*plane*) on your way to Korea. The passenger sitting next to you is a 한국 사람 (hahn-gook ssah-rahm) (*Korean*). Don't fall asleep just yet — it may be an opportunity to practice your new language skills! 걱정 마세요! (guhk-jjuhng mah-seh-yoh) (*Don't worry!*) We'll touch upon the 질문 (jeel-moon) (*questions*) that Korean speakers are most likely to ask you, as well as how to answer them. (To check out how to form questions, also read Chapter 3 on Korean grammar.)

Stating where you're from

One topic that's bound to come up during your first conversations in Korean is where you're from — your 나라 (nah-lah) (*country*) or 도시 (doh-shee) (*city*) of origin. There are a couple of ways to ask this based on who you're talking to — most commonly, one of the following two questions:

어디에서 왔어요? (uh-dee-eh-suh wah-ssuh-yoh?) (*Where are you from?*)

어디에서 오셨어요? (uh-dee-eh-suh oh-shyuh-ssuh-yoh?) (honorific)

TIP

어디에서 means "from where." The particle, 에서 (eh-suh) means "from" in this context. The verb 오셨어요 (oh-shyuh-ssuh-yoh) (*came*) contains the honorific suffix -시, so it's used when you speak to elderly people or when you want to show extra politeness.

Answering is super simple! Just switch out 어디 (uh-dee) (*where*) with the name of the place you're from, and then say 왔어요 (wah-ssuh-yoh) (*came*) with a falling intonation. Are you from 미국 (mee-gook) (*United States*)? 캐나다 (kae-nah-dah) (*Canada*)? Or more specifically, from 뉴욕 (nyoo-yohk) (*New York*)? 밴쿠버 (behn-koo-buh) (*Vancouver*)? See the examples here:

미국에서 왔어요. (mee-goo-geh-suh wah-ssuh-yoh.) (*I'm from the U.S.*)

(캐나다) 밴쿠버에서 왔어요. ((kae-nah-dah) behn-koo-buh-eh-suh wah-ssuh-yoh.) (*I'm from Vancouver (Canada).*)

(저는) 호주 캔버라에서 왔어요. ((juh-neun) hoh-joo kaen-buh-rah-eh-suh wah-ssuh-yoh.) (*I'm from Canberra, Australia.*)

REMEMBER

In Korean, it's common to drop pronouns like 저 (juh) (*I*) from sentences when the context already implies the subject. These pronoun-less sentences can also be used to ask Yes/No questions. Simply raise your intonation at the end of the sentence. For instance, 미국에서 왔어요? (mee-goo-geh-suh wah-ssuh-yoh?) with a rising intonation means "*Are you from the U.S.?*"

CULTURAL WISDOM

Remember that Korean is a macro-to-micro language. When talking about where you're from, the 나라 (nah-lah) (*country*) comes first, and then 도시 (doh-shee) (*city*), which may be opposite order you usually use in your own native language.

TIP

People may ask directly if you're a citizen of a particular country. It's easy to express one's nationality or citizenship: 나라 (nah-rah) (*nation*) + 사람 (sah-rahm) (*person*). And then add 이에요 (ee-eh-yoh) (*am/is/are*), or, for more formal tone, 입니다 (eem-nee-dah) to complete your sentence. Examples:

> (저는) 한국 사람이에요. ((juh-neun) hahn-gook ssah-rah-mee-eh-yoh) (*I am Korean.*)
>
> 캐나다 사람이에요. (kae-nah-dah sah-rah-mee-eh-yoh) (*I am Canadian.*)
>
> 미국 사람입니다. (mee-gook ssah-rah-meem-nee-dah) (*I am American.*)
>
> 인도 사람입니다. (een-doh sah-rah-meem-nee-dah) (*I am Indian.*)

REMEMBER

Remember that, by using a rising intonation, you can turn these statements into a Yes/No question. Read on for example conversation.

> 호주 사람이에요? (hoh-joo sah-rah-mee-eh-yoh?) (*Are you Australian?*)
>
> 네, 호주 사람이에요. (neh, hoh-joo sah-rah-mee-eh-yoh.) (*Yes, I'm Australian.*)
>
> 아니요, 뉴질랜드 사람이에요. (ah-nee-yoh. nyoo-jeel-laen-deu sah-rah-mee-eh-yoh.) (*No, I'm a New Zealander.*)
>
> 영국에서 왔어요? (yuhng-goo-geh-suh wah-ssuh-yoh?) (*Are you from the UK?*)
>
> 네, 런던에서 왔어요. (neh, luhn-duh-neh-suh wah-ssuh-yoh.) (*Yes, I'm from London.*)

TIP

When traveling outside of your country, you may run into someone from the same 나라 (nah-rah) (*nation*). (What a small world!) In such cases, instead of resorting to your native language, you can use the particle 도 (doh) (*also*) after 저. For example, to say "I'm also from Canada," you can say "**저도** 캐나다 사람이에요" or "**저도** 캐나다에서 왔어요." Alternatively, you can simply say **저도**요 (juh-doh-yoh) (*Me, too!*). Short and sweet!

Asking about destinations

If you're traveling, another favorite topic of conversation is the destination and purpose of your trip. Whether it's for a visit to a 친구 (cheen-goo) (*friend*) or 친척 (cheen-chuhk) (*relatives*), 출장 (chool-jjahng) (*business travel*), or just to enjoy your 휴가 (hyoo-gah) (*vacation*), talking about travel is a great way to keep a conversation going. First, you can start out with a destination question:

어디(에) 가세요? (uh-dee(-eh) gah-seh-yoh?) (*Where are you going?*)

You can also ask directly whether they're going to a particular destination:

서울에 가세요? (suh-woo-reh gah-seh-yoh?) (*Are you heading to Seoul?*)

LA에 가세요? (eh-leh-ee-eh gah-seh-yoh?) (*Are you going to L.A.?*)

Again, answering is simple! Substitute 어디 with your destination and add 에 가요: "[destination]에 가요" (eh gah-yoh) (*I'm going to [destination].*)

제주도에 가요 (jeh-joo-doh-eh gah-yoh) (*I'm going to Jeju Island.*)

부산에 가요. 집이 부산에 있어요. (boo-sah-neh gah-yoh. jee-bee boo-sah-neh ee-ssuh-yoh) (*I'm going to Busan. My home is in Busan.*)

Talking about the purpose of visit

As a follow-up, people may ask, "무슨 일로 가세요?" (moo-seun neel-loh gah-seh-yoh) (*Why are you going there?*), which literally means, *Because of what matter are you going?*

If you've already made it to your destination and the conversation is taking place in that area, replace 가세요 (gah-seh-yoh) (*go — honorific*) with 오셨어요 (oh-shuh-ssuh-yoh) (*came — honorific*). That is, 무슨 일로 오셨어요? (*What brought you hear? [honorific, past tense]*)

If you're going on business trip, you can simply say 출장 가요 (chool-jjahng gah-yoh) (*I am going on a business trip*), or 출장 중이에요 (chool-jjahng joong-ee-eh-yoh) (*I am currently on a business trip*), or 출장 왔어요 (chool-jjahng wah-ssuh-yoh) (*I came on a business trip*).

For other reasons, a handy pattern to express your purpose of going or coming to somewhere is [verb stem]+(으)러 가다/오다 (eu-ruh gah-dah/oh-dah) (*to go/come (somewhere) in order to . . .*). If the verb stem ends in a consonant, use 으러 가다. If the stem ends in a vowel or ㄹ, use 러 가다. Table 7-1 shows the conjugated form with some verbs.

TABLE 7-1 ## Verb Conjugation: -(으)러 가다/오다

Korean Verbs	English	Informal Polite Form: -(으)러 가다/오다
가르치다 (gah-reu-chee-dah)	to teach	가르치러 가요/와요 (gah-reu-chee-ruh gah-yoh/wah-yoh)
구경하다 (goo-gyung-hah-dah)	to sightsee	구경하러 가요/와요 (goo-gyung-hah-ruh gah-yoh/wah-yoh)
만나다 (mahn-nah-dah)	to meet	만나러 가요/와요 (mahn-nah-ruh gah-yoh/wah-yoh)
만들다 (mahn-deul-dah)	to make	만들러 가요/와요 (mahn-deul-luh gah-yoh/wah-yoh)
먹다 (muhk-ttah)	to eat	먹으러 가요/와요 (muh-geu-ruh gah-yoh/wah-yoh)
배우다 (bae-oo-dah)	to learn	배우러 가요/와요 (bae-oo-ruh gah-yoh/wah-yoh)
일하다 (eel-hah-dah)	to work	일하러 가요/와요 (eel-hah-ruh gah-yoh/wah-yoh)

Think about the reasons for your potential trip to Korea while reading these next examples!

한국에 무슨 일로 가세요? (hahn-goo-geh moo-seun neel-loh gah-seh-yoh?) (*Why are you going to Korea?*)

여행하러 가요. (yuh-haeng-hah-ruh gah-yoh.) (*I am going to travel.*)

공부하러 가요. (gohng-boo-hah-ruh gah-yoh.) (*. . . to study.*)

쇼핑하러 가요. (shyoh-peeng-hah-ruh-gah-yoh.) (*. . . to shop.*)

쉬러 가요. (shwee-ruh gah-yoh.) (*. . . to take a rest/relax.*)

한국어 배우러 가요. (hahn-goo-guh bae-oo-ruh gah-yoh.) (*. . . to learn Korean.*)

영어 가르치러 가요. (yuhng-uh gah-reu-chee-ruh gah-yoh.) (*. . . to teach English.*)

친구 만나러 가요. (cheen-goo mahn-nah-ruh gah-yoh.) (*. . . to meet my friends.*)

K-pop 콘서트 보러 가요. (K-pop kohn-ssuh-teu boh-ruh gah-yoh.) (*. . . to see a K-pop concert.*)

If you're already in the area where your destination is, replace 가요 with -왔어요 (wah-ssuh-yoh) (*came*) to express "*I came (here) to...*".

> (여기에) 일하러 왔어요. ((yuh-gee-eh) eel-hah-ruh wah-ssuh-yoh.) (*I came (here) to work.*)
>
> (부산에) 바다 보러 왔어요. ((boo-sah-neh) bah-dah boh-ruh wah-ssuh-yoh.) (*I came (to Busan) to see the ocean.*)

Asking about trip duration

As a possible follow-up, you may talk about how long you'll stay at your destination. *How long are you there for?* in Korean is "[place]에 얼마나 있어요?" ([place]-eh uhl-mah-nah ee-ssuh-yoh?). For extra politeness, replace 있어요 with 계세요 (gyeh-seh-yoh), the honorific form, in your question.

To answer to this question, use the following pattern: [duration] + (이)요 ((ee-) yoh). To express duration, use Sino-Korean numbers with units/counters like 일 (eel) (*days*), 주 (joo) (*weeks*), 개월 (gae-wuhl) (*months*), or 년 (nyuhn) (*year*). To make a short and polite sentence, add (이)요, the polite ending marker: 이요 after a consonant-ending noun and 요 after a vowel-ending noun.

> 서울에 얼마나 있어요 / 계세요? (suh-oo-reh uhl-mah-nah ee-ssuh-yoh / gyeh-seh-yoh?) (*How long are you staying in Seoul?*)
>
> 5일이요. (oh-ee-ree-yoh) (*Five days.*)
>
> 3주요. (sahm-joo-yoh) (*Three weeks.*)
>
> 2개월이요. (ee-gae-wuh-ree-yoh) (*Two months.*)
>
> 1년이요. (eel-nyuh-nee-yoh) (*One year.*)

Chatting about where you live

You might continue your conversation by talking about where you live. "To live in" in Korean is "[place](에 or 에서) 살아요 (sah-rah-yoh)." 살아요 (살다) (*live*) is one of the rare verbs that can take both 에 and 에서 particles. But people may drop those particles in casual conversations. The honorific form is 사세요 (sah-seh-yoh). See the example conversation down below:

> 어디(에) 사세요? (uh-dee(-eh) sah-seh-yoh?) (*Where do you live?*)
>
> 부산(에) 살아요. (boo-sahn-(eh) sah-rah-yoh.) (*I live in Busan.*)

WHERE TO VISIT IN KOREA

If you're visiting Korea for a short time — a few days, for example — the first pick to visit will be 서울 (suh-ool) (*Seoul*), the most crowded and most dynamic city in Korea. It has more than 600 years of history as the former capital city of 조선 왕조 (joh-suhn wahng-joh) (*Joseon Dynasty*) and the current capital of 대한민국 (dae-hahn-meen-gook) (*Republic of Korea*). You'll have endless things to do and see, be it traditional Korean culture or the vibrant modern culture.

If you have a little more time to visit other cities, hop on a KTX (Korea Train eXpress), one of the fastest bullet trains in the world, to visit the largest port city in Korea, 부산 (boo-sahn) (*Busan*). (This "train to Busan" is nothing like the movie, we promise.) Located in the southeast of Korea, 부산 has beautiful 바닷가 (bah-dah-kkah) (*beaches*), huge 해산물 시장 (hae-sahn-mool shee-jahng) (*seafood markets*) and lots of 해산물 식당 (sheek-ttahng) (*seafood restaurants*)!

If you have time to check out some islands, 제주도 (jeh-joo-doh) (*Jeju Island*) is another fantastic recommendation. Just like Hawaii, 제주도 is a popular 신혼 여행 (sheen-hohn nyuh-haeng) (*honeymoon*) city, with lots of 아름다운 경치 (ah-reum-dah-oon gyuhng-chee) (*beautiful scenery*). If you're looking for some coastal relaxation and unique cuisine, especially the seafood caught by the 제주 해녀 (jeh-joo hae-nyuh), Jeju's famous deep-sea diver women, 제주도 won't disappoint!

Well, we could go on and on here fantasizing about our hypothetical dream vacations on the Korean coast, but it's probably time to get back to studying. It'll be much easier making your way around these places if you know the language! (For info on planning a trip, flip to Chapter 14.)

Praising Your Language Skills

You'll soon realize how impressed people are by your Korean skills after even just a few sentences. You can talk about your skills and share your learning experience.

To express "to speak [language]," use this pattern: [Language] + 하다 (hah-dah). *To speak Korean* is 한국말/한국어 하다 (hahn-goong-mahl/hahn-goo-guh hah-dah). To ask if someone speaks Korean, use a rising intonation and say 한국말 해요? (hahn-goong-mahl hae-yoh?), or in an honorific form, 한국말 하세요? (hahn-goong-mahl hah-seh-yoh?).

If you add -어 (uh) or 말 (mahl) (*language*) at the end of the country name, it becomes the language of the country. For example, 프랑스 (peu-rahng-sseu) is *France*, and 프랑스말 (peu-rahng-sseu-mahl) or 프랑스어 (peu-rahng-sseu-uh) means *French (language)*. (Simple, right?) 말, native Korean, has a more casual tone than 어, Sino-Korean. What does 스페인어 mean then? Yes, it's the *Spanish language*. One exception to this rule is *English*: It's 영어 (yuhng-uh), NOT 미국어 (mee-goo-guh) ("*USA language*"), 영국어 (yuhng-goo-guh) ("*UK language*"), or 호주어 (hoh-joo-uh) ("*Australian language*").

To indicate your language skill, use adverbs like 잘 (jahl) (*well*), 조금 (joh-geum) (*a little*), or 못 (moht) (*can't*) before 하다. See the examples here:

한국말 하세요? (hahn-goong-mahl hah-seh-yoh?)

네, 잘해요. (neh, jahl-hae-yoh.) (*Yes, I do well / I'm good at it.*)

조금 해요. (joh-geum hae-yoh.) (*I do a little bit.*)

아니요, 못해요. (ah-nee-yoh, moh-tae-yoh.) (*No, I can't.*)

When you speak just a few simple phrases in Korean to 한국 사람 (hahn-gook ssah-rahm) (*Korean people*), you'll almost always hear, 한국말 잘하네요! (hahn-goong-mahl jahl-hah-neh-yoh!) (*You speak Korean very well!*) or, in an honorific form, 한국말 잘하시네요! (hahn-goong-mahl jahl-hah-shee-neh-yoh!). "네요" (neh-yoh) is known as the "mood ending" because it adds surprise or admiration to the speaker's tone in a casual conversation. (Yes, a verb ending can carry the emotion of the speaker!) People will genuinely appreciate your effort to learn a new language, and you'll be amazed with the amount of praise that pours in!

As a response to a compliment on your Korean skills, you can say 고맙습니다 (goh-mahp-sseum-nee-dah) (*Thank you!*). But in Korea, people tend to use more modest phrases when they receive compliments. In some cultures, 겸손 (gyuhm-sohn) (*humility, modesty*) is more highly valued, and Korea is one of them. Don't worry about sounding like your self-confidence is on the floor; these phrases will help show your modesty (and maybe even earn you an extra compliment). Take a look at more example responses:

영어 잘하시네요! (yuhng-uh jahl-hah-shee-neh-yo!) (*Your English is so good!*)

아니에요. 아직 잘 못해요. (ah-nee-eh-yoh, ah-jeek jahl moh-tae-yoh.) (*Not at all. I'm not so good yet.*)

고맙습니다. 아직 배울 게 많아요. (goh-mahp-sseum-nee-dah. ah-jeek bae-ool kkeh mah-nah-yoh.) (*Thank you, but I still have a lot to learn.*)

Talking about learning resources

As a follow-up, people may be curious about where and how you learned Korean. If someone asks you, 한국어, 어디에서 배웠어요? (hahn-goo-guh, uh-dee-eh-suh bae-wuh-ssuh-yoh?) (*Where did you learn Korean?*) and 어떻게 배웠어요? (uh-ttuh-keh bae-wuh-ssuh-yoh?) (*How did you learn it?*), what would be your response? Anything from the list below?

> 학교에서 배웠어요. (hahk-kkyoh-eh-suh bae-wuh-ssuh-yoh.) (*I learned it at school.*)
>
> 한국 드라마 많이 봤어요. (hahn-gook deu-rah-mah mah-nee bwah-ssuh-yoh.) (*I watched a lot of Korean dramas.*)
>
> 한국 친구한테서 배웠어요. (hahn-gook cheen-goo-hahn-teh-suh bae-wuh-ssuh-yoh) (*I learned it from my Korean friends.*)
>
> 혼자 인터넷으로 공부했어요. (hohn-jah een-tuh-neh-seu-roh gohng-boo-hae-ssuh-yoh.) (*I self-studied using the Internet.*)
>
> K-pop 많이 들었어요. (K-pop mah-nee deu-ruh-ssuh-yoh.) (*I listened to K-pop a lot.*)
>
> *Korean For Dummies* 책으로 공부했어요. (Korean For Dummies chae-geu-roh gohng-boo-hae-ssuh-yoh.) (*I studied using the book, Korean For Dummies.*)

GRAMMATICALLY SPEAKING

When you learn, hear, or receive something *from someone*, you use the particle 한테서 (hahn-teh-suh) (*from (someone)*). For example, to express "I learned it *from* my mother" is 어머니**한테서** 배웠어요 (uh-muh-nee-hahn-teh-suh bae-wuh-ssuh-yoh). "I heard it from my friend" would be "친구**한테서** 들었어요." (cheen-goo-hahn-teh-suh deu-ruh-ssuh-yoh.)

Note: 한테서 is only used for people. To express *from* an inanimate source, use 에서 (eh-suh), as in 인터넷**에서** 배웠어요 (een-tuh-neh-seh-suh bae-wuh-ssuh-yoh) (*I learned it from the Internet*).

Now that you are learning Korean using *Korean For Dummies*, you can also utilize the particle **으로** (eu-roh) (*with, by means of, using*) as in 책으로 (chae-geu-roh) (*using/with the book*). So, now you can confidently say "저는 *Korean For Dummies* **책으로** 공부해요." (juh-neun Korean For Dummies chae-geu-roh gohng-boo-hae-yoh.) (*I study using the book, Korean For Dummies*). Awesome!

Talkin' the Talk

PLAY

Minho is a hair stylist in Seoul, and Lia came to his hair salon for the first time. While doing her hair, Minho struck up a conversation with her.

Minho: 어디에서 오셨어요?
uh-dee-eh-suh oh-shyuh-ssuh-yoh?
Where are you from?

Lia: 호주에서 왔어요.
hoh-joo-eh-suh wah-ssuh-yoh.
I came from Australia.

Minho: 호주 어디요?
hoh-joo uh-dee-yoh?
Where in Australia?

Lia: 시드니요.
shee-deu-nee-yoh.
Sydney.

Minho: 그래요? 한국말 잘하시네요!
geu-rae-yoh? hahn-goong-mahl jahl hah-shee-neh-yoh!
Is that right? Your Korean is really good!

Lia: 아니에요. 그냥 조금 해요.
ah-nee-eh-yoh. geu-nyahng joh-geum hae-yoh.
No. I do just a little bit.

Minho: 어디에서 배웠어요?
uh-dee-eh-suh bae-wuh-ssuh-yoh?
Where did you learn it?

Lia: 호주에서 한국어 수업 들었어요. 그리고 한국 드라마 많이 봐요.
hoh-joo-eh-suh hahn-goo-guh soo-uhp deu-ruh-ssuh-yoh.
geu-ree-goh hahn-gook deu-rah-mah mah-nee bwah-yoh.
I took Korean classes in Australia. And I watch a lot of Korean dramas.

Minho: 한국 드라마 좋아해요?
hahn-gook deu-rah-mah joh-ah-hae-yoh?
Do you like Korean dramas?

Lia: 네, 정말 좋아해요.
neh, juhng-mahl joh-ah-hae-yoh.
Yes, I really like them.

WORDS TO KNOW

호주	hoh-joo	Australia
배웠어요 (배우다)	bae-wuh-ssuh-yoh	learned
수업	soo-uhp	class
들었어요 (듣다)	deu-ruh-ssuh-yoh	took (a course); listened
그리고	geu-ree-goh	and
봐요 (보다)	bwah-yoh	watch, see
좋아해요 (좋아하다)	joh-ah-hae-yoh	like

Making New Friends

Sometimes people may ask you questions that are considered to be quite forward in the Western culture. In the following sections, you find topics that are rather a bit more personal.

Talking about jobs

If you want to ask what someone does for a living, start off with this question:

무슨 일 하세요? (moo-seun-neel hah-seh-yoh?) (*What do you do?*)

Answering this is simple: [job term] + 이에요/예요 (is/am/are). For a more formal tone, use 입니다, which is the formal version of 이에요/예요.

[occupation]이에요 (ee-eh-yoh) with a consonant-ending noun:

[학생]**이에요** ([hahk-ssaeng]-ee-eh-yoh) (*I am [a student]*.)

[occupation]예요 (yeh-yoh) with a vowel-ending noun:

[요리사]**예요** ([yoh-ree-sah]-yeh-yoh) (*I am [a cook]*.)

[occupation]입니다 (eem-nee-dah) with any noun:

군인**입니다** (goo-nee-neem-nee-dah) (*I am a soldier.*)

간호사**입니다** (gahn-hoh-sah-eem-nee-dah) (*I am a nurse.*)

Table 7-2 shows some occupations you or your conversation partner may hold:

TABLE 7-2

Occupations

Occupation	Pronunciation	Meaning
간호사	gahn-hoh-sah	nurse
공무원	gohng-moo-wuhn	government official
경찰	kyuhng-chahl	police officer
군인	goo-neen	soldier
대학생	dae-hahk-ssaeng	college student
대학원생	dae-hah-gwuhn-saeng	graduate student
변호사	byuhn-hoh-sah	lawyer
선생님	suhn-saeng-neem	teacher
소방관	soh-bahng-gwahn	firefighter
승무원	seung-moo-wuhn	flight attendant
연예인	yuh-nyeh-een	entertainer
요리사	yoh-ree-sah	chef, cook
의사	eui-sah	doctor
엔지니어	ehn-jee-nee-uh	engineer
작가	jahk-kkah	writer
취업준비생	chwee-uhp-joon-bee-saeng	job seeker
프로그래머	peu-roh-geu-rae-muh	programmer
회사원	hwae-sah-wuhn	office worker

TIP

If you're in between jobs and seeking a job at the moment, you can say 취업 준비하고 있어요 (chwee-uhp joon-bee-hah-goh ee-ssuh-yoh) or 지금 직장 구하고 있어요 (jee-geum jeek-jjahng goo-hah-goh ee-ssuh-yoh) (*I'm looking for a job now*). 취업 준비하다, in a literal sense, means *to prepare for employment*, and 직장 구하다 means *to seek a job*.

TIP

If you want to further ask where someone works, try this question:

어디에서 일하세요? (uh-dee-eh-suh eel-hah-seh-yoh?) (*Where do you work?*)

The answer to this question looks like this:

[place]에서 일해요. (eh-suh eel-hae-yoh.) (*I work at/from/for [place]*).

GRAMMATICALLY
SPEAKING

에서 (eh-suh) means "at" or "for" in this context. And remember to use 일해요 (eel-hae-yoh), a non-honorific form, instead of 일하세요, when referring to yourself. Here are examples:

저는 삼성에서 일해요. (juh-neun sahm-suhng-eh-suh eel-hae-yoh.) (*I work at Samsung.*)

KB 은행에서 일해요. (KB eun-haeng-eh-suh eel-hae-yoh) (*I work at KB bank.*)

편의점에서 일해요. (pyuh-nee-juh-meh-suh eel-hae-yoh.) (*I work at a convenience store.*)

Talking about school stuff

Whether or not you like to study, the topic of school may come up as well. For 학생 (hahk-ssaeng) (*students*), if you want to be more specific and tell people about where and what you study, and what year you are, keep reading.

If someone wants to know where you're studying, they may ask:

어디에서 공부하세요? (uh-dee-eh-suh gohng-boo-hah-seh-yoh?) (*Where do you study?*)

Answering is a piece of cake! Replace 어디 with the name of school or just the city where you study, and switch the verb to 공부해요 (gohng-boo-hae-yoh). For instances, 보스턴 대학교에서 공부해요. (boh-seu-tuhn dae-hahk-kkyoh-eh-suh gohng-boo-hae-yoh.) (*I study at Boston College.*) or 보스턴에서 공부해요 (boh-seu-tuhn-eh-suh gohng-boo-hae-yoh.) (*I study in Boston.*).

As a follow-up, they may ask what you're studying:

뭐 공부하세요? (mwuh gohng-boo hah-seh-yoh?) (*What do you study?*)

뭐 전공하세요? (mwuh juhn-gohng-hah-seh-yoh?) (*What do you major?*)

Again, answering is easy! Replace 뭐 with your field of study and use the verb, 공부해요 (gohng-boo-hae-yoh) (*study*) or 전공해요 (juhn-gohng-hae-yoh) (*major*). For instance, if you're an 경제학 (gyuhng-jeh-hahk) (*Economics*) major, say 경제학 공부해요 or 경제학 전공해요. Table 7-3 contains some of the majors or areas of study.

TABLE 7-3

Areas of Study

Study Areas	Pronunciation	Meaning
간호학	gahn-hoh-hahk	nursing
경영학	gyuhng-yuhng-hahk	business
공학	gohng-hahk	engineering
교육학	gyoh-yoo-kahk	education
국제학	gook-jjeh-hahk	international studies
법학	buh-pahk	law
사회학	sah-hwae-hahk	sociology
생물학	saeng-mool-hahk	biology
심리학	sheem-nee-hahk	psychology
영문학	yuhng-moon-hahk	English literature
역사학	yuhk-ssah-hahk	history
정치학	juhng-chee-hahk	political science
커뮤니케이션	kuh-myoo-nee-keh-ee-shyuhn	communication and media studies
컴퓨터 과학	kuhm-pyoo-tuh-gwah-hahk	computer science
화학	hwah-hahk	chemistry

If someone asks you about your 학년 (hahng-nyuhn) (*school grade*), don't worry! Just remember to use Sino-Korean numbers, like 일 (eel), 이 (ee), 삼 (sahm), 사 (sah), 오 (oh), 육 (yook). . . . For instance, if you're in the 1st grade or freshman, say 일 학년이에요 (eel hahng-nyuh-nee-eh-yoh). 6th grade? 육 학년이에요 (yoo kahng-nyuh-nee-eh-yoh). (Replace the bracketed words with any Sino-Korean numbers.)

몇 학년이에요? (myuh tahng-nyuh-nee-eh-yoh?) (*What grade are you in?*)

고등학교 [삼] 학년이에요. (goh-deung-hahk-kkyo [sahm] hahng-nyuh-nee-eh-yoh) (*I'm in my [third] year of high school.*)

대학교 [사] 학년이에요. (dae-hahk-kkyoh [sah] hahng-nyuh-nee-eh-yoh) (*I'm in my [fourth] year of college = I'm a senior in college.*)

CULTURAL WISDOM

In Korea, there are six years of 초등학교 (choh-deung-hahk-kkyoh) (*elementary school; grade 1 through 6*), three years of 중학교 (joong-hahk-kkyoh) (*middle school; grade 7 through 9*), three years of 고등학교 (goh-deung-hahk-kkyoh) (*high school; grade 10 through 12*) and two to four years of 대학교 (dae-hahk-kkyoh) (*college*). So if a Korean student tells you they are in 중학교 이 학년 (ee hahng-nyuhn), that means they are in 8th grade. If they are in 고등학교 삼 학년 (sahm hahng-nyun), they are high school seniors, that is, 12th grade in the U.S., so on and so forth.

Chatting About Family

가족 (gah-johk) (*family*) matters, and so does the use of kinship terms in Korean culture. Koreans have several dozen 단어 (dah-nuh) (*words*) for family members, many of which may not exist in English. A few family words have rules that the English language doesn't. For instance, sometimes you say certain words depending on your gender and whether or not the person you're talking about is your own family member or someone else's. Read on for some common kinship terms for immediate family.

>> 부모님 (boo-moh-neem) (*parents*)

>> 할머니 (hahl-muh-nee) (*grandmother*)

>> 할아버지 (hah-rah-buh-jee) (*grandfather*)

>> 어머니/엄마 (uh-muh-nee/uhm-mah) (*mother/mom*)

>> 아버지/아빠 (ah-buh-jee/ah-ppah) (*father/dad*)

>> 아내 (ah-nae) (*wife*)

>> 남편 (nahm-pyuhn) (*husband*)

>> 자녀 (jah-nyuh) (*children*)

>> 딸 (ttahl) (*daughter*)

>> 아들 (ah-deul) (*son*)

>> 손주 (sohn-joo) (*grandchild*)

>> 형제 (hyuhng-jeh) (*brothers, sibling*)

>> 자매 (jah-mae) (*sisters*)

>> 남매 (nahm-mae) (*brothers and sisters*)

>> 언니 (uhn-nee) (*older sister of females*)

>> 누나 (noo-nah) (*older sister of males*)

>> 오빠 (oh-ppah) (*older borther of famales*)

>> 형 (hyuhng) (*older brother of males*)

>> 동생 (dohng-saeng) (*younger sibling*)

>> 이모 (ee-moh) (*aunt from mom's side/mom's sisters*)

>> 고모 (goh-moh) (*aunt from dad's side/dad's sisters*)

>> 삼촌 (sahm-chohn) (*uncle*)

CULTURAL WISDOM

In Korea, people often use kinship terms to address others, even if they aren't blood-related. It can add warmth and friendliness to daily interactions. For example, when meeting older friends, it's common to address them as 언니/누나 (*older sister*) or 오빠/형 (*older brother*). Similarly, when meeting elderly people, they call them 할아버지 (hah-rah-buh-jee) (*grandfather*) or 할머니 (hahl-muh-nee) (*grandmother*). Even mother's friends are referred to as 이모 (ee-moh) (*aunties/mom's sisters*). At times, in cozy local eateries, you might even hear people call middle-aged waitstaff women 이모님 (ee-moh-neem) (*aunt — honorific form*) as a friendly way to address them. You can see how language can create a sense of warmth and closeness. (Note that this practice is not common though in fancy, formal restaurants!)

Expressing possession and existence

To talk about what family members you have and where they are, you can use some easy-to-remember verbs: 있어요 (ee-ssuh-yoh) (*to have/to exist*) and 없어요 (uhp-ssuh-yoh) (*to not have/to not exist*).

REMEMBER

The default particle before 있어요 / 없어요 is the subject particle, 이/가: 이 (ee) after a consonant-ending noun, such as 삼촌 (sahm-chohn) (*uncles*), and 가 (gah) after a vowel-ending noun, such as 누나 (noo-nah) (*older sister*). The 이/가 particle is used in formal writing but often omitted in spoken Korean, so you won't hear them often in casual conversations.

[kinship term] (이/가) 있어요.

동생이 있어요. (dohng-saeng-ee ee-ssuh-yoh.) (*I have a younger sibling.*)

[kinship term] (이/가) 없어요.

누나가 없어요. (noo-nah-gah uhp-ssuh-yoh.) (*I don't have an older sister.*)

To specify how many you have, just add native Korean numbers between the kinship term and 있어요, as in 동생(이) 둘 있어요. (dohng-saeng(-ee) dool ee-ssuh-yoh.) (*I have two younger siblings.*)

If someone asks you 형제(가) 있어요? (hyuhng-jeh-(gah) ee-ssuh-yoh?) (*Do you have siblings?*), what would be your response? Here're examples:

형 하나 있어요. (hyuhng hah-nah ee-ssuh-yoh.) (*I have an older brother.*)

여동생 둘하고 오빠 하나 있어요. (yuh-dohng-saeng dool-hah-goh oh-ppah hah-nah ee-ssuh-yoh.) (*I have two younger sisters and an older brother.*)

형제(가) 없어요. 저 혼자예요. (hyuhng-jeh(-gah) uhp-ssuh-yoh. juh hohn-jah-yeh-yoh.) (*I don't have siblings. I'm an only child.*)

The verb 있어요 and 없어요 are indeed quite handy for expressing possession or non-possession. 있어요 primarily means *to exist*, which is also used to mean *to have* in Korean; 없어요 is the opposite. For example, if you want to say "Jenny doesn't have a boyfriend" in Korean, you can say 제니는 남자친구가 없어요 (jenny-neun nahm-jah-cheen-goo-gah uhp-ssuh-yoh), which literally translates to "As for Jenny, a boyfriend doesn't exist."

Here are some sample conversations. You can give a simple response like "네, 있어요" (neh, ee-ssuh-yoh) (*Yes, I have*) or "아니요, 없어요" (ah-nee-yoh, uhp-ssuh-yoh) (*No, I don't*), or you can get more detailed if you'd like.

Q: 반려동물 있어요? (bahl-lyuh-dohng-mool ee-ssuh-yoh) (*Do you have a pet?*)

A: 네, 강아지 두 마리 있어요. (neh, gahng-ah-jee doo mah-ree ee-ssuh-yoh) (*Yes, I have two puppies.*)

Q: 고양이도 있어요? (goh-yahng-ee-doh ee-ssuh-yoh) (*Do you have a cat too?*)

A: 아니요. 강아지만 있어요. (ah-nee-yoh. gahng-ah-jee-mahn ee-ssuh-yoh) (*No. I have puppies only.*)

The verb 있어요 / 없어요 can also express the location of someone or something. Note that the location is marked with the static location particle 에. (For more info on describing location, flip to Chapter 17.)

친구가 광주**에 있어요**. 그래서 친구 만나러 가요. (cheen-goo-gah gwahng-joo-eh ee-ssuh-yoh. geu-rae-suh cheen-goo mahn-nah-ruh gah-yoh) (*My friend is in Gwangju, so I'm going (there) to meet her.*)

우리 회사가 인천**에 있어요**. 그래서 매일 인천으로 출퇴근해요. (oo-ree hwae-sah-gah een-chuh-neh ee-ssuh-yoh. geu-rae-suh mae-eel een-chuh-neu-neu-roh chool-twae-geun-hae-yoh) (*My company is in Incheon, so I commute to Incheon every day.*)

TIP

When referring to elderly people or higher-ups, use the honorific verbs: (에) 계세요/안 계세요 for location, and (이/가) 있으세요/없으세요 for posession. See Table 7-4 for conjugations, and more examples here:

Q: 할아버지는 어디 계세요? (hah-rah-buh-jee-neun uh-dee gyeh-seh-yoh?) (*Where is your grandfather?*)

A: 지금 하와이에 계세요. (jee-geum hah-wah-ee-eh gyeh-seh-yoh.) (*He is in Hawaii now.*)

Q: 가족이 다 하와이에 계세요? (gah-joh-gee dah hah-wah-ee-eh gyeh-seh-yoh?) (*Does your family all live in Hawaii?*)

A: 아니요. 부모님은 한국에 계세요. 한국에 일이 있으세요. (ah-nee-yoh. boo-moh-nee-meun hahn-goo-geh gyeh-seh-yoh. hahn-goo-geh ee-ree ee-sseu-seh-yoh) (*No. My parents are in Korea now. They have some business there.*)

REMEMBER

Keep in mind that the choice of particle can drastically change the meaning of a sentence. For instance, consider the following. Just one tiny particle can flip the whole meaning of a sentence on its head!

저는 집**에** 있어요. (juh-neun jee-beh ee-ssuh-yoh.) (*I am at home.*)

저는 집**이** 있어요. (juh-neun jee-bee ee-ssuh-yoh.) (*I have/own a house.*)

So depending on what you want to say, the honorific form also differs.

할머니는 호텔**에** 계세요. (hahl-muh-nee-neun hoh-teh-reh gyeh-seh-yoh.) (*My grandmother is in a hotel.*)

할머니는 호텔**이** 있으세요. (hahl-muh-nee-neun hoh-teh-ree ee-sseu-seh-yoh.) (*My grandmother owns a hotel.*)

TABLE 7-4   ## Verb of Possession and Existence

Word	Meaning	Informal Polite 요 ending non-honorific	honorific
있다	To have	있어요 (ee-ssuh-yoh)	있으세요 (ee-sseu-seh-yoh)
	To exist/be located		계세요 (gyeh-seh-yoh)
없다	To not have	없어요 (uhp-ssuh-yoh)	없으세요 (uhp-sseu-seh-yoh)
	To not exist		안 계세요 (ahn gyeh-seh-yoh)

Asking about Age

Another topic that may arise is 나이 (nah-ee) (*age*). 몇 살이에요? (myuht ssah-lee-eh-yoh?) (*How old are you?*) is a straightforward question. A more polite alternative is 나이가 어떻게 되세요? (nah-ee-gah uh-ttuh-keh dwae-seh-yoh). 어떻게 되세요? is the honorific question, meaning "what is...?". If you're talking to someone who appears to be senior, like grandparents, or discussing them, you can replace 나이 with 연세 (yuhn-seh) (*age. honorific*), and ask 연세가 어떻게 되세요?

CULTURAL WISDOM

First of all, don't take offense if you're asked this question — there's a few reasons people may ask your age, and those reasons shouldn't be malicious. They're probably trying to determine how to address you properly, and they're also likely just trying to get to know you better. (It's also entirely possible that no age-related question comes up!)

If you ever feel uncomfortable divulging your exact age, no obligation to do so! You can simply mention you're in your 이십 대 (ee-sheep ttae) (*20s*), 삼십 대 (sahm-sheep ttae) (*30s*), and so on. Optionally, you can also specify whether you're in the 초반 (choh-bahn) (*early*), 중반 (joong-bahn) (*mid*), or 후반 (hoo-bahn) (*late*) part of that age range. Here're sentence examples:

> 40대예요. (sah-sheep ttae-yeh-yoh) (*I'm in my 40s.*)
>
> 50대 중반이에요. (oh-sheep ttae joong-bah-nee-eh-yoh) (*I'm in my mid 50s.*)

TIP

If you're up for giving the exact number, use the [native Korean number] + 살이에요 (sah-ree-eh-yoh). If you're 20 years old, then say 스무 살이에요 (seu-moo sah-ree-eh-yoh). 33 years old? 서른세 살이에요 (suh-reun-seh sah-ree-eh-yoh). In a casual conversation, you can even drop the counter and just say the native Korean numbers, as in 서른셋이에요 (suh-reun-seh-shee-eh-yoh) (*I'm 33.*). (Also see Chapter 5 for the native Korean numbers.)

Five "Save Me!" Phrases

When you first converse in Korean, it's totally natural to not understand much of what you hear. But don't be too hard on yourself. Instead, keep these nifty phrases in your back pocket. You may go simple with just saying 네? (neh?) (*What?*) Or you may use all of them to get your point across.

> 네? 뭐라고 하셨어요? (neh? mwuh-rah-goh hah-shuh-ssuh-yoh?) (*What? What did you say?*)

죄송해요. 이해 못 했어요. (jwae-sohng-hae-yoh. ee-hae moh-tae-ssuh-yoh.) (*I'm sorry. I didn't understand.*)

좀 천천히 말해 주세요. (johm chuhn-chuhn-hee mahl-hae joo-seh-yoh.) (*Please speak slowly.*)

다시 한번 말해 주세요. (dah-shee hahn-buhn mahl-hae joo-seh-yoh.) (*Please say it one more time.*)

TIP

If you need to ask what something means in 영어 (yuhng-uh) (*English*) or how to say something in 한국어 (hahn-goo-guh) (*Korean*) or in 영어, use one of the following expressions:

[word] 뭐예요? ([word] mwuh-yeh-yoh?) (*What is* [word]?)

[word] 무슨 뜻이에요? (moo-seun tteu-shee-eh-yoh?) (*What does* [word] *mean?*)

[word] 영어로/한국어로 뭐예요? (yuhng-uh-roh/hahn-goo-guh-roh mwuh-yeh-yoh?) (*What is* [word] *in English/in Korean?*)

Replace [word] with whatever word you want to ask about. For instance, imagine that you're in a 식당 (sheek-ttahng) (*restaurant*) and a serving staff brings you some dishes or drinks that you didn't order and says "서비스예요." (ssuh-bee-sseu-yeh-yoh.) It sounded like *service* in English, but you may wonder if you heard it right. What could "service" mean in this context? Go ahead and ask! Try saying "서비스, 뭐예요?" or "서비스, 무슨 뜻이에요?"

CULTURAL WISDOM

서비스 (ssuh-bee-sseu) (*service*), by the way, means "free items." (Yes, it's a Korean–English hybrid word, a.k.a. Konglish.) If you order in Korean, sometimes the restaurant owners are so impressed that they might offer you "서비스" items in the form of delicious 반찬 (bahn-chahn) (*side dishes*) like 계란 찜 (geh-rahn jjeem) (*egg custards*) or whatever else they can whip up. Isn't it cool? People will genuinely appreciate your efforts to learn a new language!

Sharing Your Contact information

After your first conversation with some people who speak Korean, you may decide that you'd like to keep in touch with them. You can ask as follows:

전화번호가 뭐예요? (juhn-hwah-buhn-hoh-gah mwuh-yeh-yoh?) (*What is your phone number?*)

이메일 주소가 뭐예요? (ee-meh-eel joo-soh-gah mwuh-yeh-yoh?) (*What is your email address?*)

You can also use the honorific form, 어떻게 되세요? (uh-ttuh-keh dwae-seh-yoh?), instead of 뭐예요? We discuss 어떻게 되세요 in the preceding section when learning how to ask someone's age.

To respond, you just say each Sino-Korean number from your 전화번호 one by one. The numbers you need to know are from zero to nine. That is, 공 (gohng), 일 (eel), 이 (ee), 삼 (sahm), 사 (sah), 오 (oh), 육 (yook), 칠 (cheel), 팔 (pahl), 구 (goo). (Flip to Chapter 5 for numbers.)

CULTURAL WISDOM

If you're staying in Korea, another handy-dandy tool for keeping in touch with someone is 카카오톡 (kah-kah-oh-tohk) (*KakaoTalk*). It's a must-have mobile messenger 앱 (aep) (*app*) for personal or group chats.

카카오톡 있어요? 아이디가 뭐예요? (kakaotalk ee-ssuh-yoh? ah-ee-dee-gah mwuh-yeh-yoh?) (*Do you have KakaoTalk? What's your ID?*)

WHAT'S SNS AND KAKAOTALK?

소셜 미디어 해요? (ssoh-shyuhl mee-dee-uh hae-yoh) (*Do you do social media?*) In Korea, you'll often hear the words like 에스엔에스 (eh-sseu-ehn-eh-sseu) (*SNS*) and 카카오톡 (*KakaoTalk*).

- **SNS:** An acronym of *Social Networking Service*, it refers to social media in general as one of those fun *Konglish* words.

- **KakaoTalk** (카카오톡 or 카톡 shortened form): The No. 1 messaging app in Korea. Not only is it for personal or group messages, audio and video calls, it also has integrated features like shopping, reservations, mobile payment, mobile games, taxi calls, and remittance services. If you plan to live or work in Korea, this is one of the first apps to download.

FUN & GAMES

This is Lia's family. Match the family members with the correct terms that identify them from Lia's perspective. Turn to Appendix C for the answers.

galastudio/Adobe Stock Photos

a. 어머니 (uh-muh-nee)

b. 할머니 (hahl-muh-nee)

c. 여동생 (yuh-dohng-saeng)

d. 아버지 (ah-buh-jee)

e. 오빠 (oh-ppah)

f. 할아버지 (hah-rah-buh-jee)

Chapter 8

Money: Easy as *Won*, Two, Three

돈 (dohn) (*money*) — in its multitude of currencies, shapes, and forms — is at the root of countless purchases. Going a day without it? Challenging. Especially for travelers in a foreign country, it's hard to imagine. Mastering a foreign monetary system is crucial for smooth transactions and enjoyable experiences.

In this chapter, we take you on a financial journey, guiding you from exchanging currencies to making purchases with 현금 (hyuhn-geum) (*cash*) or 신용카드 (shee-nyohng-kah-deu) (*credit card*) while exploring Korea. Get ready to manage your finances with ease!

Knowing Korean Currency

The official currency of South Korea is the 원 (wuhn) (*won*), abbreviated as KRW (Korean Republic Won). Pronounced like the English "won" as in "We *won* the World Series," the currency symbol is ₩, like an uppercase "W" with two horizontal lines. Like many national currencies, the Korean 원 includes both 동전 (dohng-juhn) (*coins*) and 지폐 (jee-pyeh) (*bills*). Table 8-1 presents a breakdown of the denominations of Korean currency. (To avoid any legal issues, the depictions of the paper currency are slightly cropped.)

TABLE 8-1   ## Korean Currency

Currency	Value	Notes	Images
일원 (ee-rwuhn)	₩1	Features the Rose of Sharon (무궁화), South Korea's national flower. Rarely used as prices are typically rounded to the nearest 10 won.	
십원 (shee-bwuhn)	₩10	The pennies of Korea, featuring the Dabotap Pagoda from the UNESCO World Cultural Heritage site, Bulguksa Temple in Gyeongju; bronze color.	
오십원 (oh-shee-bwuhn)	₩50	Displays a stalk of rice, a crucial crop in Korean agriculture, symbolizes prosperity and growth; silver color; worth about nickel.	
백원 (bae-gwuhn)	₩100	Portrays Admiral Yi Sun-sin (이순신), a revered Korean naval commander during the Joseon Dynasty; similar in size and color to a U.S. quarter but valued like a dime.	
오백원 (oh-bae-gwuhn)	₩500	Features a flying red-crowned crane, known as hak (학) or durumi (두루미), a symbol of peace, purity, and longevity; comparable in size to a U.S. half dollar but more commonly used.	
천원 (chuh-nwuhn)	₩1,000	A blue bill depicting Yi Hwang (이황), a noted philosopher and scholar from the Joseon Dynasty.	
오천원 (oh-chuh-nwuhn)	₩5,000	An orange bill, depicting Yi I (이이), another respected philosopher and scholar from the Joseon Dynasty; roughly equivalent to a U.S. $5 bill.	

Currency	Value	Notes	Images
만원 (mah-nwuhn)	₩ 10,000	A green bill with King Sejong the Great, historically the largest denomination until the issuance of the 50,000 won bill in 2009.	
오만원 (oh-mah-nwuhn)	₩ 50,000	A yellow bill featuring Shin Saimdang (신사임당), a 16th-century artist. Uniquely, both she and her son (Yi I) are honored on Korea's currency.	

Going to the Bank

Banking in a foreign country may seem daunting, but you'll be pleased to know that 은행 (eun-haeng) (*bank*) in Korea go out of their way to make you feel valued. No need to make an appointment here — just walk in whenever you need service. Once there, grab a 번호표 (buhn-hoh-pyoh) (*numbered ticket*), find a seat, and wait for your turn. When your number is displayed or called at one of the counters, approach the 은행원 (eun-haeng-wuhn) (*teller*) to handle your business.

CULTURAL WISDOM

Some of the major banks in Korea are KB 국민은행 (KB goong-meen-eun-haeng) (*KB Kookmin Bank*), 하나은행 (hah-nah-eun-haeng) (*Hana Bank*), 신한은행 (sheen-hahn-eun-haeng) (*Shinhan Bank*), and 우리은행 (oo-ree-eun-haeng) (*Woori Bank*). These banks are well-known for their reliable and comprehensive banking services, and they also offer services in 영어 (yuhng-uh) (*English*).

Understanding polite requests

TIP

Bank tellers in Korea typically use highly honorific language, including honorific formal endings like 십니다 (sheem-nee-dah) for statements, 십니까? (sheem-nee-kkah) for questions, and 십시오 (sheep-ssee-oh) for requests. Don't worry about matching this level of formality; responding in the informal polite (아요/어요) form is perfect! Read on for more examples and insights.

Here're some phrases you may encounter during your visit to a bank:

안녕하십니까? 무슨 일로 오셨습니까? (ahn-nyuhng-hah-sheem-nee-kkah? moo-seun eel-loh oh-shyuh-sseum-nee-kkah) (*Hello, what brings you here?*)

이쪽에서 번호표 뽑으시고 잠시 기다려 주십시오. (ee-jjoh-geh-suh buhn-hoh-pyoh ppoh-beu-shee-goh jahm-shee gee-dah-ryuh joo-sheep-ssee-oh) (*Please take a number ticket here and wait a moment.*)

[27]번 고객님 [3]번 창구로 오십시오. ([ee-sheep-cheel]-buhn goh-gaeng-neem [sahm]-buhn chahng-goo-roh oh-sheep-ssee-oh) (*Customer number [27], please come to counter number [3].*)

어떻게 도와 드릴까요? (uh-ttuh-keh doh-wah deu-reel-kkah-yoh) (*How may I help you?*)

Table 8-2 provides a quick overview of honorific request conjugations.

TABLE 8-2

Honorific Request Conjugations

Verb	Informal	Formal
기다리다 (gee-dah-ree-dah) (to wait)	기다리세요	기다리십시오
	기다리시겠어요?	기다리시겠습니까?
	기다려 주세요	기다려 주십시오
	기다려 주시겠어요?	기다려 주시겠습니까?
환전하다 (hwahn-juhn-hah-dah) (to exchange money)	환전하세요	환전하십시오
	환전하시겠어요?	환전하시겠습니까?
	환전해 주세요	환전해 주십시오
	환전해 주시겠어요	환전해 주시겠습니까?
앉다 (ahn-ttah) (to sit)	앉으세요	앉으십시오
	앉으시겠어요 ?	앉으시겠습니까?
	앉아 주세요	앉아 주십시오
	앉아 주시겠어요?	앉아 주시겠습니까?

GRAMMATICALLY
SPEAKING

As shown in the conjugated forms in Table 8-2, the level of politeness in requests can vary. Direct polite requests often use the 세요 (seh-yoh) and 십시오 (sheep-ssee-oh) endings. For a softer (more polite) approach, you can frame your request as an inquiry using 시겠어요? (shee-geht-ssuh-yoh) or 시겠습니까? (shee-geht-sseum-nee-kkah), which politely ask if someone is willing to perform an action.

To further increase the level of politeness, incorporate the 아/어 주다 form, which means "to do something for someone else's benefit." This ending conjugates to 아/어 주세요 (joo-seh-yoh) or 아/어 주십시오 (joo-sheep-ssee-oh), both of which convey a respectful request.

For the highest level of formality, opt for 아/어 주시겠어요? (joo-shee-geh-ssuh-yoh) or 아/어 주시겠습니까? (joo-shee-geht-sseum-nee-kkah), translating to "Would you please do it [for me]?" (For detailed guidance on 아/어 conjugation, see Chapter 3 and Appendix B.)

Phew! Going over the politeness levels is like a workout, isn't it? But there's no need to rush or get it perfect from the start. With more exposure, it'll naturally feel easier. Just keep practicing at your own pace!

Using common terms and phrases

Now, let's check out some key Korean banking terms to enhance your banking experience in Korea! Many of them can turn into verbs by adding 하다 (hah-dah) (*to do*) to express the action.

- >> 개설(하다) (gae-suhl(-hah-dah)) (*(to) open*)
- >> 계좌 (gyeh-jwah) (*account*)
- >> 비밀번호 (bee-meel-buhn-hoh) (*password, pin number*)
- >> 서류 (suh-ryoo) (*document*)
- >> 송금(하다) (sohng-geum(-hah-dah)) (*(to) wire transfer/remit*)
- >> 서명(하다) (suh-myuhng(-hah-dah)) (*(to) sign*)
- >> 수수료 (soo-soo-ryoh) (*fee, charge*)
- >> 신분증 (sheen-boon-jjeung) (*ID*)
- >> 신용카드 (shee-nyohng-kah-deu) (*credit card*)
- >> 이체(하다) (ee-cheh(-hah-dah)) (*(to) transfer money*)
- >> 입금(하다) (eep-kkeum(-hah-dah)) (*(to) deposit money*)
- >> 작성(하다) (jahk-ssuhng(-hah-dah)) (*(to) fill out*)
- >> 잔액조회 (jah-naek-joh-hwae) (*balance inquiry*)
- >> 직불/체크카드 (jeek-ppool/cheh-keu-kah-deu) (*debit card*)
- >> 출금(하다) (chool-geum(-hah-dah)) (*(to) withdraw(al)*)
- >> 통장 (tohng-jahng) (*bank book*)

>> 현금 (hyuhn-geum) (*cash*)

>> 현금자동입출금기 (hyuhn-geum-jah-dohng-eep-chool-geum-gee) (*ATM*)

>> 환율 (hwah-nyool) (*exchange rate*)

>> 환전(하다) (hwahn-juhn(-hah-dah)) (*(to) exchange currency*)

>> 환전소 (hwahn-juhn-soh) (*currency exchange booth*)

Opening a bank account

If you plan to work or study in Korea, you may want to open a bank account in Korea. Here're the 서류 (suh-ryoo) (*documentation*) you'll need: 여권 (yuh-kkwuhn) (*passport*), 비자 (bee-jah) (*visa*), and 한국 전화번호 (hahn-gook juhn-hwah-buhn-hoh) (*Korean phone number*). Depending on your purpose in Korea, additional 증명서 (jeung-myuhng-suh) (*verification/certificate*) for employment or student status may be required.

Banks may also require an 외국인 등록증 (wae-goo-geen deung-nohk-jjeung) (*Alien Residence Card/ARC*) for stays longer than 3개월 (sahm-gae-wuhl) (three months). Your 외국인 등록증 serves as your official 신분증 (sheen-boon-jjeung) (*ID*) in Korea, allowing you to do online or mobile banking. Since it can take up to a month to be issued, plan accordingly. Some banks might still allow you to open an account without it, but with limited services.

Here're some example interactions you might have with bank 직원 (jee-kwuhn) (*staff/employee*).

> 계좌 개설하러 왔어요. (gyeh-jwah gae-suhl-hah-ruh wah-ssuh-yoh) (*I came to open a bank account.*)

> 서류 작성해 주시겠습니까? (suh-ryoo jahk-ssuhng-hae joo-shee-geht-sseum-nee-kkah) (*Would you please fill out the form?*)

> 신분증 좀 주시겠습니까? (sheen-boon-jjeung johm joo-shee-geht-sseum-nee-kkah) (*Would you please give me your ID?*)

Making deposits and withdrawals

Banking in Korea is generally affordable, with many banks offering 계좌 (gyeh-jwah) (*accounts*) that have no-fee and no minimum deposit requirements. But, be mindful of potential small 수수료 (soo-soo-ryoh) (*fees*) for 출금 (chool-geum) (*withdrawals*) from other bank's ATMs.

Once your account is open, you're ready to manage your money right away with your new bank card and PIN for instant transactions. Here're some useful phrases to know:

[오만-] 원 입금해 주세요. ([oh-mahn-]wuhn eep-kkeum-hae joo-seh-yoh) (*Please make a deposit of [50,000 won].*)

계좌 이체하고 싶어요. (gyeh-jwah ee-cheh-hah-goh shee-puh-yoh) (*I'd like to make a wire-transfer.*)

송금 수수료가 얼마예요? (sohng-geum soo-soo-ryoh-gah uhl-mah-yeh-yoh) (*How much is the wire transfer fee?*)

Exchanging money

Most 은행 (eun-haeng) (*banks*) in Korea offer competitive exchange rates, better than 환전소 (hwahn-juhn-soh) (*currency exchange booths*) or 호텔 (hoh-tehl) (*hotels*). Don't worry if you arrive in Korea without exchanging your money; you can do 환전 (hwahn-juhn) (*currency exchange*) at the airport banks. See possible phrases that may occur at the 은행 below.

환전하러 왔어요. (hwahn-juhn-hah-ruh wah-ssuh-yoh) (*I came to exchange some currency.*)

얼마나 환전하시겠어요? (uhl-mah-nah hwahn-juhn-hah-shee-geh-ssuh-yoh) (*How much would you like to exchange?*)

1000달러, 원화로 환전해 주세요. (chuhn-dahl-luh wuhn-hwah-roh hwahn-juhn-hae joo-seh-yoh) (*Please exchange $1,000 to wons.*)

오늘 미국 달러 환율, 얼마예요? (oh-neul mee-gook dahl-luh hwah-nyool, uhl-mah-yeh-yoh) (*What's today's exchange rate for the U.S. dollar?*)

여행자 수표, 원화로 바꿀 수 있어요? (yuh-haeng-jah soo-pyoh, wuhn-hwah-roh bah-kkool ssoo ee-ssuh-yoh) (*Can I exchange traveler's checks to Korean won?*)

Using an ATM or CD

If you're running low on 현금 (hyuhn-geum) (*cash*) in Korea, you can make a quick 출금(chool-geum)(*withdrawals*)usingyourcreditcardata현금자동입출금기(hyuhn-geum-jah-dohng-eep-chool-geum-gee) (*ATM*) or 현금인출기 (hyuhn-geum een-chool-gee) (*cash dispensers, often abbreviated as CD*).

TIP

The ATMs are commonly referred to by the English acronym, "ATM," so, if you need to locate one, just ask, "ATM, 어디 있어요?" (eh-ee-tee-ehm, uh-dee ee-ssuh-yoh) (*Where is an ATM?*)

These machines are conveniently located in various places, including the airport, subway stations, convenience stores, and banks. Whether you need to withdraw 현금 (hyuhn-geum) (*cash*), deposit funds, check your 잔액 (jah-naek) (*balance*), or transfer, you're never far from one. If you're using a card issued overseas, look for an ATM with the "Global ATM" sign to withdraw cash. Many ATMs offer menu options in 영어 (yuhng-uh) (*English*).

Talkin' the Talk

PLAY

Judy, an American tourist, goes to a bank teller to exchange some money. She approaches counter number 3.

Teller: 어서 오십시오, 고객님. 무엇을 도와 드릴까요?
uh-suh oh-sheep-ssee-oh, goh-gaeng-neem. moo-uh-seul doh-wah-deu-reel-kkah-yoh?
Welcome, ma'am. What can I help you with?

Judy: 달러 환전하고 싶은데요.
dahl-luh hwahn-juhn hah-goh shee-peun-deh-yoh
I'd like to exchange some dollars.

Teller: 미국 달러 말씀이십니까?
mee-gook dahl-luh mahl-sseu-mee-sheem-nee-kkah?
Do you mean US dollars?

Judy: 네. 오늘 환율이 얼마예요?
neh. oh-neul hwahn-nyoo-ree uhl-mah-yeh-yoh
Yes. How much is the exchange rate today?

Teller: 오늘 환율은 일 달러에 천삼백오십 원입니다.
oh-neul hwahn-nyoo-reun eel-ddahl-luh-eh chuhn-sahm-baek-oh-shee-bwuh-neem-nee-dah
Today's exchange rate is $1 to 1,350 won.

Judy: 그럼 오백 달러 바꿔 주세요.
geu-ruhm oh-baek-ddahl-luh bah-kkwuh joo-seh-yoh
Then, please exchange $500 for me.

Teller:	네, 도와 드리겠습니다. 달러하고 여권 주시겠습니까?
	neh, doh-wah-deu-ree-geht-sseum-nee-dah. dahl-luh-hah-goh yuh-kkyuhn joo-shee-geht-sseum-nee-kkah
	Yes, I'll help you. Would you please give me your dollars and passport?
Judy:	여기요.
	yuh-gee-yoh.
	Here it is.

• •

WORDS TO KNOW

고객	goh-gaek	customer, client
환전하고 싶은데요 (환전하고 싶다)	hwahn-juhn-hah-goh shee-peun-deh-yoh	I want to exchange currency
환율	hwah-nyool	exchange rate
바꿔 주세요 (바꿔 주다)	bah-kkwuh joo-seh-yoh	Please (ex)change (for me)
여권	yuh-kkwuhn	passport

Paying for Your Purchases

Whether you've had an hours–long shopping spree and found something you just have to buy, or enjoyed a nice meal at a restaurant, the time comes to pay. Here're some useful phrases to smoothly handle the transaction, whether you're paying by cash or card:

결제/계산 도와 드리겠습니다. (gyuhl-jjeh/gyeh-sahn doh-wah deu-ree-geht-sseum-nee-dah) (*I'll help you with payment.*)

뭘로 결제/계산하시겠어요? (mwuhl-loh gyuhl-jjeh-/gyeh-sahn-hah-shee-geh-ssuh-yoh) (*How would like to pay?*)

현금으로 낼게요. (hyuhn-geu-meu-roh nael-kkeh-yoh) (*I'll pay in cash.*)

카드로 할게요. (kah-deu-roh hahl-kkeh-yoh) (*I'll do it by card; I'll pay with a credit card.*)

Remember that, the particle 로 (roh) is used after a noun ending in a vowel or ㄹ, while 으로 (eu-roh) follows a noun ending in a consonant. These particles indicate that the noun is being used as a tool, means, method, or choice, as in the preceding examples.

Keep in mind the versatile use of the verb, 하다 (hah-dah) (*to do*), the most frequently used verb in Korean. It can be used for a wide range of actions. If you're unsure of the specific verb for something you need to "do," try using 하다. It will work most of the time. For instance:

카드로 **할게요**. (kah-deu-roh hahl-kkeh-yoh) (*I'll do/go with a credit.card.*): replacing 내다 (nae-dah) (*to pay*) or 결제하다/계산하다 (gyuhl-jjeh-hah-dah/gyeh-sahn-hah-dah) (*to make a payment*)

오늘 가게 **해요**? (oh-neul gah-geh hae-yoh) (*Does the store open today?*): replacing 열다 (yuhl-dah) (*to open*) or 영업하다 (yuhng-uh-pah-dah) (*to operate business*)

점심 같이 **할까요**? (juhm-sheem gah-chee hahl-kkah-yoh) (*Shall we have lunch together?*): replacing 먹다 (muhk-ttah) (*to eat*)

하다 is also combined with many nouns to create new verbs, even with English words, as in 쇼핑하다, (shyoh-peeng-hah-dah) (*to shop*), 사인하다 (ssah-een-hah-dah) (*to sign*), 업데이트하다 (uhp-deh-ee-teu-hah-dah) (*to update*), 프린트하다 (peu-reen-teu-hah-dah) (*to print*), and more. Get creative with 하다! (For more on conjugation, see Chapter 3.)

Using cash

While card payments are prevalent in Korea, carrying some 현금 (hyuhn-geum) (*cash*) is advisable, especially for places like street vendors that may only accept cash. See some useful phrases:

죄송해요. 카드 안 돼요. 현금만 받아요. (jwae-sohng-hae-yoh. kah-deu ahn dwae-yoh. hyuhn-geum-mahn bah-dah-yoh) (*Sorry. We don't take card. We only accept cash.*)

현금 얼마 있어요? (hyuhn-geum uhl-mah ee-ssuh-yoh) (*How much cash do you have?*)

[만 원]밖에 없어요. (mah-nwuhn-bah-kkeh uhp-ssuh-yoh) (*I only have [10,000 won].*)

돈 좀 빌려 주세요. 내일 갚을게요. (dohn johm beel-lyuh joo-seh-yoh. nae-eel gah-peul-kkeh-yoh) (*Please lend me some money. I'll pay you back tomorrow.*)

거스름돈 여기 있어요. (guh-seu-reum-ttohn yuh-gee ee-ssuh-yoh) (*Here's your change.*)

GRAMMATICALLY
SPEAKING

The particle 밖에 (bah-kkeh) (*only*) is used exclusively in negative sentences, appearing with verbs like 없다 (uhp-ttah) (*to not have*) or 모르다 (moh-reu-dah) (*to not know*), or alongside negative adverbs such as 안 (ahn) (*not*) and 못 (moht) (*cannot*). So, to express "I only have 10,000 won," you say 만 원밖에 없어요 (mahn-nwuhn-bah-kkeh uhp-ssuh-yoh), not 만 원밖에 있어요.

Using credit cards and e-wallets

Cashless payment are very popular in Korea, widely accepting both traditional 카드 (kah-deu) (*credit/debit cards*) and 휴대폰/모바일 결제 (hyoo-dae-pohn/moh-bah-eel gyuhl-jjeh) (*cell phone/mobile payments*). While most international 카드 are accepted in most places, some smaller shops might not accept specific foreign cards. When unsure, simply ask, [디스커버] 카드 돼요? ([dee-seu-kuh-buh] kah-deu dwae-yoh) (*Is [Discover] card accepted?*). And you will hear either good news: 네, 돼요. (neh, dwae-yoh) (*Yes, it's accepted.*), or bad news: 아니요, 안 돼요. (ah-nee-yoh, ahn dwae-yoh) (*No, it's not accepted.*).

Mobile payments are also prevalent, with popular e-wallet apps like 네이버페이 (*Naver Pay*), 카카오페이 (*Kakao Pay*), and 삼성페이 (sahm-suhng-peh-ee) (*Samsung Pay*). To confirm availability, you can ask 휴대폰 결제 돼요? (hyoo-dae-pohn gyuhl-jjeh dwae-yoh) (*Are mobile payments accepted?*).

GRAMMATICALLY
SPEAKING

Like the versatile 하다 (hah-dah) verb, "되다" (dwae-dah) (*to work, make, become, be available, do*) is your go-to for functionality checks and availability inquires. Here're some practical examples:

[카드] 돼요? (kah-deu dwae-yoh) (*Does [the card] work?; Do you accept [card]?*): Use [item] 돼요 to discuss if something works or functions properly, or if something is acceptable.

[에어컨] 안 돼요. (eh-uh-kuhn ahn dwae-yoh) (*The [AC] doesn't work/is broken.*): Use [item] 안 돼요 when something isn't working.

[라면] 돼요? ([rah-muhn] dwae-yoh) (*Is [ramen] available/served?*): Use [menu/service] 돼요 to discuss the availability of a menu item or service.

잘 될 거예요/잘 됐어요 (jahl dwael kkuh-yeh-yoh/jahl dwae-ssuh-you) (*It will work well/It worked well.*): Idiomatic expressions of 잘 되다 (*to go well/work out well*), used in various contexts.

BUY NOW, PAY LATER: PAYING IN INSTALLMENTS

In Korea, installment payments, known as 할부 (hahl-boo), are very common for almost any purchase, from groceries to gadgets. If a store accepts your 신용카드 (shee-nyohng-kah-deu) (credit card), which is the case in most places, the clerk will often ask whether you want to settle the bill now, known as 일시불 (eel-ssee-bool), or spread the cost over time with 할부 (hahl-boo). Many plans even offer the sweet deal of no interest, called 무이자할부 (moo-ee-jah-hahl-boo). Here are some useful phrases that can be used at checkout:

- 일시불로 하시겠어요? (eel-ssee-bool-loh hah-shee-geh-ssuh-yoh) (*Will you pay the full amount at once?*)

- [몇 개월] 할부로 하시겠어요? ([myuht kkae-wuhl] hahl-boo-roh hah-shee-geh-ssuh-yoh) (*[How many months] for the installments?*)

- 3개월 할부 할게요. (sahm-gae-wuhl hahl-boo hahl-kkeh-yoh) (*I'll go for the 3-month plan.*)

Using personal checks

Korean personal checks, known as 수표 (soo-pyoh), operates quite differently from those in the U.S. In Korea, 수표 are bank-issued on request and must be pre-funded either with cash or directly from your bank account. And, these 수표 aren't used directly in stores for purchases; instead, they must be cashed at a bank or at an ATM. 수표 are generally used for transactions exceeding 100,000 won, with common denominations including 십만 원 (sheem-mah-nwuhn) (*100,000 won*), 오십만 원 (oh-sheem-mah-nwuhn) (*500,000 won*), and 백만 원 (baeng-mah-nwuhn) (*1,000,000 won*), typically in business settings. Navigating the check system in Korea is straightforward once you grasp these key differences, ensuring you handle larger payments with ease.

Talkin' the Talk

PLAY

Jeongsu and Robert are co-workers, and they have just finished a meal at a restaurant.

Jeongsu: 저기요. 여기 계산서 좀 주실래요?
juh-gee-yoh. yuh-gee gyeh-sahn-suh johm joo-sheel-lae-yoh?
Excuse me. Would you give us a check?

Waiter:	네, 손님. 잠시만요.
	neh, sohn-neem. jahm-shee-mahn-yoh.
	Yes, sir. One moment, please.

Robert:	오늘은 제가 낼게요.
	oh-neu-reun jeh-gah nael-kkeh-yoh.
	I'll pay for the meal today.

Jeongsu:	아니에요. 제가 낼게요.
	ah-nee-eh-yoh. jeh-gah nael-kkeh-yoh.
	No, it's fine. I'll pay.

Robert:	정수 씨가 지난 번 저녁 샀으니까 오늘은 제가 살게요.
	juhng-soo ssee-gah jee-nahn buhn juh-nyuhk sah-sseu-nee-kkah oh-neu-reun jeh-gah sahl-kkeh-yoh.
	You paid for the dinner last time, so I'll buy today.

Jeongsu:	그러실래요? 오늘 덕분에 잘 먹었습니다.
	geu-ruh-sheel-lae-yoh? oh-neul duhk-ppoo-neh jahl muh-guht-sseum-nee-dah.
	Would you? I had a good meal today, thanks to you.

The waiter brings back the bill. Robert and Jeongsu go to the cashier.
Robert hands the check to the cashier.

Cashier:	7번 테이블 불고기 하나, 비빔밥 하나, 소주 한 병, 모두 2만5천원입니다.
	cheel-buhn teh-ee-beul bool-goh-gee hah-nah, bee-beem-bahp hah-nah, soh-joo hahn byuhng, moh-doo ee-mahn oh-chuh-nwuh-neem-nee-dah
	At Table 7, the total is 25,000 won for one bulgogi, one bibimbap, and one bottle of soju.

Robert:	여기요.
	yuh-gee-yoh
	Here.

Cashier:	3만원 받았습니다. 거스름돈 5천원 여기 있습니다. 현금 영수증 필요하세요?
	sahm-mah-nwuhn bah-daht-sseum-nee-dah. guh-seu-reum-ttohn oh-chuh-nwuhn yuh-gee eet-sseum-nee-dah. hyuhn-geum yuhng-soo-jeung pee-ryoh-hah-seh-yoh
	I received 30,000 won. Here's your change, 5,000 won. Would you like a cash receipt?

Robert: 네. 감사합니다. 맛있게 잘 먹었습니다.

neh. gahm-sah-hahm-nee-dah. mah-sheet-kkeh jahl muh-guht-sseum-nee-dah

Yes, please. Thank you. We had a good meal.

Cashier: 감사합니다. 또 오세요.

gahm-sah-hahm-nee-dah. ttoh oh-seh-yoh

Thank you. Please come again.

WORDS TO KNOW

계산서	gyeh-sahn-suh	bill, check
낼게요 (내다)	nael-kkeh-yoh	put out, pay
거스름돈	guh-seu-reum-ttohn	change
현금	hyuhn-geum	cash
영수증	yuhng-soo-jeung	receipt

FUN & GAMES

Look at the illustrations of the Korean bills and coins here and calculate the sum of the money for each. See Appendix C for correct answers.

1. _____

2. _____

3. _____

4. _____

5. _____

Look at the illustrations of the Korean bills and coins here and calculate the sum of the money for each set. Appendix C for correct answers.

Chapter 9

Eating and Drinking

A re you a foodie who goes on a quest for popular local foods and restaurants whenever you visit a new country or city? Exploring cuisine is an excellent way to immerse yourself in a new 문화 (moon-hwah) (*culture*) and 언어 (uh-nuh) (*language*). This couldn't be truer than with 한국 요리 (hahn-gook yoh-ree) (*Korean cuisine*), where the dining experience intertwines the community, 전통 (juhn-tohng) (*tradition*), and rich 역사 (yuhk-ssah) (*history*) of an ancient culture that predates refrigeration and electricity.

This chapter elaborates on Korean dining and how it differs from dining in 서양 문화 (suh-yahng moon-hwah) (*Western culture*). You learn words and phrases related to Korean foods, learn about proper 식탁 예절 (sheek-tahk yeh-juhl) (*table manners*) and 음주 예절 (eum-joo yeh-juhl) (*drinking etiquette*), and discover how to communicate your hunger or thirst. Plus, you learn how to place orders at restaurants or through delivery apps.

Whether you like 외식 (weh-sheek) (*dining out*), 집밥 (jeep-ppahp) (*homemade meals*), or 배달 음식 (bae-dahl eum-sheek) (*delivered food*), whether or not you have a high tolerance for 매운 음식 (mae-oon eum-sheek) (*spicy food*), and whether or not you're 채식주의자 (chae-sheek-jjoo-ee-jah) (*vegetarian*), learning how to talk about food is an essential part of your learning journey. Let's dig in and uncover how to talk about, order, and savor some great Korean dishes!

Dig In! Let's Eat!

The Korean word for a meal is 밥 (bahp). In general, 밥 means *meal*. However, it can also specifically refer to a bowl of *steamed rice*, a staple of Korean food. The variety of 반찬 (bahn-chahn) (*side dishes*) and 주요리 (joo-yoh-ree) (*main dishes*) — often called 주메뉴 (joo-meh-nyu) (*main menus*) — makes every Korean meal a different experience. Everyone can find something to eat at a Korean table. From sweet, to savory, to spicy, the flavor profiles are top-notch. The wide variety of flavors and ingredients used in 한국 음식 makes it great for picky eaters or people with dietary restrictions.

CULTURAL WISDOM

Korea is 농업 (nohng-uhp) (*agriculture*)-based, with rice as a staple grain. Because of this, there are specific terms for each stage of rice: 모 (moh) (*sprouts*), 벼 (byuh) (*rice plant*), 쌀 (ssahl) (*rice crop or uncooked rice*), and 밥 (bahp) (*cooked rice*). 쌀 is integrated into Korean cuisine in many different ways, like 떡 (tteok) (*rice cakes*), 죽 (jook) (*rice porridge*), 한과 (hahn-gwah) (*traditional Korean cookies*), 엿 (yuht) (*traditional Korean taffy*), 쌀음료수 (ssah-leum-nyoh-soo) (*rice-based drinks*) like 식혜 (shee-keh) (*sweet rice drink*) and 막걸리 (mahk-kkuhl-lee) (*rice wine*), and many more!

Trying Korean foods

The first thing you may notice about a Korean 밥상 (bahp-ssahng) (*dining table*) is that it is very, very busy. A typical Korean meal includes 밥 (bahp) (*rice*), 반찬 (bahn-chahn) (*side dishes*), and often 국 (gook) (*soup*) and/or 찌개 (jjee-gae) (*stew*). You usually have a bowl of 밥 in front of you, possibly a small bowl of 국, a pair of 젓가락 (juh-kkah-rahk) (*chopsticks*), and a 숟가락 (soot-kkah-rahk) (*spoon*) sitting to your right.

Surrounding your bowls of 밥 and 국 are little plates called 반찬 (bahn-chahn) (*side dishes*). They include various 나물 (nah-mool) (*vegetable dishes*), 해산물 (hae-sahn-mool) (*seafood*), 두부 (doo-boo) (*tofu*), 계란 (geh-rahn) (*eggs*), and sometimes 고기 (goh-gee) (*meats*). 반찬 come in a splendid array of rich flavors and vibrant colors.

The most iconic Korean 반찬 of all is 김치 (geem-chee) (*Kimchi*). While many may know 김치 only as being the red, spicy cabbage dish, 김치 can actually be made from a wide assortment of salted and fermented vegetables. A meal without 김치 is unthinkable for most Koreans.

At the center of the table, you may see 찌개 (jjee-gae) (*stew*), 전골 (juhn-gohl) (*hot pot*), or other main dishes made of 고기 (goh-gee) (*meat*) or 생선 (saeng-suhn) (*fish*). There's a 국자 (gook-jjah) (*ladle*) or serving spoon for 찌개, 전골 and other

주메뉴, and an 앞접시 (ahp-jjuhp-ssee) (*small plate*) is often provided for you to bring a portion of the 주메뉴 closer to you to eat.

CULTURAL WISDOM

Sharing is an important part of the Korean 밥상 (bahp-ssahng) (*table*). There's even an old saying in Korea that goes, "콩 한쪽도 나눠 먹는다" (kohng hahn-jjohk-ttoh nah-nwuh-muhng-neun-dah) (*to share/split even a single bean*). The whole 가족 (gah-johk) (*family*) shares meals every day. It's the same if you go to a 한국 식당 (hahn-gook sheek-ttahng) (*Korean restaurant*) with friends. Most 반찬 are shared using your own 젓가락 (juht-kkah-rahk) (*chopsticks*), which enhances the sense of community or family in the dining experience. But while the meals are meant to be shared, you don't want to poke or dig around in the 반찬 with your chopsticks. Sharing is caring, but not when it comes to germs!

Understanding meal time

To have a meal is 밥 먹다 (bahm muhk-ttah). If someone asks you 지금 뭐 해요? (jee-geum mwuh-hae-yoh?) (*What are you doing now?*) when you're eating, you can say 지금 밥 먹어요 (jee-geum bahm muh-guh-yoh) (*I'm eating/having a meal now*). The meals are also referred to according to the time of day:

>> 아침 (ah-cheem) (*morning, breakfast*)

>> 점심 (juhm-sheem) (*lunch time, lunch*)

>> 저녁 (juh-nyuhk) (*evening, dinner*)

So, instead of 밥 먹어요, you can specify which meal of the day, as in 아침 먹어요 (ah-cheem muh-guh-yoh) (*I'm having breakfast*) and 저녁 먹어요 (juh-nyuhk muh-guh-yoh) (*I'm having dinner*).

Expressing eating with the verb Muhk-ttah

GRAMMATICALLY SPEAKING

Try making some questions in Korean using the verb 먹다 (muhk-ttah) (*to eat*). Remember that 네/아니요 (neh/ah-nee-yoh) (*yes/no*) questions in Korean are super easy — just raise the intonation! For example, 먹었어요 (muh-guh-ssuh-yoh) is the past tense form of 먹어요. If you raise the intonation to say 저녁 먹었어요? (juh-nyuhk muh-guh-ssuh-yoh?), it becomes the question, *Did you have dinner?* (Flip to Chapter 3 for Yes/No and WH-questions in Korean.) Stay tuned for more examples:

Q: 점심 먹었어요? (juhm-sheem muh-guh-ssuh-yoh) (*Did you eat lunch?*)

A: 아니요. 바빠서 못 먹었어요. (ah-nee-yoh. bah-ppah-suh mohn muh-guh-ssuh-yoh.) (*No, I was busy, so I couldn't eat.*)

Q: 저녁 뭐 먹고 싶어요? (juh-nyuhk mwuh muhk-kkoh shee-puh-yoh?) (*What do you want to have for dinner?*)

A: 냉면 먹고 싶어요. (naeng-myuhn muhk-kkoh shee-puh-yoh.) (*I want to have naeng-myun/Korean style cold-noodle.*)

Q: 어디에서 먹을까요? (uh-dee-eh-suh muh-geul-kkah-yoh?) (*Where shall we eat?*)

A: 그냥 집에서 먹어요. (geu-nyahng jee-beh-suh muh-guh-yoh.) (*Let's just eat at home.*)

TIP

In formal settings and relationships, use 식사하다 (sheek-ssah-hah-dah), a formal version of 밥 먹다 (bahm muhk-ttah) (*to have a meal*). 식사하셨어요? (sheek-ssah-hah-shuh-ssuh-yoh?) (*Have you eaten?*) is used when talking to business partners, in-laws, or teachers, for instance. When the meal is ready to eat, you can say 식사하세요 (sheek-ssah hah-seh-yoh) (*Please eat.*).

CULTURAL WISDOM

You may hear, 언제 한번 같이 식사해요 (uhn-jeh hahn-buhn gah-chee sheek-ssah-hae-yoh), or more casually, 언제 한번 같이 밥 먹자! (uhn-jeh hahn-buhn gah-chee bahm muhk-jjah). They both translate into *Let's have a meal sometime*. 언제 (uhn-jeh) (*when, sometime*) here means *sometime*, and 한번 (hahn-buhn) means *a try*. In casual Korean usage, it's an expression used to stay in touch with acquaintances without actually committing to a plan. An English equivalent would be, "We should get together for dinner sometime."

Satisfying your hunger

The ability to express your hunger and thirst is a crucial skill. Your 배 (bae) is your *stomach* and 고파요 (goh-pah-yoh) means *yearn* or *crave*. So, 배고파요 (bae goh-pah-yoh) means *I'm hungry*. To ask if someone is hungry, raise the intonation and ask, 배고파요? Possible responses are 네 (neh) (*yes*), or 아니요 (ah-nee-yoh) (*no*), or (배) 안 고파요 ((bae) ahn goh-pah-yoh) (*I'm not hungry*). If you're full, say 배불러요 (bae-bool-luh-yoh) (*I'm full*).

Your 목 (mohk) is your *neck* or *throat*. 말라요 (mahl-lah-yoh) means *dry* or *parched*. Put those two together to get, 목말라요 (mohng-mahl-lah-yoh), meaning *My throat is parched*, or *I'm thirsty*.

To suggest going out to eat something, you could say, 배고파요. 밥 먹으러 갈래요? (bae goh-pah-yoh. bahm-muh-geu-ruh gahl-lae-yoh?) (*I'm hungry. Would you like to go eat?*) If you want to offer water to your friend, you can kindly ask "목말라요? 물 마실래요?" (mong-mahl-lah-yoh? mool mah-sheel-lae-yoh?) (*Are you thirsty? Would you like some water?*)

What if you aren't that hungry but feel like snacking? Then say 입이 심심해요 (ee-bee sheem-sheem-hae-yoh). 입 (eep) is *mouth*, and 심심해요 means *bored*. So the expression literally means, your "mouth is bored."

Table 9-1 displays some examples of how to conjugate and use the verbs, 먹다 (muhk-ttah) (*to eat*), 마시다 (mah-shee-dah) (*to drink*), and 드시다 (deu-shee-dah) (*the honorific form of* 먹다 *and* 드시다).

TABLE 9-1   Common Endings for 먹다, 마시다, and 드시다

Korean Word	Meaning	Examples
먹다	*to eat*	
먹어요 (muh-guh-yoh)	*(I) eat*	저는 고기를 안 먹어요. (juh-neun goh-gee-reul ahn muh-guh-yoh) (*I don't eat meat.*)
먹었어요 (muh-guh-ssuh-yoh)	*ate*	아직 안 먹었어요. (ah-jeek ahn muh-guh-ssuh-yoh) (*I haven't eaten yet.*)
먹을래요 (muh-geul-lae-yoh)	*I'm going to/gonna eat . . .; are you going to/gonna eat . . .?*	뭐 먹을래요? (mwuh muh-geul-lae-yoh) (*What are you going to eat?*)
먹을까요? (muh-geul-kka-yoh?)	*shall I/we eat?*	어디에서 먹을까요? (uh-dee-eh-suh muh-geul-kka-yoh) (*Where shall we eat?*)
먹으러 가요 (muh-geu-ruh gah-yoh)	*go to eat*	점심 먹으러 가요. (juhm-sheem muh-geu-ruh gah-yoh) (*Let's go to eat lunch.*)
먹고 싶어요 (muhk-kkoh-shee-puh-yoh)	*want to eat*	매운 음식 먹고 싶어요. (mae-oon eum-sheek muhk-kko shee-puh-yoh) (*I want to eat spicy food.*)
마시다	*to drink*	
마셔요 (mah-shyuh-yoh)	*(I) drink*	맥주 안 마셔요. (maek-jjoo ahn mah-shyuh-yoh) (*I don't drink beer.*)
마셨어요 (mah-shyuh-ssuh-yoh)	*drank*	차 마셨어요. (chah mah-shuh-ssuh-yoh) (*I drank tea.*)
마실래요 (mah-sheel-lae-yoh)	*I want to drink. . .; do you want to drink. . .?*	뭐 마실래요? (mwuh mah-sheel-lae-yoh) (*What would you like to drink?*)

(continued)

TABLE 9-1 *(continued)*

Korean Word	Meaning	Examples
마실까요? (mah-sheel-kkah-yoh?)	*Shall I/we drink?*	라테 마실까요? (lah-tteh mah-sheel-kkah-yoh) *(Shall we drink lattes?)*
마시러 가요 (mah-shee-ruh gah-yoh)	*go to drink*	커피 마시러 가요. (kuh-pee mah-shee-ruh gah-yoh) *(Let's go to drink coffee.)*
마시고 싶어요 (mah-shee-goh shee-puh-yoh)	*want to drink*	물 마시고 싶어요. (mool mah-shee-goh shee-puh-yoh) *(I want to drink water.)*
드시다	***to eat, drink (honorific)***	
드세요 (deu-seh-yoh)	*please eat/drink*	맛있게 드세요. (mah-shee-kkeh deu-seh-yoh) *(Enjoy the food.)*
드셨어요 (deu-shyuh-ssuh-yoh)	ate, drank	맛있게 드셨어요? (mah-shee-kkeh deu-shyuh-ssuh-yoh) *(Did you enjoy the food?)*
드실래요? (deu-sheel-lae-yoh)	*Would you like to eat/drink. . .?*	뭐 드실래요? (mwuh deu-sheel-lae-yoh) *(What would you like to have?)*

TIP

You may hear restaurant waitstaff say, 맛있게 드세요 (mah-shee-kkeh deu-seh-yoh) (*Enjoy the food!*, literally, *Eat deliciously*). It's the Korean version of "Bon appétit," a common phrase wishing for the guests to enjoy the food. People also say 많이 드세요 (mah-nee deu-seh-yoh) (*Have a good meal!*, literally, *Please eat a lot*). You can replace 드세요 with 먹어요 (polite ending) or 먹어 (intimate ending) depending on whom you're talking to. Check out this dialogue between a host and a guest:

Guest: 초대 감사합니다. (choh-dae gahm-sah-hahm-nee-dah.) (*Thank you for the invitation!*)

Host: 맛있게 드세요! (mah-shee-kkeh deu-seh-yoh.) (*Enjoy the food!*)

Guest: 네, 잘 먹겠습니다. 음식이 많네요! (neh, jahl muhk-kkeht-sseum-nee-dah. eum-shee-gee mahn-neh-yoh) (*Thank you; I will. There are so many dishes!*)

Host: 많이 드세요. (mah-nee deu-seh-yoh.) (*Have a good meal!*)

Guest: (after meal) 잘 먹었습니다! 정말 맛있었어요. (jahl muh-guh-sseum-nee-dah. juhng-mahl mah-shee-ssuh-ssuh-yoh) (*Thank you; I really enjoyed it. It was really delicious.*)

Talkin' the Talk

PLAY

Sooho and Jane bump into each other during their lunch break at their company's lounge.

Sooho: 제인 씨, 식사하셨어요?

jeh-een-ssee, sheek-ssah hah-shyuh-ssuh-yoh?

Jane, have you eaten lunch?

Jane: 아뇨, 아직요. 미팅이 있었어요. 수호 씨는요?

ah-nyoh, ah-jeeng-nyoh. mee-teeng-ee ee-ssuh-ssuh-yoh.
soo-hoh-ssee-neun-yoh?

No, not yet. I had a meeting. How about you?

Sooho: 저는 먹었어요. 제인 씨, 오늘 저녁에 뭐 해요? 같이 저녁 먹을래요?

juh-neun muh-guh-ssuh-yoh. jeh-een-ssee, oh-neul
juh-nyuh-geh mwuh hae-yoh? gah-chee juh-nyuhk
muh-geul-lae-yoh?

I did. What are you doing this evening? Would you like to have dinner together?

Jane: 그래요! 뭐 먹으러 갈까요?

geu-rae-yoh! mwuh muh-geu-ruh gahl-kkah-yoh?

Sure! What should we go eat?

Sooho: 요즘 너무 더워요. 치맥 어때요?

yoh-jeum nuh-moo duh-wuh-yoh. chee-maek uh-ttae-yoh?

It's been too hot lately. How about chi-maek?

Jane: 치맥이 뭐예요? 안 먹어 봤어요.

chee-mae-gee mwuh-yeh-yoh? ahn muh-guh-bwah-
ssuh-yoh.

What's chi-maek? I haven't tried it.

Sooho: 치킨하고 맥주 줄임말이에요.

chee-keen-hah-goh maek-jjoo joo-reem-mah-lee-eh-yoh.

It's the shortened word for "chicken and beer."

Jane: 아! 드라마에서 봤어요. 저 치킨 정말 좋아해요!

ah! deu-rah-mah-eh-suh bwah-ssuh-yoh. juh chee-keen
juhng-mahl joh-ah-hae-yoh!

I saw it in a drama. I really like chicken.

WORDS TO KNOW

아직	ah-jeek	not yet
저녁	juh-nyuhk	evening, dinner
요즘	yoh-jeum	lately, recently, these days
더워요 (덥다)	duh-wuh-yoh	it's hot
먹어 봤어요 (먹어 보다)	muh-guh bwah-ssuh-yoh	have eaten, tried eating
줄임말	joo-reem-mahl	abbreviation, portmanteau

Getting to Know Korean Cuisine

쌀 (ssahl) (*rice*) and 야채 (yah-chae) (*vegetables*) are the main staple of Korean cuisine, but 고기 (goh-gee) (*meats, poultry*) and 생선 (saeng-suhn) (*fish*) are also enjoyed in moderation and often cooked with seasonal vegetables. Since Korea is surrounded by the ocean, it's no surprise that they consume a lot of 해산물 (hae-sahn-mool) (*seafood*).

Popular dishes

Korean cuisine practically revolves around 김치 (kimchi; *pickled vegetables*) which are known to be packed with 유산균 (yoo-sahn-gyoon) (*probiotics*). While the term 김치 is generally used to describe one made from 배추 (bae-choo) (*napa cabbage*) or 무 (moo) (*Korean radish*), it's made with many different vegetables and has more than 200 region-specific variations. For example, 총각 김치 (chohng-gahk geem-chee) uses small turnips instead of cabbage. Other types of 김치 include 오이 소박이 (oh-ee soh-bah-gee) (*cucumber kimchi*), 백김치 (baek-geem-chee) (*white kimchi*), 물김치 (mool-geem-chee) (*water kimchi*), 동치미 (dohng-chee-mee) (*watery radish kimchi*), 보쌈 김치 (boh-ssahm geem-chee) (*kimchi wrapped with a large cabbage leaf*), and 깍두기 (kkahk-ttoo-gee) (*diced radish kimchi*), just to name a few.

You can basically put 김치 in any dishes you want, like 김치 찌개 (jjee-gae) (*stew*), 김치 볶음밥 (boh-kkeum-bahp) (*fried rice*), 김치 만두 (mahn-doo) (*dumpling*), 김치 전/부침개 (juhn/boo-cheem-gae) (*Korean style pancake*), 김치 국수 (gook-ssoo) (*noodles*), and many more!

CULTURAL WISDOM

Traditionally, 김치 were stored in Korean earthenware pots called (옹기) 항아리 ((ohng-gee) hahng-ah-ree) which aided in the natural fermentation process by allowing 김치 to "breathe" through the jars while keeping the temperature consistent. The pots were buried in the ground to prevent their contents from freezing during the 겨울 (gyuh-ool) (*winter*), and to keep cool during the 여름 (yuh-reum) (*summer*). Today, many families have a 김치 냉장고 (kimchi naeng-jahng-goh), a special refrigerator dedicated to keeping home-made 김치 in their home.

Enough about 김치 — there are plenty of other Korean dishes to try! Another very popular dish is meaty BBQ, a.k.a. 불고기 (bool-goh-gee) (*marinated beef, "fired meat"*). 불고기 usually refers to strips of 소고기 (soh-goh-gee) (*beef*) marinated in a sauce and grilled over an open flame. The marinades for different kinds of meat can vary, and the 돼지고기 (dwae-jee goh-gee) (*pork*) and 닭고기 (dahk-kkoh-gee) (*chicken*) variations of 불고기 tend to be a bit spicier, whereas the traditional 소고기 불고기 is sweet and savory.

Dietary restrictions

By any chance, 채식주의자예요? (chae-sheek-jjoo-ee-jah-yeh-yoh?) (*Are you a vegetarian?*) Don't worry. Korea has so many options for a 채식 식단 (chae-sheek sheek-ttahn) (*vegetarian diet*). 비빔밥 (bee-beem-ppahp) (*bibimbap; a rice bowl topped with an array of seasoned vegetables and optional meat*), 김밥 (geem-ppahp) (*kimbap; seaweed rice roll with a variety of stuffings*), 순두부 찌개 (soon-doo-boo jjee-gae) (*soft-tofu stew*), 잡채 (jahp-chae) (*japchae; clear/sweet potato noodle stir-fry with vegetables with optional meat*), 파전 (pah-juhn) (*scallion pancake*), 야채죽 (yah-chae-jook) (*vegetable rice porridge*), 떡볶이 (ttuhk-ppoh-kkee) (*spicy rice cakes*), to name a few; all have versions for 채식주의자.

If you have any dietary preferences or restrictions and need any ingredients to be removed, let them know by stating explicitly as follows:

[dish]에 [item] 들어가요? ([dish]eh [item] deu-ruh-gah-yoh) (*Does [dish] contain [item]?*)

[item] 빼 주세요. (ppae joo-seh-yoh) (*Please leave out [item].*)

[item] 안/못 먹어요. ([item] ahn/mohn muh-guh-yoh) (*I don't/can't eat [item].*)

For pescatarians, for example, you can tell your needs like this:

고기 안 먹어요. 생선은 괜찮아요. 고기 빼 주세요. (goh-gee ahn muh-guh-yoh. saeng-suh-neun gwehn-chah-nah-yoh. go-gee ppae joo-seh-yoh.) (*I don't eat meat. Fish is okay. Please leave out the meat.*)

If you're allergic to something like 우유 (oo-yoo) (*milk*) or 땅콩 (ttahng-kohng) (*peanuts*), you can add "[allergen] 알레르기(가) 있어요." Examples:

계란 알레르기 있어요. 계란 빼 주세요. (geh-rahn ahl-leh-reu-gee ee-ssuh-yoh. geh-rahn ppae joo-seh-yoh) (*I'm allergic to eggs. Please leave them out.*)

Spiced up with seasoning

The three most essential condiments in Korean cuisine are 간장 (gahn-jahng) (*soy sauce*), 된장 (dwaen-jahng) (*fermented soybean paste*), and 고추장 (goh-choo-jahng) (*gochujang; hot pepper paste*).

These fermented sauce and pastes, called 장 (jahng), were also stored in earthenware pots, (옹기) 항아리, alternatively known as 장독 (jahng-ttohk), just like 김치. Traditional food preservation methods are still in use in the 시골 (shee-gohl) (*countryside*) of Korea. You can see rows and rows of wide, traditional pots placed in front of houses in rural areas. Table 9-2 displays Korean 양념 재료 (yahng-nyuhm jae-ryoh) (*seasoning ingredients*).

TABLE 9-2   **Korean Essential Seasoning Ingredients**

Seasoning	Pronunciation	Translation
간장	gahn-jahng	soy sauce
고추장	goh-choo-jahng	red pepper paste
고춧가루	goh-choo-kkah-roo	red pepper powder
된장	dwaen-jahng	soybean paste
소금	soh-geum	salt
설탕	suhl-tahng	sugar
식초	sheek-choh	vinegar
액젓	aek-jjuht	fish sauce
조청	joh-chuhng	traditional sweetener (made of rice and malt barley)
참기름	chahm-gee-reum	(roasted) sesame seed oil
후추	hoo-choo	black pepper

Describing food with descriptive verbs

Do you like what you're eating? Perhaps you don't care much for it. To communicate that and more, check out Table 9-3 for handy words and phrases to describe foods.

TABLE 9-3   **Words and Phrases to Describe Liking Food . . . Or Not!**

Descriptive Verbs	Pronunciation	Translation
맛있어요 (맛있다)	mah-dee-ssuh-yoh/ mah-shee-ssuh-yoh	It is tasty
맛없어요 (맛없다)	mah-duhp-ssuh-yoh	It is not tasty
달아요 (달다)	dah-rah-yoh	It's sweet
매워요 (맵다)	mae-wuh-yoh	It's spicy
짜요 (짜다)	jjah-yoh	It's salty
싱거워요 (싱겁다)	sheeng-guh-wuh-yoh	It's bland/plain
셔요 (시다)	shyuh-yoh	It's sour
고소해요 (고소하다)	goh-soh-hae-yoh	It's nutty, buttery, creamy
뜨거워요 (뜨겁다)	tteu-guh-wuh-yoh	It's hot
차요 (차다)	chah-yoh	It's cold
시원해요 (시원하다)	shee-wuhn-hae-yoh	cool; refreshing (food being cold or hot enough to make one feel refreshed)
너무	nuh-moo	too (used to emphasize very)
정말	juhng-mahl	really, truly
진짜	jeen-jjah	real, genuine; really (colloquial)
조금	joh-geum	a little bit

Is the 김치찌개 you ordered too spicy? Try saying, 매워요! (mae-wuh-yoh) (*it's spicy!*), or 너무 매워요 (nuh-moo mae-wuh-yoh) (*It's too spicy!*). Is it tasty? 정말 맛있어요! (jung-mahl mah-shee-ssuh-yoh). If you feel refreshed after a spoonful of hot 국 (gook) (*soup*), you can say 시원해요! (shee-wuhn-hae-yoh) (*refreshing!*).

Describe your meal using adverbs like 너무, 정말 or 진짜, 조금 and 안 (ahn) (*not*). In terms of saltiness intensity, you can characterize your food with one of the following phrases; 너무 짜요 (*It's too salty*), 정말/진짜 짜요 (*It's really salty*), 조금 짜요

(It's a bit salty), 안 짜요 *(It's not salty),* 딱 좋아요 (ttahk joh-ah-yoh) *(It's just right),* 조금 싱거워요 *(It's a little bland/plain),* 너무 싱거워요 *(It's too bland/plain).*

Practicing Good Table Manners

Honoring elders is an important aspect in Korean culture and is even reflected in the eating habits of Koreans. But there's more to table manners than simply honoring your elders. In Korea, the following slight gestures and mannerisms will show the people you are dining with that you took the time to learn the proper etiquette and will go a long way in impressing them, no matter their age:

>> Don't pick up your 숟가락 (soot-kkah-rahk) *(spoon)* or 젓가락 (juh-kkah-rahk) *(chopsticks)* until the elders at the table pick up theirs.

>> Before the meal, always thank your host by saying, "잘 먹겠습니다" (jahl muhk-kkeht-sseum-nee-dah) (Literally, *I will eat it well*).

>> After the meal, compliment the cook or the host by saying, "잘 먹었습니다" (jahl muh-guht-sseum-nee-dah) (Literally, *I have eaten it well = I enjoyed the food*).

>> Don't pick your bowl up from the table.

>> Don't make slurping or smacking sounds while eating. In Korea, eating quietly is considered polite, as opposed to some cultures where eating loudly is a sign of appreciation.

>> Don't hold your 숟가락 and 젓가락 together in one hand. 숟가락 is for rice and soup, and 젓가락 is for 반찬 (bahn-chahn) *(side dishes).*

>> After finishing your meal, put the 수저 (soo-juh) *(spoon and chopsticks),* shortened form of 숟가락 and 젓가락, back to their original setting and do not leave them in your bowl.

CULTURAL WISDOM

숟가락 and 젓가락 are all you ever need when eating Korean food. However, feel free to ask for a 포크 (poh-keu) *(fork)* if you're not familiar with 젓가락, and most restaurants are happy to accommodate you. Unlike other Asian countries where 수저 are made of 나무 (nah-moo) *(wood)* or bamboo, Korean 수저 are made of 쇠 (shwae) *(metal)* — iron in the past, steel today; steel is one of the top industries in Korea.

The shape of Korean 쇠젓가락 are thin and flat, which makes them hard to roll down the table. Though they require some dexterity, 쇠수저 are durable, environmentally friendly, and perfect for grabbing sizzling hot meat straight off of the Korean BBQ grill.

Check out a few vocabulary terms in Table 9-4 to familiarize yourself with various utensil-related terms. When asking for a certain utensil, all you need to do is add 좀 주세요 (johm joo-seh-yoh) (*please give*), as in 접시 좀 주세요 (juhp-ssee johm joo-seh-yoh). (*Please give us some plates.*) To specify how many, put the native Korean number between the utensil and 주세요, as in 포크 하나 주세요 (poh-keu hah-nah joo-seh-yoh) (*one fork, please*).

TABLE 9-4

Utensil Terms

Utensil	Pronunciation	Translation
숟가락	soot-kkah-rahk	spoon
젓가락	juh-kkah-rahk	chopsticks
수저	soo-juh	spoon and chopstick
포크	poh-keu	fork
칼	kahl	knife
컵	kuhp	mug, cup
잔	jahn	tea cup, glass for liquor
접시	juhp-ssee	plate
쟁반	jaeng-bahn	tray, platter
공기	gohng-gee	bowl for rice
그릇	geu-reut	bowl
국자	gook-jjah	ladle
(밥) 주걱	(bahp) joo-guhk	spatula (for rice)

Dining Out

The service mentality in the Korean food and their service industry is second to none. You can easily get the attention of the 종업원 (johng-uh-bwuhn) (*waitstaff*) by making eye contact with them, but you can simply call them over to your table as well by saying, 여기요 (yuh-gee-yoh). Conveniently, many restaurants also have call button on each table. The following sections give you the key info you need to successfully and confidently navigate public eateries in Korea.

Understanding what's on the menu

When 종업원 comes, they may say, 뭐 드실래요? (mwuh deu-sheel-lae-yoh) (*What would you like to eat?*), or in a more formal tone, 주문하시겠어요? (joo-moon hah-shee-geh-ssuh-yoh) (*Would you like to order?/Are you ready to order?*). If the 메뉴 (meh-nyoo) (*menu*) contains only Korean words and you're having a hard time understanding, try the following phrases to communicate with the 종업원.

여기 뭐가 맛있어요? (yuh-gee mwuh-gah mah-shee-ssuh-yoh) (*What's good here?*)

Many Koreans are happy to suggest something for you, but it's good to know what you're about to eat before venturing into a wild culinary experience. You could be leaving the 식당 (sheek-ttahng) (*restaurants*) with your mouth on fire because of the spices, or be left staring at a plate of meat, wondering where you went wrong. Try some of these questions to find what you want:

뭐가 안 매워요? (mwuh-gah ahn mae-wuh-yoh) (*What's not spicy?*)

이거 매워요? (ee-guh mae-wuh-yoh) (*Is this spicy?*)

이거는 맛이 어때요? (ee-guh-neun mah-shee uh-ttae-yoh) (*How does it taste?*)

채식 메뉴 있어요? (chae-sheek meh-nyoo ee-ssuh-yoh) (*Do you have vegetarian options?*)

채식 메뉴가 뭐예요? (chae-sheek meh-nyoo-gah mwuh-yeh-yoh) (*What are your vegetarian options?*)

Ordering at a restaurant

You can use 주세요 (joo-seh-yoh) (*Please give*) or 주실래요? (joo-sheel-lae-yoh) (*Could you give...?*) when asking for things at restaurants. Put whatever you want to ask for in front, as in 물 주세요 (mool joo-seh-yoh) (*Water, please*).

Sometimes you may hear "[item] 좀 더 주세요" ([item] johm duh joo-seh-yoh) (*More [item], please*). 좀 (johm) functions as a politeness marker, and 더 (duh) means *more*. Stay tuned for more phrases you may use at a restaurant.

>> (여기) 주문할게요. ((yuh-gee) joo-moon-hahl-kkeh-yoh) (*We're ready to order.*)

>> 메뉴판 좀 주세요. (meh-nyoo-pahn johm joo-seh-yoh) (*Menu, please.*)

>> 냅킨 좀 더 주세요. (naep-keen johm duh joo-seh-yoh) (*More napkins, please.*)

>> 반찬 좀 더 주실래요? (bahn-chahn johm duh joo-sheel-lae-yoh) (*Could you give more side dishes please?*)

>> 이거 좀 더 주실래요? (ee-guh johm duh joo-sheel-lae-yoh) (*May I have some more of this (one)?*)

Paying for your meal

CULTURAL WISDOM

To pay after your meal, you can ask 여기 얼마예요? (yuh-gee uhl-mah-yeh-yoh) (*How much is our food?*) Koreans use the word 여기 (yuh-gee) (*here*) to refer to themselves. But be prepared for some fierce resistance if you offer to foot the bill when out with your Korean friends! They may insist on 더치페이 (duh-chee-peh-ee) (*going Dutch; splitting the bill*).

Tipping at a restaurant

You might be familiar with 팁 (teep) (*tip* jars or a screen showing options for giving a 팁 of 15 percent to 30 percent). Korea doesn't have these, as the waitstaff's salary alone covers their services. This comes from the idea that every service should be done at its best, whether there is extra pay or not. So, if you ever visit Korea and offer a 팁, the receiver may be confused and uncomfortable. To show your appreciation, say 잘 먹었습니다! (jahl muh-guh-sseum-nee-dah) (*I enjoyed the food very much!*), 진짜 맛있었어요! (jeen-jjah mah-shee-ssuh-ssuh-yoh) (*It was really tasty*). A couple of words can brighten their day.

Talkin' the Talk

PLAY

Jin and her friend, Charlotte, went to a Korean restaurant and ordered food.

Waitstaff:	어서 오세요. 몇 분이세요?
	uh-suh oh-seh-yoh. myuht-ppoo-nee-seh-yoh?
	Come on in. How many people?

Jin:	두 명이요.
	doo-myuhng-ee-yoh.
	Two.

Waitstaff:	이쪽으로 오세요.
	ee-jjoh-geu-roh oh-seh-yoh.
	Please come this way.

(After looking at the menu)

Waitstaff:	주문하시겠어요?
	joo-moon-hah-shee-geh-ssuh-yoh?
	Would you like to order?

(continued)

(continued)

Jin:	삼겹살 2인분하고 파전 하나, 된장찌개 하나 주세요. 그리고 밥 하나 더 주세요. sahm-gyuhp-ssahl ee-een-boon-hah-goh pah-juhn hah-nah, dwaen-jahng-jjee-gae hah-nah joo-seh-yoh. geu-ree-goh bahp hah-nah duh joo-seh-yoh. *Two servings of pork belly, one Korean scallion pancake, and one soybean stew please. And one more rice please.*
Waitstaff:	네, 알겠습니다. 음료수는요? neh, ahl-geht-sseum-nee-da. eum-nyoh-soo-neun-nyoh? *Sure. Any beverages?*
Jin:	그냥 물 주세요. geu-nyahng mool joo-seh-yoh. *Just water please.*
Waitstaff:	(계산대 앞에서) 맛있게 드셨어요? mah-shee-kkeh deu-shuh-ssuh-yoh? (In front of the register) *Did you enjoy the food?*
Charlotte:	네, 잘 먹었습니다. 얼마예요? neh, jahl muh-guh-sseum-nee-dah. uhl-mah-yeh-yoh? *Yes. We really enjoyed it. How much is it?*
Waitstaff:	98,000원입니다. 결제는 어떻게 하시겠어요? goo-mahn-pahl-chun-won-eem-nee-dah. gyuhl-jjeh-neun uh-ttuh-keh hah-shee-geh-ssuh-yoh? *It's 98,000 won. How would you like to pay?*
Charlotte:	카드요. kah-deu-yoh. *By card.*
Waitstaff:	네, 결제했습니다. 여기 사인해 주세요. 영수증 여기 있습니다. 감사합니다. neh, gyuhl-jjeh-haet-sseum-nee-dah. yuh-gee ssa-een-hae joo-seh-yoh. yuhng-soo-jeung yuh-gee ee-sseum-nee-dah. gahm-sah-hahm-nee-dah. *Sure. All paid. Please sign here. Here is the receipt. Thank you.*
Charlotte:	안녕히 계세요. 고맙습니다. ahn-nyuhng-hee gyeh-seh-yoh. goh-mahp-sseum-nee-dah. *Bye. Thank you.*

. . . .

WORDS TO KNOW

주문하시겠어요	joo-moon-hah-shee-geh-ssuh-yoh	Would you like to order?
2인분	ee-een-boon	two servings
음료수	eum-nyoh-soo	beverage
얼마예요?	uhl-mah-yeh-yoh?	How much is it?
결제	gyuhl-jjeh	payment
영수증	yuhng-soo-jeung	receipt

Ordering Delivery Food

Korea is practically a heaven of 배달 음식 (bae-dahl eum-sheek) (*delivery food*). You can order almost any food, at any time, from almost anywhere. Feeling 배고파요 (bae-goh-pah-yoh) (*hungry*) at the beach? Sure thing! Having cravings at 새벽 세 시 (sae-byuhk seh-shee) (*3am*)? No problem. Make some room to enjoy a variety of restaurants specializing in 야식 (yah-sheek) (*late night snacks*) when you go to Korea.

Got apps?

The most convenient way to have your food delivered is through 앱 (aep) (*apps*), also called 어플 (uh-peul). Here are three of Korea's most popular mobile 배달 앱 (bae-dahl aep) (*delivery apps*).

» **Coupang Eats (쿠팡이츠):** This app supports Korean and English. It's well-known for quick delivery.

» **Baemin (배민):** The name is the shortened form of 배달의 민족 (bae-dah-leh meen-johk), which translates to *People of Delivery*. This is the largest 배달 앱 in Korea. Don't let the Korean-only (at least at the moment) app stop you from exploring hundreds of thousands of foods!

» **Yogiyo (요기요):** Although the app is in Korean, you can still access the English version through the website. Don't forget to take advantage of their 쿠폰 (koo-pohn) (*coupons*) and 할인 이벤트 (hah-reen ee-behn-teu) (*discount events*).

Check out Table 9-5 for the handy vocabulary related to 배달 앱.

TABLE 9-5   Delivery App Words

Delivery Term	Pronunciation	Translation
인기 메뉴	een-kkee meh-nyoo	popular menu
(현)주소	(hyuhn) joo-soh	(current) address
주문하기	joo-moon-hah-gee	order
결제하기	gyuhl-jjeh-hah-gee	pay
배달비	bae-dahl-bee	delivery fee
포장주문	poh-jahng-joo-moon	takeout
포장가능	poh-jahng-gah-neung	available for takeout
1인분	eel een-boon	one serving
3인분	sahm een-boon	three servings
재주문	jae-joo-moon	re-order
고객추천 가게	goh-gaek-choo-chuhn gah-geh	customer recommended store
최소주문	chweh-soh-joo-moon	minimum order
할인	hah-leen	discount, sale
주문 수락	joo-moon soo-lahk	order received
메뉴 준비중	meh-nyoo joon-bee-joong	menu in preparation
배달중	bae-dahl-joong	in delivery
배달 완료	bae-dahl wahl-lyoh	delivered

GRAMMATICALLY
SPEAKING

When ordering by phone, a handy verb ending to use is 해 주세요 (*Please do. . .for me*). To ask the restaurant to prepare the food for takeout, you can say 포장해 주세요 (poh-jahng-hae joo-seh-yoh). Check out more examples:

짜장면 네 그릇 배달해 주세요 (jjah-jahng-myuhn neh geu-leut bae-dahl-hae joo-seh-yoh) (*Please deliver four (bowls of) black bean noodles.*)

맛있는 음식 좀 추천해 주세요 (mah-sheen-neun eum-sheek jjohm choo-chuhn-hae joo-seh-yoh) (*Please recommend some delicious food.*)

Choosing what to eat

Now for the hardest part . . . choosing what to order! Your choices with 배달 음식 (bae-dahl eum-sheek) (*delivery foods*) are almost limitless, from authentic 한식

(hahn-sheek) (*Korean food*), 양식 (yahng-sheek) (*Western food*), 중식 (joong-sheek) (*Chinese food*), or 일식 (eel-sheek) (*Japanese food*), to 분식 (boon-sheek) (*casual/ street food*), even fast foods like 롯데리아 (loht-tteh-ree-ah) (*Lotteria*). Don't forget to leave room for 디저트 (dee-juh-teu) (*desserts*). Here are some of the most popular 배달 음식.

- » 김치찌개 (geem-chee jjee-gae) (*Kimchi stew*)
- » 김밥 (geem-ppahp) (*Korean seaweed rice roll with various stuffings*)
- » 감자탕 (gahm-jah-tahng) (*pork backbone stew*)
- » 떡볶이 (ttuhk-ppoh-kkee) (*rice cake cooked in spicy gochujang sauce*)
- » 보쌈 (boh-ssahm) (*boiled pork*)
- » 볶음밥 (boh-kkeum-bahp) (*fried rice*)
- » 삼계탕 (sahm-gyeh-tahng) (*chicken soup with ginseng and other herbs*)
- » 짜장면 (jjah-jahng-myuhn) (*black bean sauce noodles*)
- » 짬뽕 (jjahm-ppohng) (*spicy seafood noodle soup*)
- » 치킨 (chee-keen) (*fried chicken seasoned with various sauce*)
- » 피자 (pee-jah) (*pizza*)
- » 회 (hwae) (*thinly sliced raw fish*)
- » 햄버거 (haem-buh-guh) (*hamburger*)
- » 해물 파전 (hae-mool pah-juhn) (*seafood scallion pancake*)

CULTURAL WISDOM

The earliest recorded instance of food delivery in Korea dates back to the 18th century. Interesting enough, the popular delivery food at that time was 냉면 (naeng-myuhn), cold noodles made of buckwheat or other starches. You may wonder how the cold noodles were delivered in an era with no 냉장고 (naeng-jahng-goh) (*refrigerators*). 냉면 was actually enjoyed in winter back then. This historical context helps to explain why the cold northern cities of North Korea, such as *Pyungyang* (평양) and *Hamheung* (함흥), were renowned for their 냉면. Today, thanks to the invention of 냉장고, 냉면 has become one of the most beloved 여름 음식 (yuh-reum eum-sheek) (*summer foods*), enjoyed by many.

TIP

Question: What's the most popular 배달 음식 in Korea now? Answer: 닭튀김 (dahk-twee-geem) (*fried chicken*), or in modern terminology, 치킨 (chee-keen) (*fried chicken*). Try ordering 반반 치킨 (bahn-bahn chee-keen) (*half-and-half chicken*) to try two flavors at the same time — the chef will fry half of the order to crispy, golden perfection and coat the other half in a delicious, sweet and spicy 고추장 소스 (goh-choo-jahng ssoh-sseu) (*gochujang sauce*).

KOREAN STREET FOOD

길거리 음식 (geel-kkuh-ree eum-sheek) (*street foods*) are a must when traveling in Korea. Street food vendors sell everything from spicy rice cakes, to sweet pancakes, to chicken skewers, and more, all at prices your wallet will love. The trio you usually see is 떡볶이 (ttuhk-ppoh-kkee) (*chewy rice cakes cooked in gochujang sauce*), 어묵 (uh-mook) (*fish cakes*), and 호떡 (hoh-ttuhk) (*sweet dessert pancakes*), but that's just the tip of the delicious street food iceberg.

After your satisfying afternoon snack, say 얼마예요? (uhl-mah-yeh-yoh?) (*How much is it?*) or 계산해 주세요 (gyeh-sahn-hae joo-seh-yoh) (*I would like to pay now*), and the owner will tell you how much you owe. Remember to say 잘 먹었습니다 (jahl muh-guh-sseum-nee-dah) (*I enjoyed the food.*). You may also hear locals say 많이 파세요 (mah-nee pah-seh-yoh) (literally, *Please sell a lot*) when leaving a store or food stand. It's a way to say good bye and extend warm wishes.

Drinking, Korean style

If a friend asks you to go bar hopping or clubbing, you'll probably be in a situation where 술 (sool) (*alcoholic beverages*) are in the mix. Koreans raise their glasses and say "건배" (guhn-bae) (*cheers*) before drinking, though your younger friends may say "짠" (jjahn) instead, which is the onomatopoeia for the sound of glasses clinking together, or "와이파이" (wah-ee pah-ee) (*wi-fi*) if they're too far away to touch their glass to yours. Remember these drinking etiquette tips:

>> It's customary for the younger people to pour drinks for their elders.

>> When pouring someone else's drink, hold the bottle with your 오른손 (oh-leun-sohn) (*right hand*) while supporting your right wrist with the 왼손 (waen-sohn) (*left hand*) as you pour.

>> When receiving a drink from an elder, the hand positions should be the same, with your 오른손 holding the cup and your 왼손 supporting your right wrist.

>> It's polite for younger people to turn their heads away from their elders when taking a drink and to hold the cup with both hands.

Following the etiquette of other cultures goes a long way when meeting new people during your travels, but don't get too stressed. People will forgive lapses in etiquette amongst foreigners, as it is not expected of them. For Korean terms for some of the drinks, check out Table 9-6.

TABLE 9-6   ## Popular Beverages in Korea

Beverage	Pronunciation	Translation
녹차	nohk-chah	green tea
막걸리	mahk-kkuhl-lee	Korean traditional unrefined rice wine
맥주	maek-jjoo	beer
미수 (미숫가루)	mee-soo (mee-soo-kkah-roo)	beverage made of Korean grain powder
보리차	boh-ree-chah	barley tea
소주	soh-joo	distilled Korean rice wine
수정과	soo-juhng-gwah	Korean traditional cinnamon-ginger punch
술	sool	alcoholic beverage
식혜	shee-keh	Korean traditional rice punch
우유	oo-yoo	milk
음료수	eum-nyoh-soo	beverages (non-alcoholic)
인삼차	een-sahm-chah	ginseng tea
주스	joo-sseu	juice
커피	kuh-pee	coffee
탄산음료	tahn-sahn-eum-nyoh	soda

FUN & GAMES

A. You're invited to your Korean friend's house. Choose the two phrases you say before and after the meal. The answers are in Appendix C.

1. 맛있게 드세요

2. 잘 먹겠습니다

3. 많이 드세요

4. 잘 먹었습니다

B. Match each type of food and utensil with the Korean word.

© John Wiley & Sons, Inc.

1. 젓가락	Rice
2. 국	Soup
3. 생선	Spoon
4. 밥	Chopsticks
5. 숟가락	Stew
6. 찌개	Side dish
7. 반찬	Fish

Chapter **10**

Shopping Made Easy

쇼핑 좋아해요? (shyoh-peeng joh-ah-hae-yoh) (*Do you enjoy shopping?*) Venturing abroad for shopping is more than mere transactions — it's a cultural journey. Picture yourself bargaining in Korea's bustling 시장 (shee-jahng) (*outdoor markets*), or exploring a vast selection of products online and in-store. Each place you visit offers a unique glimpse into the local culture and lifestyle, perfect for both experienced shoppers and those hunting for that ideal 기념품 (gee-nyuhm-poom) (*souvenir*).

This chapter guides you through various shopping venues, from cozy corner shops to grand department stores, and from traditional markets to modern online platforms. It also provides essential information on 사이즈 (ssah-ee-jeu) (*sizes*), 색 (saek) (*colors*), and various types of merchandise, ensuring your shopping spree is as enjoyable and interactive as it is fruitful.

Exploring Shopping Venues in Korea

Korea offers a diverse array of shopping experiences, catering to various tastes and preferences. No matter which part of Korea you're in, you're never far from a shopping spot, big or small — especially near 관광지 (gwahn-gwahng-jee) (*tourist attractions*), where a shopping complex is likely just a stroll away.

TIP

If you're shopping in Seoul, consider starting at these popular spots:

>> 명동 (myuhng-dohng) (*Myeongdong*), 동대문시장 (dohng-dae-moon-shee-jahng) (*Dongdaemun Market*): These bustling hubs are packed with a wide range of goods, from 화장품 (hwah-jahng-poom) (*cosmetics*) to 옷 (oht) (*clothes*), street food, and everything in between.

>> 인사동 (een-sah-dohng) (*Insadong*), 남대문시장 (nahm-dae-moon-shee-jahng) (*Namdaemun Market*): Tourist favorites for traditional Korean crafts and 기념품 (gee-nyuhm-poom) (*souvenirs*).

>> 이태원 (ee-tae-wuhn) (*Itaewon*): Known for its international vibe, this district is filled with trendy shops, upscale cafes, bars and restaurants. English is widely spoken.

>> 홍대 (hohng-dae) (*Hongdae*): Named after the nearby Hongik University, renowned for its art program, 홍대 is located in the western end of Seoul. Known for its youthful, artsy vibe, and trendy fashion boutiques.

Navigating stores with ease

Here's a guide to different types of shopping destinations across Korea:

Department stores

Major city 백화점 (bae-kwah-juhm) (*department stores*) often feature high-end brands, upscale décor, and possibly art galleries, similar to those in your home country. For specific items, start with the floor guide on the first floor. Here are some handy words to know:

>> 매장 (mae-jahng) (*sales section*): Use this word after the name of one of the following items to ask about its location at a 백화점.

- 가구 (gah-goo) (*furniture*)
- 가전제품 (gah-juhn-jeh-poom) (*home appliances*)
- 남성복 (nahm-suhng-bohk) (*men's clothes*)
- 명품 (myuhng-poom) (*luxury brand goods*)
- 보석 (boh-suhk) (*jewelry*)
- 생활용품 (saeng-hwahl-yohng-poom) (*household goods*)
- 아동복 (ah-dohng-bohk) (*children's clothes*)
- 액세서리/잡화 (aek-seh-suh-ree/jah-pwah) (*accessory/miscellaneous goods*)
- 여성복 (yuh-suhng-bohk) (*women's clothes*)

- 속옷 (soh-goht) (*undergarments*)
- 스포츠용품 (seu-poh-cheu-yohng-poom) (*sporting goods*)
- 식품 (sheek-poom) (*food products/grocery*)
- 신발 (sheen-bahl) (*shoes*)
- 화장품 (hwah-jahng-poom) (*cosmetics*)

» 식당가 (sheek-ttahng-gah) (*restaurant section/food court*)

» 주차장 (joo-chah-jahng) (*parking lot*)

» 지하 [일] 층 (jee-hah [eel] cheung) (*underground, basement [1st] floor*): Combine 지하 (*underground*) with the [Sino-Korean number]-층 for basement floors where you can usually find a grocery section, food court, and parking garage.

Large discount stores and supermarkets

For grocery and household shopping in Korea, head to nearby 슈퍼마켓/슈퍼/마트 (shyoo-puh-mah-keht/shyoo-puh/mah-teu) (*supermarkets*) or 대형할인마트 (dae-hyuhng-hah-reen-mah-teu) (*large discount stores*) like 이마트 (*E-Mart*) or 홈플러스 (*HomePlus*). 배달 (bae-dahl) (*delivery*) services are often available; check their website or apps for details. For bulk shopping, *Costco* is also available, albeit with fewer locations, as well as *E-mart Traders*, which doesn't require a membership. Here are some essential terms to know when shopping at these places.

» 가격 (gah-gyuhk) (*price*)

» 교환 (gyoh-hwahn) (*exchange*)

» 고객 센터 (goh-gaek sehn-tuh) (*customer service center*)

» 계산대 (geh-sahn-dae) (*checkout*)

» 상품 (sahng-poom) (*product/item*)

» 시식 (shee-sheek) (*tasting/sample*)

» 영수증 (yuhng-soo-jjeung) (*receipt*)

» 자동 결제기 (jah-dohng gyuhl-jeh-gee) (*self-checkout*)

» 장바구니 (jahng-bah-goo-nee) (*shopping baskets*)

» 환불 (hwahn-bool) (*refund*)

» 판매 (pahn-mae) (*sale*)

» 품절 (poom-juhl) (*sold out*)

» 1+1 할인 (wuhn peul-luh-sseu wuhn hah-reen) (*BOGO discount*)

TIP

At the 계산대, a cashier might ask, "봉투 필요하세요?" (bohng-too pee-ryoh-hah-seh-yoh) (*Do you need a bag?*) Since bags at stores aren't free, many shoppers opt to bring their own reusable ones. If you have yours, simply say "아니요, 괜찮아요" (ah-nee-yoh, gwaen-chah-nah-yoh) (*No, it's okay*). Forgot your bag? You can respond with "네, 주세요" (neh, joo-seh-yoh) (*Yes, please*).

You might consider buying 쓰레기 봉투 (sseu-reh-gee bohng-too) (*designated garbage bags*) which can be reused for sorting trash at home — a common practice in Korea. (For more on trash sorting in Korea, check out Chapter 20.)

Small stores and shops

While large 백화점, 할인마트, or 슈퍼마켓 offer convenience and variety, for a dash of local flavor and adventure, explore quaint neighborhood 가게 (gah-geh) (*store, shop*). These small stores, with their vibrant awnings and street-facing windows displaying goods, provide a picturesque glimpse into daily life. You may find them inside your neighborhood 시장 (shee-jahng) (*markets*) or on the street.

Each 가게 usually reflects its specialty right in its name, often utilizing suffixes like 점 (juhm) (*store*), 집 (jeep) (*home/house*), or 방 (bahng) (*room*), as alternatives to 가게. Here are a few examples to look out for:

>> 기념품 가게/기념품점 (gee-nyuhm-poom-kkah-geh/-juhm) (*souvenir store*)

>> 과일 가게 (gwah-eel-kkah-geh) (*fruit shop*)

>> 꽃 가게/꽃집 (kkoht-kkah-geh/kkoht-jjeep) (*flower shop*)

>> 반찬 가게 (bahn-chahn-kkah-geh) (*side dish stores*)

>> 생선 가게 (saeng-suhn-kkah-geh) (*fish shop*)

>> 옷 가게 (oht-kkah-geh) (*clothes stores*)

>> 정육점 (juhng-yook-jjuhm) (*butcher's shop*)

>> 빵집/제과점 (ppahng-jjeep/jeh-gwah-juhm) (*bakery*)

>> 책방/서점 (chaek-ppahng/suh-juhm) (*bookstore*)

>> 학용품 가게/문구점 (hah-gyohng-poom-kkah-geh/moon-goo-juhm) (*stationary store*)

Traditional markets

Searching for more vibrant outdoor shopping experience? Check out Korean 전통시장 (juhn-tohng-shee-jahng) (*traditional markets*), often simply called 시장 (shee-jahng) (*markets*).

These markets vary by how often they operate: 상설시장 (sahng-suhl-shee-jahng) (*daily market*) found in neighborhood every day, and 정기시장 (juhng-gee-shee-jahng) (*periodic market*) like the 5일장 (oh-eel-jjahng) (*market held every 5 days*) or 7일장 (chee-reel-jjahng) (*market held every 7 days*). Don't overlook the 벼룩시장 (byuh-rook-ssee-jahng) (*flea markets*), which pop up on weekends for day-long treasure hunting.

In Seoul, check out iconic spots like the 남대문시장 (nahm-dae-moon-shee-jahng) (*Namdaemun Market*), bustling for nearly 700 years since Seoul became the capital, 동대문시장 (dohng-dae-moon-shee-jahng) (*Dongdaemun Market*), and nearby 광장시장 (gwahng-jahng-shee-jahng) (*Gwangjang Market*), a food lover's delight offering an array of traditional Korean dishes and street food, frequently featured on global food shows.

Every 시장 here has its own story, inviting you to check out — so grab 편한 신발 (pyuhn-hahn sheen-bahl) (*comfy shoes*) and start exploring! For directions to these 시장, refer to 네이버 지도 (neh-ee-buh jee-doh) (*Naver Map*) or 카카오 지도 (kah-kah-oh jee-doh) (*Kakao Map*).

Convenience stores

If you need to grab something quick, easy, and affordable, 편의점 (pyuh-nee-juhm) (*convenience stores*) are there on nearly every street corner. True to their name — "편의" meaning *convenience* — these stores offer a wide range of items, from 즉석 음식 (jeuk-ssuhk eum-sheek) (*ready-to-eat meals*) and toiletries to underwear and transportation cards, pretty much all essential 생필품 (saeng-peel-poom) (*daily necessities*). Many 편의점 have seating areas inside and/or outside, perfect for a quick break with a snack or drink. They also provide amenities like microwaves and 뜨거운 물 (tteu-guh-oon mool) (*hot water*), ensuring your convenience at every turn.

Underground shopping centers

The 지하상가 (jee-hah-sahng-gah) (*underground shopping center*) is a unique shopping place, tucked under the city, often linked to subway stations. No need to worry about the weather — you're covered for any rainy days! Check out "고투몰"

(goh-too-mohl) (*GotoMall*), the largest 지하상가 in Korea, located under 강남 고속터미널 (gahng-nahm goh-sohk-tuh-mee-nuhl) (*Gangnam Express Bus Terminal*) in Seoul. With over 1,000 stores offering everything from trendy clothes to souvenirs, accessories, wedding essentials, flowers, and electronics, you'll never get bored.

Duty-free shop and outlet malls

You can also explore 면세점 (myuhn-seh-juhm) (*duty free shops*) located in airports, seaports, and major cities, along with 아울렛몰 (ah-ool-leht-mohl) (*outlet malls*), situated on the outskirts of metropolitan areas. Only those who can present their passport and boarding pass (within 60 days of your departure date) at checkout can purchase at 면세점. Many 면세점 offer online platforms with multilingual services and user-friendly payment options. At 아울렛몰, you can find luxury brands at affordable prices. To avoid the weekend rush, consider visiting on weekdays.

CLICK, SHOP, LOVE: ONLINE SHOPPING

Online shopping has been a huge trend in Korea, with platforms ranging from 인터넷/온라인 쇼핑몰 (een-tuh-neht/ohn-nah-een shyoh-peeng-mohl) (*Internet/online shopping malls*) to 홈쇼핑몰 (hohm-shyoh-peeng-mohl) (*home shopping malls*), which are TV-based shopping services.

Korea's advanced Internet infrastructure and high mobile usage make shopping on mobile devices incredibly popular. You can easily find anything you need online, from daily essentials to unique finds. Some of the popular 온라인 쇼핑몰 include 쿠팡 (*Coupang*) (www.coupang.com), 네이버쇼핑 (*Naver Shopping*) (http://shopping.naver.com), G 마켓 (*G Market*) (www.gmarket.co.kr), and 11번가 (*11street*) (www.11st.co.kr).

For those interested in second-hand items, the go-to online platforms are 당근마켓 (dahng-geun-mah-keht) (*Danggeun Market*) and 중고나라 (joong-goh-nah-rah) (*Jungonara*). 당근마켓, an app-focused on local, neighborhood-based transaction, also supports 영어 (yuhng-uh) (*English*), ensuring you navigate easily and snag great deals without language barriers. Whether you're looking for a bargain or something unique, these platforms serve as your gateway to Korea's vibrant 중고품 시장 (joong-goh-poom shee-jahng) (*second-hand markets*).

Talkin' the Talk

PLAY

Jane and Mina need to go shopping. They decide where to go.

Mina: 제인 씨, 오늘 뭐 해요?
jeh-een ssee, oh-neul mwuh hae-yoh?
Jane, what are you going to do today?

Jane: 과일 사러 시장에 가려고요.
gwah-eel sah-ruh shee-jahng-eh gah-ryuh-goh-yoh.
I plan to go to the market to buy some fruits.

Mina: 저도 반찬 사야 되는데 같이 갈래요?
juh-doh bahn-chahn sah-yah dwae-neun-deh gah-chee
gahl-lae-yoh?
I need to go get some side dishes, so do you want to go together?

Jane: 좋아요. 저는 화장품도 필요해요.
joh-ah-yoh. juh-neun hwah-jahng-poom-doh pee-ryoh-hae-yoh.
Sure. I need some cosmetics, too.

Mina: 백화점에 과일, 반찬, 화장품 다 있으니까 백화점으로 갈까요?
bae-kwah-juh-meh gwah-eel bahn-chahn hwah-jahng-poom
dah ee-sseu-nee-kkah bae-kwah-juh-meu-roh gahl-kkah-yoh?
*There are fruits, side dishes, and cosmetics at department stores,
so shall we go to the department store?*

Jane: 그거 좋은 생각이네요.
geu-guh joh-eun saeng-gah-gee-neh-yoh.
That's a good idea.

WORDS TO KNOW

과일	gwah-eel	fruit
사러 가려고요 (사러 가다)	sah-ruh gah-ryuh-goh-yoh	go (in order) to buy
사야 되는데 (사야 되다)	sah-yah dwae-neun-deh	need to buy
시장	shee-jahng	market
반찬	bahn-chahn	side dish
화장품	hwah-jahng-poom	cosmetics
필요해요 (필요하다)	pee-ryoh-hae-yoh	I need; necessary

Knowing the hours of operation

Most shops keep standard hours, opening around 10am and closing by 9pm. But places like 슈퍼마켓 (shyoo-puh-mah-keht) (*supermarkets*) or 편의점 (pyuh-nee-juhm) (*convenience stores*) often run longer. 전통시장 (juhn-tohng-shee-jahng) (*traditional markets*) might have varied times, so it's good to check ahead. Here are some handy phrases to help you find out the business hours of where you're shopping. Just swap out the word in brackets for the specific place you're curious about!

[백화점] 몇 시부터 몇 시까지 해요? (bae-kwah-juhm myuht ssee-boo-tuh myuht ssee-kkah-jee hae-yoh) (*From what time until what time does [the department store] operate?*)

[편의점] 몇 시부터 해요? (pyuh-nee-juhm myuht ssee-boo-tuh hae-yoh) (*From what time does [the convenient store] store operate?*)

[시장] 몇 시에 열어요? (shee-jahng myuht ssee-eh yuh-ruh-yoh) (*What time does [the market] open?*)

[가게] 몇 시까지 해요? (gah-geh myuht ssee-kkah-jee hae-yoh) (*Until what time does [the store] operate?*)

[슈퍼마켓] 몇 시에 닫아요? (shyoo-puh-mah-kae myuht ssee-eh dah-dah-yoh) (*What time does [the supermarket] close?*)

Asking for what you are looking for

If you need help in a store, you can always flag down 점원 (juh-mwuhn) (*store employees*) by saying, 저기요. (juh-gee-yoh) for "*Excuse me.*" Looking for something specific? Just ask:

[item] 있어요? ([item] ee-ssuh-yoh) (*Do you have/carry [item]?*)

[item] 어디(에) 있어요? ([item] uh-dee(-eh) ee-ssuh-yoh?) (*Where is [item]?*).

At a high-rise department store or shopping complex, you can ask about floor information, by replacing 어디 with 몇 층 (myuht cheung) (*what floor*). Here are a few go-tos:

[양말] 있어요? ([yahng-mahl] ee-ssuh-yoh) (*Do you have [socks]?*)

[기념품] 어디에 있어요? ([gee-nyuhm-poom] uh-dee-eh ee-ssuh-yoh) (*Where are [souvenirs]?*)

[여자 신발] 몇 층에 있어요? ([yuh-jah sheen-bahl] myuht cheung-eh ee-ssuh-yoh) (*On which floor are [women's shoes]?*)

Talkin' the Talk

PLAY

Mike asks an attendant for help at a department store.

Mike: 실례합니다. 좀 도와 주세요.
sheel-lyeh hahm-nee-dah. johm doh-wah joo-seh-yoh.
Excuse me. I'd like some help please.

Attendant: 네, 고객님. 어떻게 도와 드릴까요?
neh, goh-gaeng-neem. uh-ttuh-keh doh-wah
deu-reel-kkah-yoh?
Yes, sir. How can I help you?

Mike: 넥타이 어디 있어요?
nehk-tah-ee uh-dee ee-ssuh-yoh?
Where are the ties?

Attendant: 네, 넥타이 찾으십니까? 5층 남성복 매장으로 가시면 됩니다.
neh, nehk-tah-ee chah-jeu-sheem-nee-kkah? oh-cheung
nahm-suhng-bohk mae-jahng-eu-roh gah-shee-myuhn
dwaem nee-dah.
*Oh, are you looking for ties? You can go to the men's
clothing department on the fifth floor.*

Mike: 감사합니다. 식당은 몇 층에 있어요?
gahm-sah-hahm-nee-dah. sheek-ttahng-eun myuht
cheung-eh ee-ssuh-yoh?
Thank you. On which floor are the restaurants?

Attendant: 네, 고객님. 식당은 지하 1층에도 있고 8층에도 있습니다.
neh, goh-gaeng-neem. sheek-ttahng-eun jee-hah
eel-cheung-eh-doh eet-kkoh pahl-cheung-eh-doh
eet-sseum-nee-dah.
*Yes, sir. Restaurants are on the first basement floor and also
on the eighth floor.*

Mike: 엘리베이터 어디에 있어요?
ehl-lee-beh-ee-tuh uh-dee-eh ee-ssuh-yoh?
Where are elevators?

Attendant: 네, 고객님. 엘리베이터는 오른쪽에 있습니다.
neh, goh-gaeng-neem. ehl-lee-beh-ee-tuh-neun oh-reun-
jjoh-geh eet-sseum-nee-dah.
Yes, sir. Elevators are on the right side.

Mike: 도와 주셔서 감사합니다.
doh-wah joo-shyuh-suh gahm-sah-hahm-nee-dah.
Thank you for your help.

WORDS TO KNOW

고객	goh-gaek	customer
찾으십니까? (찾다)	chah-jeu-sheem-nee-kkah	are you looking for. . .?
남성복	nahm-suhng-bohk	men's clothing
매장	mae-jahng	sales section
식당	sheek-ttahng	restaurant
지하	jee-hah	basement

Comparing Merchandise

When choosing the best fit for your comfort and preferences, mastering a few key words is your first step. Let's start with three handy terms, pulled straight from the demonstrative pronouns, 이, 그, and 저 (see Chapter 3 for more info). Use these terms to easily point out and compare items, whether they're right next to you or across the way:

» 이거 (ee-guh) (*this one*; the one right next to me)

» 그거 (geu-guh) (*that one*; the one closer to you)

» 저거 (juh-guh) (*that one over there*; farther away from you and me)

Comparing items

When comparing items, you may use opposites words. You can also utilize negative adverbs like 별로 (byuhl-loh) and 안 (ahn) to convey "not really" or "not much." See the examples in Table 10-1.

TABLE 10-1   Positive and Negative Comparisons

Positive	Negative
좋아요. (joh-ah-yoh) (*It's good; I like it*)	싫어요. (shee-ruh-yoh) (*I dislike it*)
	(별로) 안 좋아요. (byuhl-loh ahn joh-ah-yoh) (*It's not that good; I don't really like it.*)
마음에 들어요. (mah-eu-meh deu-ruh-yoh) (*I like it.*) (*Literally, it enters my heart*) * *Used when you see it for the first time*	(별로) 마음에 안 들어요. (byuhl-loh mah-eu-meh ahn deu-ruh-yoh) (*I don't really like it.*)
예뻐요. (yeh-ppuh-yoh) (*It's pretty.*)	(별로) 안 예뻐요. (byuhl-loh ahn yeh-ppuh-yoh) (*It' not that pretty.*)
커요. (kuh-yoh) (*It's big.*)	작아요. (jah-gah-yoh) (*It's small.*)
	안 커요. (ahn kuh-yoh) (*It's not big.*)
비싸요 (bee-ssah-yoh) (*It's expensive.*)	싸요. (ssah-yoh) (*It's cheap.*)
	안 비싸요. (ahn bee-ssah-yoh) (*It's not expensive,*)
잘 맞아요. (jahl mah-jah-yoh) (*It fits well.*)	잘 안 맞아요. (jahl ahn mah-jah-yoh) (*it doesn't fit well.*)

GRAMMATICALLY
SPEAKING

Enhancing comparisons

To enhance comparisons, there are two things you can try:

>> Add 더 (duh) (*more*) before a verb for emphasis:

- 마트가 더 싸요. (mah-teu-gah duh ssah-yoh) (*Market is cheaper.*)

- 이게 더 좋아요. (ee-geh duh joh-ah-yoh) (*This one is better.*)

(이게 combines 이거 and the subject particle 가, emphasizing key information. Always use the contracted form, 이게, not 이거가. For more details on the 이/가 subject particle, see Chapter 3.)

>> Use "[item] 보다" (boh-dah) to say "compared to/than [the item]." This phrase can be placed before or after the item you're comparing:

- 이게 [저거]보다 더 좋아요. (ee-geh [juh-guh]-boh-dah duh joh-ah-yoh) (*This is better than [that].*)

- [저거]보다 이게 더 예뻐요. ([juh-guh]-boh-dah ee-geh duh yeh-ppuh-yoh) (*This is prettier than [that].*)

- [백화점]보다 마트가 더 싸요. ([bae-kwah-jujhm]-boh-dah mah-teu-gah duh ssah-yoh) (*The market is cheaper than [department stores].*)

Now, can you try saying "The department store is more expensive than the mart" in Korean? The word for "*expensive*" is 비싸요 (bee-ssah-yoh). Yes, you'd say, "백화점이 마트보다 더 비싸요." You can also switch the word order like this: "마트보다 백화점이 더 비싸요." You got it!

TIP

When shopping, take your time to compare items based on 가격 (gah-gyuhk) (*price*), 품질 (poom-jeel) (*quality*), and style. Uncertain about which to choose? Seek guidance from store attendants by inquiring, 뭐가 더 좋아요? (mwuh-gah duh joh-ah-yoh) (*Which one is better?*). They'll be happy to help and offer insights about their merchandise. If you wonder which item is more budget-friendly, simply ask, 뭐가 더 싸요? (mwuh-gah duh ssah-yoh) (*What is cheaper?*).

If you're just browsing and prefer to do so without assistance, you can politely let store employees know by saying, 그냥 구경 좀 할게요 (geu-nyahng goo-gyuhng johm hahl-geh-yoh) (*I'll just look around a bit*) or 그냥 구경해도 돼요? (geu-nyahng goo-gyuhng hae-doh dwae-yoh) (*Can I just browse?*).

Making your choice

Ready to decide? When one item stands out, you can indicate your preference with:

이거로 할게요. (ee-guh-roh hahl-kkeh-yoh) (*I'll go with this one.*)

이게 제일 좋아요. (ee-geh jeh-eel joh-ah-yoh) (*This is the best; I like this one the best.*)

이게 제일 괜찮은 거 같아요. (ee-geh jeh-eel gwaen-chah-neun guh gah-tah-yoh) (*This seems like the best one.*)

저게 제일 마음에 들어요. (juh-geh jeh-eel mah-eu-meh deu-ruh-yoh) (*That one is my favorite; literally, that one enters my heart the most.*)

Shopping for Outfits

Korea is a global fashion hotspot, home to a wide variety of 의류 (eui-ryoo) (*clothing, outfit*) shops, ranging from quaint boutiques to upscale stores, and from traditional to trendy. As you explore these shopping destinations, knowing key terms related to size and color is crucial to ensure you find exactly what you're looking for.

Talking about what you need

To kick off your clothing shopping, it's useful to know some Korean terms for the items you're looking for. Check out the following list for some basic clothing items in Korean. Some are staples for everyone, and some are gender specific.

>> 상의/윗도리 (**sahng-eui/weet-ttoh-ree**) (*top*) 티셔츠 (tee-shyuh-cheu) (*t-shirts*), 와이셔츠 (wah-ee-shyuh-cheu) (*dress shirts*), 코트 (koh-teu) (*coat*), 블라우스 (beul-lah-oo-seu) (*blouse*), 스웨터 (seu-weh-tuh) (*sweater*), 자켓 (jah-keht) (*jacket*)

>> 하의/아랫도리 (**hah-eui/ah-raet-ttoh-ree**) (*bottom*): 바지 (bah-jee) (*pants*), 반바지 (bahn-bah-jee) (*shorts*), 청바지 (chuhng-bah-jee) (*blue jeans*), 치마 (chee-mah) (*skirt*)

>> 기타 (**gee-tah**) (*others*): 정장 (juhng-jahng) (*suit*), 유니폼 (yoo-nee-pohm) (*uniform*), 교복 (gyoh-bohk) (*school uniform*), 원피스 (wuhn-pee-sseu) (*dress*), 속옷 (soh-goht) (*undergarments*), 잠옷 (jah-moht) (*pajamas*), 수영복 (soo-yuhng-bohk) (*swimsuits*), 비옷/우비 (bee-oht/oo-bee) (*raincoat*)

>> 잡화 (**jah-pwah**) (*fashion accessories*): 모자 (moh-jah) (*hat*), 목도리 (mohk-ttoh-ree) (*scarf, muffler*), 넥타이 (nehk-tah-ee) (*ties*), 시계 (shee-gyeh) (*watch*), 벨트/허리띠 (behl-teu/huh-ree-ttee) (*belt*), 장갑 (jahng-gahp) (*gloves*), 양말 (yahng-mahl) (*socks*)

>> 신발 (**sheen-bahl**) (*shoes*): 구두 (goo-doo) (*formal shoes*), 운동화 (oon-dohng-hwah) (*sneakers*), 부츠 (boo-cheu) (*boots*), 샌들 (saen-deul) (*sandal*), 슬리퍼 (seul-lee-puh) (*slippers*)

Understanding Korean sizing

In Korea, sizing units are very different from those used in North America or Europe. 신발 (sheen-bahl) (*shoes*) sizes are measured in millimeters in Korea (for example, a men's size 9 and 10 in the US are equivalent to 270 and 280 in Korea; a women's size 7 and 8 are 240 and 250 in Korea). It's helpful to familiarize yourself with the metric system for 사이즈/치수 (ssah-ee-jeu/chee-soo) (*size*) before shopping in Korea.

Women's clothing sizes are sometimes labeled 44/55/66/77/88/99, corresponding to XS through XXL. No stress if you're unsure — size comparison charts are widely available online to help you out. When discussing sizes with 점원 (juh-mwuhn) (*store employees*), here are some useful phrases:

사이즈가 어떻게 되세요? (ssah-ee-jeu-gah uh-ttuh-keh dwae-seh-yoh) (*What size do you need?*)

더 큰/작은 사이즈 있어요? (duh keun/jah-geun ssah-ee-jeu ee-ssuh-yoh) (*Do you have a larger/smaller size?*)

한 치수 (더) 큰 거 주세요. (hahn chee-soo duh keun guh joo-seh-yoh) (*Can you give me one size bigger?*)

한 치수 (더) 작은 거 주세요. (hahn chee-soo duh jah-geun guh joo-seh-yoh) (*Please give me one size smaller.*)

Asking about colors

색 (saek) or 색깔 (saek-kkahl) is the Korean word for color. Table 10-2 lists basic colors in Korean.

TABLE 10-2 **Colors in Korean**

검은색/검정색 (guh-meun-saek/guhm-juhng-saek) (*black*)	하얀색/흰색 (hah-yahn-saek/heen-saek) (*white*)
노란색 (noh-rahn-saek) (*yellow*)	밤색 (bahm-saek) (*brown*)
보라색 (boh-rah-saek) (*purple*)	빨간색 (ppahl-gahn-saek) (*red*)
주황색 (joo-hwahng-saek) (*orange*)	초록색 (choh-rohk-ssaek) (*green*)
파란색 (pah-rahn-saek) (*blue*)	분홍색 (boon-hohng-saek) (*pink*)
회색 (hwae-saek) (*gray*)	하늘색 (hah-neul-saek) (*skyblue*)

If you have specific color preferences, ask store employees about the availability of those colors, saying, 있어요 (ee-ssuh-yoh) (*Do you have [it]?*) after the color term. For example, [흰색] 있어요? (heen-saek ee-ssuh-yoh?) (*Do you have a white color?*).

Trying something on

Korea is known for its unique fashion and high-quality fabrics. Explore a variety of materials and styles to see if they suit your comfort and style preferences. When you want to try something on in a store, simply ask:

[옷] 입어 봐도 돼요? ([oht] ee-buh bwah-doh dwae-yoh) (*May I try on [these clothes]?*)

[신발] 신어 봐도 돼요? ([sheen-bahl] shee-nuh bwah-doh dwae-yoh) (*May I try on [these shoes]?*)

[모자] 써 봐도 돼요? ([moh-jah] ssuh bwah-doh dwae-yoh) (*May I try on [this hat]?*)

After trying them on, the 점원 (juh-mwuhn) (*store employees*) might ask how it is: 어떠세요? (uh-ttuh-seh-yoh) (*How is it? — honorific*). You can also ask 어때요? if you're seeking feedback from the staff or your shopping buddy. Feel free to use any of the phrases from Table 10-1. Here are additional responses to the "어때요?" question:

멋있어요. (muh-shee-ssuh-yoh) (*It looks cool/looks stylish.*)

잘 어울려요. (jahl uh-ool-lyuh-yoh) (*It looks good on you.*)

이거 사요. (ee-guh sah-yoh) (*Get this one.*)

좀 커요/작아요. (johm kuh-yoh/jah-gah-yoh) (*It's a bit big/small.*)

다른 색 한번 입어 봐요. (dah-reun saek hahn-buhn ee-buh-bwah-yoh) (*Try a different color.*)

REMEMBER

Note that 멋있어요 can extends beyond mere appearance. The term 멋 (muht) in Korean can convey a sense of sophistication in style, behavior, or even the inherent qualities of an object or action. When paired with the verb, 있어요 (ee-ssuh-yoh) (*to have*), 멋있어요 effectively gives a thumbs up, acknowledging more than just visual appeal. It's a versatile compliment used to admire not only someone's looks but also their conduct or the impressive nature of their actions.

GRAMMATICALLY SPEAKING

When offering feedback or expressing opinions, people sometimes use the pattern, "(stem)+은/는/을 거(것) 같아요." (eun/neun/eul guh gah-tah-yoh) (*It seems/It looks like/I think. . .*), to softens their statements. Table 10-3 outlines how to use this pattern:

TABLE 10-3 ## Softening Statements in Korean

Tense	Conjugation	Dictionary form	Examples
Present	**Adjective stem + 은** (*ending in a consonant*)	작다 (*small*)	좀 작은 거 같아요. (johm jah-geun guh gah-tah-yoh) (*It seems a bit small.*)
Present	**이다/아니다, Adjective stem + ㄴ** (*ending in a vowel*)	별로이다 (*to be not my taste/to be not that good*)	별로인 거 같아요. (byuhl-loh-een guh gah-tah-yoh) (*It doesn't seem that good.*)
Present	**Verb stem + 는**	어울리다 (*suit/match*)	이게 더 잘 어울리는 거 같아요. (ee-geh duh jahl uh-ool-lee-neun guh gah-tah-yoh) (*I think this one suits you/me better.*)
Future	**Verb/Adjective stem + ㄹ/을**	어울리다 (*suit/match*)	잘 어울릴 거 같아요. (jahl uh-ool-leel guh gah-tah-yoh) (*I think it will suit you/me well.*)

Talkin' the Talk

PLAY

Natalie and Kate are at a department store shopping for clothes.

Kate: 반바지 어디 있어요?
bahn-bah-jee uh-dee ee-ssuh-yoh?
Where are shorts?

Attendant: 네. 이쪽에 있습니다.
neh. ee-jjoh-geh eet-sseum-nee-dah.
They are here.

Natalie: 이 반바지 어때요?
ee bahn-bah-jee uh-ttae-yoh?
How are these shorts?

Kate: 멋있어요. 근데 파란색이 더 잘 어울릴 것 같아요.
muh-shee-ssuh-yoh. geun-deh pah-rahn-sae-gee duh
jahl uh-ool-leel kkuht gah-tah-yoh.
It's stylish. I think blue would suit you better.

Natalie: 이거 파란색 77사이즈 있어요?
ee-guh pah-rahn-saek cheel-cheel ssah-ee-jeu
ee-ssuh-yoh?
Do you have this a size 77 in blue?

Attendant: 네. 잠시만 기다려 주세요.
neh. jahm-shee-mahn gee-dah-ryuh joo-seh-yoh.
Yes. Wait a moment.

Natalie: 이거 입어 봐도 돼요?
ee-guh ee-buh bwah-doh dwae-yoh?
Can I try this on?

Attendant: 그럼요. 탈의실에서 입어 보세요.
geu-ruhm-nyoh. Tah-ree-shee-reh-suh ee-buh
boh-seh-yoh.
Of course. Please try it on in the fitting room.

WORDS TO KNOW

반바지	bahn-bah-jee	shorts
멋있어요 (멋있다)	muh-shee-ssuh-yoh	cool, stylish
파란색	pah-rahn-saek	blue
어울릴 것 같아요 (어울리다)	uh-ool-leel kkuht gah-tah-yoh	I think it'll suit
입어 봐도 돼요 (입어 보다)	ee-buh-bwah-doh dwae-yoh	Can I try on; you may try on
탈의실	tah-ree-sheel	fitting, dressing room

Shopping for Groceries

Many modern 슈퍼마켓 (shyoo-puh-mah-keht) (*supermarkets*), 슈퍼 (shyoo-puh) in short, or 마트 (mah-teu) (*mart*), both large chains and smaller neighborhood stores, carry a wide range of groceries, including fresh and packaged foods and international eateries.

We cover some basics of grocery shopping here. First things first, if you know the names of some essential grocery items in Korean, you're already ahead, and grocery shopping will be as fun and easy as sightseeing! (Also check out Chapter 9 for more on food.)

>> **고기 (goh-gee) (*meat*):** 생선 (saeng-suhn) (*fish*), 해산물 (hae-sahn-mool) (*seafood*), 소고기 (soh-goh-gee) (*beef*), 돼지고기 (dwae-jee-goh-gee) (*pork*), 닭고기 (dahk-kkoh-gee) (*chicken*)

>> **과일/채소 (gwah-eel/chae-soh) (*fruit/vegetable*):** 사과 (sah-gwah) (*apple*), 배 (bae) (*pear*), 딸기 (ttahl-gee) (*strawberry*), 파 (pah) (*scallion*), 오이 (oh-ee) (*cucumber*), 감자 (gahm-jah) (*potato*)

>> **유제품 (yoo-jeh-poom) (*dairy*):** 계란/달걀 (geh-rahn/dahl-gyahl) (*egg*), 우유 (oo-yoo) (*milk*), 치즈 (chee-jeu) (*cheese*), 버터 (buh-tuh) (*butter*), 요거트 (yoh-guh-teu) (*yogurt*)

>> **곡물 (gohng-mool) (*grains*):** 국수 (gook-ssoo) (*noodles*), 쌀 (ssahl) (*rice*), 라면 (lah-myuhn) (*ramen*), 잡곡 (jahb-kkohk) (*assorted grains*)

>> 과자 **(gwah-jah)** *(confectionery, snack chips)*: 빵 (ppahng) *(bread)*, 케이크 (keh-ee-keu) *(cake)*, 도넛 (doh-nuht) *(donuts)*, 사탕 (sah-tahng) *(candy)*, 껌 (kkuhm) *(chewing gum)*

>> 반찬 **(bahn-chahn)** *(side dishes)*: 두부 (doo-boo) *(tofu)*, 김 (geem) *(dried seaweed)*, 김치 (geem-chee) *(Kimchi)*, 멸치 (myuhl-chee) *(anchovy)*, 오징어 (oh-jeeng-uh) *(squid)*

>> 기타 *(others)*: 건조식품 (guhn-joh-sheek-poom) *(dried food)*, 냉동식품 (naeng-dohng-sheek-poom) *(frozen food)*, 견과류 (gyuhn-gwah-ryoo) *(nuts)*, 음료 (eum-nyoh) *(drink)*, 통조림 (tohng-joh-reem) *(canned food)*, 유기농 제품 (yoo-gee-nohng jeh-poom) *(organic products)*, 밀키트 (meel-kee-teu) *(meal kit)*

CULTURAL WISDOM

For more authentic Korean experience, consider visiting 전통시장 (juhn-tohng-shee-jahng) *(traditional market)*. Here, you can explore a variety of ready-to-eat 반찬 (bahn-chahn) *(side dishes)* and 김치 (geem-chee) *(Kimchi)*, along with fresh produce and live seafood.

A unique cultural treat you might encounter is "덤" (duhm), where 가게 주인 (gah-geh joo-een) *(store owners)* give you a little extra, like an additional piece of fruit or a little extra produce as a way to express gratitude, build goodwill, and enhance customer satisfaction.

When it comes to bargaining, useful phrases include 좀 비싸요 (johm bee-ssah-yoh) *(It's a bit expensive)*, 좀 깎아 주세요. (johm kkah-kkah joo-seh-yoh) *(Please give me a discount.)*, or 좀 싸게 해주세요. (johm ssah-geh hae joo-seh-yoh) *(Could you make it cheaper?)*.

Paying for Your Purchases

Ready to pay? Various payment options are available in Korea. For cashless 결제 (gyuhl-jjeh) *(payment)*, Naver Pay, Kakao Pay, or Samsung Pay are widely used in Korea. Apply Pay also works in larger stores. In smaller, mom-and-pop type stores or 전통시장 (juhn-tohng shee-jahng) *(traditional markets)*, standard (신용)카드 ((shee-nyohng-)kah-deu) *(credit cards)* or 현금 (hyuhn-geum) *(cash)* are still preferred. (For more details and expressions on payment options, see Chapter 8.)

WARNING

Prices are inclusive of 부가가치세 (boo-gah-gah-chee-seh) (*Value Added Tax (VAT)*), so what you see is what you pay — no extra calculations needed! Remember to ask for a 영수증 (yuhng-soo-jeung) (*receipt*).

카드로 결제할게요. (kah-deu-roh gyuhl-jjeh-hahl-kkeh-yoh) (*I'll pay by credit card.*)

현금으로 계산할게요. (hyuhn-geu-meu-roh gyeh-sahn-hahl-kkeh-yoh) (*I'll settle the bill/pay with cash.*)

일시불로 할게요. (eel-ssee-bool-loh hahl-kkeh-yoh) (*I'll pay in full.*)

3개월 할부로 해 주세요. (sahm-gae-wuhl hahl-boo-roh hae joo-seh-yoh) (*Please let me make a three-month installment payment.*)

Tax Refund

Check if the store offers a 세금 환급 (seh-geum hwahn-geup) (*tax refund*) by looking for signs ("Tax Refund" or "Tax Free") around the store or on your receipt. You can also ask "세금 환급 돼요?" (seh-geum hwahn-geup dwae-yoh) (*Is a tax refund available?*). Claim your tax refund at departure by presenting your 영수증 (yuhng-soo-jeung) (*receipts*), 여권 (yuh-kkwuhn) (*passport*), and purchased items. Some stores, like Olive Young in metropolitan cities, offer immediate tax refunds. You can also find city tax refund booths/kiosks in large tourist areas — a savvy shopper's bonus! For more details, visit the VisitKorea website (`https://english.visitkorea.or.kr`) under "Duty Free & Tax Refunds."

FUN & GAMES

Please match the type of store with the item you would find in the store.
The answers are found in Appendix C.

a. 꽃집 (kkoht-jjeep) _____

b. 문구점 (moon-goo-juhm) _____

c. 제과점 (jeh-gwah-juhm) _____

d. 옷가게 (oht-kkah-geh) _____

e. 정육점 (juhng-yook-jjuhm) _____

f. 생선가게 (saeng-suhn-gah-geh) _____

g. 서점 (suh-juhm) _____

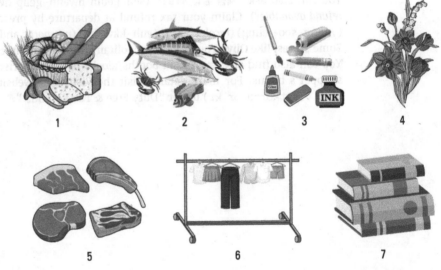

1   2   3   4

5   6   7

© John Wiley & Sons, Inc.

Chapter **11**

Exploring the Town

When traveling, what's your go-to activity after settling into your room and unpacking your luggage? Perhaps you head out for a meal or explore the town if your 시차 (shee-chah) (*jet lag*) hasn't kicked in yet. No worries if you're unsure where to start! From historical cultural venues to vibrant nightlife, Korea has something for everyone at every hour of the day.

You might be keen on exploring 한국 역사 (hahn-gook yuhk-ssah) (*Korean history*) and 문화 (moon-hwah) (*culture*) at various museums or historical sites. Alternatively, you might enjoy 문화 체험 (moon-hwah cheh-huhm) (*cultural hands-on activities*). If relaxation is more your speed, consider catching a movie, or exploring unique cafés and various "방 문화" (bahng moon-hwah) (*room cultures; room-based activities*).

This chapter covers the essentials you need to navigate the art and culture of Korea. So, without further ado, let's dive right in!

Exploring Fun Places

CULTURAL WISDOM

First off, it's good to familiarize yourself with some key local 검색 엔진 (guhm-saek ehn-jeen) (*search engines*) and apps before you set out to explore the area. Korea's No.1 portal site, 네이버 (*Naver*) (www.naver.com), is available as an app that can be viewed in English. Additionally, 파파고 (*Papago*) (papago.naver.com), the most popular AI translator in Korea, can be a pretty handy tool for overcoming language barriers. For navigation, 네이버 지도 (Naver Maps) (map.naver.com) offers a reliable, most widely used mapping service in English.

Other handy apps include *VisitKorea*, *VisitSeoul*, and *Discover Seoul Pass* for comprehensive travel insights, *Kakao Taxi* and *TABA* (exclusive to foreigners) for taxi-hailing services, and *Subway Korea* for detailed subway maps and schedules, among others.

When searching for places to visit, consider exploring:

>> **(놀이)공원** ((noh-ree-)gohng-wuhn) (*(amusement) park*)

>> **미술관** (mee-sool-gwahn) (*art museum*)

>> **박물관** (bahng-mool-gwahn) (*museum*)

>> **서점** (suh-juhm) (*bookstore*)

>> **영화관** (yuhng-hwah-gwahn) (*movie theater*)

>> **전시장** (juhn-shee-jahng) (*exhibit hall*)

>> **문화체험관** (moon-hwah-cheh-huhm-gwahn) (*cultural experience center*)

For performance-related experiences, add these to your vocabulary:

>> **공연/콘서트** (gohng-yuhn/kohn-ssuh-teu) (*performance, show, concert*)

>> **뮤지컬** (myoo-jee-kuhl) (*musical*)

>> **연극** (yuhn-geuk) (*drama/play*)

>> **영화** (yuhng-hwah) (*movie*)

>> **전시회** (juhn-shee-hwae) (*exhibition*)

Visiting museums and galleries

CULTURAL WISDOM

Exploring 박물관 (*museums*) or 미술관 (*art museums*) is a great way to kick off your trip. 서울 (suh-ool) (*Seoul*) has numerous large-scale 박물관, but don't miss out on the smaller, intriguing ones outside of the capital, too. Some are even 무료 (moo-ryoh) (*free of charge*), including the 국립중앙박물관 (goong-neep-joong-ahng-bahng-mool-gwahn) (*National Museum of Korea*), 한글 박물관 (hahn-geul bahng-mool-gwahn) (*National Hangeul Museum*), and the 전쟁 기념관 (juhn-jaeng-gee-nyuhm-gwahn) (*War Memorial of Korea*).

For a unique experience, check out some 이색 박물관 (ee-saek bahng-mool-gwahn) (*unique museums*) like the *Museum of Kimchikan*, where you can immerse yourself in all things 김치 (*Kimchi*) and even learn to make some yourself! Keep an eye out for museums that offer guided tours and English-supported apps, like the National Museum of Korea app.

Before heading out, here are some useful phrases to keep in mind. Some places are closed on 월요일 (wuh-ryoh-eel) (*Mondays*). *To open* is 열어요 (yuh-ruh-yoh), *to close* is 닫아요 (dah-dah-yoh), and *to run/operate* is 해요 (hae-yoh). With these verbs, you can ask important questions about their 운영 시간 (oo-nyuhng shee-gahn) (*business hours*) or special exhibit periods:

Q: 역사박물관, [월요일]에 열어요? (yuhk-ssah-bahng-mool-gwahn, [wuh-ryoh-ee]-reh yuh-ruh-yoh) (*Is the history museum open on [Monday]?*)

A: 아니요, 닫아요. (ah-nee-yoh, dah-dah-yoh) (*No, it's closed.*)

Q: 미술관, 몇 시에 열어요? (mee-sool-gwahn myuht ssee-eh yuh-ruh-yoh) (*What time does the art museum open?*)

A: 아홉 시에 열어요. (ah-hohp ssee-eh yuh-ruh-yoh) (*It opens at 9.*)

Q: 몇 시에 닫아요? (myuht ssee-eh dah-dah-yoh) (*What time does it close?*)

A: [여섯] 시요. ([yuh-suht] ssee-yoh) (*[6] o'clock.*)

You can also inquire about the range of hours or dates using the particles 부터 (boo-tuh) (*from*) and 까지 (kkah-jee) (*until*):

Q: 박물관, 몇 시부터 몇 시까지 해요? (bahng-mool-gwahn myuht ssee-boo-tuh myuht ssee-kkah-jee hae-yoh) (*From what time to what time does the museum operate?*)

A: 열 시부터 네 시까지 해요. (yuhl ssee-boo-tuh neh shee-kkah-jee hae-yoh) (*It runs from 10 to 4.*)

Q: 특별전시회, 언제부터 언제까지 해요? (teuk-ppyuhl-juhn-shee-hwae, uhn-jeh-boo-tuh uhn-jeh-kkah-jee hae-yoh) (*From when to when does the special exhibition run?*)

A: 2월 10일부터 24일까지 해요. (ee-wuhl shee-beel-boo-tuh ee-sheep-ssah-eel-kkah-jee hae-yoh) (*It runs from February 10th to 24th.*)

Feel free to explore other questions you might want to ask, such as:

박물관 지도 있어요? (bahng-mool-gwahn jee-doh ee-ssuh-yoh) (*Do you have a museum map?*)

사진 찍어도 돼요? (sah-jeen jjee-guh-doh dwae-yoh) (*Can I take photos?*)

입장료 있어요? 얼마예요? (eep-jjahng-nyoh ee-ssuh-yoh? uhl-mah-yeh-yoh) (*Is there an admission fee? How much is it?*)

영어 오디오 안내 서비스 있어요? (yuhng-uh oh-dee-oh ahn-nae ssuh-bee-sseu ee-ssuh-yoh) (*Is there an English audio guide service?*)

영어 가이드투어 몇 시에 해요? (yuhng-uh gah-ee-deu too-uh myuht ssee-eh hae-yoh) (*What time do you have the English guided tour?*)

Touring historical sites

Besides 박물관 and 미술관, consider exploring the rich history of Korea by visiting its historical sites. Many have been transformed to parks and historical landmarks, offering guided tours. 서울 (suh-ool) (*Seoul*) alone is home to five remaining (고)궁 ((goh-)goong) (*palaces*) from the 조선 왕조 (joh-suhn wahng-joh) (*Joseon Dynasty*). 경복궁 (gyuhng-bohk-kkoong) (*Gyeongbokgung Palace*), dating back to 1395, is the largest among them and offers a glimpse into traditional Korean architecture and landscapes. For those seeking a fun cultural experience, consider renting 한복 (hahn-bohk) (*Korean traditional costumes*) from a nearby rental place, for photos in these palaces.

For another immersive cultural experience, venture to 민속촌 (meen-sohk-chohn) (*folk villages*) and 한옥 마을 (hah-nohk mah-eul) (*Hanok villages; traditional villages*). 용인 한국민속촌 (*Yongin Korean Folk Village*) is the largest of its kind, where you can partake in 전통 혼례 (juhn-tohng hohl-lyeh) (*traditional wedding ceremonies*), enjoy various 전통 공연 (juhn-tohng gohng-yuhn) (*traditional performances*), and engage in 체험 활동 (cheh-huhm hwahl-ttohng) (*hands-on activities*). Be sure not to miss the 야간 개장 (yah-gahn gae-jahng) (*nighttime openings*) during the summer, extending the fun beyond regular hours!

Here are some handy phrases to utilize:

[매표소] 어디예요? ([mae-pyoh-soh] uh-dee-yeh-yoh) (*Where is the [ticket office]?*)

[안내소] 어디예요? (ahn-nae-soh uh-dee-yeh-yoh) (*Where is the [information desk]?*)

[물품보관함] 있어요? (mool-poom-boh-gwahn-hahm ee-ssuh-yoh) (*Do you have [storage lockers]?*)

[오디오 가이드] 대여하려고 해요. (oh-dee-oh gah-ee-deu dae-yuh-hah-ryuh-goh hae-yoh) (*I'm going to rent an audio guide.*)

[한복] 대여하려고 해요. ([hahn-bohk] dae-yuh-hah-ryuh-goh hae-yoh) (*I'm going to rent [Hanbok].*)

[체험 활동] 예약하려고 해요. ([cheh-huhm hwahl-ttohng] yeh-yahk-kah-ryuh-goh hae-yoh) (*I'm going to reserve [hands-on activity programs].*)

인터넷에서 표 예매했어요. (een-tuh-neh-seh-suh pyoh yeh-mae-hae-ssuh-yoh) (*I purchased a ticket on the Internet in advance.*)

Talkin' the Talk

PLAY

Peter and his friends visited the Korean folk village in Yongin. Peter is buying tickets at the ticket booth.

Clerk: 몇 장 드릴까요?
myuht jjahng deu-reel-kkah-yoh?
How many tickets do you need?

Peter: 어른 세 장 주세요. 얼마예요?
uh-reun seh-jahng joo-seh-yoh. uhl-mah-yeh-yoh?
Three adults, please. How much is it?

Clerk: 십만 오천 원입니다.
sheem-mahn oh-chuhn wuh-neem-nee-dah.
It's 105,000 won.

Peter: 오디오 가이드 있어요?
oh-dee-oh gah-ee-deu ee-ssuh-yoh?
Do you have an audio guide?

Clerk: 네. 여기 있습니다.
neh. yuh-gee eet-sseum-nee-dah.
Yes. Here it is.

Peter: 물품보관함 어디 있어요?
mool-poom-boh-kwahn-hahm uh-dee ee-ssuh-yoh?
Where are the lockers?

Clerk: 저기 안내소 안에 있어요.
juh-gee ahn-nae-soh ah-neh ee-ssuh-yoh.
It's inside the information center over there.

Peter: 고맙습니다.
goh-mahp-sseum-nee-dah.
Thank you.

WORDS TO KNOW

몇 장	myuht jjahng	how many tickets (장: noun counter)
드릴까요? (드리다)	deu-reel-kkah-yoh	shall I give. . .? (드리다: humble form of 주다)
어른	uh-reun	adult
얼마예요?	uhl-mah-yeh-yoh	how much is it?
안내소	ahn-nae-soh	information center

Taking in the Korean Popular Culture

Shifting gears to pop culture, even if you're not an avid fan of K-pop or K-dramas, exploring Korean pop culture-themed tours and activities can be a fun adventure! Korea's entertainment industry and 대중 문화 (dae-joong moon-hwah) (*pop culture*) have gained significant global recognition, sparking the phenomenon known as 한류 (hahl-lyoo) (*Hallyu; Korean Wave*). You've probably come across global hits like Psy's "강남스타일" (gahng-nahm seu-tah-eel) (*Gangnam Style*) from 2013 or music from idol groups like BTS (방탄소년단; bahng-tahn soh-nyuhn-dahn). Additionally, you may have enjoyed in the Netflix mega-hit "오징어 게임" (oh-jeeng-uh geh-eem) (*Squid Game*). Nowadays, 한류 extends beyond K-pop and K-dramas to encompass other aspects like food and films. The next section introduces you some engaging activities, useful resources, and handy phrases for your 한류-themed adventures.

Delving into the K-pop and K-dramas

Explore the following websites for a variety of hands-on activities, from K-pop 댄스 수업 (daen-sseu soo-uhp) (*dance classes*) and K-food 요리 (yoh-ree) (*cooking*) sessions to 전통주 (juhn-tohng-joo) (*traditional liquor*), 전통 공예 (juhn-tohng gohng-yeh) (*traditional crafts*), and even K-beauty 메이크업 (meh-ee-keu-uhp) (*makeup*) classes. You can also discover 드라마 촬영지 (deu-rah-mah chwah-ryuhng-jee) (*drama filming locations*) online:

» VisitSeoul (https://english.visitseoul.net/hallyu)

» VisitKorea (https://english.visitkorea.or.kr/svc/thingsToDo/hallyu.do)

Excitingly, some of these activities are free! Be sure to book in advance as seats and dates are limited. Additionally, travel blogs like Trazy.com (https://blog.trazy.com) offer helpful guides for K-pop enthusiasts, covering tour programs, entertainment companies, nearby activities, and more.

GRAMMATICALLY
SPEAKING

To express your desire to participate in these activities in Korean, you can use this pattern: "[verb stem]고 싶어요 (goh shee-puh-yoh) (*I want to [verb]*). For instance, if you want to say "I want to go," the verb for *to go* is 가다 (gah-dah). Combine the verb stem, 가, with 고 싶어요, and you get 가고 싶어요 (gah-goh shee-puh-yoh). Read on for more examples in Table 11-1.

TABLE 11-1 고 싶다 Conjugations and Examples

Verb	Meaning	Examples
하다 (hah-dah)	to do	뭐 하고 싶어요? (mwuh hah-goh shee-puh-yoh) (*What do you want to do?*)
가다 (gah-dah)	to go	어디(에) 가고 싶어요? (uh-dee(-eh) gah-goh shee-puh-yoh) (*Where do you want to go?*)
가보다 (gah-boh-dah)	to visit/check out the place	드라마 촬영지에 가보고 싶어요. (deu-rah-mah chwah-ryuhng-jee-eh gah-boh-goh sheep-puh-yoh) (*I want to visit the drama filming place.*)
듣다 (deut-ttah)	(1) to listen (2) to take (a class)	무슨 음악 듣고 싶어요? K-pop 자주 들어요? (moo-seun eu-mahk deut-kkoh shee-puh-yoh? K-pop deu-ruh-yoh) (*What music do you want to listen to? Do you often listen to K-pop?*) 케이팝 댄스 수업 듣고 싶어요. (k-pop daen-sseu soo-uhp deut-kkoh shee-puh-yoh) (*I want to take a K-pop dance class.*)
배우다 (bae-oo-dah)	to learn	한국 요리 배우고 싶어요. (hahn-gook yoh-ree bae-oo-goh shee-puh-yoh) (*I want to learn Korean cooking.*)
만들다 (mahn-deul-dah)	to make	전통 공예 만들고 싶어요. (juhn-tohng gohng-yeh mahn-deul-goh shee-puh-yoh) (*I want to make traditional crafts.*)
먹어보다 (muh-guh-boh-dah)	to try the food	길거리 음식 먹어보고 싶어요. (geel-kkuh-ree eum-sheek muh-guh-boh-goh shee-puh-yoh) (*I want to try street food.*)

On the big screen: Going to theaters

한국 영화 (hahn-gook yuhng-hwah) (*Korean movies*) are also a huge part of 한류. You may have heard of the award-winning black comedy thriller "기생충" (gee-saeng-choong) (*Parasite*) and many others that have also been the spotlight at various 국제 영화제 (gook-jjeh yuhng-hwah-jeh) (*international film festivals*).

CULTURAL WISDOM

However, the movie industry has been significantly affected by the COVID-19 pandemic. While streaming services at home offer great convenience, watching 새 개봉 영화 (sae gae-bohng yuhng-hwah) (*newly released movies*) in a 영화관 (yuhng-hwah-kwahn) (*movie theater*) is still a unique experience. Some multiplex theaters have creatively amped up the moviegoing experience with unique theme interiors, such as living-room themes with reclining beds and butler service. CGV, one of the largest multiplex cinema brands in Korea, has even transformed some of its theaters into climbing gyms, hoping to attract movie watchers to the theater. (Their high ceilings and slanted floors are perfect for climbing walls!) Check if there are any cool 영화관 near your hotel for a unique experience!

The verb most commonly associated with going to a 영화 or any 공연 (gohng-yuhn) (*performance*) is 보다 (boh-dah) (*to watch/see*). See Table 11-2 to learn how 보다 is conjugated to convey different meanings.

TABLE 11-2 **보다 Conjugations and Examples**

Endings	Conjugated Form	Examples
아/어요 (informal polite: present)	봐요 (bwah-yoh)	영화 자주 봐요? 네, 자주 봐요. (yuhng-hwah jah-joo bwah-yoh? neh, jah-joo bwah-yoh) (*Do you watch movies often? Yes, I watch (movies) often.*)
았/었어요 (informal polite: past)	봤어요 (bwah-ssuh-yoh)	공연 잘 봤어요? (gohng-yuhn jahl bwah-ssuh-yoh) (*Did you watch the performance well? = Did you enjoy the performance?*)
(으)세요 (polite request)	보세요 (boh-seh-yoh)	그 영화 재미있어요. 꼭 보세요. (geu yuhng-hwah jae-mee-ee-ssuh-yoh. kkohk boh-seh-yoh) (*The movie is fun. You really should watch it.*)
(으)ㄹ까요? (*Shall we/I?*)	볼까요? (bohl-kkah-yoh)	뭐 볼까요? 무슨 영화 좋아해요? (mwuh bohl-kkah-yoh? moo-seun yuhng-hwah joh-ah-hae-yoh) (*What shall we watch? What kinds of movie do you like?*)
(으)ㄹ래요? (*Would you like to?*)	볼래요? (bohl-lae-yoh)	몇 시 영화 볼래요? (myuht ssee yuhng-hwah bohl-lae-yoh) (*What time would you like to watch the movie?*)
고 싶다 (*want to*)	보고 싶어요 (boh-goh shee-puh-yoh)	뭐 보고 싶어요? 연극 보고 싶어요. (mwuh boh-goh shee-puh-yoh? yuhn-geuk boh-goh shee-puh-yoh) (*What do you want to watch? I want to watch a drama play.*)
(으)ㄹ 거예요 (future plan)	볼 거예요 (bohl kkuh-yeh-yoh)	뭐 볼 거예요? (mwuh bohl kkuh-yeh-yoh?) (*What are you going to watch?*)

Hopping Around Cafés and Pubs

If you're interested in exploring areas in Seoul with a youthful vibe or vibrant nightlife scenes, then you may want to check out 홍대 (hohng-dae) (*Hongdae*), 강남 (gahng-nahm) (*Gangnam*), 명동 (myuhng-dohng) (*Myeongdong*), or 이태원 (ee-tae-wuhn) (*Itaewon*). These neighborhoods are well-known for their 식당 (sheek-ttahng) (*restaurants*), 카페 (kah-peh) (*cafés*), 클럽 (keul-luhp) (*clubs*), bars and shops. In particular, 홍대 is popular for indie art. You'll find busking musicians, street dance performers, local shops, and art markets, along with many trendy 카페.

CULTURAL WISDOM

When exploring cafés and pubs in Seoul, get ready for a unique experience. You'll notice cafés lining the streets everywhere. For something special, seek out 이색 카페 (ee-saek kah-peh) (*unique cafés*). Imagine sipping coffee with friendly 개 (gae) (*dogs*), 고양이 (goh-yahng-ee) (*cats*), or even 양 (yahng) (*sheep*). Enjoy tea while crafting 반지 (bahn-jee) (*rings*), building with Legos, or relaxing in a 해먹 (hae-muhk) (*hammock*) reminiscent of a Spanish Siesta. Try "salt healing" in a 소금 (soh-geum) (*salt*) 카페. Korea's 카페 culture is creative and diverse, adding a fun twist to your coffee experience!

Another distinct feature is 안주 (ahn-joo) found in pubs. It refers to varying dishes paired with drinks, ranging from complimentary snacks like 땅콩 (ttahng-kohng) (*peanuts*) and 마른 오징어 (mah-reun oh-jeeng-uh) (*dried squid*) to heartier options like 파전 (pah-juhn) (*scallion pancakes*) and 삼겹살 (sahm-gyuhp-ssahl) (*grilled pork belly*), perfect for accompanying your drinks. Plus, many spots have a handy call button at each table for calling waitstaff. How convenient! For some useful phrases while navigating cafés and pubs, check out Table 11-3.

CULTURAL WISDOM

If you're out at a restaurant or a pub and end up consuming some alcohol, remember that 음주 운전 (eum-joo oon-juhn) (*driving under the influence*) is 불법 (bool-ppuhp) (*illegal*), as it is worldwide. (The legal drinking age is 19 in Korea). If you're unable to find a sober ride home, you can always call for 대리 운전 (dae-lee oon-juhn) (*designated driver service, proxy driving*), available 24/7. A 대리 운전 기사 (dae-ree oon-juhn gee-sah) (*substitute driver*) will come to your location, drive your car, and get you to your destination. Many pubs and restaurants have 명함 (myuhng-hahm) (*business cards*) of these 대리 운전 기사. It's a hassle-free, reliable service that people turn to after a night of drinking.

TABLE 11-3 **Activities Related to Exploring**

Verbs	Meaning	Examples
계산하다 (gyeh-sahn-hah-dah)	to pay	**계산할게요.** 계산서 주세요. (gyeh-sahn-hahl-kkeh-yoh. gyeh-sahn-suh joo-seh-yoh) (*I would like to pay. Can I have the bill, please?*)
놀다 (nohl-dah)	to hang out	주말에 홍대에서 **놀았어요.** (joo-mah-leh hong-dae-eh-suh noh-rah-ssuh-yoh) (*We hung out at the Hondae area on the weekend.*)
마시다 (mah-shee-dah)	to drink	커피 **마실래요?** (kuh-pee mah-sheel-lae-yoh) (*Would you like to drink coffee?*)
만나다 (mahn-nah-dah)	to meet	어디에서 **만날까요?** [신촌]에서 **만나요.** (uh-dee-eh-suh mahn-nahl-kkah-yoh sheen-choh-neh-suh mahn-nah-yoh) (*Where shall we meet? Let's meet at [Shinchon].*)
자리가 있다 (jah-ree-gah eet-ttah)	a seat to be available	여기 **자리 있어요.** (yuh-gee jah-ree ee-ssuh-yoh) (*There is a seat here/This seat is available.*)
앉다 (ahn-ttah)	to sit	여기 **앉아도 돼요?** (yuh-gee ahn-jah-doh dwae-yoh?) (*Can I sit here?*)
주문하다 (joo-moon-hah-dah)	to order	여기요! **주문할게요.** (yuh-gee-yoh! joo-moon-hahl-kkeh-yoh) (*Excuse me! We'd like to order.*)
얘기하다 (yae-gee-hah-dah)	to talk	카페에서 **얘기해요.** (kah-peh-eh-suh yae-gee-hae-yoh) (*Let's talk at a coffeeshop.*)
취하다 (chwee-hah-dah)	to be drunk	좀 **취했어요.** 그만 마셔요. (johm chwee-hae-ssuh-yoh. geu-mahn mah-shyuh-yoh) (*You're a bit drunk. Stop drinking.*)

Experiencing Korean "Bahng" Culture

In Korea, you frequently hear the word 방 (bahng) (*room*), which doesn't necessarily mean the rooms at home. The variety of public 방 offers different types of entertainment. They are everywhere, accessible, and very affordable. Let's check out Korean 방 to get you ready for your trip!

Noh-rae-bahng

노래방 (noh-rae-bahng) (*Korean-style karaoke room*), literally meaning "song room," is a popular destinations for Koreans of all ages. Unlike Western karaoke, where a machine is set up in the corner of a venue or restaurant, 노래방 is a room specifically designed for karaoke. Koreans like to go to 노래방 to unwind from the hard work week and to belt out tunes to relieve stress. Nowadays, 코인 (koh-een) (*coin*) 노래방, where you can pay a tiny fee per song instead of renting a room by the hour, is very popular. Don't worry if you don't know the 가사 (gah-sah) (*lyrics*) to any Korean songs because 노래방 offers a selection spanning over many languages!

Even if you're not a good singer, don't shy away when a Korean friend suggests this activity. Although it could potentially be embarrassing for both of you, it can be a disarming activity that brings you closer to your friend or partner. Also, don't get discouraged if the 노래방 machine gives you a low 점수 (juhm-soo) (*score*) at the end of your song. It doesn't have anything to do with your actual vocal talent. (Here's a secret: The louder you sing, the higher the 점수 you get!) Check out these handy 노래방-related phrases:

노래방에 갈래요? (noh-rae-bahng-eh gahl-lae-yoh) (*Would you like to go to noraebang?*)

무슨 노래 하고 싶어요? (moo-seun noh-rae hah-goh shee-puh-yoh) (*What (kinds of) songs do you want to sing?*)

[이 노래] 알아요? [이거] 같이 부를래요? ([ee noh-rae] ah-rah-yoh? [ee-guh] gah-chee boo-reul-lae-yoh?) (*Do you know [this song]? Would you like to sing [this] together?*)

[이 노래] 들어 봤어요? (ee noh-rae deu-ruh bwah-ssuh-yoh) (*Have you listened to [this song]?*)

30분 더 (노래)할래요? (sahm-sheep-ppoon duh (noh-rae-)hahl-lae-yoh) (*Do you want to do/sing 30 more minutes?*)

노래 잘하네요! (noh-rae jahl-hah-neh-yoh) (*You're so good at singing!*)

You can replace [이 노래] with a specific song title.

Jjeem-jeel-bahng

찜질방 (jjeem-jeel-bahng) (*Korean sauna/bathhouses*) are another must-try in Korea. The act of "찜질" can best be described as a massage using a hot or cold pack, or going into hot water, sand, or a sauna to sweat it out. It helps detoxify, relieve pain, and improve circulation. 찜질방 is like a 5-in-1 package with 사우나 (ssah-oo-nah) (*sauna*). Inside the 찜질방 are 사우나, 목욕탕 (moh-gyohk-tahng) (*baths*), 식당 (sheek-ttahng) (*restaurant*), 오락 시설 (oh-rahk shee-suhl) (*entertainment facilities*), and even a 수면실 (soo-myuhn-sheel) (*sleeping room*). 목욕탕 and 수면실 are separated by gender, but the other facilities are co-ed and require you to wear 찜질복 (jjeem-jeel-bohk) (*Korean bathhouse uniforms*).

목욕탕 (moh-gyohk-tahng) (*baths*) is where you take a deep bath, exfoliate, or shower. Big bathhouses offer herbal tubs like 쑥 (ssook) (*mugwort*). Make sure you shower before plunging into the bathtub or entering a 사우나. Want to try something very new? 목욕탕 has professional exfoliators who are trained to scrub and massage. For 사우나, multiple rooms kept at a range of temperatures from piping hot to freezing cold are available, so find the room that suits you. The rooms are also filled with materials like jade stones, charcoal, mud, crystals, or special types of wood.

Another fun part of 찜질방 is 식당 or 분식점 (boon-sheek-jjuhm) (*snack bar*). Popular 분식 메뉴 (boon-sheek meh-nyoo) (*snack menu*) include 구운 계란 (goo-oon gyeh-rahn) (*baked eggs*), 식혜 (sheek-kyeh) (*sweet rice drink*), and 미역국 (mee-yuhk-kkook) (*seaweed soup*), alongside a variety of meal options at reasonable prices.

Don't miss out on their 오락 시설 (oh-rahk shee-suhl) (*entertainment facilities*) like TV and movie rooms, comic book libraries, and game rooms, among others. For a budget-friendly option, look for 24/7 찜질방 in big cities, where you can stay over-night instead of at a pricey hotel!

All in all, 찜질방 offers a unique blend of 한국 문화 (hahn-gook moon-hwah) (*Korean culture*), traditional wellness practices, and modern entertainment. Enjoy the experience! For essential terms related to 찜질방, check out the following list.

>> **목욕 용품 (moh-gyohk yohng-poom) (*bath products*):** 때수건 (ttae-soo-guhn) (*exfoliating mitten*), 바디워시 (bah-dee-wuh-shee) (*body wash*), 비누 (bee-noo) (*soap*), 린스 (leen-sseu) (*conditioner*), 샴푸 (shyahm-poo) (*shampoo*), 수건/타월 (soo-guhn/tah-wuhl) (*towel*), 칫솔 (cheet-ssohl) (*toothbrush*), 치약 (chee-yahk) (*toothpaste*)

>> **서비스 & 시설 (ssuh-bee-sseu & shee-suhl) (*services & facilities*):** 냉탕 (naeng-tahng) (*cold bath*), 온탕 (ohn-tahng) (*hot bath*), 세신 (seh-sheen) (*exfoliation (service)*), 사물함 (sah-mool-hahm) (*locker*), 신발장 (sheen-bahl-jjahng) (*shoe locker*), 열쇠/키 (yuhl-sswae/kee) (*key*), 탈의실 (tah-ree-sheel) (*exchange room*), 찜질방옷/찜질복 (jjeem-jeel-bahng-oht/jjeem-jeel-bohk) (*jjeem-jeel-bahng clothes*)

TIP

The items are provided or available for purchase on-site. When you need any of these, simply use the pattern, [item] 있어요? (ee-ssuh-yoh) (*Do you have [item]?*) or [item] 주세요 (joo-seh-yoh) (*Please give [item]*).

[치약]하고 [칫솔] 있어요? ([chee-yahk-]hah-goh [cheet-ssohl] ee-ssuh-yoh) (*Do you have [toothpaste] and [toothbrush]?*)

[찜질복, 라지 사이즈] 주세요. (jjeem-jeel-bohk, lah-jee ssah-ee-jeu joo-seh-yoh) (*Can you give me a [large size jjeem-jeel-bohk]?*)

PC-bahng and Mahn-hwah-bahng

PC 방/피시방 (pee-ssee-bahng) are similar to 인터넷 카페 (een-tuh-neht kah-peh) (*internet cafés*), where you can check your 이메일 (ee-meh-eel) (*emails*) or search for travel info. Yet, PC 방 differs from the typical 인터넷 카페; it's catered more toward 컴퓨터 게임 (kuhm-pyoo-tuh geh-eem) (*computer games*). Feeling hungry while you're there? No problem! You can order yummy 분식 (boon-sheek) (*snack food*) on the spot.

Similarly, if you're a cartoon lover and want to kick back with a wide variety of 만화 (mahn-hwah) (comics), swing by 만화방 (mahn-hwah-bahng). They've got you covered for both entertainment and snacks to order, just like other 방s. Some places even combine 피시방 and 만화방 for double the fun!

Here are some handy phrases to ask about 시간당 요금 (shee-gahn-dahng yoh-geum) (hourly rates) at these 방s. (For more on Korean numbers, check out Chapter 5.)

한 시간에 얼마예요? (hahn shee-gah-neh uhl-mah-yeh-yoh?) (How much is it per hour?)

[패키지 요금], 얼마예요? (pae-kee-jee yoh-geum, uhl-mah-yeh-yoh?) (What is the [package rate]?)

평일은 [3500]원, 주말은 [4000]원입니다. (pyuhng-ee-reun [sahm-chuh-noh-baek]-wuhn, joo-mah-reun [sah-chuhn]-wuh-neem-nee-dah) (It's [3,500] won for weekdays, and [4,000] won for weekends.)

회원은 [2500]원, 비회원은 [3000]원입니다. (hwae-wuh-neun [ee-chuh-noh-baek]-wuhn, bee-hwae-wuh-neun [sahm-chuhn]-wuhn-eem-nee-dah) (It's [2,500] won for members, and [3,000] won for non-members.)

FUN & GAMES

Match the following fun places with their English translation. You probably know more answers than you realize!

1. 박물관   a. movie theater

2. 피시방   b. comic book room

3. 찜질방   c. museum

4. 민속촌   d. Korean bathhouse

5. 만화방   e. folk village

6. 영화관   f. internet café

7. 노래방   g. art gallery

8. 미술관   h. Korean-style karaoke

Turn to Appendix C for the answers.

Chapter **12**

Connecting Across the World: Phones, Mail, and the Internet

전화 (juhn-hwah) (*phones*) and the 인터넷 (een-tuh-neht) (*internet*) are integral to our daily lives, from local catch-ups to global interactions. While emails, texts, and DMs are widespread, traditional phone calls and 일반 우편 (eel-bahn oo-pyuhn) (*snail mail, postal mail*) still hold significance for their personal touch.

Whether you're calling across 시간대 (shee-gahn-dae) (*time zones*) or sending a sweet 소포 (soh-poh) (*package*) halfway around the world, this chapter helps you make those connections in Korean. It's packed with key words and phrases for different 통신 수단 (tohng-sheen soo-dahn) (*means of communication*). Get ready to enhance your Korean communication skills with newfound confidence!

Phoning Made Easy

Kicking off with phone etiquette, the typical greeting 여보세요? (yuh-boh-seh-yoh) (*Hello?*) is your go-to way to start a phone conversation. It's simple yet effective. You can also add 안녕하세요 (ahn-nyuhng-hah-seh-yoh) (*Hello/How are you?*) before introducing yourself.

The upcoming sections explore essential phone vocabulary, including how to make calls and leave messages in Korean.

Brushing up on phone vocabulary

The key verbs for phone communication are 전화하다 (juhn-hwah-hah-dah) (*to call, to talk on the phone*), and 문자하다 (moon-jjah-hah-dah) (*to text*), both ending in 하다 (hah-dah) (*to do*). As you might have guessed, 전화 means "phone" and 문자 means "text."

When calling or texting, use different particles: [person]한테 (*to a [person]*), [person]하고 (*with a [person]*), and [place]에 (*to a [place]*). Table 12-1 presents how to use these verbs in sentences:

THE HANDY DANDY "HANDPHONE"

In Korea, a cell phone is called 휴대폰 (hyoo-dae-pohn), 휴대 전화 (hyoo-dae juhn-hwah) (*carry around phone*), or more literally, 핸드폰 (haen-deu-pohn) (*hand phone*). As soon as you land, you can rent one at airports or most major hotels. The three major telecom companies are KT, SK, and LG U+. You can snag a physical SIM card at 공항 편의점 (gohng-hahng pyuh-nee-juhm) (*airport convenience stores*), order one online from *EGsimcard.co.kr* or *KRSim.net*, or opt for an eSIM from *eSimKorea.net*.

Over here, 휴대폰 is key. As the birthplace of tech giants like 삼성 (sahm-suhng) (*Samsung*) and LG, coupled with high internet penetration, features like contactless payment were available in Korea long before they became widespread elsewhere. With just a few taps, you can handle a lot of things from banking to real-time bus tracking, and much more. Consequently, many household have replaced their home landlines with individual 휴대폰.

TABLE 12-1   **How to Use To Call and To Text**

	Informal polite	Example Sentences
Present	해요	[친구]한테 자주 전화해요/문자해요. ([cheen-goo]-**hahn-teh** jah-joo juhn-hwah-hae-yoh/moon-jjah-hae-yoh) (*I often call/text [a friend]*.)
Past	했어요	[친구]하고 매일 전화했어요. ([cheen-goo]-**hah-goh** mae-eel juhn-hwah-hae-ssuh-yoh) (*I talked **with** [a friend] on the phone everyday.*)
Future	할 거예요	언제 전화할 거예요? (uhn-jeh juhn-hwah-hahl kkuh-yeh-yoh) (*When are you going to call?*)
Promisory	할게요	내일 전화할게요/문자할게요. (nae-eel juhn-hwah-hahl-kkeh-yoh/moon-jjah-hahl-kkeh-yoh) (*I will call/text you tomorrow.*)
Obligation	해야 돼요	[집]에 전화해야 돼요. ([jee-b]**eh** juhn-hwah-hae-yah dwae-yoh) (*I need to call [home]*.)
Permission	해도 돼요	[8시쯤] 전화해도 돼요? 네. 아무 때나 괜찮아요. ([yuh-duhl ssee-jjeum] juhn-hwah-hae-doh dwae-yoh? neh, ah-moo ttae-nah gwaen-chah-nah-yoh) (*Is it okay to call you [around 8 o'clock]? Yes, anytime is okay.*)
Prohibition	하지 마세요	[밤늦게] 전화하지 마세요. ([bahm-neu-kkeh] juhn-hwah-hah-jee mah-seh-yoh) (*Please don't call [late at night]*.)
Polite command	하세요	도움이 필요하면 [저한테/서비스 센터에] 전화하세요. (doh-oo-mee pee-ryoh-hah-myuhn [juh-hahn-teh/ssuh-bee-sseu-ssehn-tuh-eh) juhn-hwah-hah-seh-yoh) (*If you need help, please call [me/service center]*.)

TIP

Here are some more key verbs. You can replace the terms in brackets with any means of communication like 문자, 이메일 (ee-meh-eel) (emails), 카드 (kah-deu) (cards), 편지 (pyuhn-jee) (letters) or DM.

[전화] 오다 (juhn-hwah oh-dah) (literally "[a call] comes"=to receive [a call].) * from: [person]한테서, [place]에서

[전화] 받다 (juhn-hwah baht-ttah) (to receive/answer [the phone])

[문자] 보내다 (moon-jjah boh-nae-dah) (to send [a text])

See the examples below to learn how these phrases can be used in conversation:

[동생]한테서 전화가 와요. 잠시만요. 전화 좀 받을게요. ([dohng-saeng]-hahn-teh-suh juhn-hwah-gah wah-yoh. jahm-shee-mahn-yoh. juhn-hwah johm bah-deul-kkeh-yoh) (A call is coming from [my younger sibling]. Hold on. Let me answer the phone.)

괜찮아요. 전화 받으세요. (gwaen-chah-nah-yoh. juhn-hwah bah-deu-seh-yoh) (It's OK. Go ahead and answer the phone.)

아까 [문자] 보냈어요. 받았어요? (ah-kkah [moon-jjah] boh-nae-ssuh-yoh. bah-dah-ssuh-yoh?) (I sent a [text] earlier. Did you get it?)

네, 잘 받았어요. 고마워요. (neh, jahl bah-dah-ssuh-yoh. goh-mah-wuh-yoh) (Yes, I got your message. Thank you.)

Making calls in or to Korea

Korean landline numbers are seven or eight digits long, and begin with two- or three-digit 지역번호 (jee-yuhk-buhn-hoh) (area code) that begins with 0. For instance, 02 for 서울 (suh-ool) (Seoul), 051 for 부산 (boo-sahn) (Busan), and 032 for 인천 (een-chuhn) (Incheon).

휴대폰 번호 (hyoo-dae-pohn buhn-hoh) (mobile numbers) all start with 010, followed by a seven- or eight-digit number (for example, 010-1234-5678). Within Korea, just dial the numbers as is.

Wondering how to read these phone numbers? Visit Chapter 5 for a comprehensive guide on numbers. Here is a quick recap of the Sino-Korean number 0 through 9 for use with phone numbers.

0	1	2	3	4	5	6	7	8	9
공 (gohng)	일 (eel)	이 (ee)	삼 (sahm)	사 (sah)	오 (oh)	육 (yook)	칠 (cheel)	팔 (pahl)	구 (goo)

The country code for South Korea is 82. If your 가족 (gah-johk) (*family*) want to make an 국제전화 (gook-jjeh-juhn-hwah) (*international call*) from North America, first, dial + (plus sign) on digital devices, or 011 on traditional phones, then 82 (South Korea's country code), then 10 (dropping the initial 0 of the mobile prefix number) and the remaining seven- to eight-digit 휴대폰 번호. This will look something like this:

011-82-10-xxxx-xxxx (for traditional phones)

+82-10-xxxx-xxxx (for digital devices)

REMEMBER

Keep the versatile expression 여보세요 (yuh-boh-seh-yoh) handy for your phone conversations. Use it as a response when someone greets you with 여보세요. Not hearing anything on the other end? Repeat 여보세요 to gently ask, "Are you there?"

Phone introductions & troubleshooting

Even with caller ID, introducing yourself may still be necessary. For names ending in a vowel (based on Korean pronunciation of the name), use "[name]예요." For names ending with a consonant, use "[name]이에요." In formal or business settings, opt for the more formal "[name]입니다," regardless of whether the noun ends in a consonant or vowel. For further details on introductions, refer to Chapter 4. Here are some examples:

여보세요, 누구세요? (yuh-boh-seh-yoh, noo-goo-seh-yoh) (*Hello, who is this?*)

저, 사라예요. (juh, sah-rah-yeh-yoh) (*I'm Sarah.*)

마이클이에요. (mah-ee-keul-ee-eh-yoh) (*This is Michael.*)

알렉스입니다. (ahl-lehk-sseu-eem-nee-dah) (*This is Alex.*)

REMEMBER

When calling someone close, there's no need for formal introductions. Simply say "It's me" as "저예요" (juh-yeh-yoh) in polite form, or "나야" (nah-yah) in 반말 (bahn-mahl) (*intimate speech*) for very close friends or siblings. Optionally, you can add your name, like "저예요, 사라." (*It's me, Sarah*) and "나야, 마이클." (*It's me, Michael*).

TIP

If you can't hear the other party or if there's a misdial, use one of the following phrases:

잘 들려요? (jahl deul-lyuh-yoh) (*Do you hear me okay?*)

잘 안 들려요. (jahl ahn deul-lyuh-yoh) (*I can't hear you well.*)

다시/천천히 말씀해 주세요. (dah-shee/chuhn-chuhn-hee mahl-sseum-hae joo-seh-yoh) (*Please say that again/slowly.*)

잘못 걸었어요. (jahl-moht guh-ruh-ssuh-yoh) (*I/You dialed the wrong number.*)

Talkin' the Talk

PLAY

Will is at a department store trying to make a call to his friend, Hyunsoo, because he forgot to bring his cell phone. He is looking for a phone to borrow because he forgot to bring his cell phone.

Will: 전화기 좀 쓸 수 있을까요?
juhn-hwah-gee johm sseul ssoo ee-sseul-kkah-yoh?
May I please use the phone?

Sales clerk: 네, 여기 이 전화기 쓰세요.
neh, yuh-gee ee juhn-hwah-gee sseu-seh-yoh.
Yes, you can use this phone here.

Will dials the number, and Hyunsoo picks up the phone.

Hyunsoo: 여보세요?
yuh-boh-seh-yoh.
Hello?

Will: 여보세요? 현수 씨, 저 윌이에요. 지금 통화 괜찮아요?
yuh-boh-seh-yoh? hyuhn-soo ssee, juh wee-ree-eh-yoh. jee-geum tohng-hwah gwaen-chah-nah-yoh.
Hello? Hyunsoo, this is Will. Can you talk now?

Hyunsoo: 네, 괜찮아요. 무슨 일이에요?
neh, gwaen-chah-nah-yoh. moo-seun ee-ree-eh-yoh.
Yes, it's okay. What's up?

Will: 오늘 약속에 좀 늦을 것 같아요.
oh-neul yahk-ssoh-geh johm neu-jeul kkut gah-tah-yoh.
I'm afraid I'll be late for today's appointment.

WORDS TO KNOW

전화기	juhn-hwah-gee	phone (machine)
쓸 수 있을까요?	sseul-ssoo ee-sseul-kkah-yoh	Can I use it?
쓰세요 (쓰다)	sseu-seh-yoh	Please use
통화	tohng-hwah	phone conversation
약속	yahk-ssohk	appointment
늦을 것 같아요 (늦다)	neu-jeul kkuh gah-tah-yoh	I think I'll be late

Confirming the right contact

When contacting a new place or person, it's crucial to ensure you've reached the intended contact. To confirm, you can use one of the following endings:

>> [vowel-ending noun]지요? (*This is [Noun], right?*)

>> [consonant-ending noun]이지요? (*This is [Noun], right?*)

Here are some examples. Feel free to replace the brackets with other names or places to further your practice.

[고객 센터]**지요**? ([goh-gaek ssehn-tuh]-jee-yoh) (*This is the [customer service], right?= Is this the [. . .]?*)

[서울 식당]**이지요**? ([suh-ool sheek-ttahng]-ee-jee-yoh) (*Is this [Seoul Restaurant]?*)

[남준 씨] 휴대폰**이지요**? ([nahm-joon ssee] hyoo-dae-pohn-ee-jee-yoh)
(*Is this [Namjoon]'s cell?*)

Here are additional phrases for various common situations.

[매니저]하고 통화할 수 있을까요? ([mae-nee-juh]-hah-goh tohng-hwah hahl ssoo ee-sseul-kkah-yoh) (*Can I talk to [the manager]?*)

전데요. (juhn-deh-yoh) (*This is she/he.*)

지금 통화중이에요. (jee-geum tohng-hwah-joong-ee-eh-yoh.) (*She/He is on the phone now.*)

잠깐만 기다리세요. (jahm-kkahn-mahn gee-dah-ree-seh-yoh) (*Please wait a moment.*)

[최 선생님] 지금 안 계세요. 나중에 다시 해 보세요. ([chwae suhn-saeng-neem] jee-geum ahn gyeh-seh-yoh. nah-joong-eh dah-see hae boh-seh-yoh) (*[Teacher Choi] is not here now. Please call again later.*)

REMEMBER

Use 있어요/없어요 (ee-ssuh-yoh/uhp-ssuh-yoh) when talking about presence or absence casually, like for siblings or friends. For the elderly or higher-ups, switch to 계세요/안 계세요 (gyeh-seh-yoh/ahn gyeh-seh-yoh) to discuss existence or presence.

Leaving a message

If the person you're trying to reach isn't available, leaving a message is a practical alternative. Here are some useful phrases when you're leaving a message with someone else:

메시지 남기시겠어요? (meh-see-jee nahm-gee-shee-geh-ssuh-yoh) (*Would you like leave a message?*)

나중에 다시 전화할게요. (nah-joong-eh dah-shee juhn-hwah-hahl-kkeh-yoh) (*I will call again later.*)

Here are some phrases to use when recording an 음성메세지 (eum-suhng meh-sseh-jee) (*voicemail*).

안녕하세요? [벤]이에요/[수]예요. (ahn-nyuhng-hah-seh-yoh? [behn]-ee-eh-yoh/[soo]-yeh-yoh) (*Hi. This is [Ben]./This is [Sue].*)

질문이 있어서 전화했어요. (jeel-moo-nee ee-ssuh-suh juhn-hwah-hae-ssuh-yoh) (*I called you because I had a question.*)

[프로젝트] 때문에 전화했어요. ([peu-roh-jehk-teu] ttae-moo-neh juhn-hwah-hae-ssuh-yoh) (*I called because of [the project].*)

제 전화번호는 [010-321-7654]예요/이에요. (jeh juhn-hwah-buhn-boh-neun [gohng-eel-gohng sahm-ee-eel cheel-yook-oh-sah]-yeh-yoh) (*My phone number is [010-321-7654].*)

시간 될 때, 전화 주세요. (shee-gahn dwael ttae, juhn-hwah joo-seh-yoh) (*When you're available, please give me a call.*)

안녕히 계세요. (ahn-nyuhng-hee gyeh-seh-yoh) (*Goodbye.*)

Talkin' the Talk

PLAY

Greg Moore called Ms. Han, his teacher, at her office, and Ms. Han's colleague, Ms. Choi, picks up the phone.

Greg: 여보세요?

yuh-boh-seh-yoh?

Hello?

Ms.Choi: 여보세요?

yuh-boh-seh-yoh?

Hello?

Greg: 거기 한국어학당이지요?

guh-gee hahn-goo-guh-hahk-ttahng-ee-jee-yoh

Is this the Korean Language Institute?

Ms.Choi: 네. 누구 찾으세요?

neh. noo-goo chah-jeu-seh-yoh?

Yes. Who are you trying to reach?

Greg: 한수진 선생님 계세요? 저는 한 선생님 학생 그렉 무어예요.

hahn-soo-jeen suhn-saeng-neem gyeh-seh-yoh? juh-neun hahn suhn-saeng-neem hahk-ssaeng geu-rehk moo-uh-yeh-yoh.

Is Ms. Han, Soojin in? I'm Greg Moore, Ms. Han's student.

Ms.Choi: 아니요, 지금 안 계세요. 수업에 가셨어요. 2시쯤 오실 거예요.

ah-nee-yoh. jee-geum ahn gyeh-seh-yoh. soo-uh-beh gah-shyuh-ssuh-yoh. doo-shee-jjeum oh-sheel kkuh-yeh-yoh.

No, she's not here now. She went to class. She'll be back around 2.

Greg: 그럼 이따가 다시 전화 드릴게요.

geu-ruhm ee-ttah-gah dah-shee juhn-hwah deu-reel-kkeh-yoh.

Then, I will call again later today.

WORDS TO KNOW

선생님	suhn-saeng-neem	teacher
한국어학당	hahn-goo-guh-hahk-ttahng	Korean language institute
누구	noo-goo	who, whom, whose
찾으세요 (찾다)	chah-jeu-seh-yoh	look for
학생	hahk-ssaeng	student
수업	soo-uhp	class
이따가	ee-ttah-gah	later (same day)
전화 드릴게요 (드리다)	juh-hwah deu-reel-kkeh-yoh	will give a call (politer form of 전화하다)

You've Got Mail!

Despite a global decline in 우편 (oo-pyuhn) (*postal mail*) due to digital communication, Korea's 우체국 (oo-cheh-gook) (*post offices*) remain a vital part of the community. They're common, convenient, and offer more than just mail and package services. From banking to e-shopping and budget phone plans, they provide a wide array of services. For more info, visit https://www.epost.go.kr (English is available).

REMEMBER

The 우체국 in Korea are closed on 토요일 (toh-yoh-eel) (*Saturday*) and 일요일 (ee-ryoh-eel) (*Sunday*), so plan your visits for 평일 (pyuhng-eel) (*weekdays*) to catch them open!

Getting familiar with postal terms

To make the most of Korea's reliable postal services, get acquainted with the essential postal terms:

>> 우체국 (oo-cheh-gook) (*post office*)

>> 우체통 (oo-cheh-tohng) (*post box/drop box*)

>> 우편함 (oo-pyuhn-hahm) (*letter box, mailbox*)

>> 편지 (pyuhn-jee) (*letter*)

>> 봉투 (bohng-too) (*envelope*)

>> 엽서 (yuhp-ssuh) (*postcard*)

>> 우표 (oo-pyoh) (*postage stamps*)

>> 소포 (soh-poh) (*parcel*)

>> 깨지는 물건 (kkae-jee-neun mool-guhn) (*fragile items*)

>> 등기 우편 (deung-gee oo-pyuhn) (*registered mail*)

>> 일반/보통 우편 (eel-bahn/boh-tohng oo-pyuhn) (*standard/regular mail*)

>> 빠른 우편 (ppah-reunoo-pyuhn) (*express mail*)

>> 보내는 사람 (boh-nae-neun sah-rahm) (*sender*)

>> 받는 사람 (bahn-neun sah-rahm) (*receiver*)

>> 보내는 주소 (boh-nae-neun joo-soh) (*sender's address*)

>> 받는 주소 (bahn-neun joo-soh) (*shipping address*)

>> 우편 번호 (oo-pyuhn-buhn-hoh) (*zip code*)

>> 연락처 (yuhl-lahk-chuh) (*contact info*)

Sending mail from Korea

Need to ship items overseas or send 기념품 (gee-nyuhm-poom) (*souvenirs*) back home? Utilize the following phrases to efficiently navigate the 우체국 (oo-cheh-gook) (*post office*). Feel free to replace the words in brackets with other destinations or postal services.

어디로 보내실 거예요? (uh-dee-roh boh-nae-sheel kkuh-yeh-yoh) (*Where would you like to send it?*)

[뉴욕]으로 보낼 거예요. ([nyoo-yohk]-eu-roh boh-nael kkuh-yeh-yoh) (*I'm going to ship this off to [New York].*)

[보통 우편], 며칠/얼마나 걸려요? ([boh-tohng oo-pyuhn], myuh-cheel/uhl-mah-nah guhl-lyuh-yoh) (*For [regular mail], how many days does it take?*)

[빠른 우편]으로 보내 주세요. ([ppah-reun oo-pyuhn]-eu-roh boh-nae joo-seh-yoh) (*Please send this by [express mail].*)

[EMS], 얼마예요? ([EMS], uhl-mah-yeh-yoh?) (*How much is [EMS]?*)

우표 [다섯] 장 주세요. (oo-pyoh [dah-suht] jjahng joo-seh-yoh) (*Please give me [five] stamps.*) * Replace [다섯] with other native Korean numbers, like in 한, 두, 세. . . 열.

CULTURAL WISDOM

Remember, the Korean 주소 (joo-soh) (*address*) is written in a "macro to micro" format. After the sender's or receiver's 이름 (ee-reum) (*name*) (last name first), the address starts with the country and ends with the house or apartment number. Think of it as zooming in from space all the way down to your doorstep!

The official suffixes for administrative divisions/regions are: -도 (doh) (-*do; province*), -시 (shee) (-*si; city*), -구 (goo) (-*gu; district in a metropolitan city*), -동 (dohng) (-*dong; area within a city or district*), -대로 (dae-roh) (-*daero; big road with 8 or more lanes, similar to boulevard*), -로 (roh) (-*ro; street with 2 to 7 lanes*), -길 (geel) (-*gil; road with 1 lane*).

You also need a 5-digit Korean 우편번호 (oo-pyuhn-buhn-hoh) (ZIP code, postal code) for sorting mail. You can look up the correct 우편번호 online, such as at www.ePost.go.kr (Postal Code Search).

Let's Go Online!

Korea is a paradise for internet enthusiasts. Here is a list of the basic computer and internet terms. See how many you can recognize; many are 외래어 (wae-rae-uh) (*loanwords*) from English.

- » 검색 (guhm-saek) (*search*)
- » 노트북 (noh-teu-book) (*laptop*)
- » 컴퓨터 게임 (kuhm-pyoo-tuh geh-eem) (*computer game*)
- » 키보드 (kee-boh-deu) (*keyboard*)
- » 인터넷 (een-tuh-neht) (*internet*)
- » 와이파이 (wah-ee-pah-ee) (*Wi-Fi*)
- » 블루투스 (beul-loo-too-sseu) (*Bluetooth*)
- » 브라우저 (beu-rah-oo-juh) (*browser*)
- » 웹사이트 (wehp-ssah-ee-teu) (*website*)
- » 로그인/로그아웃 (loh-geu-een/loh-geu-ah-oot) (*login/logout*)
- » 아이디 (ah-ee-dee) (*ID*)
- » 비밀번호 (bee-meel-buhn-hoh) (*password*)
- » (첨부) 파일 ((chuhm-boo-)pah-eel) ((*attachment*) *file*)
- » (화상) 채팅 ((hwah-sahng) chae-teeng) ((*video*) *chatting*)

>> 앱/어플 (aep/uh-peul) (*application*)

>> 다운로드 (dah-oon-loh-deu) (*download*)

>> 저장 (juh-jahng) (*save*)

>> 스트리밍 (seu-teu-ree-meeng) (*streaming*)

>> 소셜미디어/SNS (soh-shyuhl-mee-dee-uh/S-N-S) (*social media/ "Social Networking Service"*)

TIP

Some terms above can be paired with the verbs 하다 (hah–dah) (*to do*) or 되다 (dwae–dah) (*to be available, to work*). Read on for sentence examples.

하다:

SNS 해요? (SNS hae-yoh?) (*Do you do/use social media?*)

컴퓨터 게임할까요? (kuhm-pyoo-tuh geh-eem-hahl-kkah-yoh) (*Shall we play computer games?*)

인터넷에서 검색해 봐요. (een-tuh-neh-seh-suh guhm-saek-kae bwah-yoh) (*Try searching on Naver.*)

앱 다운로드했어요?/다운 받았어요? (aep dah-oon-loh-deu hae-ssuh-yoh/dah-oon bah-dah-ssuh-yoh) (*Did you download the app?*)

화상 채팅 자주 해요? 가끔 해요. (hwah-sahng chae-teeng jah-joo hae-yoh? gah-kkeum hae-yoh) (*Do you often video chat? I do it sometimes.*)

되다:

와이파이 돼요? (wah-ee-pah-ee dwae-yoh) (*Does the Wi-Fi work?*)

인터넷 잘 돼요? (een-tuh-neht jahl dwae-yoh) (*Is the internet working well?*)

파일 업로드가 안 돼요. (pah-eel uhp-loh-deu-gah ahn dwae-yoh) (*The file won't upload.*)

갑자기 로그아웃 됐어요. (gahp-jjah-gee loh-geu-ah-oot dwae-ssuh-yoh) (*Suddenly, I was logged out.*)

이 컴퓨터에서 로그인이 안 돼요. (ee kuhm-pyoo-tuh-eh-suh loh-geu-een-ee ahn dwae-yoh) (*Login isn't working on this computer.*)

파일 첨부가 안 됐어요. (pah-eel chuhm-boo-gah ahn dwae-ssuh-yoh) (*The file is not attached/the attachment didn't work.*)

TIP

So much information on the 인터넷 and countless 웹사이트 at your fingertips! To enhance your 검색 (guhm-saek) (*search*) experience, consider purchasing Korean 키보드 stickers online or downloading a free layout print!

FUN & GAMES

If you love trivia and word hunting, this is the game for you! Find Korean words for the English terms related to technology and communication in the following puzzle. Words are up, down, diagonal, or backwards. Become a master word searcher! (See Appendix C for the answers.)

Words to find: *post office, internet, cellphone, password, ID, door-to-door parcel delivery, phone conversation, address, download, letter, hello (on the phone), computer, parcel, email, PC room, postcard, postage stamp, laptop, browser, webtoon, phone, website*

브	라	우	저	툰	노	아	편
비	우	표	웹	사	이	트	지
밀	엽	체	택	디	집	메	북
번	서	방	국	배	주	소	일
호	컴	시	원	화	전	포	핸
맹	퓨	피	통	다	운	로	드
넷	터	인	여	보	세	요	폰

Chapter **13**

Korean at Work and School

D iving into a new language is like unlocking a treasure chest of opportunities, from making new friends to embarking on 여행 (yuh-haeng) (*traveling*), 유학 (yoo-hahk) (*studying abroad*), and even launching an international career. If you're interested in working for a 한국 회사 (hahn-gook hwae-sah) (*Korean company*) or teaching at a school in Korea, this chapter is right up your alley!

Adapting to work life in a 외국 (wae-gook) (*foreign country*) might seem daunting, but fear not. In this chapter, you'll find guidance on navigating Korea's 직장 문화 (jeek-jjahng moon-hwah) (*work culture*), covering essentials from job applications to work-friendly phrases. And for those eyeing a teaching position in a Korean school, we've got you covered too. Remember to explore the recommended websites for more job-related info!

Getting Down to Work

Ever considered working abroad? Why not? Korea is home to some big players in the market, like 삼성 (sahm-suhng) (*Samsung*), 현대 (hyuhn-dae) (*Hyundai*), 기아 (gee-ah) (*Kia*), LG, CJ, and 포스코 (poh-seu-koh) (*POSCO*). Many other companies also contribute significantly to Korean's global economy. The entertainment, IT, beauty, and healthcare industries are thriving, with numerous other exciting fields to explore as well.

While the job market can be competitive, there's no harm in trying, especially if you're keen on immersing yourself in a new culture and lifestyle. Depending on your 기술 (gee-sool) (*field of expertise; technique*), 자격 (jah-gyuhk) (*qualifications*), 경력 (gyuhng-nyuhk) (*work experience*), 적성 (juhk-ssuhng) (*aptitude*), and 관심 분야 (gwahn-sheem boo-nyah) (*interested field*), you are bound to find something that fits you. (See Chapter 7 for job terms.)

Preparing applications

Here are common 지원 서류 (jee-wuhn suh-ryoo) (*application documents*) for Korean companies.

- » 이력서 (ee-ryuhk-ssuh) (*resume, CV*)
- » 자기소개서 (jah-gee-soh-gae-suh) (*personal statement*)
- » 입사 지원서 (eep-ssah jee-wuhn-suh) (*application/cover letter*)
- » 자격증 사본 (jah-gyuhk-jjeung sah-bohn) (*copy of certifications*)
- » 추천서 (choo-chuhn-suh) (*recommendation letter*)

For examples of how these nouns can be used with different action or descriptive verbs, like *to write* or *to be necessary*, see Table 13-1.

GRAMMATICALLY SPEAKING

Just remember, personal pronouns like 나/저 (nah/juh) (*I*) are often omitted in Korean sentences. This adds versatility, allowing sentences to apply to different subjects in various situations. For instance, the sentence, 이력서 내야 돼요 (ee-ryuhk-ssuh nae-yah-dwae-yoh), which literally means "*Resume needs to be submitted*," can be used to express "I have to submit a resume" (as if you're saying what you need to do) or "You need to submit a resume" (as if a recruiter says it to you), depending on the context. By raising intonation, it can also be turned into a question like "Do I/you have to submit a resume?"

TABLE 13-1 **Talking about Job Applications**

Verbs	아요/어요 Informal Polite	아야/어야 돼요 (Should, Must)	Examples
쓰다 (sseu-dah) (to write)	(-을/를) 써요 (ssuh-yoh)	써야 돼요 (ssuh-yah-dwae-yoh)	자기 소개서(를) 써야 돼요. (jah-gee soh-gae-suh(-reul) ssuh-yah dwae-yoh) (*I need to write a personal statement.*)
내다 (nae-dah) (to submit)	(-을/를) 내요 (nae-yoh)	내야 돼요 (nae-yah dwae-yoh)	언제까지 내야 돼요? (uhn-jeh-kkah-jee nae-yah dwae-yoh) (*When do I have to submit (it) by?*)
있다 (eet-ttah) (to have; exist)	(-이/가) 있어요 (ee-ssuh-yoh)	있어야 돼요 (ee-ssuh-yah dwae-yoh)	추천서(가) 있어야 돼요? (choo-chuhn-suh-(gah) ee-ssuh-yah dwae-yoh) (*Do you have to have a reference letter?*)
보다(boh-dah) (to take (exam) to see/ watch)	(-을/를) 봐요 (bwah-yoh)	봐야 돼요 (bwah-yah dwae-yoh)	면접(을) 봐야 돼요. (myuhn-juhb-(eul) bwah-yah-dwae-yoh) (*I must have a job interview.*)
필요하다 (pee-ryoh-hah-dah) (to be needed, necessary)	(-이/가) 필요해요 (pee-ryoh-hae-yoh)	—	이력서하고 자기 소개서(가) 필요해요. (ee-ryuhk-ssuh-hah-goh jah-gee soh-gae-suh(-gah) pee-ryoh-hae-yoh) (*You need a resume and a statement.*)

Adding questions words such as 언제까지 (uhn-jeh-kkah-jee) (*by when*), 어디에 (uh-dee-eh) (*to where*), or 누구한테 (noo-goo-hahn-teh) (*to who*) allows for extended questioning like 언제까지 (이력서) 내야 돼요? (*By when do I/you need to submit (it/the resume)?*). (By the way, you're doing a great job of exploring new sentences! Keep it up!)

POPULAR JOB-SEARCH WEBSITES

For an effective job search, check out popular 채용 정보 웹사이트 (chae-yohng juhng-boh web-ssah-ee-teu) (*recruitment info sites*) and 앱 (aep) (*apps*) in Korea:

- PeopleNjob (https://www.peoplenjob.com)
- Kotra Job Fair (https://www.kotra.or.kr/ck_eng/index.do)
- Study in Korea: K-employment (https://www.studyinkorea.go.kr/)
- Job Korea (https://www.jobkorea.co.kr)
- SaramIN (https://www.saramin.co.kr)

Remember, you'll need a visa to work in Korea. To ask, "What (kind of) visa do you need?", you can say 무슨 비자(가) 필요해요? (moo-seun bee-jah-gah pee-ryoh-hae-yoh). For teaching in Korea, you need an E-2 Teaching Visa. You can say, "E-2 비자가 필요해요" (E-2 bee-jah-gah pee-ryoh-hae-yoh) (*I/You need an E-2 visa*). Check out these websites for visa info: www.hikorea.go.kr, www.visa.go.kr.

If the job you're interested in requires Korean language proficiency, you might want to consider taking the *Test of Proficiency in Korean (TOPIK)*. First time hearing about it? No worries! You can find more info about it in the future when the need arises at: www.topik.co.kr.

Interview do's and don'ts

Now, imagine you've scored an invite to a 면접 (myuhn-juhp) (*interview*), or as an alternative term, 인터뷰 (een-tuh-byoo). Feeling those butterflies fluttering? Totally normal! But, no need to stress too much. Remember, 너무 긴장하지 마세요. (nuh-moo geen-jahng-hah-jee mah-seh-yoh) (*don't be too nervous.*) After all, 인터뷰 에티켓 (eh-tee-keht) (*etiquette*) doesn't differ that much from country to country.

Non-verbal communication, like your 태도 (tae-doh) (*attitude*), 몸짓 (mohm-jjeet) (*gestures*), 얼굴 표정 (uhl-gool pyoh-juhng) (*facial expressions*), and 목소리 톤 (mohk-ssoh-ree tohn) (*tone of voice*) and 속도 (sohk-ddoh) (*speed*) are just as important as verbal communication.

When you enter the interview room, remember to establish eye contact with the 면접관 (myuhn-juhp-kkwahn) (*interviewer*) and offer a slight bow. Here are some more tips for interviews:

시간을 지키세요. (shee-gah-neul jee-kee-seh-yoh) (*Get there on time.*)

자신감 있게 말하세요. (jah-sheen-gahm eet-kkeh mahl-hah-seh-yoh) (*Speak confidently.*)

단정하게 입으세요. (dahn-juhng-hah-geh ee-beu-seh-yoh) (*Dress nicely.*)

팔짱을 끼지 마세요. (pahl-jjahng-eul kkee-jee mah-seh-yoh) (*Don't cross your arms.*)

다리를 꼬지 마세요. (dah-lee-reul kkoh-jee mah-seh-yoh) (*Don't cross your legs.*)

Common interview questions

Preparing for common interview topics beforehand can significantly boost your confidence and help you ace that interview! These topics include 자기 소개 (jah-gee soh-gae) (*self-introduction*), 지원 동기 (jee-wuhn dohng-gee) (*reasons for applying*), 장단점 (jahng-dahn-jjuhm) (*strength and weakness — both in personality and work skills*), 팀워크 경험 (teem-wuh-keu gyuhng-huhm) (*teamwork experiences*) and 입사 후 계획 (eep-ssah hoo gyeh-hwaek) (*future plans after joining the company*).

Now, let's transform those topics into potential interview questions. Here's what you might encounter:

자기 소개를 해 주세요. (jah-gee soh-gae-reul hae joo-seh-yoh) (*Please tell us about yourself.*)

우리 회사 지원 동기가 무엇입니까? (oo-ree hwae-sah jee-wuhn-dohng-gee-gah moo-uh-sheem-nee-kkah) (*What motivates you to apply to our company?*)

장점과 단점을 말씀해 주세요. (jahng-jjuhm-gwah dahn-jjuh-meul mahl-sseum-hae joo-seh-yoh) (*Tell us about your strengths and weaknesses.*)

상사와 갈등이 있으면 어떻게 하겠습니까? (sahng-sah-wah gahl-ddeung-ee ee-sseu-myuhn uh-ttuh-keh hah-geht-sseum-nee-kkah) (*If you have a conflict with your boss, how would you handle?*)

팀워크 경험을 말씀해 주세요. (teem-wuh-keu gyuhng-huh-meul mahl-sseum-hae joo-seh-yoh) (*Please share your experiences of teamwork.*)

입사 후 계획이 무엇입니까? (eep-ssah hoo gyeh-hwae-gee moo-uh-sheem-nee-kkah) (*What are your plans after joining our company?*)

Talkin' the Talk

PLAY

Lisa is at a job fair and is talking to a recruiter at a Korean company.

Lisa: 안녕하세요! 리사 스미스라고 합니다. 이 회사에 지원하려고 하는데요. 이력서는 한글하고 영어 둘 다 내야 돼요?

ahn-nyung-hah-seh-yoh! lee-sah seu-mee-seu-lah-goh hahm-nee-dah. ee hwae-sah-eh jee-wuhn-hah-ryuh-goh hah-neun-deh-yoh. ee-ryuk-ssuh-neun hahn-geul-hah-goh yuhng-uh dool dah nae-yah-dwae-yoh?

Hello! I am Lisa Smith. I am going to apply to this company. Do I need to turn in the resume in both Korean and English?

Recruiter: 아니요, 영어 이력서만 내세요. 영어 자기 소개서도 내야 돼요.

ah-nee-yoh. yuhng-uh ee-ryuhk-ssuh-mahn nae-seh-yoh. yuhng-uh jah-gee soh-gae-suh-doh nae-yah-dwae-yoh.

No, just turn in an English resume. You also need to submit a statement in English.

Lisa: 네. 알겠습니다. 추천서도 필요해요?

neh. ahl-geht-sseum-nee-dah. choo-chuhn-suh-doh pee-ryo-hae-yoh?

Okay. I see. Do you need recommendation letters, too?

Recruiter: 지금은 안 필요해요. 추천인 연락처만 이력서에 적어 주세요.

jee-geu-meun ahn pee-ryo-hae-yoh. choo-chuh-neen yuhl-lahk-chuh-mahn ee-ryuhk-ssuh-eh juh-guh joo-seh-yoh.

No need for now. You just put the reference's contact info on your resume.

Lisa: 네. 근데 명함 있으세요?

neh. geun-deh myuhng-hahm ee-sseu-seh-yoh.

Okay. By the way, do you have a business card?

Recruiter: 네. 여기 있습니다. 질문 있으시면 이메일 주세요.

neh. yuh-ghee eet-sseum-nee-dah. jeel-moon ee-sseu-shee-myuhn ee-meh-eel joo-seh-yoh.

Here it is. If you have any questions, please email me.

Lisa: 네. 감사합니다. 안녕히 계세요.

neh. gahm-sah-hahm-nee-dah. ahn-nyuhng-hee gyeh-seh-yoh.

Yes. Thank you. Goodbye.

WORDS TO KNOW

지원하려고 합니다 (지원하다)	jee-wuhn-hah-ryuh-goh hahm-nee-dah	intend/plan to apply (* 려고 하다 expresses intention)
내세요 (내다)	nae-seh-yoh	please submit
연락처	yuhl-lahk-chuh	contact information
명함	myuhng-hahm	business card
있으세요 (있다)	ee-sseu-seh-yoh	possess/have (honorific form)

Interacting with Your Colleagues

Suppose you've nailed your 이력서 (ee-ryuk-ssuh) (*resume*) and sailed through the 면접 (myuhn-juhp) (*interview*). Finally, you 취직했어요 (chwee-jeek-hae-ssuh-yoh) (*got the job*)! Now you're all set to start your new journey at your new 직장 (jeek-jjahng) (*workplace*).

GRAMMATICALLY SPEAKING

To work is 일하다 (eel-hah-dah) in Korean. To specify *where* you work, mark the place using the 에서 (eh-suh) particle. For example, "I work for a trading company" is 무역 회사에서 일해요 (moo-yuhk hwae-sah-eh-suh eel-hae-yoh). "I work at LG" is LG에서 일해요 (LG-eh-suh eel-hae-yoh). Check out the following questions and responses you can use when chatting with Korean speakers:

Q: 어느 부서에서 일해요? (uh-neu boo-suh-eh-suh eel-hae-yoh) (*Which department do you work in?*)

A: 해외 마케팅 부서에서 일해요. (hae-wae mah-keh-teeng boo-suh-eh-suh eel-hae-yoh) (*I work in the overseas marketing department.*)

A: 저는 홍보부에서 일해요. (juh-neun hohng-boh-boo-eh-suh eel-hae-yoh) (*I work in the public relations department.*)

Q: 거기에서 일한 지 얼마나 됐어요? (guh-gee-eh-suh eel-hahn jee uhl-mah-nah dwae-ssuh-yoh) (*How long have you been working there?*)

A: 일 년 됐어요. (eel-lyuhn dwae-ssuh-yoh) (*It's been a year.*)

A: 얼마 안 됐어요. (uhl-mah ahn dwae-ssuh-yoh) (*It hasn't been long.*)

Addressing people at work

CULTURAL WISDOM

Korean society and work culture are hierarchical, and addressing someone properly is crucial in the Korean 직장 (jeek-jjahng) (*workplace*). Learning how to address people at work in Korea may feel difficult at first, but all you need is some time.

Addressing superiors

When talking to your 상사 (sahng-sah) (*boss, supervisor*), use their 직함 (jeek-kahm) (*job titles, positions*) and never go by their first name. Remember, the Korean language doesn't allow second-person pronouns like 너 (nuh)/당신 (dahng-sheen) (*you*) or one's name to be used for someone you need to show respect to.

Use one of the following options — full name+[position], last name+ [position], or just [position].

For example, say your 팀장 (teem-jahng) (*team leader*) is 박지민 (*Park Jimin*). 박 is the 성 (suhng) (*family name*), and 지민 is the 이름 (ee-reum) (*first name*). You address them as 박지민 팀장님, 박 팀장님, or just 팀장님. The suffix, 님 (neem), which gets placed after a person's position, is a sign of further respect.

Here are some common 직함 (jeek-kahm) (*job titles, positions*). Larger companies may have more 직함 systems, which can take time to get used to. Remember to add 님 after each of these words when addressing each of your 상사.

>> 사장 (sah-jahng) CEO, president

>> 부사장 (boo-sah-jahng) vice president

>> 부장 (boo-jahng) department chair

>> 과장 (gwah-jahng) section chief

>> 대리 (dae-ree) assistant manager

>> 사원 (sah-wuhn) staff member

>> 인턴 (een-tuhn) intern

Addressing equals or subordinates

Addressing someone of equal or lower position at work is more flexible. You can use their job title or position (for example, 박 팀장, 김 과장). Or you can use their *full* or *first name* followed by the suffix, 씨 (ssee) which can be best translated as an equivalent to "Mr/Ms/Mrs/Miss" in English. Say your teammate at work is 전정국 (Jeon Jungkook). You can call him 전정국 씨 (i.e., [full name] 씨) or 정국 씨 (i.e., [first name] 씨). This keeps it not too formal, but still respectful.

However, adding 씨 to the last name only (for example, 전 씨) is a no-no, unlike English. You'll only hear 성 (suhng) (*last name*) with 씨 in very limited situations, like referring to criminal suspects on the news. Also, remember not to use 씨 after job titles — 팀장님 씨 and 선생님 씨 don't exist.

Talking about activities at work

So many things to do at your 직장 (jeek–jjahng) (*workplace*), so little time. Here are some of the activities you do at 직장.

>> 출근하다 (chool-geun-hah-dah) (*to go/come to work*)

>> 퇴근하다 (twae-geun-hah-dah) (*to leave work for the day*)

>> 야근하다 (yah-geun-hah-dah) (*to work overtime*)

>> 결근하다 (gyuhl-geun-hah-dah) (*to be absent from work*)

>> 회의하다 (hwae-ee-hah-dah) (*to have a meeting*)

>> 발표하다 (bahl-pyoh-hah-dah) (*to present*)

>> 복사하다 (bohk-ssah-hah-dah) (*to make copies*)

>> 연락하다 (yuhl-lahk-kah-dah) (*to contact*)

>> 전화하다 (juhn-hwah-hah-dah) (*to phone*)

>> 확인하다 (hwah-geen-hah-dah) (*to check, to confirm/verify*)

>> 이메일하다 (ee-meh-eel-hah-dah) (*to email*)

>> 계약하다 (gyeh-yahk-kah-dah) (*to make a contract*)

>> 서명하다/사인하다 (suh-myuhng-hah-dah/ssah-een-hah-dah) (*to sign*)

>> 연차 내다/쓰다 (yuhn-chah nae-dah/sseu-dah) (*to take (days) off*)

>> 출장 가다 (chool-jjahng gah-dah) (*to go on a business trip*)

>> (하루) 쉬다 ((hah-roo) shwee-dah) (*to rest/have (a day) off*)

GRAMMATICALLY SPEAKING

Many of the activities in the previous list use the [noun]+하다 (hah–dah) (*to do*) pattern. For example, 회의 (hweh-ee) (*meeting/conference*) + 하다 = 회의하다 (*to have a meeting*). The 하다-ending verbs conjugate as follows:

해요 (hae-yoh) (informal polite: present tense)

했어요 (hae-ssuh-yoh) (past tense)

할 거예요 (hahl kkuh-yeh-yoh) (future tense)

하세요 (hah-seh-yoh) (command)

해 주세요 (hae joo-seh-yoh) (*Please do it [for me/someone else]*)

Read on for full-sentence examples:

몇 시에 출근해요? (myuht ssee-eh chool-geun-hae-yoh) (*What time do you go to work?*)

이메일 확인했어요? (ee-meh-eel hwah-geen-hae-ssuh-yoh) (*Did you check the email?*)

아프면 일찍 퇴근하세요. (ah-peu-myuhn eel-jjeek twae-geun-hah-seh-yoh) (*If you're sick, you should get off work early.*)

여기에 사인해 주세요. (yuh-gee-eh ssah-een-hae joo-seh-yoh) (*Please sign here.*)

직장 (jeek-jjahng) (*your workplace*) is a place that requires you to take care of your 책임 (chae-geem) (*responsibilities*) and 의무 (eui-moo) (*obligations*). Very fun. To express obligation, you can use the ending, 해야 돼요 (hae-yah dwae-yoh) (*must/should*). Here are some sentence examples.

몇 시까지 출근해야 돼요? (myuht ssee-kkah-jee chool-geun-hae-yah dwae-yoh?) (*What time do I/you have to come to work by?*)

몇 장 복사해야 돼요? (myuht jjahng bohk-ssah-hae-yah dwae-yoh?) (*How many copies should I make?*)

오늘 야근해야 돼요. (oh-neul yah-geun-hae-yah dwae-yoh.) (*I need to work overtime today.*)

다음 주에 출장 가야 돼요. (dah-eum jjoo-eh chool-jjahng-gah-yah dwae-yoh.) (*I have to go for the business trip next week.*)

Attending meetings

회의 (hweh-ee) (*meetings*) are an inevitable part of any job. If you're doing business with Korean clients, there will most likely be 통역사 (tohng-yuhk-sah) (*interpreter*). Still, using a little 한국어 (hahn-goo-guh) (*Korean*) on your own at the beginning of a meeting can make a positive impression. The following are some common introductions used in meetings. They're in the formal speech ending.

>> 안녕하십니까. (ahn-nyuhng-hah-sheem-nee-kkah) (*Hello.*)

>> 반갑습니다. (bahng-gahp-sseum-nee-dah) (*Nice to meet you.*)

>> 회의를 시작하겠습니다. (hwae-ee-reul shee-jahk-kah-geht-sseum-nee-dah) (*Let's start the meeting.*)

The following phrases should come in handy during meetings:

» 질문(이) 있습니다. (jeel-moon-(ee) eet-sseum-nee-dah) (*I have a question.*)

» 제안(이) 있습니다. (jeh-ahn-(ee) eet-sseum-nee-dah) (*I have a suggestion.*)

» 좀 쉬었다 할까요? (johm shwee-uht-ttah hahl-kkah-yoh) (*Shall we take a little break?*)

» 좋은 생각입니다. (joh-eun saeng-gah-geem-nee-dah) (*That's a great idea.*)

» 10분 휴식 후에 회의를 계속하겠습니다. (sheep-ppoon hyoo-sheek hoo-eh hwae-ee-reul gyeh-soh-khah-geht-sseum-nee-dah) (*We'll continue after a 10-minute break.*)

» 오늘 회의를 마치겠습니다. (oh-neul hwae-ee-reul mah-chee-geht-sseum-nee-dah) (*Let's wrap up the meeting.*)

Working from Home

By any chance, 집에서 일해요? (jee-beh-suh eel-hae-yoh) This question can mean "Do you work from home/telework?" or "Do you work at home?" In a more formal tone, you can say 재택근무해요 (jae-taek-geun-moo-hae-yoh). 재택근무 (jae-taek-geun-moo) (*working from home*) has become more popular than ever since the COVID-19 pandemic. Here are handy phrases for talking about where you work:

재택근무해요? (jae-taek-kkeun-moo-hae-yoh) (*Do you work from home?*)

일주일에 며칠 재택근무해요? (eel-jjoo-ee-leh myuh-cheel jae-taek kkeun-moo-hae-yoh) (*How many days a week do you work remotely?*)

일주일에 3일 재택근무해요. (eel-jjoo-ee-leh sah-meel jae-taek-kkeun-moo-hae-yoh) (*I work from home 3 days a week.*)

일주일에 하루 사무실에 가요. (eel-jjoo-ee-leh hah-roo sah-moo-shee-leh gah-yoh) (*I go to the office one day a week.*)

집에서 화상 회의해요. (jee-beh-suh hwah-sahng hwae-ee-hae-yoh) (*I do virtual meetings from home.*)

TIP

화상 회의 (hwah-sahng hwae-ee) (*virtual meetings; video conferencing*) are more popular and accessible than ever. Here's what to say during a 화상 회의 over a video conferencing platform (bloopers included):

카메라(를) 켜 주세요 (kah-meh-rah-(reul) kyuh joo-seh-yoh) (*Please turn on your camera.*)

여러분, 마이크(를) 꺼 주세요. (yuh-ruh-boon, mah-ee-keu-(reul) kkuh joo-seh-yoh) (*Everyone, please turn off your mics.*)

잠시만요. (jahm-shee-mahn-nyoh) (*Please wait a second.*)

먼저 말씀하세요 (muhn-juh mahl-sseum-hah-seh-yoh) (*Please go ahead first.*)

소리가 안 들려요. (soh-ree-gah ahn deul-lyuh-yoh) (*I can't hear you.*)

화면 공유해 주세요. (hwah-myuhn gohng-yoo-hae joo-seh-yoh) (*Please share your screen.*)

화면이 정지됐어요. (hwah-myuh-nee juhng-jee-dwae-ssuh-yoh) (*The screen is frozen/ You're frozen.*)

제 화면 보이세요? (jeh hwah-myuhn boh-ee-seh-yoh?) (*Can you see my screen?*)

질문은 채팅 창에 써 주세요. (jeel-moo-neun chae-teeng chahng-eh ssuh joo-seh-yoh) (*Please write your questions in the chatbox.*)

죄송합니다. 저희 아이들이었습니다. (jwae-sohng-hahm-nee-dah. juh-hee ah-ee-deul-ee-uh-sseum-nee-dah.) (*Sorry, that was my kids.*)

Talkin' the Talk

PLAY

James isn't feeling too great today and he was hoping to leave work early. He went to talk to his team leader, Amy, about it.

James: 팀장님, 드릴 말씀이 있습니다.
teem-jahng-neem, deu-reel mahl-sseu-mee eet-sseum-nee-dah.
I have something to tell you.

Amy: 네. 무슨 일이에요?
neh. moo-seun ee-ree-eh-yoh?
Yes. What's the matter?

James: 제가 몸이 안 좋아서 오늘 좀 일찍 퇴근하고 싶은데요.
jeh-gah moh-mee ahn joh-ah-suh oh-neul johm eel-jjeek twae-geun-hah-goh shee-peun-deh-yoh.
I'm not feeling well, so I'd like to leave a little early today.

Amy: 아, 그래요? 어디가 안 좋아요?
Ah, geu-rae-yoh? gahm-ghee-eh guhl-lyuht-ssuh-yoh?
Oh, really? Where does it hurt?

James: 감기에 걸린 거 같아요. 목이 아프고 기침이 많이 나요.
gahm-ghee-eh guhl-leen guh gah-tah-yoh. mo-ghee ah-peu-goh ghee-chee-mee mah-nee nah-yoh.
I think I got a cold. I have sore throat and am coughing a lot.

Amy: 그럼 일찍 퇴근하세요. 내일까지 푹 쉬세요.
geu-ruhm eel-jjeek twae-geun-hah-seh-yoh. nae-eel-kkah-jee pook shee-seh-yoh.
Then, please go home early. And take a good rest until tomorrow.

James: 네. 그럼 내일 하루 연차 쓰겠습니다. 감사합니다.
neh. geu-ruhm nae-eel hah-roo yuhn-chah sseu-geht-sseum-nee-dah. gahm-sah-hahm-nee-dah.
Yes. I will take a day off tomorrow then. Thank you.

• •

WORDS TO KNOW

몸이 안 좋아서 (안 좋다)	moh-mee ahn joh-ah-suh	because I don't feel well
일찍	eel-jjeek	early
퇴근하고 싶 은데요 (퇴근하다)	twae-geun-hah-go shee-peun-deh-yoh	want to leave work for the day (* 고 싶은데요 expresses one's desire/wish)
감기에 걸린 거 같아 요 (감기에 걸리다)	gahm-ghee-eh guhl-leen-guh gah-tah-yoh	I think/it seems that I got a cold
푹 쉬세요	pook shwee-seh-yoh	Take a good rest
하루 연차 쓰겠습 니다 (연차 쓰다)	hah-rooo yuhn-chah sseu-geht-sseum-nee-dah	I will take a day off (work)

Working at School

Teachers of 영어 (yuhng-uh) (*English*) are in high demand in Korea. *To teach* is 가르치다 (gah-reu-chee-dah), which conjugates in the following ways:

가르쳐요 (gah-reu-chyuh-yoh) (*(I) teach*) — present tense

가르쳤어요 (gah-reu-chyuh-ssuh-yoh) (*taught*) — past tense

가르칠 거예요 (gah-reu-cheel-kkuh-yeh-yoh) (*will teach*) — future plan; probability

가르치고 싶어요 (gah-reu-chee-goh shee-puh-yoh) (*want to teach*)

To express *where* you teach, use the 에서 particle after the name of the place. For example, to say "I teach at a high school," you can say "고등학교에서 가르쳐요" (goh-deung-hahk-kkyoh-eh-suh gah-reu-chyuh-yoh). It's that easy!

To specify what you teach, squeeze in the subject before the verb. For example, if you teach 영어 (yuhng-uh) (*English*), say 고등학교에서 영어 가르쳐요. Stay tuned for more Korean terms related to education.

Schools and students

CULTURAL WISDOM

교육 (gyoh-yook) (*education*) is perhaps one of the hottest topics in Korea, and there is even a term for this phenomenon — 교육열 (gyoh-yoong-nyuhl) (literally, *education fever — passion for education*).

The schools follow a 6-3-3 system, meaning that students go to elementary school for six years, middle school and high school for three years each. Check out Table 13-2 for more on school levels and how to refer to students in each level:

TIP

If you want to find out if someone's a student, try out the pattern "[Noun]이에요" ([hahk-ssaeng]ee-eh-yoh) (*is/are [noun]*):

Q: 대학생이에요? (dae-hahk-ssaeng-ee-eh-yoh) (*Are you a college student?*)

A: 네, 대학생이에요. (neh, dae-hahk-ssaeng-ee-eh-yoh) (*Yes, I'm a college student.*)

A: 아니요, 대학생 아니에요. 고등학생이에요. (ah-nee-yoh, dae-kahk-sseang ah-nee-eh-yoh. goh-deung-hahk-ssaeng-ee-eh-yoh) (*No, I'm not a college student. I'm a high schooler.*)

TIP

A handy verb to use when talking about *going to school* or *working for a company* is 다니다 (dah-nee-dah) (*to attend regularly*). If you're a graduate student, you can say "대학원에 다녀요" (dae-hah-gwuh-neh dah-nyuh-yoh) (*I go to graduate school*), which means the same as "대학원생이에요" (dae-hah-gwuhn-saeng-ee-eh-yoh) (*I'm a graduate student*).

TABLE 13-2

Schools in Korea

School (pronunciation)	Meaning	Students
어린이집 (uh-lee-nee-jeep)	daycare/nursery	원생 (wuhn-saeng)
유치원 (yoo-chee-wuhn)	kindergarten	유치원생
학교 (hahk-kkyoh)	school	학생 (hahk-ssaeng)
초등학교 (choh-deung-hahk-kkyoh)	elementary school	초등학생
중학교 (joong-hahk-kkyoh)	middle school	중학생
고등학교 (goh-deung-hahk-kkyoh)	high school	고등학생
전문대 (juhn-moon-dae)	2-year college	전문대생
대학교 (dae-hahk-kkyoh)	4-year college	대학생
대학원 (dae-hah-gwuhn)	graduate school	대학원생

If someone says "마케팅 회사에 다녀요" (mah-keh-teeng hwae-sah-eh dah-nyuh-yoh), it means they work for a marketing company. It has the same meaning as "마케팅 회사에서 일해요" (mah-keh-teeng hweh-sah-eh-suh eel-hae-yoh). Ready to practice in conversation? See below:

Q: 어느 학교에 다녀요? (uh-neu hahk-kkyoh-eh dah-nyuh-yoh?) (*Which/what school do you go to?*)

A: 부산 중학교에 다녀요. (boo-sahn joong-hahk-kkyoh-eh dah-nyuh-yoh) (*I go to Busan Middle School.*)

Q: 딸이 몇 학년이에요? (ttah-lee myuht tahng-nyuh-nee-eh-yoh?) (*What grade is your daughter?*)

A: 지금 유치원에 다녀요. (jee-geum yoo-chee-wuh-neh dah-nyuh-yoh) (*She goes to a kindergarten now.*)

Q: 어느 회사에 다녀요? (uh-neu hwae-sah-eh dah-nyuh-yoh?) (*Which/what company do you work for?*)

A: 삼성에 다녀요. (sahm-suhng-eh dah-nyuh-yoh) (*I work for Samsung.*)

REMEMBER

Another important school/work-related terms to know are 선배 (suhn-bae) (*friends in higher grade, senior colleagues*) and 후배 (hoo-bae) (*friends in lower grade, junior colleagues*). 선배 means someone who started attending school or working earlier than you. 후배 is the opposite.

남준 선배, 지금 어디 가요? (nahm-joon suhn-bae, jee-geum uh-dee gah-yoh) (*Namjoon, where are you going now?*)

이쪽은 제 회사 후배예요. (ee-jjoh-geun jeh hwae-sah hoo-bae-yeh-yoh) (*This is my junior colleague.*)

Teachers matter

Remember that favorite 선생님 (suhn-saeng-neem) (*teacher*) from your school days? Teachers hold a special place in shaping our lives. Seee if your favorite teacher was one of the following:

» 교장 선생님 (gyoh-jahng suhn-saeng-neem) (*principal*)

» 교감 선생님 (gyoh-gahm suhn-saeng-neem) (*vice principal*)

» 교생 선생님 (gyoh-saeng suhn-saeng-neem) (*student teacher*)

» 유치원 / 초등학교 / 중학교 / 고등학교 선생님 (yoo-chee-wuhn / choh-deung-hahk-kkyoh / joong-hahk-kkyoh / goh-deung-hahk-kkyoh suhn-saeng-neem) (*kindergarten / elementary / middle school / high school teacher*)

» 교수님 (gyoh-soo-neem) (*professor*)

TIP

Another term for "teacher" is 교사 (gyoh-sah), mainly used to describe the occupation, not for a specific teacher. In informal contexts, students might call their teacher "쌤" (ssaem), instead of 선생님.

Here's a quick quiz: In Korean, a *medical doctor* is 의사 (eui-sah). How would you address your 의사 when you visit them? 의사? Maybe 의사님? The answer is 선생님. Why? 선생님 literally means "someone born before you," and it's commonly used to show respects to professionals, older individuals, and even strangers in certain situations. It's a versatile term used to show deference and courtesy.

TEACHING ENGLISH

영어 선생님 (yuhng-uh suhn-saeng-neem) (*English teachers*) are in high demand in Korea, as is the case in many Asian countries. If you are interested in teaching English in Korean public schools, there are various programs available, like EPIK (English Program in Korea), SMOE (Seoul Metropolitan Office of Education), and GEPIK (Gyeonggi English Program in Korea). EPIK is the most well-known program, sponsored by the Ministry of Education.

Don't worry if you don't know where to start because there are also third-party recruiters like Korean Horizons, Teach ESL Korea, Footprints Recruiting, Korvia, and Gone2Korea, that can help you find teaching positions in Korea.

Subjects, semesters, and vacations

I bet you have lots of (hopefully fond) memories from your student days. 무슨 과목을 좋아했어요? (moo-seun gwah-moh-geul joh-ah-hae-ssuh-yoh) (*What subjects did you like?*) Check out the Korean terms for some of the school subjects.

» 국어 (goo-guh) (*language arts*)

» 영어 (yuhng-uh) (*English*)

» 수학 (soo-hahk) (*math*)

» 과학 (gwah-hahk) (*science*)

» 역사 (yuhk-ssah) (*history*)

» 사회 (sah-hwae) (*social studies*)

» 미술 (mee-sool) (*art*)

» 음악 (eu-mahk) (*music*)

» 체육 (cheh-yook) (*physical education*)

Knowing Korean academic years and semesters will also come in handy. Table 13-3 presents some essential vocabulary on school years.

TABLE 13-3   Academic Calendar Vocabulary

School	Meaning	Examples
학기 (hahk-kkee)	semester, quarter	1학기 (eel-hahk-kkee) (*first semester*)
		2학기 (ee-hahk-kkee) (*second semester*)
학년 (hahng-nyuhn)	school year	일 학년 (eel hahng-nyuhn) (*1st grade/freshman*)
		삼 학년 (sahm hahng-nyuhn) (*3rd grade/junior*)
방학 (bahng-hahk)	(school) vacation	여름 방학 (yuh-reum ppahng-hahk) (*summer vacation*)
		겨울 방학 (gyuh-ool ppahng-hahk) (*winter vacation*)
개학 (gae-hahk)	start of school	언제 개학해요? 다음주 월요일에 해요.
		(uhn-jeh gae-hahk-kae-yoh? dah-eum-joo wuh-ryo-ee-reh hae-yoh)
		(*When does your school start? It starts next Monday.*)
개강 (gae-gahng)	start of semester (for college/ graduate school)	한국 대학교는 3월 초에 개강해요.
		(hahn-gook dae-hahk-kkyoh-neun sah-mwuhl choh-eh gae-gahng-hae-yoh)
		(*Colleges in Korea start in early March.*)

FUN & GAMES

A. Imagine that you're planning to work in Korea. Match these Korean job application or work-related words with their English equivalents.

1. 이력서	a. personal statement
2. 자기소개서	b. conference meeting
3. 면접	c. business trip
4. 추천서	d. company
5. 회의	e. resume
6. 출장	f. interview
7. 회사	g. recommendation letter
8. 연차 쓰다	h. to go to work
9. 출근하다	i. to leave work for the day
10. 퇴근하다	j. to take (days) off

B. Assume that you're planning to work at a Korean school. Match these school-related words with their English equivalents.

1. 학생	a. school vacation
2. 선생님	b. English
3. 초등학교	c. elementary school
4. 영어	d. teacher
5. 방학	e. student

See Appendix C for the answers.

3

Korean on the Go

Chapter **14**

Planning a Trip

Deciding to travel isn't just about throwing darts at a 지도 (jee-doh) (*map*), though that can be quite fun. Are you packing flip-flops or a power suit? Is it a 휴가 (hyoo-gah) (*vacation*) or a 출장 (chool-jjahng) (*business trip*)? Have you marked a 명소 (myuhng-soh) (*landmark*) or a local festival as a must-visit? Setting clear 여행 (yuh-haeng) (*travel*) goals and smart 계획 (gyeh-hwaek) (*planning*) can stretch your budget and make your time abroad more rewarding.

This chapter is your guide to choosing the optimal time to visit Korea, discovering places to explore, packing the essentials (and perhaps some extras), and engaging with locals. So grab your 여권 (yuh-kkwuhn) (*passport*) and 목베개 (mohk-ppeh-gae) (*neck pillow*). Adventure calls!

Picking a Good Time to Travel

Obviously, you wouldn't visit Korea in 한겨울 (hahn-gyuh-ool) (*midwinter*) for hiking, nor would you bring skis in 한여름 (hahn-nyuh-reum) (*midsummer*). The upcoming sections guide you in choosing optimal travel times, by exploring the seasons and holidays. (For information on how to say dates, see Chapter 5; for weather descriptions, see Chapter 4.)

Checking out the seasons

Checking out the 날씨 (nahl-ssee) (*weather*) is one of the to-do items when planning a trip. Korea has four very distinct seasons. Table 14-1 shows some key words on the 사계절 (sah-gyeh-juhl) (*four seasons*):

TABLE 14-1   **Korean Seasons and Weather**

Seasons	When	Weather
봄 (bohm) (*spring*)	3월~5월 (sah-mwuhl~oh-wuhl) (*March–May*)	Warm and dry. Korea bursts into bloom with flowers and leafy trees, ideal for enjoying the country's vibrant 꽃축제 (kkoht-chook-jjeh) (*flower festivals*). There's big temperature gap between day and night.
여름 (yuh-reum) (*summer*)	6월~8월 (yoo-wuhl~pah-rwuhl) (*June–August*)	Hot and humid. People beat the heat by retreating to the beaches and mountains. Summer festivals like the 머드축제 (muh-deu-chook-jjeh) (*mud festival*) highlights the season's festivities. 장마 (jahng-mah) (*monsoon rains*) typically span from late June to mid July.
가을 (gah-eul) (*fall*)	9월~11월 (goo-wuhl~shee-bee-rwuh) (*September–November*)	Cool and sunny. Best season to visit Korea. During 10월 (shee-wuhl) (*October*), the leaves turn color, known as 단풍 (dahn-poong) (*autumn foliage*), and the whole countryside turns a vivid orange, red, and yellow. As temperatures begin to drop, Korea gradually transitions into winter.
겨울 (gyuh-ool) (*winter*)	12월~2월 (shee-bee-wuhl~ee-wuhl) (*December–February*)	Cold and dry. Historically, Korea experienced a few days of intense cold followed by milder weather, but climate change has disrupted the typical winter pattern, affecting weather conditions worldwide.

Here are some sample sentences about seasons and weather. Feel free to replace the brackets with other seasons or months:

어느 계절을 (제일) 좋아하세요? (uh-neu gyeh-juh-reul (jeh-eel) joh-ah-hah-seh-yoh) (*Which season do you like (the most)?*)

저는 [여름]을 제일 좋아해요. (juh-neun [yuh-reum]-eul jeh-eel joh-ah-hae-yoh) (*I like [summer] the most.*)

한국 [6월] 날씨가 어때요? (hahn-gook [yoo-wuhl] nahl-ssee-gah uh-ttae-yoh) (*How is the [June] weather in Korea?*)

따뜻해요 (ttah-tteu-tae-yoh) (*It's warm.*)

덥고 습해요 (dup-kkoh seu-pae-yoh) (*It's hot and humid.*)

시원하고 맑아요 (shee-wuhn-hah-goh mahl-gah-yoh) (*It's cool and clear/sunny.*)

춥고 좀 건조해요 (choop-kkoh johm guhn-joh-hae-yoh) (*It's cold and a little dry.*)

Celebrating Korean holidays

Koreans officially follow the 양력 (yahng-nyuhk) (*Gregorian, solar calendar*), though some holidays, like New Year's Day and Korean Thanksgiving, are observed through the 음력 (eum-nyuhk) (*lunar calendar*) of that year.

On 공휴일 (gohng-hyoo-eel) (*public holidays*), while offices and banks take a break, palaces, museums, amusement facilities, and shops stay open. Millions of people return to their 고향 (goh-hyahng) (*hometown*) to celebrate with family. But these 공휴일 are also a popular time for trips, leading to hustle and bustle everywhere, from shopping centers to highways and airports. Here are some contexts in which you might talk about 공휴일:

오늘 무슨 날이에요? (oh-neul moo-seun nah-ree-eh-yoh) (*What holiday is today?; Is today a special day?*)

오늘 [어린이날]이에요. (oh-neul [uh-ree-nee-nahl]-ee-eh-yoh) (*Today is Children's Day.*)

[부산] 여행 언제 갈 거예요? ([booh-sahn] yuh-haeng uhn-jeh gahl kkuh-yeh-yoh) (*When are you going on a trip to [Busan]?*)

[크리스마스 연휴]에 갈 거예요. ([keu-ree-sseu-mah-sseu yuhn-hyoo]-eh gahl kkuh-yeh-yoh) (*I'm going during the [Christmas holiday].*)

Learn about some Korean 공휴일 listed in Table 14-2—those marked with an asterisk follow the lunar calendar. (For months and dates, see Chapter 5.)

On 설날 (suhl-lahl) (*New Year's Day*), people perform 세배 (seh-bae) (*New Year's deep bow*) as a New Year's greeting. During 세배, they often say 새해 복 많이 받으세요 (sae-hae bohk mah-nee bah-deu-seh-yoh) (*May you receive lots of luck in the new year*) and 건강하세요 (guhn-gahng-hah-seh-yoh) (*Please stay healthy*). In return, elders typically give 세뱃돈 (seh-baet-ttohn) (*New Year's monetary gifts*) and shar 덕담 (duhk-ttahm) (*warm wishes*).

TABLE 14-2 **Korean Holidays**

Korean	Date	Description
설날 (suhl-lahl) (*Lunar New Year*)	1/1* (일월 일일) (ee-rwuhl ee-reel)	Celebrated on the first day of the lunar calendar, this is one of Korea's most significant traditional holidays. It's three day holiday and people travel to reunite with family. Traditionally people eat 떡국 (ttuhk-kkook) (*sliced rice cake soup*) on 설날.
삼일절 (sah-meel-jjuhl) (*Independence Movement Day*)	3/1 (삼월 일일) (sah-mwuhl ee-reel)	Commemorates the March 1, 1919 Declaration of Independence during Japanese colonization, with ceremonies at 탑골공원 (tahp-kkohl-gohng-wuhn) (*Tapgol Park*) in Seoul, the site where the movement began. Notably, the new academic year in Korea starts shortly after 삼일절.
부처님오신날 (boo-chuh-neem-oh-sheen-nahl) (*Buddha's Birthday*)	4/8* (사월 팔일) (sah-wuhl pah-reel)	Also referred to as 석가탄신일 (suhk-kkah-tahn-shee-neel). Rituals are held at many 절 (juhl) (*temples*) nationwide. 연등 (yuhn-deung) (*lotus lanterns*) decorate 절 courtyards and are lit and paraded on the eve.
어린이날 (uh-ree-nee-nahl) (*Children's Day*)	5/5 (오월 오일) (oh-wuhl oh-eel)	On this day, 어린이 (*children*) enjoy outings to amusement parks, zoos, or cinemas. Just three days after 어린이날, on May 8th, is 어버이날 (uh-buh-ee-nahl) (*Parents' Day*), which is not a 공휴일 (gohng-hyoo-eel) (*public holiday*).
현충일 (hyuhn-choong-eel) (*Memorial Day*)	6/6 (유월 육일) (yuh-wuhl yuh-geel)	Dedicated to honoring fallen soldiers and civilians, the main ceremonies are held at the 국립묘지 (goong-neep-myoh-jee) (*National Cemetery*) in Seoul and Daejeon.
광복절 (gwahng-bohk-jjuhl) (*Liberation Day*)	8/15 (팔월 십오일) (pah-rwuhl shee-boh-eel)	August 15 marks the acceptance of the Allies' surrender terms by Japan in 1945, leading to Korea's liberation. The term 광복절 translates to "Restoration of Light Day," reflecting Korea's revival and proud history and emphasizing its restoration. 북한 (boo-kahn) (*North Korea*) also commemorates this day.
추석 (choo-suhk) (*Chuseok*)	8/15* (팔월 십오일) (pah-rwuhl shee-boh-eel)	Korean Thanksgiving Day: Also known as 한가위 (hahn-gah-wee) (*Hangawi*), this three-day holiday is time for families to gather, share traditional meals like 송편 (sohng-pyuhn) (*half moon-shaped rice cake*), 갈비찜 (gahl-bee-jjeem) (braised short ribs), and give thanks for the 추수 (choo-soo) (*harvest*).
개천절 (gae-chuhn-juhl) (*National Foundation Day*)	10/3 (시월 삼일) (shee-wuhl sah-meel)	Commemorating the foundation of Korea's first kingdom, 고조선 (goh-joh-suhn) (*Gojoseon*), in 2333 BC by 단군 (dahn-goon) (*Dangun*), who is often described as a mythical figure, 개천절 celebrates the creation of the nation.
한글날 (hahn-geul-lahl) (*Hangul Day*)	10/9 (시월 구일) (shee-wuhl goo-eel)	Celebrates the 한글 (hahn-geul) (*Korean alphabet*), invented by 세종대왕 (seh-johng-dae-wahng) (*King Sejong*) in 1443. 북한 (boo-kahn) (*North Korea*) also honors this on January 15th, calling it 조선글날 (joh-suhn-geul-lahl) (*Joseon Language Day*).
크리스마스 (keu-ree-sseu-mah-sseu) (*Christmas*)	12/25 (십이월 이십오일) (shee-bee-wuhl ee-shee-boh-eel)	Also known as 성탄절 (suhng-tahn-juhl), it's observed more quietly in Korea, compared to some Western countries. Many participate in secular festivities, yet it also holds special significance for those who engage in cherished and religious services, especially within the Christian community.

Holidays marked with an asterisk follow the lunar calendar.

TIP

To wish someone a happy holiday in Korean, or to talk about your holiday, you can use the verb 보내다 (boh-nae-dah) (*to spend (time)*):

[추석] 잘 보내세요! ([choo-suhk] jahl boh-nae-seh-yoh) (*Have a great [Choosuk]!*)

[연휴] 잘 보냈어요? 뭐 했어요? ([yuhn-hyoo] jahl boh-nae-ssuh-yoh mwuh hae-ssuh-yoh) (*Did you have a good [holiday]? What did you do?*)

네, 잘 보냈어요. 고향에서 가족 만나고 여행도 했어요. (neh, jahl boh-nae-ssuh-yoh goh-hyahng-eh-suh gah-johk mahn-nah-goh yuh-haeng-doh hae-ssuh-yoh) (*Yes, I had a good one. I met my family in my hometown and traveled as well.*)

Choosing Your Destination

If your visit is business-related, your destination may be predetermined. But if you're there to unwind, the entire country is available for your exploration. So, what catches your interest? Bustling events and vibrant festivals, serene historical sites, relaxing natural settings, or a mix of everything? All these and more await you. Despite its modest size, Korea is rich in 역사 (yuhk-ssah) (*history*) and 문화 (moon-hwah) (*culture*), offering a wealth of opportunities for exploration.

» **Urban Explorer:** For those who thrive in vibrant cityscapes and possibly some retail therapy, check out Seoul's dynamic districts like 강남 (gahng-nahm) (*Gangnam*), 이태원 (ee-tae-wuhn) (*Itaewon*), 명동 (myuhng-dohng) (*Myeongdong*), 홍대 (hohng-dae) (*Hongdae*), and 동대문 (dohng-dae-moon) (*Dongdaemun*), where shopping, dining, and entertainment await. For more on town exploration, see Chapter 11; for shopping adventures, see Chapter 10.

» **History Buffs:** Travel back in time in 경주 (gyuhng-joo) (*Gyeongju*), the heart of the ancient 신라 (sheel-lah) (*Silla Dynasty*), home to numerous 역사 유물 (yuhk-ssah yoo-mool) (*historical relics, artifacts*), 고분 (goh-boon) (*ancient tombs*), and 절 (juhl) (*temples*) dating back over a millennium. Known as a "museum without walls," 경주 is the city with the most UNESCO World Cultural Heritage Sites.

In 서울 (suh-ool) (*Seoul*), explore over 600 years of history amidst vibrant modernity through 고궁 (goh-goong) (*palaces*) like 경복궁 (gyuhng-bohk-kkoong) (*Gyeongbokgung Palace*) and 창덕궁 (chahng-duhk-kkoong) (*Changdeokgung Palace*), along with many 박물관 (bahng-mool-gwahn) (*museums*). Other historical cities like 강릉 (gahng-leung) (*Gangneung*), 안동 (ahn-dohng) (*Andong*), and 전주 (juhn-joo) (*Jeonju*) also offer rich cultural insights.

» **Coastal Retreats:** 해산물 (hae-sahn-mool) (*seafood*) lovers and 해변 (hae-byuhn) (*beaches*) enthusiasts visit the beautiful coastal cities along the 한반도

(*Korean Peninsula*), bordered by the 남해 (nahm-hae) (*South Sea*), 서해 (suh-hae) (*West Sea*), and 동해 (dohng-hae) (*East Sea*). Notable cities include 부산 (boo-sahn) (*Busan*), 남해 (nahm-hae) (*Namhae*), 통영 (tohng-yuhng) (*Tongyeong*), 거제 (guh-jeh) (*Geoje*), 인천 (een-chuhn) (*Incheon*), 보령 (boh-ryuhng) (*Boryeong*), 강릉 (gahng-leung) (*Gangneung*), and 속초 (sohk-choh) (*Sokcho*). Plus, there are many 섬 (suhm) (*islands*), like the renowned 제주도 (jeh-joo-doh) (*Jeju Island*).

>> **Nature Trails:** For those seeking to refresh and rejuvenate, Korea's 국립 공원 (goong-neep gohng-wuhn) (*national park*) such as 설악산 (suh-rahk-ssahn) (*Seoraksan*), 지리산 (jee-ree-sahn) (*Jirisan*), 북한산 (boo-kahn-sahn) (*Bukhansan*), and 한라산 (hahl-lah-sahn) (*Hallasan*) are great for nature walks, packed with wildlife surprises and attractions like cable car or temples. 등산 (deung-sahn) (*hiking, "mountain climbing"*) is Koreans' favorite leisure activity, with hidden culinary gems awaiting after a day on the trails.

These are just a few options. No matter where you go, each destination has a unique story and history, offering chances to immerse in diverse cultures and perhaps discover new aspects of yourself!

TIP

For a tailored experience, consider these search terms when looking up destination ideas online.

Natural exploration:

>> 국립/도립 공원 (goong-neep/doh-leep gohng-wuhn) (*national/provincial parks*)

>> 산/등산로 (sahn/deung-sahn-noh) (*mountains/hiking trails*)

>> 강/호수/바다/해변/해수욕장 (gahng/hoh-soo/bah-dah/hae-byuhn/hae-soo-yohk-jahng) (*rivers/lakes/seas/beaches/bathing beaches*)

>> 자연 경치 (jah-yuhn gyuhng-chee) (*natural scenery*)

>> 온천 (ohn-chuhn) (*hot springs*)

Traditional culture:

>> 민속촌 (meen-sohk-chohn) (*folk village*)

>> 유적지 (yoo-juhk-jjee) (*historical sites*)

>> 역사 유물 (yuhk-ssah yoo-mool) (*historical relics, artifacts*)

>> 박물관 (bahng-mool-gwahn) (*museums*)

- » 전통 문화/공예 체험 (juhn-tohng moon-hwah/gohng-yeh cheh-huhm) (*traditional culture/crafts experiences*)
- » 풍물 시장 (poong-mool shee-jahng) (*folk flea markets*)

Urban lifestyle:

- » 공연/행사 (gohng-yuhn/haeng-sah) (*performances/events*)
- » 야경 (yah-gyuhng) (*night views*)
- » 지역 축제 (jee-yuhk chook-jjeh) (*local festivals*)
- » 한류 관광 (hahl-lyoo gwahn-gwahng) (*Hallyu tourism*)

Miscellaneous travel terms:

- » 기차 여행 (gee-chah yuh-haeng) (*train travel*)
- » 명소/관광지 (myuhng-soh/gwahn-gwahng-jee) (*attractions/tourism spots*)
- » 배낭여행 (bae-nahng-yuh-haeng) (*backpacking*)
- » 음식 여행 (맛집 탐방) (eum-sheek yuh-haeng [maht-jjeep tahm-bahng]) (*food tours [gourmet exploring]*)
- » 추천 여행지 (choo-chuhn yuh-haeng-jee) (*recommended travel destinations*)
- » 테마 여행 (teh-mah yuh-haeng) (*themed travels*)

Talkin' the Talk

PLAY

Soojin and Jimmy plan to do something fun for the weekend.

Soojin: 지미 씨, 이번 주말에 뭐 할까요?
jee-mee ssee, ee-buhn joo-mah-leh mwuh hahl-kkah-yoh?
Jimmy, what shall we do this weekend?

Jimmy: 지난 주말에 등산했으니까 이번에는 다른 거 해요.
jee-nahn joo-mah-leh deung-sahn-hae-sseu-nee-kkah ee-buh-neh-neun dah-leun guh hae-yoh.
Since we hiked last weekend, let's do something different this time.

Soojin: 한강에 자전거 타러 갈래요?

hahn-gahng-eh jah-juhn-guh tah-ruh gahl-lae-yoh?

Would you like to go to the Hangang River for a bike ride?

Jimmy: 좋아요. 근데 저는 자전거가 없어요.

joh-ah-yoh. geun-deh juh-neun jah-juhn-guh-gah up-ssuh-yoh.

Good! But I don't have a bike.

Soojin: 빌리면 돼요. 싸고 편해요.

beel-lee-myuhn dwae-yoh. ssah-goh pyuhn-hae-yoh.

We can rent a bike. It's cheap and convenient.

Jimmy: 잘 됐네요. 어디에서 만날까요?

jahl dwaen-neh-yoh. uh-dee-eh-suh mahn-nahl-kkah-yoh?

Perfect. Where should we meet?

Soojin: 여의도 한강공원에서 만나요.

yuh-eui-doh hahn-gahng-gohng-wuh-neh-suh mahn-nah-yoh.

Let's meet at Yeouido Hangang Park.

Jimmy: 여의도에서 어디까지 가요?

yuh-eui-doh-eh-suh uh-dee-kkah-jee gah-yoh?

Where are we going up to from Yeouido?

Soojin: 반포대교까지 갈까요?

bahn-poh-dae-gyoh-kkah-jee gahl-kkah-yoh?

Shall we go up to Banpodaegyo Bridge?

Jimmy: 얼마나 걸려요?

uhl-mah-nah guhl-lyuh-yoh?

How long does it take?

Soojin: 한 시간쯤 걸릴 거예요.

hahn shee-gahn-jjeum guhl-leel kkuh-yeh-yoh.

It will take about an hour.

Jimmy: 우리 다음 주말에는 캠핑 가요.

oo-ree dah-eum joo-mah-leh-neun caem-peeng gah-yoh.

Let's go camping next weekend.

Soojin: 캠핑 좋지요. 캠핑장 예약할게요.

caem-peeng joh-chee-yoh. caem-peeng-jahng
yeh-yah-kahl-kkeh-yoh.

Camping sounds good. I'll make a reservation for a camp site.

• •

WORDS TO KNOW

주말	joo-mahl	weekend
등산했으니까 (등산하다)	deung-sahn-hae-sseu-nee-kkah	since we hiked
자전거	jah-juhn-guh	bicycle
빌리면 (빌리다)	beel-lee-myuhn	If you lend, borrow
편해요 (편하다)	pyuhn-hae-yoh	is convenient
걸려요 (걸리다)	guhl-lyuh-yoh	it takes (time)
캠핑(장)	kaem-peeng(-jahng)	camping (site)
예약할게요 (예약하다)	yeh-yah-kahl-kkeh-yoh	will make a reservation

Dealing with Passports and Visas

Many short-term visitors can enter Korea without a 비자 (bee-jah) (*visa*) through K-ETA (Korea Electronic Travel Authorization), and some nationalities are even exempt from this requirement. Check the specifics at www.k-eta.go.kr.

Planning to travel abroad from Korea? Verify the 비자 requirements of your destination by visiting their websites. You can apply directly through the relevant 대사관 (dae-sah-gwahn) (*embassy*) or use a 여행사 (yuh-haeng-sah) (*travel agency*). Don't forget to check your 여권 유효기간 (yuh-kkwuhn yoo-hyoh-gee-gahn) (*passport's expiration date*) well in advance to allow time for processing.

Following are some words and phrases that come in handy when you're dealing with passports and visas:

>> 국내/해외 여행 (goong-nae/hae-wae-yuh-haeng) (*domestic/overseas travel*)

>> 단기/장기 체류 (dahn-gee/jahng-gee cheh-ryoo) (*short-term/long-term stay*)

>> 대사관/총영사관 (dae-sah-gwahn/chohng-yuhng-sah-gwahn) (*embassy/consulate general*)

>> 비자 (bee-jah) (*visa*)

>> 사진 (sah-jeen) (*photo*)

>> 수수료 (soo-soo-ryoh) (*fee*)

» 신청서 (sheen-chuhng-suh) (*application form*)

» 여권 (yuh-kkwuhn) (*passport*)

» 입국 목적 (eep-kkook mohk-jjuhk) (*purpose of entry*)

» (개인) 정보 ([gae-een] juhng-boh) (*[personal] information*)

» 체류 기간 (cheh-ryoo gee-gahn) (*duration of stay*)

What to Pack?

Once your itinerary is all set, it's time to pack! Grab your 여행 가방 (yuh-haeng gah-bahng) (*travel bags/suitcases*) ready, and let's get started. Check out the list of some essentials you might need. Don't worry if you forget something or can't find an item at home; you can easily pick them up at a nearest 가게 (gah-geh) (*store*) or 공항 편의점 (gohng-hahng pyuh-nee-juhm) (*airport convenience store*).

» 모자 (moh-jah) (*hat*)

» 면도기 (myuhn-doh-gee) (*razor*)

» 빗 (beet) (*brush, comb*)

» 비상약 (bee-sahng-yahk) (*emergency medicines*)

» 선글라스 (ssuhn-geul-lah-sseu) (*sunglasses*)

» 속옷 (soh-goht) (*underwear*)

» 수영복 (soo-yuhng-bohk) (*swimsuit*)

» 신발 (sheen-bahl) (*shoes*)

» 양말 (yahng-mahl) (*socks*)

» 옷 (oht) (*clothes*)

» 우산 (oo-sahn) (*umbrella*)

» 자외선차단제 (jah-wae-suhn-chah-dahn-jeh) (*sunscreen*)

» 충전기 (choong-juhn-gee) (*charger*)

» 치약/칫솔 (chee-yahk/cheet-ssohl) (*toothpaste/toothbrush*)

» 화장품 (hwah-jahng-poom) (*cosmetics*)

Table 14-3 shows three essential verbs for packing luggage, along with example sentences. Replace the brackets with other items to practice.

TABLE 14-3 **Verbs of Packing**

Korean Verb	Meaning	Examples
싸다	to pack	[가방] 싸세요. ([gah-bahng] ssah-seh-yoh) (*Please pack [your bag].*)
		[양말] 쌌어요? ([yahng-mahl] ssah-ssuh-yoh) (*Did you pack [socks]?*)
챙기다	to bring, pack, take	[여권] 챙기세요. ([yuh-kkwuhn] chaeng-gee-seh-yoh) (*Please take your [passport].*)
		[충전기] 챙겼어요? ([choong-juhn-gee] chaeng-gyuh-ssuh-yoh) (*Did you bring the charger?*)
필요하다	to be necessary	[뭐] 필요해요? ([mwuh] pee-ryoh-hae-yoh) (*[What] do you need?*)
		[수영복] 안 필요해요? ([soo-yuhng-bohk] ahn pee-ryoh-hae-yoh) (*Don't you need [swimsuit]?*)

Talkin' the Talk

PLAY

Heather is planning a trip for a holiday. She is getting help from a travel agent, Mr. Kim, for her trip.

Mr. Kim: 어떻게 도와 드릴까요?
uh-ttuh-keh doh-wah deu-leel-kkah-yoh?
How can I help you?

Heather 추석 연휴에 여행 가려고 하는데요.
choo-suhk yuhn-hyoo-eh yuh-haeng gah-ryuh-goh hah-neun-deh-yoh.
I'm trying to go on a trip during the Chuseok holidays.

Mr. Kim: 국내여행이요, 해외여행이요?
goong-nae-yuh-haeng-ee-yoh, hae-wae-yuh-haeng-ee-yoh?
Domestic or overseas travel?

Heather: 아직 안 정했어요. 추천 좀 해 주세요.
ah-jeek ahn juhng-hae-ssuh-yoh. choo-chuhn johm hae joo-seh-yoh.
I haven't decided yet. What would you recommend?

Mr. Kim:	국내여행은 제주도, 경주, 부산 2박3일, 해외여행은 홍콩 3박4일 패키지가 있어요.

Mr. Kim: 국내여행은 제주도, 경주, 부산 2박3일, 해외여행은 홍콩 3박4일 패키지가 있어요.
goong-nae-yuh-haeng-eun jeh-joo-doh, gyuhng-joo, boo-sahn ee-bahk-sah-meel, hae-wae-yuh-haeng-eun hohng-kohng sahm-bahk-sah-eel pae-kee-jee-gah ee-ssuh-yoh.
For a domestic trip, there's a 2-night and 3-day package trip to Jeju Island, Gyungju or Busan, and for an overseas trip, we have a 3-night and 4-day trip to Hong Kong.

Heather: 2박3일이 좋겠어요. 제주도하고 경주는 가 봤어요. 부산 어때요?
ee-bahk-sah-mee-ree joh-keh-ssuh-yoh. jeh-joo-doh-hah-goh gyuhng-joo-neun gah bwah-ssuh-yoh. boo-sahn uh-ttae-yoh?
The 2-day-3-night trip will be good. I've been to Jeju Island and Gyungju. How about Busan?

Mr. Kim: 부산 좋아요. 후회 안 하실 거예요.
boo-sahn joh-ah-yoh. hoo-wae ahn hah-sheel kkuh-yeh-yoh.
Busan is good. You won't regret.

Heather: 패키지에 뭐가 포함돼요?
pae-kee-jee-eh mwuh-gah poh-hahm-dwae-yoh?
What's included in the package?

Mr. Kim: 항공권, 호텔, 투어 다 포함돼요.
hahng-gohng-kkwuhn, hoh-tehl, too-uh dah poh-hahm-dwae-yoh.
Airplane tickets, hotel, and a tour are all included.

Heather: 잘 됐네요. 인천공항에서 출발해요?
jahl dwaen-neh-yoh. een-chuhn-gohng-hahng-eh-suh chool-bahl-hae-yoh?
That's great. Do I depart from the Incheon Airport?

Mr. Kim: 아니요. 김포공항에서 출발해요. 여권 꼭 챙기세요.
ah-nee-yoh. geem-poh-gohng-hahng-eh-suh chool-bahl-hae-yoh. yuh-kkwuhn kkohk chaeng-gee-seh-yoh.
No. You'll depart from the Kimpo Airport. Please make sure to pack your passport.

• •

WORDS TO KNOW

연휴	yuhn-hyoo	long holiday
국내여행	goong-nae-yuh-haeng	domestic travel
해외여행	hae-wae-yuh-haeng	overseas travel
모르겠어요 (모르다)	moh-reu-geh-ssuh-yoh	don't know
추천	choo-chuhn	recommendation
2박3일	ee-bahk-sah-meel	2 nights, 3 days
후회	hoo-hwae	regret
포함돼요 (포함되다)	poh-hahm-dwae-yoh	be included
항공권	hahng-gohng-kkwuhn	air ticket

FUN & GAMES

You have free time for a day in Seoul and want to go around the city. Referring to the map below, write down your detailed plans for the day, including (1) places you will visit and (2) activities you plan to do, in Korean. Try to be ambitious and vigorous with as many activities as you can come up with. (Answers vary; see Appendix C for possible answers.)

TRAVEL
SEOUL

bbtreesubmission / 123RF

1. (1) _____ (2) _____

2. (1) _____ (2) _____

3. (1) _____ (2) _____

4. (1) _____ (2) _____

5. (1) _____ (2) _____

6. (1) _____ (2) _____

Chapter **15**

Finding a Place to Stay

When planning a 여행 (yuh-haeng) (*trip*) to a far-off destination, it's easy to dream about all the exciting activities awaiting you. But, before starting your adventures, you need a cozy 숙소 (sook-ssoh) (*accommodation*) to relax and recharge. If you end up in a run-down or dilapidated 숙소, your experience might not be as enjoyable. So, choosing your 숙소 carefully is 중요해요 (joong-yoh-hae-yoh) (*important*), whether you travel 혼자 (hohn-jah) (*alone*) or with others.

This chapter covers the ins and outs of choosing the right 숙소 that fits your personal preferences and budget. We've got you covered with various options and helpful phrases for making reservations and check in/out. We want to make sure that your choice of 숙소 doesn't disappoint you, so stay tuned!

Sorting Accommodation Options

Korea offers a wide range of 숙소 types to suit diverse preferences, spanning budget guesthouses to high-end hotels, catering to various 예산 (yeh-sahn) (*budget*) and 기간 (gee-gahn) (*period*). The following section guides you in choosing the right 숙소 to help you avoid any unpleasant surprises.

Hotels

Just like anywhere else around the world, you can find franchise 호텔 (hoh-tehl) (*hotels*) in Korea. These hotels provide the usual, predictable 편의 시설 (pyuh-nee shee-shuhl) (*facilities*) and 서비스 (ssuh-bee-sseu) (*services*). If you're traveling on a generous budget and prefer familiar experiences, these places are perfect. The 직원들 (jee-gwuhn-deul) (*staff members*) are fluent in 영어 (yuhng-uh) (*English*), so you'll have little problem at these places.

If you're looking for more of a Korean-style adventure or are interested in exploring a less-beaten path, you can find numerous 숙소 options. These are often more affordable than franchise hotels.

Hanok stay

If you want to experience Korea's rich cultural heritage in a unique and immersive way while enjoying modern comfort, a 한옥 (hah-nohk) (*traditional Korean house*) is your go-to accommodation. Known for its 친환경 (cheen-hwahn-gyuhng) (*eco-friendly*) materials like 흙 (heuk) (*earth*), 나무 (nah-moo) (*wood*), and 돌 (dohl) (*rock*), 한옥 offers a distinctive stay. Some 한옥 스테이 (hah-nohk seu-teh-ee) (*Hanok stays*) also provide workshops on 전통 공예 (juhn-tohng gohng-yeh) (*traditional crafts*), 전통 요리 (juhn-tohng yoh-ree) (*traditional cooking*), 다도 (dah-doh) (*tea ceremonies*), and more. Check out the following websites, and get ready to be transported back in time!

» https://english.visitkorea.or.kr/svc/main/index.do

» https://hanok.seoul.go.kr/front/eng/index.do

» https://hanok.jeonju.go.kr

CULTURAL WISDOM

The traditional sleeping arrangement doesn't include a 침대 (cheem-dae) (*bed*). Instead, you find a 요 (yoh) (*a thick, heavy folding mattress*) and 이불 (ee-bool) (*blanket*) in the 장롱 (jahng-nohng) (*closet*) of a room. Spread the 요 out on the floor and use the 이불 to keep yourself warm. This arrangement may sound uncomfortable, but it is much softer than you think. Also, when you wake up, fold the 요 and 이불 as you found them and put them back in the closet or stack them in the corner. In Korea, "making your bed" means "folding your bed." This act is called 이불 개다 (ee-bool gae-dah) (*to fold the blanket*)– 이불 개요 (gae-yoh) in its informal polite ending. Proper etiquette is to take care of your bed yourself as soon as you wake up.

While staying in a 한옥, remove your shoes before entering the living spaces due to Korea's floor-based culture. Concerned about cold floors during 겨울 (gyuh-ool) (*winter*)? Don't be! Korea's unique 온돌 (ohn-dohl) (*heated floor*) system keeps you warm, letting you sleep peacefully even on the coldest of nights!

Guesthouses and meen-bahk

Next are 게스트 하우스 (geh-seu-teu hah-oo-sseu) (*guesthouses*), offering accommodations from shared dormitory-style rooms to private rooms with varying levels of amenities. They are particularly popular among people who go 배낭여행 (bae-nahng-nyuh-haeng) (*backpacking*) and those seeking affordable options.

Similar are 민박 (meen-bahk) (*Korean bed & breakfasts*), which are homier and more informal than hotels or motels. Their smaller size often allows for more interaction with staff and other guests.

Motels and hostels

모텔 (moh-tehl) (*motels*) are everywhere, marked by bright neon signs. Nowadays, 무인텔 (moo-een-tehl) (*staff-less/self-check-in motel*) have gained popularity due to lower labor costs. 무인 (moo-een) means "no person" and 텔 (tehl) is from 모텔. The facilities in 무인텔 are relatively newer and more modern.

A more affordable option is 호스텔 (hoh-seu-tehl) (*hostel*). You share a room with other guests and have 공용 샤워실 (gohng-yohng shyah-wuh-sheel) (*communal showers*) and 화장실 (hwah-jahng-sheel) (*restrooms*) per floor. They may or may not have a cafeteria or a 부엌 (boo-uhk) (*kitchen*) for meals.

Temple-stay and campsites

Looking for other unique places to stay? Try 템플 스테이 (tehm-peul seu-teh-ee) (*temple-stay*). Literally meaning "staying at a temple," 템플 스테이 offers accommodations in Buddhist 절 (juhl) (*temples*) in Korea. You can enjoy peaceful surroundings, healthy 채식 (chae-sheek) (*vegetarian food*), and engage in activities like meditation or tea ceremonies. For more info, visit https://eng.templestay.com.

Another nature-friendly accommodation is 캠핑장 (kaem-peeng-jahng) (*campgrounds*). 캠핑 (camping) is a popular accommodation choice in Korea, including 도시 캠핑 (doh-shee kaem-peeng) (*urban camping*) in the city. No camping equipment? No worries! 글램핑 (geul-laem-peeng) (*glamping*) is available in many locations, from busy cities and to remote mountains and beaches. Some luxury hotels like the *Shilla Jeju Hotel* offer glamping programs, too. For more info on unique accommodations, visit https://english.visitkorea.or.kr/.

ACCOMMODATION APPS

An accommodation app is essential for finding the right place to stay. While globally popular apps like Airbnb are widely used, if you're in Korea, try these local booking apps for localized info and 할인 혜택 (hah-reen heh-taek) (*discount deals*): Yanolja (야놀자; yah-nohl-jah), Yeogi-eottae (여기 어때; yuh-gee uh-ttae), iTourSeoul+ (아이투어서울; ah-ee-too-uh suh-ool), or Interpark Tour (인터파크 투어; een-tuh-pah-keu too-uh).

These apps also offer 예약 서비스 (yeh-yahk ssuh-bee-sseu) (*reservation services*) for 항공 (hahng-gohng) (*flights*), 교통 (gyoh-tohng) (*transportation*), 해외 숙소 (hae-wae sook-ssoh) (*overseas accommodations*), 레저 활동 (leh-juh hwahl-ttohng) (*leisure activities*), and local festival tickets. Apps like 야놀자 and 여기 어때 are currently only in Korean. You can use 파파고 (pah-pah-goh) (*Papago*), the top Korean translation app, to help you out!

Jjeem-jeel-bahng

Looking for a wallet-friendly option to relax? Check out the 찜질방 (jjeem-jeel-bahng) (*Korean saunas/bathhouses*) in your area! They offer a great way to unwind in saunas without breaking the bank. Some 찜질방 are open 24/7, with sleeping rooms called 수면실 (soo-myuhn-sheel) available any time. Feel free to check in and out whenever it suits you. (For more info about their facilities, flip to Chapter 11.)

Long-term stay

If you plan to stay in Korea for a while and need long-term accommodation, some places mentioned earlier in this chapter offer long-term stays, so they're worth checking out. You can also look into 원룸 (wuhn-noom) (*studio*) or 오피스텔 (oh-pee-seu-tehl) (*officetel*), similar to studio apartments. While searching, use terms like 장기 숙박 (jahng-gee sook-ppahk) (*long-term lodging/accommodation*) or 장기 체류 (jahng-gee cheh-lyoo) (*long-term stay*).

Making Reservations

Once you've picked your area and accommodation type, it's time to make a 예약 (yeh-yahk) (*reservation*)! You can do it online, via apps, over the phone, or, though less common, in person.

Reserving online

For 온라인 예약 (ohn-nah-een yeh-yahk) (*online reservation*) on Korean websites or apps, the following terms will come in handy:

» **지역 (jee-yuhk) (*region*):** 도시 (doh-shee) (*city*), 위치 (wee-chee) (*location*), 교통 (gyoh-tohng) (*transportation*)

» **날짜 (nahl-jjah) (*dates*):** 체크인 (cheh-keu-een) (*check-in*), 체크아웃 (cheh-keu-ah-oot) (*check-out*), 1박 (eel-bahk) (*one night*) (*박 — a counter for *night*)

» **인원 (ee-nwuhn) (*number of people*):** 성인/어른 (suhng-een/uh-leun) (*adult*), 아동/어린이 (ah-dohng/uh-lee-nee) (*children*), 최대 인원 (chwae-dae ee-nwuhn) (*maximum number of people*)

» **객실 (gaek-sseel) (*room in a hotel, cabin*):** 1인실/싱글룸 (ee-leen-sheel/sseeng-geul-loom) (*1 person room*), 2인실/더블룸 (ee-een-sheel/ duh-beul-loom) (*2 people room*), 침대 (cheem-dae) (*bed*)

» **편의 시설 (pyuh-nee shee-suhl) (*facilities*):** 수영장 (soo-yuhng-jahng) (*swimming pool*), 사우나 (ssah-oo-nah) (*sauna*), 스파 (seu-pah) (*spa*), 헬스장/피트니스 (hehl-sseu-jahng /pee-teu-nee-sseu) (*fitness facilities*), 주방/부엌 (joo-bahng/boo-uhk) (*kitchen*), 에어컨 (eh-uh-kuhn) (*air conditioner*), 주차장 (joo-chah-jahng) (*parking lot*)

» **서비스 (ssuh-bee-sseu) (*services*):** 조식/아침 식사 (joh-sheek/ah-cheem sheek-ssah) (*breakfast*), 룸서비스 (loom-ssuh-bee-sseu) (*room service*), 세탁 서비스 (seh-tahk ssuh-bee-sseu) (*laundry service*), 반려동물 허용 (bahl-lyuh-dohng-mool huh-yohng) (*pet friendly*), 휠체어 시설 (hweel-cheh-uh shee-shuhl) (*wheelchair facilities*), 대여 (dae-yuh) (*rental*), 와이파이 (wah-ee-pah-ee) (*Wi-Fi*), 무료 취소 (moo-ryoh chwee-soh) (*free cancellation*)

CULTURAL WISDOM

The standard 전압 (juh-nahp) (*voltage*) in Korea is 220. If your country uses between 220 and 240, like in Australia, Europe, and most of Asia and Africa, you're fine. If your country uses between the 100- and 127-volt range, it's a good idea to pack a 2-in-1 voltage converter and power adapter.

Reserving via call

If you make a reservation on the phone or in person at the 안내 데스크 (ahn-nae deh-seu-keu) (*front desk*), the most important thing, of course, is to find out 빈방 (been-bahng) (*vacancy*). You can start with:

방 예약하려고 하는데요. (bahng yeh-yah-kah-ryuh-goh hah-neun-deh-yoh.) (*I'd like to make a reservation for a room.*)

[오늘] 방 있어요? ([oh-neul] bahng ee-ssuh-yoh?) (*Do you have a room [(for) today]?*)

Talking about when you stay

The clerk may ask you for the dates to check in and out.

날짜는요? (nahl-jjah-neun-nyoh?) (*How about the dates?*)

며칠부터 며칠까지요? (myuh-cheel-boo-tuh myuh-cheel-kkah-jee-yoh?) (*From what date to what date?*)

To give a range of dates, use the particles 부터 (*from*) and 까지 (*until*):

[7월 9일]부터 [12일]까지요. ([chee-rwuhl goo-eel]-boo-tuh [shee-bee-eel]-kkah-jee-yoh.) (*From [July 9th] to the [12th].*)

[내일]부터 [토요일]까지요. ([nae-eel]-boo-tuh [toh-yoh-eel]-kkah-jee-yoh.) (*From [tomorrow] to [Saturday].*)

You can replace the words in the brackets with other time expressions. (Visit Chapter 5 for dates and days of the week.)

To ask and respond politely in the simplest way, use the polite ending marker (이)요 ((ee)-yoh) after a [Noun/Noun+particle phrase]. If it ends in a consonant, add 이요; if it ends in a vowel, just add 요.

For instance, to say "I will stay until the 5th," your full answer in Korean would be "5일까지 있을 거예요" (oh-eel-kkah-jee ee-sseul kkuh-yeh-yoh). But you can keep it short, simple, and still polite: "5일까지요" (oh-eel-kkah-jee-yoh) (*Until the 5th.*).

Telling how many people

Another important question from the staff would be:

몇 분이세요? (myuht ppoo-nee-seh-yoh?) (*How many people?*)

To answer, use the native Korean number with 명 (myuhng) (*person: non-honorific noun counter*) or simply say the native Korean number only. (For more info on noun counters, see Chapter 5.)

한 명이요. (hahn myuhng-ee-yoh.) (*One person.*) or 하나요 (hah-nah-yoh.) (*One.*)

두 명이요. (doo myuhng-ee-yoh.) (*Two people.*) or 둘이요 (doo-ree-yoh.) (*Two.*)

어른 셋, 아이 넷이요. (uh-reun seht, ah-ee neh-shee-yoh.) (*Three adults, four children.*)

Checking out facilities

It's always a good idea to double-check if the price includes the facilities you want. To ask if they have the facilities or amenities you need, use [facilities] 있어요? (ee-ssuh-yoh) (*Do you have [facilities]?/Is there [facilities]?*). Here are some examples.

Q: 방에 [에어컨] 있어요? (bahng-eh [eh-uh-kuhn] ee-ssuh-yoh?) (*Is there an [air conditioner] in the room?*)

A: 네, 그럼요. (neh, geu-ruhm-nyoh.) (*Yes, of course.*)

Q: [침대] 몇 개 있어요? ([cheem-dae] myuht kkae ee-ssuh-yoh?) (*How many [beds] are there?*)

A: [더블 침대] 하나 있어요. ([dub-beul cheem-dae] hah-nah ee-ssuh-yoh.) (*There is one [full-size bed].*)

Q: [무료 주차장] 있어요? ([moo-ryoh joo-chah-jahng] ee-ssuh-yoh?) (*Is there a [complimentary/free parking]?*)

A: 없어요. 주차는 유료예요. (uhp-ssuh-yoh. joo-chah-neun yoo-ryoh-yeh-yoh.) (*No, there isn't. There's a fee for parking.*)

Q: [헬스장] 있어요? 몇 시까지 해요? ([hehl-sseu-jahng] ee-ssuh-yoh? myuht ssee-kkah-jee hae-yoh?) (*Do you have a [gym]? Until what time is it open?*)

A: [아침 여섯] 시부터 [밤 열] 시까지요. ([ah-cheem yuh-suht] ssee-boo-tuh [bahm yuhl] ssee-kkah-jee-yoh.) (*From [6am] to [10pm].*)

Price matters: Understanding the fee

Certainly, another important question to ask is fees:

[하루에] 얼마예요? ([hah-roo-eh] uhl-mah-yeh-yoh?) (*What's the rate [per day]?*)

[주차비] 얼마예요? ([joo-chah-bee] uhl-mah-yeh-yoh?) (*How much is [the parking fee]?*)

[취소 수수료] 있어요? ([chwee-soh] soo-soo-ryoh ee-ssuh-yoh?) (*Is there a cancellation fee?*)

TIP

If you're traveling during 성수기 (suhng-soo-gee) (*peak season*), like 여름 방학 (yuh-reum ppahng-hahk) (*summer vacation*) or 연휴 (yuhn-hyoo) (*holidays*), expect higher 요금 (yoh-geum) (*rate*). In Seoul, guesthouses range from $40 to $100+ per night, depending on type, area, size, and amenities.

Checking In Made Easy

You've secured your reservation, and now it's check-in day! Here are some questions you may want to ask during check-in:

[체크인/체크아웃 시간], 몇 시예요? ([cheh-keu-een/cheh-keu-ah-oot shee-gahn], myuht ssee-yeh-yoh?) (*What time is [check-in/check-out]?*)

[조식 메뉴], 뭐예요? ([joh-sheek meh-nyoo] mwuh-yeh-yoh?) (*What's on the [breakfast menu]?*)

[와이파이 비밀번호], 뭐예요? ([wah-ee-pah-ee bee-meel-buhn-hoh] mwuh-yeh-yoh) (*What's the [Wi-Fi password]?*)

Talkin' the Talk

PLAY

Dan is planning to travel around Korea. He calls Shilla Hanok Stay.

Dan: 신라 한옥스테이지요?
shilla hah-nohk-seu-teh-ee-jee-yoh?
Is this Shilla Hanok Stay?

Clerk: 네, 신라 한옥입니다.
neh, shilla hah-noh-geem-nee-dah.
Yes, this is Shilla Hanok.

Dan: 방 예약하려고 하는데요.
bahng yeh-yah-kah-ryuh-goh hah-neun-deh-yoh.
I would like to reserve a room.

Clerk: 네. 몇 분이세요?
neh, myuht ppoo-nee-seh-yoh?
Sure. How many people?

Dan: 두 명이요.
doo myuhng-ee-yoh.
Two people.

Clerk: 날짜는요?
nahl-jjah-neun-nyoh?
How about the dates?

Dan: 7월 5일부터 8일까지, 3박 4일요. 하루에 얼마예요?
chee-rwuhl oh-eel-boo-tuh pah-leel-kkah-jee, samh-bahk-sah-eel-yoh. hah-roo-eh uhl-mah-yeh-yoh?
From July 5th to 8th, 3 nights and 4 days. What's the rate per day?

Clerk:	더블룸은 구만 오천 원입니다. 예약하시겠어요?
	duh-beul-loo-meun goo-mahn oh-chuhn-won-eem-nee-dah. yeh-yah-kah-shee-geh-ssuh-yoh?
	A double room is 95,000 won. Would you like to make a reservation?
Dan:	아침 식사 포함돼요?
	ah-cheem-sheek-ssah poh-hahm-dwae-yoh?
	Is the breakfast included?
Clerk:	네. 포함됩니다.
	neh. poh-hahm-dwaem-nee-dah.
	Yes, it's included.
Dan:	예약할게요. 체크인 시간은 몇 시예요?
	yeh-yah-kahl-kkeh-yoh. cheh-keu-een shee-gah-neun myuht ssee-yeh-yoh?
	I will make a reservation. What time is check-in?
Clerk:	체크인은 오후 세 시부터입니다.
	cheh-keu-ee-neun oh-hoo seh-shee-boo-tuh-eem-nee-dah.
	Check-in starts at 3pm.

- -

WORDS TO KNOW

예약하려고 하는데요 (예약하다)	yeh-yah-kah-ryuh-goh hah-neun-deh-yoh	I would like to make a reservation
분	boon	person (honorific noun counter)
날짜	nahl-jjah	date
3박	sahm-bahk	three nights (* 박: counter for nights)
하루에	hah-roo-eh	per day
얼마예요?	uhl-mah-yeh-yoh	how much is it?
포함돼요 (포함되다)	poh-hahm-dwae-yoh	is included
몇 시예요?	myuht ssee-yeh-yoh	what time is (it)?

Asking about amenities and services

In-room amenities are important to check too. Here are some common amenities in Korean.

>> 세면 용품 (seh-myuhn yohng-poom) (*toiletries*)

>> 비누 (bee-noo) (*soap*)

>> 바디워시 (bah-dee-wuh-shee) (*bodywash*)

>> 샴푸 (shyahm-poo) (*shampoo*)

>> 린스 (leen-sseu) (*conditioner*)

>> 치약 (chee-yahk) (*toothpaste*)

>> 칫솔 (cheet-ssohl) (*toothbrush*)

>> 빗 (beet) (*comb*)

>> 면도기 (myuhn-doh-gee) (*razor*)

>> 수건/타월 (soo-guhn/tah-wuhl) (*towels*)

>> 화장지 (hwah-jahng-jee) (*toilet paper, tissues*)

>> 헤어 드라이기 (heh-uh deu-rah-ee-gee) (*hair dryer*)

>> 다리미 (dah-ree-mee) (*iron*)

>> 미니냉장고 (mee-nee naeng-jahng-goh) (*mini refrigerator*)

>> 전자레인지 (juhn-jah-reh-een-jee) (*microwave*)

>> 커피메이커 (kuh-pee meh-ee-kuh) (*coffee maker*)

>> 컵 (kuhp) (*cup*)

TIP

To request any of these amenities, use one of the following phrases.

[수건] 좀 주세요. ([soo-guhn] johm joo-seh-yoh) (*Please give [towels]/Can I get [towels]?*)

[수건] 좀 주실래요? ([soo-guhn] johm joo-sheel-lae-yoh) (*Could you give [towels]?*)

좀 (johm) here serves as a "politeness marker," softening the request for favor. To express "more," add 더 (duh) (*more*) before 주세요.

화장지 좀 **더** 주실래요? (hwah-jahng-jee jom duh joo-sheel-lae-yoh) (*Could you give me some more toilet paper, please?*)

샴푸하고 린스, **더** 주실래요? (shahm-poo-hah-goh leen-sseu duh joo-sheel-lae-yoh) (*Could you give more shampoo and conditioner, please?*)

TIP

To ask if they have services you want, you can use the handy pattern: [service] 돼요? (dwae-yoh?) (*Is [service] available?*).

지금 룸서비스 돼요? (jee-geum [loom-ssuh-bee-sseu] dwae-yoh?) (*Is [room service] available now?*)

[노트북 대여] 돼요? ([noh-teu-book dae-yuh] dwae-yoh) (*Do you offer a [laptop rental service]?*)

[세탁 서비스] 돼요? ([seh-tahk ssuh-bee-sseu] dwae-yoh) (*Do you offer [laundry service]?*)

[아침 식사] 돼요? 몇 시부터요? ([ah-cheem sheek-ssah] dwae-yoh? myuht-ssee-boo-tuh-yoh) (*Is [breakfast] available? From what time?*)

If it's good news, they'll say, 네, 돼요. (neh, dwae-yoh) (*Yes, it's available*). If it's bad news, you'll hear, 아니요, (지금) 안 돼요. (ah-nee-yoh, (jee-geum) ahn dwae-yoh) (*No, it's not available (now/at the moment).*)

Making the most of your stay

Looking for some insider knowledge about the area? Ask the staff for their recommendations. They'd know all the good spots and will be happy to share their tips with you. Here are some useful phrases to help you find the best spots around:

이 근처에 [맛집] 있어요? (ee geun-chuh-eh [maht-jjeep] ee-ssuh-yoh) (*Is there a [good/must-try restaurant] nearby?*)

이 근처에 [가볼 만한 곳] 어디예요? (ee geun-chuh-eh [gah-bohl mah-nahn goht] uh-dee-yeh-yoh?) (*What are the [places worth visiting] around here?*)

[place]에 어떻게 가요? ([place]-eh uh-ttuh-keh gah-yoh) (*How do I get to [place]?*)

[택시/투어] 예약 좀 도와주실래요? ([taek-ssee/too-uh] yeh-yahk jjohm doh-wah-joo-sheel-lae-yoh) (*Could you help me book [a taxi/tour]?*)

Checking Out and Paying Your Bill

Congratulations! Your stay has ended (hopefully it was a delightful experience!), and payment is due (if not already made). To pay, go to check-in and say:

체크아웃 할게요. (cheh-keu-ah-oot hahl-kkeh-yoh) (*I'm checking out.*)

카드로 / 현금으로 결제할게요. (kah-deu-roh / hyuhn-geu-meu-roh gyuhl-jjeh-hahl-kkeh-yoh) (*I'll pay by card / in cash.*)

영수증 주세요. (yuhng-soo-jeung joo-seh-yoh) (*The receipt, please.*)

영수증, 이메일로 보내 주세요. (yuhng-soo-jeung ee-meh-eel-loh boh-nae joo-seh-yoh) (*Please send the receipt via email.*)

Most accommodations have a check-out time of 11–12pm. If you have a late flight, ask the clerk, 짐 보관 돼요? (jeem boh-gwahn dwae-yoh) (*Can I leave my bag here?*) or 짐 보관 되지요? (jeem boh-gwahn dwae-jee-yoh) (*The luggage storage service is available, right?*) to leave your luggage. They'll be happy to help! And now you can enjoy your day without having to worry about your bags!

FUN & GAMES

Below are some situations and Korean expressions. Match each situation with the most appropriate Korean expression. See the answers in Appendix C.

1. You are making a phone call to a guesthouse to check if there is a vacancy.

2. You are curious if breakfast is available in the guesthouse.

3. You are calling to inquire about the nightly rate at a hotel.

4. You would like to request extra towels.

5. You go to the hotel front desk to complete the check-out process.

a. 하루에 얼마예요?

b. 방 있어요?

c. 아침 식사 돼요?

d. 체크아웃 할게요.

e. 수건 좀 더 주세요.

Chapter 16

Making Your Way Around: Transportation

Navigating Korea's bustling streets, especially in packed cities like Seoul, can be quite the adventure due to its high population density. But don't worry-Korea's 대중교통 (daeh-joong-gyoh-tohng) (*public transport*) system is quite convenient, efficient and reliable. Quickly learn the ropes of subways and buses, and you'll be navigating with ease.

This chapter will equip you with key phrases and tips to ease your travels through airports, bus terminals, subway stations, and when hailing cabs. With a little preparation, you can make your journeys smooth and swift. So buckle up, and 출발 (chool-bahl) (*Let's go*)!

Essential Terms for Every Transit

First up, the basics! Whether you're hopping on a train, boarding a plane, or anything in between, the verb 타다 (tah-dah) is your go-to for expressing "to ride," "to get on," or "to get in." And unless you're planning to permanently reside on that vehicle, you'll need to know 내리다 (nae-ree-dah) (*to get off*). Table 16-1 presents how to use these verbs, along with some other common transit-related verbs and adjectives, in sentences:

TABLE 16-1   Common Verbs and Adjectives for Transit

Korean	Meaning	Examples
타다	to ride/get on	부산까지 기차(를) 타요? (boo-sahn-kkah-jee gee-chah(-reul) tah-yoh) (*Do you take a train to Busan?*)
내리다	to get off	어디에서 내려요? (uh-dee-eh-suh nae-ryuh-yoh) (*Where do I get off?*)
갈아타다	to transfer	어디에서 2호선으로 갈아타요? (uh-dee-eh-suh ee-hoh-suh-neu-roh gah-rah-tah-yoh) (*Where do I transfer to (subway) Line No.2?*)
도착하다	to arrive	언제 도착해요? (uhn-jeh doh-chah-kae-yoh) (*When do you arrive?/when does it arrive?*)
출발하다	to depart	몇 시에 출발해요? (myuht-ssee-eh chool-bahl-hae-yoh) (*What time do you depart?/What time does it depart?*)
예매하다	to buy in advance	어디에서 표 예매해요? (uh-dee-eh-suh pyoh yeh-mae-hae-yoh) (*Where do you buy tickets in advance?*)
편하다	to be comfortable, convenient	기차 의자가 편해요. (gee-chah eui-jah-gah pyuhn-hae-yoh) (*The train seats are comfy.*)
편리하다	to be convenient	교통이 편리해요. (gyoh-tohng-ee pyuhl-lee-hae-yoh) (*The transportation is convenient.*)
복잡하다	to be crowded, complex	교통이 복잡해요. (gyoh-tohng-ee bohk-jjah-pae-yoh) (*The traffic is jammed.*) 지도가 좀 복잡해요. (jee-doh-gah johm bohk-jjah-pae-yoh) (*The map is a little complex.*)
빠르다	to be fast	서울에서 부산까지 뭐가 빨라요? (suh-oo-reh-suh boo-sahn-kkah-jee mwuh-gah ppahl-lah-yoh) (*What's the fastest way to get from Seoul to Busan?*)

GRAMMATICALLY SPEAKING

Remember that 타다 uses the object particle 을/를, but it's commonly dropped in casual speech, so you can just say "[transport] 타다." However, the 에서 (eh-suh) (*from*) particle is always included, so say "[transport]에서 내리다."

TIP

Key transit-related nouns can also come in handy. Here are a few:

>> 노선도 (noh-suhn-doh) (*route map*)

>> 매표소 (mae-pyoh-soh) (*ticket booth*)

>> 시간표 (shee-gahn-pyoh) (*schedule chart*)

- **»** 역 (yuhk) (*station*)

- **»** 연착 (yuhn-chahk) (*delayed arrival*)

- **»** 출발/도착 시간 (chool-bahl/doh-chahk shee-gahn) (*departure/arrival time*)

- **»** 편도/왕복 (pyuhn-doh/wahng-bohk) (*one-way/round-trip*)

- **»** 환승 (hwahn-seung) (*transfer*)

Here is how these nouns can be used in questions:

[왕복] 얼마예요? ([wahng-bohk] uhl-mah-yeh-yoh) (*How much is the [round-trip]?*)

[매표소]가 어디 있어요? ([mae-pyoh-soh]-gah uh-dee ee-ssuh-yoh) (*Where is the [ticket booth]?*)

[도착] 시간이 언제예요? ([doh-chahk] shee-gah-nee uhn-jeh-yeh-yoh) (*When is the [arrival] time?*)

Navigating Korean Airports

As you 한국에 도착했어요 (hahn-goo-geh doh-chah-kae-ssuh-yoh) (*arrived in Korea*), most likely by 비행기 (bee-haeng-gee) (*airplane*), hopefully you had a good flight. The following section will guide you on how to move through 공항 (gohng-hahng) (*airport*). Remember to connect to 무료 인터넷 (moo-ryoh een-tuh-neht) (*free Wi-Fi*) as soon as you land, to stay informed and explore the 공항 and beyond!

AIRPORTS: WHERE ADVENTURES BEGIN

Korea has eight 국제공항 (gook-jjeh-gohng-hahng) (*international airports*). Among them, 인천공항 (een-chuhn-gohng-hahng) (*Incheon Airport*), a highly awarded hub, is one of the largest and busiest worldwide, mainly handling 국제선 (gook-jjeh-suhn) (*international flights*). 김포공항 (*Kimpo Airport*), which used to handle 국제선, now focuses on 국내선 (goong-nae-suhn) (*domestic flights*) and short international routes within Asia.

Craving a quick snack or a caffeine boost? Just scan a QR code on airport seats to order directly from delivery robots — a playful touch in your airport experience. To learn more about their services, amenities, and more, check out 공항 site at www.airport.kr/ap/en/index.do.

Passing immigration and customs

All travelers have to go through 입국심사 (eep-kkook-sheem-sah) (*immigration screening*) and 세관심사 (seh-gwahn-sheem-sah) (*customs*). To make your entry as smooth as butter, it's a smart move to review the entry requirements and customs regulations on the Korea Customs Service website (www.customs.go.kr/english/main.do). They also offer a paperless declaration form through their app.

At 입국심사, have your 여권 (yuh-kkwuhn) (*passport*), 비자 (bee-jah) (*visa*), 탑승권 (tahp-sseung-kkwuhn) (*boarding pass*), all completed declaration forms, and any other travel documents ready. You'll also snap a quick 사진 (sah-jeen) (*photo*) and give your 지문 (jee-moon) (*fingerprints*) — just the usual procedure at any country's 입국심사.

When the 이민관 (ee-meen-gwahn) (*immigration officer*) asks about your 방문 목적 (bahng-moon mohk-jjuhk) (*purpose of visit*) and 방문 기간 (bahng-moon gee-gahn) (*duration of visit*) in English, it's the perfect opportunity to practice your Korean! Here are the Korean versions of the potential questions:

> [여권] 보여 주세요. ([yuh-kkwuhn] boh-yuh joo-seh-yoh) (*Your [passport], please.*)
>
> 한국에 무슨 일로 오셨어요? (hahn-goo-geh moo-seun neel-loh oh-shyuh-ssuh-yoh) (*What brought you to Korea?*)
>
> 한국 어디에서 지낼 거예요 (hahn-gook uh-dee-eh-suh jee-nael kkuh-yeh-yoh) (*Where will you stay in Korea?*)
>
> 얼마나 오래 있을 거예요? (uhl-mah-nah oh-rae ee-sseul kkuh-yeh-yoh) (*How long will you stay?*)

And if you're ready to respond in Korean, here are some phrases to help you artic- ulate the purpose of your visit:

> 학회/일/비지니스 때문에 왔어요 (hah-kwae/eel/bee-jee-nee-sseu ttae-moo-neh wah-ssuh-yoh) (*I came for a conference/work/business.*)
>
> 관광하러 왔어요 (gwahn-gwahng-hah-ruh wah-ssuh-yoh) (*I came to tour.*)
>
> 유학하러 왔어요 (yoo-hah-kah-ruh wah-ssuh-yoh) (*I came to study abroad.*)
>
> 친척/친구 방문하러 왔어요 (cheen-chuhk/cheen-goo bahng-moon-hah-ruh wah-ssuh-yoh) (*I came to visit relatives/friends.*)

Getting to and from the airport

Most 공항 (gohng-hahng) (*airports*) offer a variety of transportation options right from the terminal. Just follow the clear signage to find your way. If you need a bit more help, stop by any 안내데스크 (ahn-nae-deh-seu-keu) (*information desk*). They're always ready to point you in the right direction. Here're the transportation services explained in Korean terms:

>> **공항버스** (gohng-hahng-buh-sseu) (*airport bus*): Hop on the 공항버스, also known as **공항리무진** (gohng-hahng-lee-moo-jeen) (*airport limousine bus*) to travel comfortably to Seoul, nearby towns, or major 도시 (doh-shee) (*cities*) across Korea. The buses offer a smooth, convenient ride that you're sure to appreciate! For info on schedules, reservations, and locations of 매표소 (mae-pyoh-soh) (*ticket offices*) and 공항버스 정류장 (gohng-hahng-buh-sseu juhng-nyoo-jahng) (*airport bus stops*), visit their website at https://airportlimousine.co.kr. A heads-up: They don't run all night.

>> **공항철도** (gohng-hahng-chuhl-ttoh) (*airport rail link*) and **지하철** (jee-hah-chuhl) (*subway*): The AREX (*Airport Railroad Express*) connects 인천공항 (*Incheon Airport*) with 김포공항 (*Gimpo Airport*). It's also linked to the Seoul 지하철 network, making it possible to reach central Seoul in less than an hour. Find more details at https://www.airportrailroad.com.

>> **택시** (taek-ssee) (*taxis*) and **콜밴** (kohl-baen) (*vans, oversized taxis*): Available at designated taxi stops outside the terminals. 요금 (yoh-geum) (*Fares*) are reasonable, and there're even foreigner exclusive taxi services. Real-time taxi availability can be checked at www.airport.kr/ap/en/tpt/pb1cTptTaxi.do.

Talkin' the Talk

PLAY

Brian just landed at Incheon Airport and is trying to catch a taxi.

Driver:	어서 오세요. 어디로 모실까요? uh-suh-oh-seh-yoh. uh-dee-roh moh-sheel-kkah-yoh? *Welcome. Where shall I take you?*
Brian:	롯데호텔월드 가 주세요. loht-tteh-hoh-tehl-wuhl-deu gah joo-seh-yoh *Please take me to the Lotte Hotel World.*
Driver:	네, 출발하겠습니다. neh. chool-bahl-hah-geht-sseum-nee-dah *Okay, departing now.*

(The taxi arrived at the hotel.)

Driver: 손님, 롯데호텔월드 도착했습니다.
sohn-neem, loht-tteh-hoh-tehl-wuhl-deu doh-chah-kaet-sseum-nee-dah
Sir, we arrived at Lotte Hotel World.

Brian: 얼마예요?
uhl-mah-yeh-yoh
How much is it?

Driver: 사만 오천팔백 원입니다.
sah-mahn oh-chuhn pahl-bae-gwuh-neem-nee-dah
It's 45,800 won.

Brian: 카드 돼요?
kah-deu dwae-yoh
Will a credit card work?

Driver: 네, 그럼요.
neh, geu-ruhm-nyoh
Yes, of course.

Brian: 카드 여기 있어요.
kah-deu yuh-gee ee-ssuh-yoh
Here's my credit card.

Driver: 사 만 오천팔백 원 카드 결제했습니다. 카드하고 영수증 여기 있습니다.
sah-mahn oh-chuhn pahl-bae-gwuhn kah-deu gyuhl-jjeh-haet-sseum-nee-dah. kah-deu-hah-goh yuhng-soo-jeung yuh-gee ee-sseum-nee-dah
A credit card payment of 45,800 won was made. Here are your credit card and a receipt.

Brian: 수고하세요.
soo-goh-hah-seh-yoh
I appreciate it.

Driver: 감사합니다. 안녕히 가세요.
gahm-sah-hahm-nee-dah. ahn-nyuhng-hee gah-seh-yoh
Thank you. Good-bye.

• •

WORDS TO KNOW

모실까요 (모시다)	moh-sheel-kkah-yoh	take care, take (an honorific person to somewhere)
출발하겠습니다 (출발하다)	chool-bahl-hah-geht-sseum-nee-dah	will depart
손님	sohn-neem	guest, customer
도착했습니다 (도착하다)	doh-chah-kaet-sseum-nee-dah	arrived
돼요 (되다)	dwae-yoh	(service) work/is available
결제했습니다 (결제하다)	gyuhl-jjeh-haet-sseum-nee-dah	paid, made a payment
영수증	yuhng-soo-jeung	receipt
수고하세요 (수고하다)	soo-goh-hah-seh-yoh	Thank you for your efforts; Take care

Conquering Local Public Transport

You've finally 호텔에 도착했어요 (hoh-teh-reh doh-chah-kaet-ssuh-yoh) (*arrived at your hotel*), unpacked, freshened up, and are ready to explore. How do you go about doing it?

In bustling hubs like Seoul or Busan, every conceivable 교통 수단 (gyoh-tohng soo-dahn) (*mode of transportation*) is practically at your doorstep. The web and various apps are loaded with information. Chatting with the 직원 (jee-gwuhn) (*staff*) at your hotel or guesthouse can also offer great insider tips for zipping around quickly and easily. It's a great chance to practice your Korean skills too! (For more on asking for directions, see Chapter 17.)

[Lotte Tower] 에 어떻게 가요? ([Lotte Tower]-eh uh-ttuh-keh gah-yoh) (*How do I get to [Lotte Tower]?*)

[Lotte Tower] 까지 [지하철로] 얼마나 걸려요? ([Lotte Tower]-kkah-jee [jee-hah-chuhl-loh] uhl-mah-nah guhl-lyuh-yoh) (*How long does it take to get to [Lotte Tower] [by subway]?*)

(이 근처) 어디에서 교통카드 살 수 있어요? ((ee geun-chuh) uh-dee-eh-suh gyoh-tohng-kah-deu sahl ssoo ee-ssuh-yoh) (*Where (nearby) can I buy a transportation card?*)

SMART TRAVEL: USING TRANSPORTATION CARDS

As you venture out, make the most of 대중교통 (dae-joong-gyoh-tohng) (*public transportation*) with a handy, reloadable, tappable 교통카드 (gyoh-tohng-kah-deu) (*transportation card*). Beyond travel, these cards function as a "debit card," allowing you to pay for goods or services at affiliated stores. The popular T-money Cards, also known as 티머니 카드 (tee-muh-nee kah-deu), is available at many places including airports, subway stations, 편의점 (pyuh-nee-juhm) (*convenience stores*), 백화점 (bae-kwah-juhm) (*department stores*), as well as via mobile apps. Tourists-exclusive options like Korea Tour Card, NAMANE card, and WOWPASS are another 교통카드. They come in various forms, including 열쇠고리 (yuhl-sswae-goh-ree) (*key chains*), making them a cute little souvenir. When your trip wraps up, you can cash out remaining card balance. Additionally, you can link your Korean bank card for 교통카드 usage, but make sure it supports contactless payment. When reloading your T-money card at a subway station, be sure to have cash on hand. For more details, check out these links:

- **VisitKorea:** https://english.visitkorea.or.kr/ (Section on "Transportation Cards")

- **T-money:** www.t-money.co.kr/

Hailing a taxi

For the ultimate "door-to-door" ride convenience, taxis are your go-to option. You'll find 택시 승강장 (taek-ssee seung-gahng-jahng) (*taxi stands*) near busy locations like bus terminals, major subway stations, and shopping malls. You can also hail a cab on the fly by waving down one with a "빈차" (been-chah) (*vacant car*) sign in red on the windshield, and the driver may pull up for you. If a taxi is booked, you'll see a "예약" (yeh-yahk) (*reserved*) sign displayed in green.

CULTURAL WISDOM

Nowadays, however, the most popular way to grab a taxi in Korea is using the KakaoT app, also known as 카카오 택시 (*Kakao Taxi*), the No.1 taxi app in the country. UT, linked to Uber, is also available, though it's less common. With 카카오 택시, you can pay the driver directly in your preferred method — no need to store your credit card details — and get a fare estimate beforehand.

TIP

Alternatively, you can call a taxi company and request a taxi by saying, "택시 좀 보내 주세요" (taek-ssee johm boh-nae joo-seh-yoh) (*Please send a taxi.*). They'll ask your 위치 (wee-chee) (*location*) and you let them know where you are. Or, you can ask your hotel or restaurant staff to call one for you by saying, "택시 좀 불러 주세요" (taek-ssee johm bool-luh joo-seh-yoh) (*Could you call a taxi for me?*)

Once inside, 안전벨트 매세요 (ahn-juhn behl-teu mae-seh-yoh) (*buckle your seat belt*), and use these phrases with the 기사님 (gee-sah-neem) (*driver*):

[*destination*] 가 주세요. ([*destination*] gah joo-seh-yoh) (*Please take me to [destination].*)

이 주소로 가 주세요. (ee-joo-soh-roh gah joo-seh-yoh) (*Please take me to this address.*)

[저기]에서 세워 주세요. ([juh-gee]-eh-suh seh-wuh joo-seh-yoh) (*Please stop/pull over [there].*)

[여기]에서 내릴게요. ([yuh-gee]-eh-suh nae-reel-kkeh-yoh) (*I'd like to get off [here].*)

얼마예요? (uhl-mah-yeh-yoh) (*How much is it?*)

There you go! You're all set to zip through the city with ease. Ready for more adventures with other 대중교통 (dae-joong-gyoh-tohng) (*public transportation*)? Keep reading!

Taking buses

Korea has a pretty extensive 버스 (buh-sseu) (*bus*) system that connects you to just about anywhere. Hop on 시내버스 (shee-nae-buh-sseu) (*city buses*) for quick local jaunts, which make frequent stops.

TIP

Take advantage of map apps like *Naver Map* or *Kakao Map* to discover the shortest 노선 (noh-suhn) (*route*), public transit recommendation, and live bus tracking — pretty handy info. Plus, bus stops typically feature a digital "Bus Information System," where you can check 실시간 업데이트 (sheel-shee-gahn uhp-deh-ee-teu) (*real-time updates*) on:

도착 예정 시간 (doh-chahk yeh-juhng shee-gahn) (*ETA*)

현재 버스 위치 (hyuhn-jae buh-sseu wee-chee) (*current bus location*)

To confirm with locals, you can ask those around you:

[경복궁] 가려면 몇 번 버스 타야 돼요? ([gyuhng-bohk-kkoong] gah-ryuh-myuhn myuht ppuhn buh-sseu tah-yah dwae-yoh) (*To go to [Gyeongbok Palace], what bus number should I take?*)

[경복궁]까지 바로 가는 버스가 있어요? ([gyuhng-bohk-kkoong] kkah-jee bah-roh gah-neun buh-sseu-gah ee-ssuh-yoh) (*Is there a bus that goes directly to [Gyeongbok Palace]?*)

Feel free to replace [경복궁] with any other destination you're planning to visit. Before hopping on, you can also ask 기사님 (gee-sah-neem) (*driver*):

> 이 버스 [경복궁]에 가요? (ee buh-sseu [gyuhng-bohk-kkoong]-eh gah-yoh) (*Is this bus going to [Gyeongbok Palace]?*)

> 몇 정류장 (더) 가야 돼요? (myuht juhng-nyoo-jahng (duh) gah-yah dwae-yoh) (*About how many (more) stops do I need to go?*)

TIP

Important! 버스에서 내릴 때 (buh-sseu-eh-suh nae-reel ttae) (*When hopping off the bus*), don't forget to tap your 교통카드 (gyoh-tohng-kah-deu) (*transportation card*) again at the back door card reader to avoid being charged twice when transferring. Also if you're paying with 현금 (hyuhn-geum) (*cash*), have the exact fare ready as drivers usually don't carry 거스름돈 (guh-seu-reum-ttohn) (*change*), and overpayments might not be refunded. Enjoy your ride and take in the outside scenery!

Riding the subway

Can't talk about 대중교통 without mentioning the 지하철 (jee-hah-chuhl) (*subway*)! In cities like Seoul, Incheon, and Busan, the subway is a top choice for getting around. It's safe, cost-effective, and super extensive. Seoul's 지하철 system is especially impressive, linking nearly every part of the city and even stretching out to the suburbs.

TIP

Download an 지하철 앱 (aep) (*app*) or visit Seoul Metro's website (www.seoulmetro. co.kr/en/) to find everything from 지하철 노선도 (noh-suhn-doh) (*route maps*), 가까운 역 (gah-kkah-oon yuhk) (*nearby stations*), 요금 (yoh-geum) (*fare*) details to timetables and real-time train updates.

Though Seoul's 지하철 노선도 might look like a spider's web at first, don't let it intimidate you! Take a few minutes to study it, and you'll find navigating the network quite manageable. Subway lines are referred to as 호선 (hoh-suhn) (*Line No.*), designated numerically as 1호선 (eel-hoh-suhn) (*Line No.1*), 2호선 (ee-hoh-suhn) (*Line No.2*), and 3호선 (sahm-hoh-suhn) (*Line No.3*), and so on.

Here are sample conversations about getting around via subway:

> [남대문시장]은 몇 호선 타야 돼요? ([nahm-dae-moon shee-jahng]-eun, myuh toh-suhn tah-yah dwae-yoh) (*Which subway line should I take to get to [Namdaemun Market]?*)

> 4호선 타야 돼요. (sah-hoh-suhn tah-yah dwae-yoh) (*You need to take Line No. 4.*)

> 어디에서 갈아타야 돼요? (uh-dee-eh-suh gah-rah-tah-yah dwae-yoh) (*Where should I transfer?*)

몇 호선으로 갈아타요? (myuh-toh-suh-neu-roh gah-rah-tah-yoh) (*What subway line do you transfer to?*)

사당역에서 4호선으로 갈아타요. (sah-dahng-yuh-geh-suh sah-hoh-suh-neu-roh gah-rah-tah-yoh) (*You transfer to Line No. 4 at SaDang Station.*)

무슨 역에서 내려야 돼요? (moo-seun-nyuh-geh-suh nae-yuh-yah dwae-yoh) (*At which station do I need to get off?*)

회현역에서 내려야 돼요. (hwae-hyuhn-nyuh-geh-suh nae-ryuh-yah dwae-yoh) (*You need to get off at Hoehyeon Station.*)

REMEMBER

Each 역 (yuhk) (*station*) has multiple 출입구 (choo-reep-kkoo) (*exits and entrances*), numbered for convenience. Some major stations have more than a dozen exits. Choosing the right 출구 (chool-goo) (*exits*) can save you some back-and-forth. Always check the clear signage or ask around if you're unsure which 출구 to take:

[남대문시장], 몇 번 출구로 나가야 돼요? ([nahm-dae-moon shee-jahng], myuht ppuhn chool-goo-roh nah-gah-yah dwae-yoh) (*Which exit number should I take for [Namdaemun Market]?*)

5번 출구요. (oh-buhn chool-goo-yoh) (*Exit No.5.*)

CULTURAL WISDOM

지하철역 are often named after the areas or district they're in like 인사동 (een-sah-dohng) (*Insa-dong*), or landmarks like 광화문 (gwahng-hwah-moon) (*Gwanghwa-mun Gate*) and 홍대입구 (hohng-dae-eep-kkoo) (*Hongik University*). This naming strategy not only makes getting around easier but also puts these areas on the map, boosting their visibility and economic benefits!

TIP

Here are some more tips to help you navigate the subway efficiently:

>> **Rush hour alert:** During 출퇴근 시간 (chool-twae-geun shee-gahn) (*rush hour*), the 지하철 can get packed. If you're claustrophobic, try to avoid peak times because things get as packed as sardines (or "sprouts" as Koreans say). Need to get off during 출퇴근 시간? Just shout 내려요/내릴게요 (nae-ryuh-yoh/nae-reel-kkeh-yoh) (*I'm getting off!*)

>> **Smooth 환승 (hwahn-seung) (transfers):** Transfer between the subway and bus within 30 minutes (or an hour overnight) to avoid paying twice for close connections. Don't forget to tap out the same way you tap in when exiting the subway or the bus to save some Korean Won on each ride.

>> **Late-night rides:** The 지하철 runs pretty late; normally from 5:30am until midnight, though some lines may close later or earlier. Check the app for specifics. If you're out late, perhaps after 노래방 (noh-rae-bahng) (*Korean karaoke room*) with friends, the 지하철 can be a budget-friendly ride home.

>> **Don't sit** (앉지 마세요) (ahn-jjee mah-seh-yoh) on designated seats for 임산부 (eem-sahn-boo) (*pregnant women*), 노약자 (noh-yahk-jjah) (*the elderly*), or 장애인 (jahng-ae-een) (*people with disabilities*).

>> **Stand to the right on escalators** (에스컬레이터 오른쪽에 서세요). (eh-seu-kuhl-leh-ee-tuh oh-reun-jjo-geh suh-seh-yoh)

Talkin' the Talk

PLAY

Ryan is talking to Sangho on the phone about meeting up for dinner and drinks later tonight.

Ryan: 상호 씨, 오늘 저녁 같이 먹을래요?
sahng-hoh ssee, oh-neul juh-nyuhk gah-chee muh-geul-lae-yoh?
Sangho, would you like to have dinner with me today?

Sangho: 좋아요. 6시 어때요?
joh-ah-yoh. yuh-suht-ssee uh-ttae-yoh?
Good. How about six o'clock?

Ryan: 6시 좋아요. 어디에서 볼까요?
yuh-suht-ssee joh-ah-yoh. uh-dee-eh-suh bohl-kkah-yoh?
6 is good. Where do you want to meet?

Sangho: 압구정동 한일관 어때요?
ahp-kkoo-juhng-dohng hah-neel-gwahn uh-ttae-yoh?
How about Hanilkwan in Apgujeong-dong?

Ryan: 거기 어떻게 가요?
guh-gee uh-ttuh-keh gah-yoh?
How can I get there?

Sangho: 잠실역에서 2호선 타고 교대역에서 3호선으로 갈아타세요. 그리고 압구정역에서 내리세요.
jahm-sheel-lyuh-geh-suh ee-hoh-suhn tah-goh gyoh-dae-yuh-geh-suh sahm-hoh-suh-neu-roh gah-rah-tah-seh-yoh. geu-ree-goh ahp-kkoo-juhng-yuh-geh-suh nae-ree-seh-yoh.
Take the subway Line 2 at the Jamsil Station and transfer to Line 3 at the Seoul National University of Education Station. And then take off at the Apgujeong Station.

Ryan:	몇 번 출구로 나가요?
	myuht ppuhn chool-goo-roh nah-gah-yoh?
	Which exit should I take?
Sangho:	2번 출구로 나오세요.
	ee-buhn chool-goo-roh nah-oh-seh-yoh.
	Take the exit number 2.

WORDS TO KNOW

호선	hoh-suhn	(subway) line
타고 (타다)	tah-goh	ride, get on (a vehicle)
갈아타고 (갈아타다)	gah-rah-tah-goh	transfer (a vehicle)
내리세요 (내리다)	nae-ree-seh-yoh	get off (a vehicle)
몇 번	myuht ppuhn	what number
출구	chool-goo	exit
나가요 (나가다)	nah-gah-yoh	go out
나오세요 (나오다)	nah-oh-seh-yoh	please come out

Driving Around

If 대중교통 (dae-joong-gyoh-tohng) (*public transport*) doesn't cut it for you (we all have our preferences!), why not drive yourself? Especially in 시골 (shee-gohl) (*rural areas*), having your own wheels is often the best way to get around. But remember, 운전 (oon-juhn) (*driving*) in Korea can be a bit of challenge, especially in the cities. Keep cool, stay alert, and drive defensively!

TIP

Expect narrow 도로 (doh-roh) (*roads*), tight 주차장 (joo-chah-jahng) (*parking spots*), and plenty of 보행자 (boh-haeng-jah) (*pedestrians*) everywhere in Korea. Also, watch out for 오토바이 (oh-toh-bah-ee) (*motorcycles*) zipping through traffic-they can be a little unpredictable, just like anywhere else.

Renting a car

렌터카 (ren-tuh-kah) (*rental car, rental car services*) are plentiful. Here's some handy vocabulary to help making renting a car a breeze.

>> 운전면허증 (oon-juhn-myuhn-huh-jjeung) (*driver's license*)

>> 4/7/9인승 (sah/cheel/goo-een-seung) (*4/7/9-passenger car*)

>> 경차 (gyuhng-chah) (*compact car*)

>> 소형차 (soh-hyuhng-chah) (*small-size car*)

>> 중형차 (joong-hyuhng-chah) (*medium-size car*)

>> 대형차 (dae-hyuhng-chah) (*large-size car*)

>> 승합차/밴 (seung-hahp-chah/baen) (*van*)

>> 전기차/하이브리드 (juhn-gee-chah/hah-ee-beu-ree-deu) (*electric car/hybrid*)

>> 내비 (nae-bee) (*navigation, GPS*)

>> 자동차 보험 (jah-dohng-chah boh-huhm) (*car insurance*)

>> 자동차 열쇠/키 (jah-dohng-chah yuhl-sswae/kee) (*car key*)

>> 계약서 (gyeh-yahk-ssuh) (*contract*)

Need a car? Try asking:

[7인승] [전기차] 있어요? ([chee-reen-seung] [juhn-gee-chah] ee-ssuh-yoh) (*Do you have a [7-passenger] [electric car]?*)

오늘부터 [일요일]까지 [이틀] 렌트할게요. (oh-neul-boo-tuh [ee-ryoh-eel]-kkah-jee [ee-teul] rehn-teu-hahl-kkeh-yoh) (*I'll rent a car for [two days] from today 'til [Sunday].*)

You can substitute [이틀] (ee-teul), which is a native Korean word meaning *two days*, with other length of days: (For numbers and the days of the week, see Chapter 5.)

>> 하루/1일 (hah-roo/ee-leel) (*one day*)

>> 사흘/3일 (sah-heul/sah-meel) (*three days*)

>> 나흘/4일 (nah-heul/sah-eel) (*four days*)

>> 닷새/5일 (daht-ssae/oh-eel) (*five days*)

>> 엿새/6일 (yuht-ssae/yoo-geel) (*six days*)

>> 일주일/7일 (eel-jjoo-eel/chee-leel) (*one week/seven days*)

>> 열흘/10일 (yuhl-heul/shee-beel) (*ten days*)

TIP

Korea recognizes the 국제 운전 면허증 (gook-jjeh oon-juhn myuhn-huh-jjeung) (*International Driving Permit*), handy in over 100 countries. It's supplement, not a replacement for your home country's 면허증 (myuhn-huh-jjeung) (*license*), which you must also carry. It's for short-term visits; for longer stays, apply for a Korean license.

Roaming with bike or strolling

자전거 탈 줄 알아요? (jah-juhn-guh tahl jjool ah-rah-yoh) (*Do you know how to ride a bike?*) If so, cruising around the cities on a 자전거 (jah-juhn-guh) (*bike*) is another fun way to see the sights. In Seoul, you can grab a bike from convenient self-service 대여소 (dae-yuh-soh) (*rental stations*), known as 따릉이 (ttah-reung-ee) (*Seoul Public Bicycle*) (www.bikeseoul.com). Fun fact: 따릉 (ttah-reung) is an ono-matopoeia for the sound of a bell installed on a bike. In other cities, there're bike 대여 (dae-yuh) (*rental services*) like 카카오 자전거 (kah-kah-oh jah-juhn-guh) (*Kakao T bike*). Get a mobile app on your phone, find a 대여소, take your bike for a spin, and return the bike to any rental rack.

Here are some phrases you can use when using bike rental services:

자전거 대여소가 어디 있어요? (jah-juhn-guh dae-yuh-soh-gah uh-dee ee-ssuh-yoh) (*Where is the bike rental station?*)

어디에 반납해야 돼요? (uh-dee-eh bahn-nahp-hae-yah dwae-yoh) (*Where do I need to return it?*)

한 시간 이용료가 얼마예요? (hahn shee-gahn ee-yohng-nyoh-gah uhl-mah-yeh-yoh) (*How much is the rate per hour?*)

WARNING

Korea is also incredibly 도보 (doh-boh) (*walking*)-friendly, especially in the cities. With well-maintained 인도 (een-doh) (*sidewalks*), 보행자 구역 (boh-haeng-jah goo-yuhk) (*pedestrian zones*), and plenty of 횡단보도 (hwaeng-dahn-boh-doh) (*cross-walks*), getting around on foot is a breeze. Plus, it's 안전해요 (ahn-juhn-hae-yoh) (*safe*) to walk around even at night. Many historical and cultural spots are located in areas that are best explored on foot, get your walking shoes ready!

Deciphering road signs

Decoding Korea's 도로표지판 (doh-roh-pyoh-jee-pahn) (*road signs*) can be a bit like a visual puzzle. But, sooner or later, you'll recognize most just by their design because many are pretty universal! For those signs that do require a little local lingo, Figure 16-1 shows some essential road signs where knowing a bit of Korean comes in handy.

Road Sign	Pronunciation	Meaning	Road Sign	Pronunciation	Meaning
통행금지	tohng-haeng-geum-jee	Road closed	진입금지	jee-neep-geum-jee	No entry for cars
비보호	bee-boh-hoh	Unprotected left turn	주차금지	joo-chah-geum-jee	No parking
횡단금지	hwaeng-dahnh-geum-jee	Pedestrian crossing prohibited	안전속도 30	ahn-juhn-sohk-ttoh	Speed limit
일방통행	eel-bahng-tohng-haeng	One-way traffic	자전거전용	jah-juhn-guh-juh-nyohng	Road reserved for bicycles
다인승 전용	dah-een-seung-juh-nyohng	HOV (highly occupied vehicle) lane	전용	juh-nyohng	Bus only lane

FIGURE 16-1:
Korean
road signs.

Government of the Republic of Korea / Wikimedia Commons / Public domain / https://commons.wikimedia.org/
wiki/Road_signs_of_South_Korea // last accessed on 09 July 2024

Between Cities: Trains, Express Buses, and Boats

When it comes to traveling between cities, get ready to experience the convenience of 기차 (gee-chah) (*trains*) and 고속버스 (goh-sohk-buh-sseu) (*express buses*). Up next, you'll find how these popular options make your journey smooth and comfortable.

Boarding the train

If you're eying some relaxing trip, Korea's 기차 (gee-chah) (*trains*) have you covered. Speed to far-away cities on the high-speed KTX (*Korea Train eXpress*) and SRT (*Super Rapid Train*) or take a scenic route with 관광 열차 (gwahn-gwahng-yuhl-chah) (*tourists trains*). These 관광 열차 offer a range of themed journeys, from a close-up look at the DMZ to leisurely rides through beautiful natural spots. You can find more on these trains at Korail (www.letskorail.com), SRT (https://etk.srail.kr/main.do), or VisitKorea (https://english.visitkorea.or.kr

Under "Transportation – Train"). Here're some handy phrases for the 매표소 (mae-pyoh-soh) (*ticket office*):

[부산] 가는 [기차] 몇 시에 있어요? ([boo-sahn] gah-neun [gee-chah] myuht ssee-eh ee-ssuh-yoh) (*What time is the [train] for [Busan] leaving?*)

[부산] 가는 [기차]표 [한] 장 주세요. ([boo-sahn] gah-neun [gee-chah]-pyoh [hahn] jahng joo-seh-yoh) (*Please give me [one] [train] ticket for [Busan].*)

[부산] 가는 기차, 몇 번 플랫폼에서 타야 돼요? ([boo-sahn] gah-neun gee-chah, myuht ppuhn peul-laet-pohm-eh-suh tah-yah dwae-yoh) (*On which platform do I need to board the train for [Busan]?*)

[1] 번 플랫폼 어디에 있어요? ([eel]-buhn peul-laet-pohm uh-dee-eh ee-ssuh-yoh) (*Where is platform No. [1]?*)

Replace [부산] with another city, [기차] with a different form of transport, and [한] with the number of ticket(s) you need — perfect for brushing up on your Korean numbers! (Refer to Chapter 5.)

Riding an express bus

For a quick, comfortable trip between cities, 고속버스 (goh-sohk-ppuh-sseu) (*express buses*) is another option. These buses offer a non-stop journey to your destination, with more room to recline and much comfy seating than standard 시내버스 (shee-nae-buh-sseu) (*city buses*).

You can find 고속버스 at designated 고속버스 정류장 (goh-sohk-ppuh-sseu juhng-nyoo-jahng) (*express bus terminals*), which are conveniently located in accessible areas of the city. These hubs are often well-connected to other public transportation options, facilitating seamless travel. In Seoul, there are several 고속버스 정류장, each catering different destinations. (To find out which 고속버스 정류장 serves your route, or to reserve a seat, visit www.kobus.co.kr.)

CULTURAL WISDOM

During your express bus journey, don't skip the 고속도로 휴게소 (goh-sohk-ttoh-roh hyoo-geh-soh) (*freeway rest stops*). These aren't just stops to find 화장실 (hah-jahng-sheel) (*bathroom*), 주유소 (joo-yoo-soh) (*gas station*), or 편의점 (pyuh-nee-juhm) (*convenient stores*). These stops are home to delightful 식당 (sheek-ttahng) (*restaurants*), and sometimes even leisure facilities or lively markets selling 지역 특산품 (jee-yuhk tteuk-ssahn-poom) (*local specialties*). Enjoy a taste of local culture while stretching your legs!

Cruising around by boat

Hop on a boat or cruise around Korea! Nestled between the 동해 (dohng-hae) (*East Sea*), 남해 (nahm-hae) (*South Sea*), and 서해 (suh-hae) (*West Sea*), Korea is a 반도

(bahn-doh) (*peninsula*) with more than 3,000 섬 (suhm) (*islands*)! From the famous 제주도 (jeh-joo-doh) (*Jeju Island*), 울릉도 (ool-leung-doh) (*Ulleung Island*), and 독도 (dohk-ttoh) (*Dokdo*), to hidden gems perfect for fishing and scuba diving, there's an island for every taste.

Getting there is all part of the adventure — whether aboard a 여객선 (yuh-gaek-ssuhn) (*passenger boat, ferry*) or a 유람선 (yoo-rahm-suhn) (*cruise ship*). Check out 여객선 터미널 (yuh-gaek-ssuhn tuh-mee-nuhl) (*passenger ship terminal*) websites for further info including 항구 정보 (hahng-goo juhng-boh) (*port information*) and 운항 시간 (oon-hahng shee-gahn) (*operation hours*) to smoothly plan your island-hopping. (Some useful websites include http://island.haewoon.co.kr and Incheon Port Passenger Terminal: www.ipfc.or.kr/eng/index.do.)

Some islands like 진도 (*Jindo*), the third largest 섬 off the southwestern coast, 거제도 (guh-jeh-doh) (*Geoje Island*), located just on the southeastern tip of the Korea, 남이섬 (nah-mee-suhm) (*Nami Island*), a popular filming locations for dramas, and 강화도 (gahng-hwah-doh) (*Ganghwa Island*), only about 30 miles away from Seoul, are super accessible, just a bus ride or drive over a 다리 (dah-ree) (*bridge*).

Whether you end up at 백령도 (baeng-nyuhng-doh) (*Baeknyeong Island*), the northernmost point you can reach by island hopping, or at 독도 (*Dokdo*), Korea's easternmost point, take a moment to relax, soaking in the peaceful surroundings!

FUN & GAMES

Unscramble the syllables below for a name of the vehicle and write the unscrambled name in the underlined space. Then match the name to the correct picture and write down the letter in the parentheses. (See Appendix C for the answers.)

1. 철지하: _____ ( )
2. 버속고스: _____ ( )
3. 시택: _____ ( )
4. 전거자: _____ ( )
5. 비기행: _____ ( )
6. 차기: _____ ( )
7. 이토오바: _____ ( )

a.

b.

c.

d.

e.

f.

g.

© John Wiley & Sons, Inc.

Chapter 17

Asking for Directions

I n today's world, where 스마트폰 지도 앱 (seu-mah-teu-pohn jee-doh aep) (*smartphone map apps*) are your go-to navigational tools, finding your way seems straightforward. However, there're moments when technology might leave us hanging, prompting you to turn to the people nearby for assistance. Your 지도 앱 might not cut it or decide to call it quits due to a low battery. Ever wondered how to ask for the nearest 화장실 (hwah-jahng-sheel) (*restroom*), 지하철역 (jee-hah-chuhl-lyuhk) (*subway station*), 숙소 (sook-ssoh) (*accommodation*), or that highly recommended 맛집 (maht-jjeep) (*must-go restaurant*)?

This chapter serves as your "directions toolkit," providing you with practical phrases and skills for giving and receiving directions smoothly. So get ready to embark on your next adventure with confidence. On your mark, 준비 (joon-bee) (*get set*), 출발 (chool-bahl) (*go*)!

Finding Your Way

In 대도시 (dae-doh-shee) (*metropolitan cities*) like 서울 (Seoul) or 부산 (Busan), coming across 영어 (yuhng-uh) (*English*) speakers is common. But, in 시골 (shee-gohl) (*rural areas*), finding someone fluent in 영어 is less likely. While 번역 앱 (buh-nyuhk aep) (*translator apps*) can be handy, why not engage directly? It often leads to a more enjoyable and enriching experience! The following sections will guide you through asking for directions to reach your 목적지 (mohk-jjuhk-jjee) (*destination*).

Asking for directions with "where?"

Before asking a stranger for directions, you want to know the proper way of addressing the person first. You can't just go up to someone on the street and launch right into a pop quiz on the local geography. Here are polite phrases you can start with before posing a "where" question:

실례합니다 (sheel-leh hahm-nee-dah.) (*Excuse me.*)

죄송한데요 (jweh-sohng-hahn-deh-yoh.) (*I'm sorry, but. . .*)

뭐 좀 여쭤볼게요 (mwuh johm yuh-jjwuh-bohl-kkeh-yoh.) (*I'd like to ask something.*)

Presuming that they didn't say 바빠요 (bah-ppah-yoh) (*I'm busy*) and dash off, it's time to ask your question! Forming a question in Korean is a breeze. Simply start with 어디 (uh-dee) (*where*), and add the existence verb 있어요 (ee-ssuh-yoh) (*to exist*), and voilà: 어디 있어요? (*Where is [it]?*). You may see 어디에 있어요? with the location partile 에, but 어디 있어요? is the common choice in casual conversations. Just put what you're looking for at the start, and your question's good to go!

지하철역, 어디 있어요? (jee-hah-chuhl-lyuhk uh-dee ee-ssuh-yoh?) (*Where is the subway station?*)

화장실, 어디 있어요? (hwah-jahng-sheel uh-dee ee-ssuh-yoh?) (*Where is the restroom?*)

REMEMBER

Adding the subject particle 이 (ee) (after a consonant-ending noun) or 가 (gah) (after a vowel-ending noun) emphasizes the noun you're referring to. While understanding them is helpful, these particles often drop in casual conversation. So don't stress too much when speaking Korean. (For more details on the particles, see Chapter 3.)

은행(이) 어디 있어요? (eun-haeng(-ee) uh-dee ee-ssuh-yoh?) (*Where is the bank?*)

학교(가) 어디 있어요? (hahk-kkyoh(-gah) uh-dee ee-ssuh-yoh?) (*Where is the school?*)

Here are some places you may want to find:

>> 가게 (gah-geh) (*store*)

>> 공원 (gohng-wuhn) (*park*)

>> 극장 (geuk-jjahng) (*theater*)

>> 경찰서 (gyuhng-chahl-ssuh) (*police station*)

>> 도서관 (doh-suh-gwahn) (*library*)

>> 마트 (mah-teu) (*mart, market, supermarket*)

- » 미국 대사관 (mee-gook dae-sah-gwahn) (*U.S. embassy*)

- » 버스정류장 (buh-sseu-juhng-nyoo-jahng) (*bus stop*)

- » 병원 (byuhng-wuhn) (*hospital, clinic*)

- » 지하철역 (jee-hah-chuhl-lyuhk) (*subway station*)

- » 카페/커피숍 (kkah-peh/kuh-pee-shyop) (*coffee shop*)

- » 편의점 (pyuh-nee-juhm) (*convenience store*)

- » 화장실 (hwah-jahng-sheel) (*restroom*)

REMEMBER

To ask about the location of a place, you can also use 어디예요? (uh-dee-yeh-yoh?), as in 피자 가게가 어디예요? (pee-jah gah-geh-gah uh-dee-yeh-yoh) (*Where is the pizza store?*). But this form doesn't apply to objects. For instance, to ask where your pizza is, you'd say 피자가 어디 있어요? (pee-jah-gah uh-dee ee-ssuh-yoh?) (*Where is the pizza?*), not 피자가 어디예요? (pee-jah-gah uh-dee-yeh-yoh?).

Understanding simple directions

Now, let's decipher the directions you may receive. If the destination is within sight — for instance, a café across the street — directions are straightforward! People will use brief location pronouns along with a simple pointing gesture. Table 17-1 showcases three location pronouns that come in handy for such scenarios.

TABLE 17-1   **Location Pronouns**

Korean	English	Location
여기 (yuh-gee)	here	near the speaker
저기 (juh-gee)	over there	far from both the speaker and the listener
거기 (guh-gee)	there (near you); that place	near the listener but far from the speaker; the previously mentioned place

To indicate something or someone is over there, just add the verb 있어요 after the proper location pronoun, like in 저기 있어요 (juh-gee ee-ssuh-yoh) (*It's over there.*). For an even simpler expression, people may say 저기요 (juh-gee-yoh) (*Over there*) or 여기요 (yuh-gee-yoh) (*Here*), using the polite ending marker 요 (yoh). Most people will also point at the location to further clarify their directions while speaking.

서점, 저기 있어요. (suh-juhm, juh-gee ee-ssuh-yoh.) (*The bookstore is over there.*)

약국요? 저기요. (yahk-kkoong-nyoh? juh-gee-yoh.) (*A pharmacy? It's over there.*)

버스정류장요? 여기 있어요. (buh-sseu-juhng-nyoo-jahng-nyoh? yuh-gee ee-ssuh-yoh.) (*A bus stop? It's here.*)

CULTURAL WISDOM

Beyond giving directions, "저기요" and "여기요" are also used as attention getters. Think of "저기요" as your go-to "Hey" or "Excuse me" for calling someone over. "여기요" is like "Here," directing attention to your (the speaker's) location. These phrases come in handy in restaurants when you're trying to catch the waitstaff's eye. So, the next time you dine out at a Korean restaurant and need service, you're all set with the perfect call!

Pinpointing relative locations

Most of the time, giving directions involves more than simply pointing across the road and saying, "저기요" (*over there*). But don't fret! Table 17-2 presents essential terms for positions along with usage examples.

TABLE 17-2 **Terms for Position**

Korean Word	Meaning	Usage (Reference Point + Position Word)
앞 (ahp)	front	은행 앞 (eun-haeng ahp) (*in front of the bank*)
뒤 (dwee)	back	은행 뒤 (eun-haeng dwee) (*behind the bank*)
안 (ahn)	in	서점 안 (suh-juhm ahn) (*inside the book store*)
밖 (bahk)	outside	서점 밖 (suh-juhm bahk) (*outside the book store*)
위 (wee)	above	가게 위 (gah-geh wee) (*above the store*)
아래 (ah-rae)	under	가게 아래 (gah-geh ah-rae) (*below the store*)
옆 (yuhp)	next to/beside	공원 옆 (gohng-wuhn yuhp) (*beside the park*)
오른쪽 (oh-reun-jjohk)	right/right side	마트 오른쪽 (mah-teu oh-reun-jjok) (*the right (side) of the mart*)
왼쪽 (waen-jjohk)	left/left side	마트 왼쪽 (mah-teu waen-jjok) (*the left (side) of the mart*)
건너편 (guhn-nuh-pyuhn)	across, opposite side	병원 건너편 (byuhng-wuhn guhn-nuh-pyuhn) (*across the hospital*)
근처 (geun-chuh)	nearby, vicinity	병원 근처 (byuhng-wuhn geun-chuh) (*near the hospital*)
사이 (sah-ee)	between	극장하고 가게 사이 (geuk-jjahng-hah-goh gah-geh sah-ee) (*between the theater and the store*)

TIP

You'll often encounter 쪽 (jjohk) (*side*) in position words like 왼쪽 (waen-jjohk) (*left side*), 오른쪽 (oh-reun-jjohk) (*right side*), or 앞쪽 (ahp-jjohk) (*front side*). It's also commonly used in cardinal directions: 동쪽 (dohng-jjohk) (*east side*), 서쪽 (suh-jjohk) (*west side*), 남쪽 (nahm-jjohk) (*south side*), and 북쪽 (book-jjohk) (*north side*). When paired with demonstrative adjectives, it can also refer to a "way" as in 이쪽 (ee-jjohk) (*this way*), 저쪽 (juh-jjohk) (*that way over there*), and 그쪽 (geu-jjohk) (*that way; near the listener*).

GRAMMATICALLY SPEAKING

Now, let's explore how to describe a location using the position words in Table 17-2. Here are the steps to follow.

| Entity | Location | | | Verb |
	Reference point	Position	Location Particle	
식당 (*restaurant*)	카페 (*café*)	옆 (*beside*)	에 (*static location*)	있어요 (*to exist*)

식당은 카페 옆에 있어요. (sheek-ttahng-eun kah-peh yuh-peh ee-ssuh-yoh) (*The restaurant is beside the café.*)

For example, to express "The restaurant is beside the café" in Korean, start with the entity you're discussing (식당). Then, take the reference point (카페) and place it before the position word (옆), forming 카페 옆 (beside the café). Finally, add the static location particle and the verb to complete the statement: 식당은 카페 옆에 있어요. And there you go!

REMEMBER

Remember the reversed word order! "Next to the café" is 카페 옆, not 옆 카페. Now, how would you say "behind the store"? The word for "store" is 가게 (gah-geh) and "behind" is 뒤 (dwee). That's right, it should be 가게 뒤 (gah-geh dwee), not 뒤 가게. You've got it!

GRAMMATICALLY SPEAKING

Wondering which particle to use for 식당? Don't worry, you've got options: 이/가 (subject particle) or 은/는 (topic particle), depending on the emphasis you want. If you're answering the question "What's next to the café?" and 식당 is the key info, opt for the subject particle (이, here) as it sounds more natural. Otherwise, go with the topic particle (은, here) as if you're responding to "Where is the restaurant?" (For further notes on particles, refer to Chapter 3.) More examples:

병원은 [약국 위]에 있어요. (byuhng-wuh-neun [yahk-kkook wee]-eh ee-ssuh-yoh.)
(The clinic is [above the pharmacy].)

편의점은 [은행 뒤]에 있어요. (pyuh-nee-juh-meun [eun-haeng dwee]-eh ee-ssuh-yoh.)
(The convenience store is [behind the bank].)

마트는 [극장 앞]에 있어요. (mah-teu-neun [geuk-jjahng ahp]-eh ee-ssuh-yoh.)
(The supermarket is [in front of the theater].)

The position word 사이 (sah-ee) (*between*) requires two reference points that you connect with the particle, 하고 (hah-goh) (*and*).

서점은 우체국하고 경찰서 사이에 있어요. (suh-juh-meun oo-cheh-gook-hah-goh gyuhng-chahl-suh sah-ee-eh ee-ssuh-yoh.) (*The bookstore is between the post office and the police station.*)

제 호텔은 식당하고 카페 사이에 있어요. (jeh hoh-teh-reun sheek-ttahng-hah-goh kkah-peh sah-ee-eh ee-ssuh-yoh.) (*My hotel is between the restaurant and the coffee shop.*)

Clarifying reference points with ordinal numbers

When giving detailed directions, you can use ordinal numbers like 첫째 (chuht-jjae) (*first*) and 둘째 (dool-jjae) (*second*). They're handy for pinpointing locations. For example:

첫째 신호등 (chuht-jjae sheen-hoh-deung) (*first traffic light*)

둘째 집 (dool-jjae jeep) (*second house*)

셋째 건물 (seht-jjae guhn-mool) (*third building*)

(Check out Chapter 5 for more info on ordinal numbers.)

Specifying distance and travel time

Sometimes you might just want to know if a place is nearby or far away rather than getting into detailed directions. Here are some handy phrases for asking about distance and estimated travel time to your destination.

멀어요? (muh-ruh-yoh) (*Is it far?*)

가까워요? (gah-kkah-wuh-yoh) (*Is it close?*)

얼마나 걸려요? (uhl-mah-nah guhl-lyuh-yoh) (*How long does it take?*)

To inquire about the distance between two places, use 에서 (eh-suh) (*from*) and 까지 (kkah-jee) (*to*) particles. Pay attention to the word order: [Place A]에서 [Place B]까지.

[여기]**에서** [마트]**까지** 멀어요? ([yuh-gee]-eh-suh [mah-teu]-kkah-jee muh-ruh-yoh) (*Is it far from [here] to [the mart]?*)

[호텔]에서 [공항]까지 얼마나 걸려요? ([hoh-tehl]-eh-suh [gohng-hahng]-kkah-jee uhl-mah-nah guhl-lyuh-yoh) (*How long does it take from [the hotel] to [the airport]?*)

To specify the means of transport in your questions, you can add 버스로 (buh-sseu-roh) (*by bus*), 지하철로 (jee-hah-chuhl-loh) (*by subway*), 차로 (chah-roh) (*by car*), or 걸어서 (guh-ruh-suh) (*on foot*) like this:

걸어서 얼마나 걸려요? (guh-ruh-suh uhl-mah-nah guhl-lyuh-yoh) (*How long does it take by walking/on foot?*)

지하철로 얼마나 걸려요? (yuh-gee-suh jee-hah-chuhl-loh uhl-mah-nah guhl-lyuh-yoh) (*How long does it take by subway?*)

REMEMBER

When asked about distance or travel time, people may respond using 시간 (shee-gahn) (*hours*) and 분 (boon) (*minutes*). Use the native Korean numbers for hours (for example, 한/두/세/네/다섯 시간. . .) (hahn/doo/seh/neh/dah-suht shee-gahn) (*one/two/three/four/five hours*) and Sino-Korean numbers for minutes (오/십/사십오 분) (oh/sheep/sah-shee-boh boon) (*five/ten/forty five minutes*).

오 분 걸려요. (oh boon guhl-lyuh-yoh.) (*It takes five minutes.*)

걸어서 이십 분(쯤) 걸려요. (guh-ruh-suh ee-sheep-ppoon-(jjeum) guhl-lyuh-yoh.) (*It takes (about) twenty minutes on foot.*)

차로 한 시간 반(쯤) 걸려요. (chah-roh hahn-shee-gahn bahn-(jjeum) guhl-lyuh-yoh.) (*It takes (about) an hour and a half by car.*)

TIP

The word 쯤 (jjeum), meaning "*about*" is placed AFTER the counters like 분 (boon) (*minute*) and 시간 (shee-gahn) (*hours*) to indicate approximation. Is it a typo? Did our cat walk across the keyboard while we weren't looking? Nope! We don't even have one. It's just one of the features of Korean with a "reversed word order": 쯤 follows the counter, crafting phrases like 십 분쯤 (sheep-ppoon-jjeum) (*about 10 minutes*) or 100 달러쯤 (baek-dahl-luh-jjeum) (*around 100 dollars*).

Talkin' the Talk

PLAY

Angela, who is new to area, asks a man on the street for directions.

Angela: **죄송한데요. 하나은행이 어디 있어요?**
jwae-sohng-hahn-deh-yoh. hah-nah-eun-haeng-ee uh-dee ee-ssuh-yoh?
Excuse me. Where is the Hana Bank?

Jungmin:	하나은행요? 저기 신호등 보이죠? 첫째 신호등 앞에 있어요.	

Jungmin: 하나은행요? 저기 신호등 보이죠? 첫째 신호등 앞에 있어요.
hah-nah-eun-haeng-nyoh? juh-gee sheen-hoh-deung boh-ee-jyoh? chuht-jjae sheen-hoh-deung ah-peh ee-ssuh-yoh.
The Hana Bank? Do you see the traffic lights? It's in front of the first traffic light.

Angela: 고맙습니다. 근데 이 근처에 편의점이 어디 있어요?
goh-mahp-sseum-nee-dah. geun-deh ee geun-chuh-eh pyuh-nee-juh-mee uh-dee ee-ssuh-yoh?
Thank you. And where is a convenience store nearby?

Jungmin: 저기 커피숍 옆에 있어요.
juh-gee kuh-pee-shop yuh-peh ee-ssuh-yoh.
It's next to the coffee shop over there.

Angela: 이 근처에 우체국도 있어요?
ee geun-chuh-eh oo-cheh-gook-ttoh ee-ssuh-yoh?
Is there a post office around this area?

Jungmin: 이 근처에는 없어요. 버스 타야 돼요. 좀 멀어요.
ee geun-chuh-eh-neun uhp-ssuh-yoh. buh-sseu tah-yah-dwae-yoh. johm muh-ruh-yoh.
There's none around here. You need to take a bus.
It's a bit far.

Angela: 그래요? 네. 감사합니다.
geu-rae-yoh? neh. gahm-sah-hahm-nee-dah.
Is that so? Okay. Thank you.

. . . .

WORDS TO KNOW

죄송한데요 (죄송하다)	jwae-sohng-hahn-deh-yoh	I'm sorry but . . .
은행	eun-haeng	bank
신호등	sheen-hoh-deung	traffic light
보이죠? (보이다)	boh-ee-jyoh	you see. . . right?
타야 돼요 (타다)	tah-yah-dwae-yoh	should take (transportation)
멀어요 (멀다)	muh-ruh-yoh	is far

Reversing Roles: Giving Directions

Sometimes, you find yourself in the role of the direction-giver. Whether you're directing someone to your guesthouse or suggesting a hidden gem 맛집 (maht-jjeep) (*must-go restaurant*), knowing how to give directions is key.

You can use the polite command form, [verb stem]+(으)세요 ((eu-)seh-yoh) (*Please [verb]*), to give directions politely. Table 17-3 has the (으)세요 forms of verbs suitable for giving directions.

TABLE 17-3   **Verbs for Giving Directions**

Verbs	Dictionary Form	Conjugated: -(으)세요
to go	가다	가세요 (gah-seh-yoh) (*Please go*)
to transfer	갈아타다	갈아타세요 (gah-rah-tah-seh-yoh) (*Please transfer to. . .*)
to cross	건너다	건너세요 (guhn-nuh-seh-yoh) (*Please cross*)
to go on foot	걸어서 가다	걸어서 가세요 (guh-ruh-suh gah-seh-yoh) (*Please walk*)
to go down	내려가다	내려가세요 (nae-ryuh-gah-seh-yoh) (*Please go down*)
to get off	내리다	내리세요 (nae-ree-seh-yoh) (*Please get off*)
to turn	돌다	도세요 (doh-seh-yoh) (*Please turn*)
to come	오다	오세요 (oh-seh-yoh) (*Please come*)
to go up	올라가다	올라가세요 (ohl-lah-gah-seh-yoh) (*Please go up*)
to pass	지나가다	지나가세요 (jee-nah-gah-seh-yoh) (*Please pass*)
to get on/ride	타다	타세요 (tah-seh-yoh) (*Please get on/take [transportation]*)

Particles matter

When giving or receiving directions, it's important to consider more than just the nouns and verbs. Just like English prepositions like "to," "at," or "from" offer crucial details about direction and origin, Korean particles like (으)로 (eu-roh) (*to/toward*) and 에서 (eh-suh) (*at/from*) play vital roles.

TIP

First, when indicating the direction of movement, (으)로 is your go-to particle. Use 으로 after a consonant-ending noun, and 로 after a vowel-ending or ㄹ-ending noun. For instance, to politely say "*Please go forward*," pair the position word "앞" (ahp) (*front*) with 으로 to create 앞으로 (ah-peu-roh) (*toward the front*). Then combine it with the verb 가세요 (*please go*) to make 앞으로 가세요 (ah-peu-roh gah-seh-yoh). Easy as pie!

The following are phrases a 종업원 (johng-uh-bwuhn) (*waiters*) might use with 손님 (sohn-neem) (*customers*):

손님, 이쪽으로 오세요. (sohn-neem, ee-jjoh-geu-roh oh-seh-yoh) (*Sir/Ma'am, please come this way.*)

화장실은 왼쪽으로 가세요. (hwah-jahng-shee-reun waen-jjoh-geu-roh gah-seh-yoh) (*For the restrooms, please go to the left.*)

GRAMMATICALLY SPEAKING

(으)로 is actually a versatile particle that also denotes "by (means of)/using." For instance, when indicating transportation methods, you can use phrases like 택시로 (taek-ssee-roh) (*by taxi*), 기차로 (gee-chah-roh) (*by train*), or 자전거로 (jah-juhn-guh-roh) (*by bike*). Saying "*I go by taxi*" becomes "택시로 가요" (taek-ssee-roh gah-yoh).

When changing transportation modes, like "transfer to. . .", you also use (으)로 with the verb 갈아타다 (gah-rah-tah-dah) (*to transfer*):

21번 버스로 갈아타요. (ee-shee-beel-buhn buh-sseu-roh gah-rah-tah-yoh.) (*Please transfer to bus No.21.*)

TIP

To indicate where you turn, move, or transfer, mark the starting place/point with 에서 (eh-suh) (*at/from*). Here are more examples.

저기 사거리에서 오른쪽으로 도세요. (juh-gee sah-guh-ree-eh-suh oh-reun-jjoh-geu-roh doh-seh-yoh.) (*Please turn right at the intersection over there.*)

서울역에서 4호선으로 갈아타세요. (suh-ool-lyuh-geh-suh sah-hoh-suh-neu-roh gah-rah-tah-seh-yoh.) (*Please transfer to Line No.4 at Seoul Station.*)

Making directions flow

Keeping a smooth and clear flow is crucial when giving directions. Here are some handy adverbs to assist you: 그 다음에 (geu-dah-eu-meh) (*next/and then*) and

그리고 (나서) (geu-ree-goh (nah-suh)) (*afterward/and then*). They're practically interchangeable. Explore their usage with longer examples, and happy navigating!

길을 건너세요. **그 다음에** 저기 가게 앞에서 79번 버스를 타세요. **그리고 (나서)** 시청에서 내리세요. (gee-reul guhn-nuh-seh-yoh. geu dah-eu-meh juh-gee gah-geh ah-peh-suh cheel-sheep-goo-buhn buh-sseu-reul tah-seh-yoh. geu-ree-goh (nah-suh) shee-chuhng-eh-suh nae-ree-seh-yoh.) (*Cross the street. Then, in front of the store over there, take bus No.79. And then get off at City Hall.*)

명동역에서 4호선 타세요. **그 다음에** 동대문에서 2호선으로 갈아타세요. **그리고 (나서)** 홍대에서 내리세요. (myuhng-dohng-nyuh-geh-suh sah-hoh-suhn tah-seh-yoh. geu dah-eu-meh dohng-dae-moon-eh-suh ee-hoh-suhn-eu-roh gah-rah-tah-seh-yoh. geu-ree-goh (nah-suh) hohng-dae-eh-suh nae-ree-seh-yoh.) (*From Myeongdong Station, take (subway) Line No.4. Then, at Dongdaemoon (station), transfer to Line No.2. And then get off at Hongdae Station.*)

FUN & GAMES

Use the map below to complete the sentences.

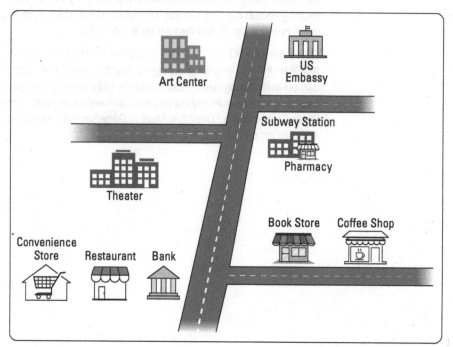

© *John Wiley & Sons, Inc.*

1. 미국 대사관은 아트 센터 _____ 에 있어요.
   The U.S. Embassy is across the art center.

2. 식당은 편의점하고 은행 _____ 에 있어요.
   The restaurant is between the convenience store and the bank.

3. 서점은 커피숍 _____ 에 있어요.
   The book store is next to the coffee shop.

4. 극장은 식당 _____ 에 있어요.
   The theater is behind the restaurant.

5. 약국은 지하철역 _____ 에 있어요.
   The pharmacy is inside the subway station.

Chapter **18**

Handling an Emergency

안전 (ahn-juhn) (*safety*) is a top priority no matter where you are, especially when travelling 해외 (hae-wae) (*abroad*). While we all strive to stay safe and promote health, unexpected 응급상황 (eung-geup-sahng-hwahng) (*emergencies*) can interrupt your adventures. Surprises are always possible, so being prepared for any situation is vital.

This chapter serves as your quick guide to efficiently handling 응급상황, from urgently calling for help to calmly informing the authorities. Even memorizing just a handful of these phrases could be crucial as it allows you to reach out to the right people when you need help the most.

Calling for Emergency Help

When caught in 응급상황 (eung-geup-sahng-hwahng) (*emergencies*), the go-to shout for help is 도와주세요! (doh-wah-joo-seh-yoh) (*Please help!*). For added effectiveness in getting attention, shout a very loud "여기요!" (yuh-gee-yoh) (*Over here!*). Depending on your predicament, you might find these additional calls surprisingly handy.

불이야!/불 났어요! (boo-ree-yah/bool nah-ssuh-yoh) (*Fire!/There's a fire!*)

도둑이야!/도둑! (doh-doo-gee-yah/doh-dook) (*It's a thief!/A thief!*)

사고 났어요! (sah-goh nah-ssuh-yoh) (*There's an accident!*)

REMEMBER

These phrases are part of your emergency toolkit. Use them well, and hopefully, you'll never have to!

Essential emergency phone numbers

In North America, 911 is the universal number for all 응급상황 (eung-geup-sahng-hwahng) (*emergency situations*). But in Korea, there are two numbers for different types of 응급상황: 119 and 112.

>> **Dial 119** (eel-leel-goo) for medical emergencies involving 응급환자 (eung-geup-hwahn-jah) (*emergency patients*), 구급차 (goo-geup-chah) (*ambulances*), 불/화재 (bool/hwah-jae) (*fires*), and other 재해 (jae-hae) (*disasters*) such as 지진 (jee-jeen) (*earthquakes*), or 태풍 (tae-poong) (*typhoons*).

>> **Call 112** (eel-leel-lee) for immediate 경찰 (gyuhng-chahl) (*police*) assistance in 범죄 (buhm-jwae) (*crime*) situations. 112 also offers the "Visible 112" service, known as "보이는 112" (boh-ee-neun eel-leel-lee). It allows you to send a live video to the 112 상담원 (sahng-dah-mwuhn) (*operator*) if you're unable to speak or unsure of your location. Click the link sent to your phone. Your 위치 (wee-chee) (*location*) and situation will be promptly addressed, and 경찰 will be dispatched.

Don't worry about language barriers. In both emergency services, the 상담원 (sahng-dah-mwuhn) (*operator*) will connect you with an 통역사 (tohng-yuhk-ssah) (*interpreter*) if needed.

Alerting the police in an emergency

"Call the police" in Korean is "경찰에 전화해요" (gyuhng-chah-reh juhn-hwah-hae-yoh). If you need someone to dial 119 for you, say "119에 전화해 주세요" (eel-leel-goo-eh juhn-hwah-hae joo-seh-yoh) (*Please call 119*). Here are some phrases you can use to explain your 위치 (wee-chee) (*location*) or situation in Korean:

여기 [서울역 근처]예요. (yuh-gee [suh-ool-lyuhk geun-chuh]-yeh-yoh) (*I am [near Seoul Station].*)

[세] 사람이 다쳤어요. ([seh]-sah-rah-mee dah-chyuh-ssuh-yoh) (*[Three] people got injured.*)

사람이 쓰러졌어요! (sah-rah-mee sseu-ruh-juh-ssuh-yoh) (*Someone has collapsed!*)

환자가 있어요. 빨리 와 주세요. (hwahn-jah-gah ee-ssuh-yoh. ppahl-lee wah joo-seh-yoh) (*There's a patient here. Please come quickly.*)

Getting Help for Less-Urgent Matters

Imagine, you've just enjoyed a delicious 비빔밥 (bee-beem-ppahp) (*mixed rice with assorted vegetables*) and discover your wallet missing! Don't panic–here's what to do.

Reporting lost belongings

If your wallet, passport, or other important items are missing, head to the nearest 파출소 (pah-chool-ssoh) (*branch police station*) or contact 경찰서 (gyuhng-chahl-ssuh) (*police station*). Provide details about your situation and location to a 경찰관 (gyuhng-chahl-gwahn) (*police officer*) to help recover your belongings. Also immediately freeze your card account if your 은행 카드 (eun-haeng kah-deu) (*bank cards*) are lost, and contact your 대사관 (dae-sah-gwahn) (*embassy*) for an Emergency Travel Certificate if your 여권 (yuh-kkwuhn) (*passport*) is missing.

Here are some useful phrases to help you communicate your loss:

> 택시에 [지갑] 두고 내렸어요. (taek-ssee-eh [jee-gahp] doo-goh nae-ryuh-ssuh-yoh) (*I left my [wallet] in the taxi.*)

> 지하철에서 [가방] 잃어버렸어요. (jee-hah-chuhl-eh-suh [gah-bahng] ee-ruh-buh-ryuh-ssuh-yoh) (*I lost my [bag] in the subway.*)

> 가방 안에 [여권]하고 [돈]하고 [카드]가 있어요. (gah-bahng ah-neh [yuh-kkwuhn]-hah-goh [dohn]-hah-goh [kah-deu]-gah ee-ssuh-yoh) (*My [passport], [money] and [cards] are inside the bag.*)

Feel free to adapt these phrases by replacing the words in brackets with other 소지품 (soh-jee-poom) (*belongings*) you may have lost.

TIP

Just in case, it's a good idea to keep your 택시 영수증 (taek-ssee yuhng-soo-jeung) (*taxi receipt*) for tracking purposes. And also check the lost-and-found in large 공공장소 (gohng-gohng-jahng-soh) (*public places*) you visited, like 박물관 (bahng-mool-gwahn) (*museums*) or 지하철역 (jee-hah-chuhl-lyuhk) (*subway station*).

You can ask, "분실물 센터가 어디예요?" (boon-sheel-mool sehn-tuh-gah uh-dee-yeh-yoh) (*Where is the lost-and-found?*) to help retrieve your items. Additionally, register your missing items at the Korean National Police Agency's Lost and Found Information System (https://www.lost112.go.kr).

Non-Emergency Assistance

For issues that aren't pressing emergent but still needs some attention, like a non-working streetlamp, call 110 (eel-leel-gohng). It's the number for non-urgent assistance, from government inquiries to civil complaints, with 통역 서비스 (tohng-yuhk ssuh-bee-sseu) (*interpreter service*) available.

Travelers seeking information on 관광지 (gwahn-gwahng-jee) (*tourist sites*), 교통 (gyoh-tohng) (*transportation*), or 식당 (sheek-ttahng) (*restaurants*) can dial the 24/7 Korea Tourism Hotline at 1330 (eel-sahm-sahm-gohng).

Talkin' the Talk

PLAY

James calls the emergency number to report an accident.

119: 119입니다. 어떻게 도와 드릴까요?
eel-leel-goo-eem-nee-dah. uh-ttuh-keh doh-wah deu-reel-kkah-yoh?
This is 119. How may I help you?

James: 차 사고가 났어요. 도와 주세요!
chah sah-goh-gah nah-ssuh-yoh. doh-wah-joo-seh-yoh!
There has been a car accident. Please help!

119: 이름과 현재 위치를 말씀해 주세요.
ee-reum-gwah hyuhn-jae wee-chee-reul mahl-sseum-hae joo-seh-yoh.
Please tell us your name and current location.

James: 제 이름은 제임스예요. 여기 시청 바로 앞이에요.
jeh ee-reu-meun jeh-eem-seu-yeh-yoh. yuh-gee shee-chuhng bah-roh ah-pee-eh-yoh
My name is James. I'm here right in front of the city hall.

119: 다친 사람이 있습니까?
dah-cheen sah-rah-mee eet-sseum-nee-kkah?
Is there anybody injured?

James: 네, 두 사람이 다쳤어요.
neh, doo sah-rah-mee dah-chyuh-ssuh-yoh.
Yes, two people got injured.

119:	잠시만 기다리세요. 구급차와 경찰이 3분 뒤에 도착할 거예요.
	jahm-shee-mahn gee-dah-ree-seh-yoh. goo-geup-chah-wah gyunhg-chah-ree sahm-boon dwee-eh doh-chah-kahl kkuh-yeh-yoh.
	Please wait a moment. An ambulance and the police will be arriving in 3 minutes.
James:	감사합니다.
	gahm-sah-hahm-nee-dah.
	Thank you.

WORDS TO KNOW

차 사고	chah sah-goh	car accident
났어요 (나다)	nah-ssuh-yoh	occured
현재	hyuhn-jae	current
위치	wee-chee	location
다친 (다치다)	dah-cheen	injured
기다리세요 (기다리다)	gee-dah-ree-seh-yoh	please wait
구급차	goo-geup-chah	ambulance
경찰	gyuhng-chahl	police
도착할 거예요 (도착하다)	doh-chah-kahl kkuh-yeh-yo	will arrive

Getting Medical Help

Falling ill is never fun, especially when you're in a 외국 (wae-gook) (*foreign country*). A sudden 감기 (gahm-gee) (*cold*) or 독감 (dohk-kkahm) (*flu*) can really throw a wrench in your well-planned trip. When traveling abroad, it's smart to bring a copy of your 처방전 (chuh-bahng-juhn) (*prescription*), along with your 처방약 (chuh-bahng-nyahk) (*prescription meds*). The following sections can help you navigate some medical issues.

Finding a doctor

For any injuries or illnesses, simply head to a 병원 (byuhng-wuhn) (*hospital, clinic*) where 의사 (eui-sah) (*doctors*) and 간호사 (gahn-hoh-sah) (*nurses*) are on hand. You can walk in neighborhood clinics without a 진료 예약 (jeel-lyoh yeh-yahk) (*medical appointment*), but for 종합병원 (johng-hahp-byuhng-wuhn) (*general hospital*) or 대학병원 (dae-hahk-byuhng-wuhn) (*university hospitals*), you'll need to book in advance. If you are looking for a specialist, Table 18-1 lists the various medical fields to guide you.

TABLE 18-1 ## Medicine Fields/Specialties

Medical Term	Pronunciation	English Meaning
내과	nae-kkwah	internal medicine
산부인과	sahn-boo-een-kkwah	obstetrics-gynecology
성형외과	suhng-hyuhng-wae-kkwah	plastic surgery
소아과	soh-ah-kkwah	pediatrics
신경과	sheen-gyuhng-kkwah	neurology
정신과	juhng-sheen-kkwah	psychiatry
안과	ahn-kkwah	optometry
이비인후과	ee-bee-een-hoo-kkwah	otolaryngology/ENT
외과	wae-kkwah	surgery
정형외과	juhng-hyuhng-wae-kkwah	orthopedic
치과	chee-kkwah	dental
피부과	pee-boo-kkwah	dermatology

CULTURAL WISDOM

Korea's 의료 서비스 (eui-ryoh ssuh-bee-sseu) (*medical service*) and 건강 보험 (guhn-gahng boh-huhm) (*health insurance*) are of exceptionally high quality. The 국민 건강 보험 (goong-meen guhn-gahng boh-huhm) (*National Health Insurance, NHI*) in Korea makes healthcare fairly affordable. Under this system, virtually all essential treatments are covered. For more info, you can visit www.nhis.or.kr/english.

TRADITIONAL KOREAN MEDICINE CLINIC

If you're interested in exploring natural or holistic treatments, consider visiting a 한의원 (hah-nee-wuhn) (*traditional Korean medicine clinic*). There, you can experience a variety of 한방 치료 (hahn-hahng chee-ryoh) (*Eastern medicine treatment*), such as 침 (cheem) (*acupuncture*), 한약 (hah-nyahk) (*oriental herbal medicine*), 부황 (boo-hwahng) (*cupping*), and 뜸 (tteum) (*moxibustion*). These therapies are known for their natural approaches, minimizing chemical use and side effects. In Korea, you have easy access to both traditional Korean and Western medical practices, tailored to your health needs. So if you ever sprain your 발목 (bahl-mohk) (*ankle*) while exploring cities on foot, consider checking out a nearby 한의원 for treatment.

Going to emergencies

In case you need to visit the 응급실 (eung–geup–sseel) (*emergency room*), Table 18–2 introduces useful phrases in informal polite speech endings.

TABLE 18-2

Medical Emergency Terms

Emergency Phrase	Pronunciation	English Meaning
구급차 불러요 (부르다)	goo-geup-chah bool-luh-yoh	call an ambulance
맥박 재요 (재다)	maek-ppahk jae-yoh	take one's pulse
심폐소생술 해요 (하다)	sheem-pyeh-soh-saeng-sool hae-yoh	perform CPR
응급실에 가요 (가다)	eung-geup-ssee-reh gah-yoh	go to the ER
응급처치 해요 (하다)	eung-geup-chuh-chee hae-yoh	give first aid
입원해요 (하다)	ee-bwuhn-hae-yoh	be hospitalized
엑스레이 찍어요 (찍다)	ehk-sseu-reh-ee jjee-guh-yoh	take an X-ray
주사 맞아요 (맞다)	joo-sah mah-jah-yoh	get a shot/an injection
체온 재요 (재다)	cheh-ohn jae-yoh	take body temperature
혈압 재요 (재다)	hyuh-rahp jae-yoh	measure blood pressure
피 나요 (나다)	pee nah-yoh	bleed
지혈해요 (하다)	jee-hyuhl-hae-yoh	stop bleeding
퇴원해요 (하다)	twae-wuhn-hae-yoh	be discharged from the hospital

Describing symptoms using body parts

In 병원 (byuhng-wuhn) (*hospital*), medical personnel may ask "어디가 아프세요?" (uh-dee-gah ah-peu-seh-yoh) (*Where does it hurt?*) or "어디가 불편하세요?" (uh-dee-gah bool-pyuhn-hah-seh-yoh) (*Where is it uncomfortable?*).

To express discomfort or pain, use "아프다" (ah-peu-dah) (*to hurt/to be in pain/to be sick*). Respond with "[body part]이/가 아파요 (ah-pah-yoh)" (*[body part] hurts*). Table 18-3 lists terms for some basic 몸 (mohm) (*body*) parts. Below is how to choose the correct subject particle, 이 or 가. (Note that in very casual speech, you may omit them.)

>> Add 이 if the noun ends in a consonant:

   눈이 아파요. (noo-nee ah-pah-yoh) (*My eye hurts.*)

>> Add 가 if the noun ends in a vowel:

   허리가 아파요. (huh-ree-gah ah-pah-yoh) (*My lower back hurts.*)

Being able to accurately describe what part of the body needs attention can be extremely helpful in medical situations.

TABLE 18-3   **Basic Body Parts**

Body Areas	Body Parts
머리 (muh-ree) (*head*)	얼굴 (uhl-gool) (*face*), 눈 (noon) (*eye*), 코 (koh) (*nose*), 귀 (gwee) (*ear*), 입 (eep) (*mouth*), 이/치아 (ee/chee-ah) (*tooth*), 목 (mohk) (*neck*)
상체 (sahng-cheh) (*upper body*)	가슴 (gah-seum) (*chest*), 어깨 (uh-kkae) (*shoulder*), 팔 (pahl) (*arm*), 팔꿈치 (pahl-kkoom-chee) (*elbow*), 손 (sohn) (*hand*), 손목 (sohn-mohk) (*wrist*), 손가락 (sohn-kkah-rahk) (*finger*), 배 (bae) (*stomach, abdomen*), 등 (deung) (*back*), 허리 (huh-ree) (*waist, lower back*)
하체 (hah-cheh) (*lower body*)	다리 (dah-ree) (*leg*), 무릎 (moo-reup) (*knee*), 발 (bahl) (*foot*), 발목 (bahl-mohk) (*ankle*), 발가락 (bahl-kkah-rahk) (*toe*)
내장 (nae-jahng) (*internal organs*)	간 (gahn) (*liver*), 뇌 (nwae) (*brain*), 심장 (sheem-jahng) (*heart*), 위 (wee) (*stomach*), 장 (jahng) (*intestines*), 폐 (pyeh) (*lung*)
기타 (gee-tah) (*others*)	근육 (geu-nyook) (*muscle*), 신경 (sheen-gyuhng) (*nerves*), 뼈 (ppyuh) (*bones*), 피부 (pee-boo) (*skin*)

TIP

To express the intensity of your pain, you can add adverbs like 너무 (nuh-moo) (*too/too much*), 많이 (mah-nee) (*a lot*), 조금 (joh-geum) (*a little bit*) before 아파요 to specify the severity, as in 배가 **너무** 아파요. (bae-gah nuh-moo ah-pah-yoh) (*My stomach hurts a lot.*).

REMEMBER

If you need the medical staff to communicate more clearly, don't hesitate to ask:

천천히 말해 주세요. (chuhn-chuhn-hee mahl-hae joo-seh-yoh.) (*Please speak slowly.*)

다시 한번 말해 주세요. (dah-shee-hahn-buhn mahl-hae joo-seh-yoh.) (*Please say it again.*)

Talking about illnesses

It's often necessary to discuss specific ailments or chronic conditions to get appropriate medical attention or prescriptions. Table 18-4 provides a list of common phrases in informal polite form for illnesses and health issues.

TABLE 18-4 **Medical Ailments**

Phrase (Dictionary Form)	Pronunciation	English Meaning
감기에 걸렸어요 (걸리다)	gahm-gee-eh guhl-lyuh-ssuh-yoh	I got a cold
기침해요 (하다)	gee-cheem-hae-yoh	I am coughing
독감에 걸렸어요 (걸리다)	dohk-kkah-meh guhl-lyuh-ssuh-yoh	I got the flu
두드러기가 나요 (나다)	doo-deu-ruh-gee-gah nah-yoh	I have hives
멀미해요 (하다)	muhl-mee-hae-yoh	I am motion sick
설사해요 (하다)	suhl-ssah-hae-yoh	I have diarrhea
식중독에 걸렸어요 (걸리다)	sheek-jjoong-doh-geh guhl-lyuh-ssuh-yoh	I have food poisoning
소화가 안 돼요 (되다)	soh-hwah-gah ahn dwae-yoh	I have indigestion
열이 나요 (나다)	yuh-ree nah-yoh	I have a fever
고혈압이 있어요 (있다)	goh-hyuh-rah-bee ee-ssuh-yoh	I have high blood pressure
당뇨가 있어요	dahng-nyoh-gah ee-ssuh-yoh	I have diabetes
두통이 있어요	doo-tohng-ee ee-ssuh-yoh	I have a headache
변비가 있어요	byuhn-bee-gah ee-ssuh-yoh	I have constipation
알레르기가 있어요	ahl-leh-reu-gee-gah ee-ssuh-yoh	I have an allergy
천식이 있어요	chuhn-shee-gee ee-ssuh-yoh	I have asthma

Following medicine prescriptions

After receiving a diagnosis, you might be prescribed various 약 (yahk) (*medication*), such as 항생제 (hahng-saeng-jeh) (*antibiotics*). To pick up your prescription, you'll need to go to a 약국 (yahk-kkook) (*pharmacy*), which is usually inside or near the hospital. The 약사 (yahk-ssah) (*pharmacist*) will explain the proper 복용법 (boh-gyohng-ppuhp) (*dosage*). Here are essential words and phrases related to 약:

>> 하루/1일 (hah-roo/ee-reel) (*a single day*)

>> 하루 두 번 (hah-roo doo buhn) (*twice daily*)

>> 1일 3회 (ee-reel sahm-hwae) (*three times a day*)

>> 회/번 (hwae/buhn) (*the number of times*)

>> 식전 (sheek-jjuhn) (*before a meal*)

>> 식후 30분 (shee-koo sahm-sheep ppoon) (*30 minutes after a meal*)

>> 알약/물약 (ahl-lyahk/mool-lyahk) (*pill/liquid medicine* or *syrup*)

>> (과다) 복용 ((gwah-dah) boh-gyohng) ((*over*) *dosage*)

>> 중단 (joong-dahn) (*discontinuation*)

>> 처방(전) (chuh-bahng (juhn)) (*prescription (sheet)*)

Here are some useful questions to have handy for your 약사:

하루에 몇 번 먹어요? (hah-roo-eh myuht ppuhn muh-guh-yoh) (*How many times a day do I take it?*)

언제 먹어요? (uhn-jeh muh-guh-yoh) (*When do I take it?*)

얼마 동안 먹어요? (uhl-mah ttohng-ahn muh-guh-yoh) (*How long do I take it?*)

부작용이 있어요? 뭐예요? (boo-jah-gyohng-ee ee-ssuh-yoh? mwuh-yeh-yoh) (*Are there any side effects? What are they?*)

약값이 얼마예요? (yahk-kkahp-ssee uhl-mah-yeh-yoh) (*How much is the medicine?*)

보험 적용돼요? (boh-huhm juh-gyohng-dwae-yoh) (*Is this covered by insurance?*)

Getting medicine over-the-counter

If you find yourself needing simple medication without any prescription, you can usually purchase it over-the-counter at a nearby 약국 (yahk-kkook) (*pharmacy*) or even 편의점 (pyuh-nee-juhm) (*convenience store*). Here are some common types of 약 you might find:

>> 감기약 (gahm-gee-yahk) (*cold medicine*)

>> 관절약 (gwahn-juhl-yahk) (*joint medicine*)

>> 두통약 (doo-tohng-yahk) (*headache medicine*)

>> 멀미약 (muhl-mee-yahk) (*motion sickness medicine*)

>> 변비약 (byuhn-bee-yahk) (*laxatives*)

>> 소화제 (soh-hwah-jeh) (*digestive aids*)

>> 안약 (ahn-yahk) (*eye drops*)

>> 알레르기약 (ahl-leh-reu-gee-yahk) (*allergy medicine*)

>> 영양제 (yuhng-yahng-jeh) (*nutritional supplements*)

>> 진통제 (jeen-tohng-jeh) (*pain reliever*)

>> 해열제 (hae-yuhl-jeh) (*fever reducer*)

Additionally, here are some common first-aid home kit items:

>> 가위 (gah-wee) (*scissors*)

>> 소독약 (soh-dohng-nyahk) (*antiseptic*)

>> (압박) 붕대 ((ahp-ppahk) boong-dae) ((*pressure*) *bandage*)

>> 항생제 연고 (hahng-saeng-jeh yuhn-goh) (*antibiotic ointment*)

>> 반창고/밴드 (bahn-chahng-kkoh/baen-deu) (*band-aid*)

>> 파스 (pah-sseu) (*pain relief patch*)

KOREAN HOME REMEDIES FOR COLDS

Each culture has its own remedies, also known as "민간요법" (meen-gahn-yoh-ppuhp) (*folk remedy*), for ailments. In Korea, common cold treatments, especially for a 기침 감기 (gee-cheem-gahm-gee) (*cough cold*) or 목 감기 (mohk gahm-gee) (*sore throat*), include 배숙 (bae-sook) (*steamed Korean pears filled with honey inside*) and 무즙 (moo-jeup) (*radish juice with honey*). Herbs like 도라지 (doh-rah-jee) (*bellflower*), 대추 (dae-choo) (*jujube*), 생강 (saeng-gahng) (*ginger*), 인삼 (een-sahm) (*ginseng*), and 유자 (yoo-jah) (*yuja, a type of citrus fruit*) are also widely used in teas to ease 감기 증상 (gahm-gee jeung-sahng) (*cold symptoms*).

For a more hearty meal, people often prepare 매운 콩나물국 (mae-oon kohng-nah-mool kkook) (*spicy bean sprout soup*) or 삼계탕 (sahm-gyeh-tahng) (*ginseng chicken soup*), both of which increase body heat, promoting the release of 땀 (ttahm) (*sweat*) and 독소 (dohk-ssoh) (*toxins*). These traditional remedies not only provide comfort but are also cherished for their natural healing benefits. So the next time you catch a cold, why not try these new options?

Talkin' the Talk

PLAY

Jane has a stomachache, and Sooho convinces her to go to the hospital.

Sooho: 제인 씨, 괜찮아요? 얼굴이 안 좋아요.
jeh-een ssee, gwaen-chah-nah-yoh? uhl-goo-ree ahn joh-ah-yoh.
Jane, are you alright? You don't look so well.

Jane: 배가 좀 아파요.
bae-gah johm ah-pah-yoh.
My stomach is aching.

Sooho: 약 먹었어요?
yahk muh-guh-ssuh-yoh.
Did you take medicine?

Jane: 네. 진통제 먹었는데도 아파요.
neh. jeen-tohng-jeh muh-guhn-neun-deh-doh ah-pah-yoh.
Yes. I took a pain reliever, but it still hurts.

Paul: 병원에 가 보세요. 제가 같이 가 줄게요.
byuhng-wuh-neh gah boh-seh-yoh. jeh-gah gah-chee gah jool-kkeh-yoh.
You'd better go to the hospital. I'll go with you.

Jane:	고마워요. 좀 걱정이 돼요.
	goh-mah-wuh-yoh. johm guhk-jjuhng-ee dwae-yoh.
	Thanks. I'm a little worried.
Paul:	걱정 마세요. 별일 아닐 거예요.
	guhk-jjuhng mah-seh-yoh. byuhl-leel ah-neel kkuh-yeh-yoh.
	Don't worry. It will be nothing serious.

WORDS TO KNOW

얼굴	uhl-gool	face
아파요 (아프다)	ah-pah-yoh	hurt, get sick
배	bae	stomach, abdomen
약	yahk	medicine
진통제	jeen-tohng-jeh	pain reliever
병원	byuhng-wuhn	hospital
걱정이 돼요 (되다)	guhk-jjuhng-ee dwae-yoh	I'm worried
별일	byuhl-leel	something serious

Getting Legal Help

Chances are, you won't need any legal help while you're in Korea. People are genuinely friendly and 관광업 (gwahn-gwahng-uhp) (*tourism*) is a big deal, so you're likely to feel right at home! However, if you do need a 변호사 (byuhn-hoh-sah) (*lawyer, legal counselor*), it's advisable to contact your 대사관 (dae-sah-gwahn) (*embassy*) or 영사관 (yuhng-sah-gwahn) (*consulate*). They can provide the most comprehensive legal support you might require while in Korea.

FUN & GAMES

Look at the picture of the body below and label the different parts of the body using the words in the box. See Appendix C for the answers.

https://www.brightsprouts.com/body-parts-activities/

코   머리   입   어깨   눈   귀   배   팔꿈치   팔   손   발   다리

4

The Part of Tens

Peruse some advice on how to get a quick handle on Korean.

Learn dos and don'ts in Korean culture.

Chapter **19**

Ten Ways to Get a Good Grip on Korean

Mastering Korean doesn't have to be daunting. With the right approach, it can be both fun and effective! In this chapter, we've lined up ten strategies to help you quickly boost your Korean skills. You'll be surprised to find that some of the best ways to learn might have seemed like distractions before — they're actually great at keeping you entertained while immersing you in the language. So let's jump in and explore these engaging and enjoyable methods to enhance your journey in learning Korean!

Learn the Korean Alphabet, Hangeul

Get a handle on 한글 (hahn-geul) (*Hangeul*). As highlighted in Chapter 2, 한글 is easy to learn, and mastering it is crucial for anyone serious about learning Korean. Relying on romanization can be tricky sometimes, as it doesn't always nail the exact sounds of Korean. We've tried to match the closest English sounds in this book, but truly knowing 한글 will elevate your learning experience. It allows you dive with ease into everything from K-pop to films and literature. Ready to unlock a world of authentic Korean content? Start with 한글.

Listen to K-Pop Music

What's on your playlist? Any 케이팝 (keh-ee-pahp) (K-pop)? Connect to the vibrant world of 케이팝, which offers a diverse array of tempos and genres. You're sure to find something that gets your foot tapping! With lyrics and translations readily available online, you can easily embed new words and phrases into your memory. It's like downloading a new language without tedious memorization. Plus, honing your listening skills can also significantly boosts your fluency.

Ready to level up? Hit a 노래방 (noh-rae-bahng) (Korean-style karaoke) with friends or create your own at home using 노래방 version videos on YouTube. Chances are, you won't stop at just one song. Singing with friends not only doubles the fun but could also turn 케이팝 a core part of your language learning routine. Get ready to get hooked on K-music!

Watch Korean Movies, Dramas, and TV Shows

Is K-pop not for you? Why not explore 한국 영화 (hahn-gook yuhng-hwah) (Korean movies), 드라마 (deu-rah-mah) (dramas), or 예능 (yeh-neung) (TV variety shows) instead? These are perfect for relaxing while you pick up the language and culture. K-dramas and K-movies offer deep insights into Korean life, language, and customs. 예능, which usually have rich 한국어 자막 (hahn-goo-guh jah-mahk) (Korean subtitles), are also great for boosting your understanding. Watching these, you'll quickly grasp cultural and linguistic nuances through the real-life interactions and behaviors on screen.

Read Korean Webtoons

Another fun way to learn Korean? Check out 웹툰 (wehp-toon) (webtoons), digital comics from Korea that not only offer engaging visuals and easy online access, but also serve as great educational tools. Many college Korean classes incorporate them for reading, writing, and cultural comprehension. Why not explore a few Korean webtoon strips to enhance your language and cultural knowledge? They're definitely worth a look, especially since many have inspired popular dramas.

For free access to a range of webtoons, visit platforms like 네이버 웹툰 (neh-ee-buh wehp-toon) (*Naver Webtoon*) and 카카오 웹툰 (kah-kah-oh wehp-toon) (*Kakao Webtoon*).

Explore the Web and Apps

In today's digital age, nearly everything's gone digital — from binge-shopping to socializing, and even earning money! Language learning is no exception. With just your smartphone or laptops, you can dive into a world of resources: vocabulary games, translators, AI chatbots, engaging video content, language exchange apps, and online classes, all aimed to enhance your language abilities. If you're interested in 무료 수업 (moo-ryoh soo-uhp) (*free courses*), check out the online 세종학당 (seh-johng-hahk-ttahng) (*King Sejong Institute*) (www.iksi.or.kr) for structured learning opportunities. Plus, YouTube offers a plethora of cultural content from the 세종학당, along with many other wonderful Korean learning videos.

Looking to boost your Korean digital literacy? Explore sites like 타닥타닥, an onomatopoeia following the sound of typing, which offers typing practice (TaDakTaDak.co.kr). From letter placement to sentence typing and games, you can practice and have fun while improving your skills.

Discover Local Classes and Events

Are you an old-school learner who likes flipping to the back of your workbook for answers and enjoys practicing pronunciation with direct feedback? If so, navigating language learning on your own can feel a little overwhelming, especially with the sea of digital resources available today. Don't just fizzle out on learning Korean but look for resources that would fit your learning style and preferences. In-person 한국어 수업 (hahn-goo-guh soo-uhp) (*Korean classes*), now more accessible than ever, might be just what you need to stay engaged, practice face-to-face, and keep progressing. Some Korean community organizations such as Korean 문화원 (moon-hwah-wuhn) (*culture centers*) or 교회 (gyoh-hwae) (*churches*) offer 한글 학교 (hahn-geul hahk-kkyoh) (*Korean language schools*). Check out community newsletters online to find more info.

TIP

한국문화원 (hahn-gook-moon-hwah-wuhn) (*Korean Cultural Center*), located in Washington D.C., New York, and Los Angeles, has a wonderful series of exhibits, talks, presentations, and classes throughout the year. When you visit these cities, check out their calendar and plan ahead.

Cook or Eat Korean Foods

음식 (eum-sheek) (*food*), rich in cultural and historical significance, offers more than sustenance — it shapes identity, culture, and society. By cooking and eating Korean dishes, you explore the cultural meanings that each recipe or dish holds. This culinary journey can connect you deeply to Korean culture.

TIP

Want a closer look at Korean cuisine? Check out food documentaries on Netflix like the *Rhapsody* series and *A Nation of* series. For 레시피 (leh-shee-pee) (*recipes*) and cooking tips, visit sites like *Kimchimari*, *Korean Bapsang*, or *Maangchi* (books and YouTube channels too). For an authentic experience, watch 백종원 (baek-johng-wuhn) (Paik Jong-won) on his YouTube channel, complete with subtitles. Plus, there's tons of other Korean cooking videos on the internet to explore.

Make Friends with Korean Speakers

Nervous about chatting with a native Korean speaker? Fear not! Be 친구 (cheen-goo) (*friends*) with them! Socializing isn't just fun — it's also one of the quickest ways to learn the language. Put aside the 교과서 (gyoh-gwah-suh) (*textbooks*) and engage into real conversations. This hands-on approach can speeds up your journey to fluency.

Wondering where to meet Korean speakers? If you're in an area with a Korean community, you can start with people you see frequently, like Korean staff at a store. Alternatively, search for terms like "Korean language exchange" online to find apps that connect you with language exchange partners.

Travel to Korea

Every tip and tactic in this book is useful, but let's face it: No matter what this book may bring to the table, immersion remains one of the most effective ways to master a foreign language. While local Korean immersion programs and virtual reality can offer a good taste of the culture and language, if you have the opportunity, visiting Korea is highly recommended. There's nothing quite like experiencing the 문화 (moon-hwah) (*culture*) firsthand. Start with the well-known destinations, but don't rule out the charm of small towns and hidden alleys that you might fall in love with. For more 여행 (yuh-haeng) (*travel*) ideas, check out Chapter 14.

Stay Positive, Creative, and Curious

Unlock your learning potential by staying positive, tapping into your 창의력 (chahng-ee-ryuhk) (*creativity*), and keeping your 호기심 (hoh-gee-sheem) (*curiosity*) alive. These aren't just catchy phrases — they're secret weapons in mastering the 한국어 (hahn-goo-guh) (*Korean language*). Even better, weave these essential elements into your daily routine for a more rewarding learning experience.

Remember, there's no one-size-fits-all formula for mastering 한국어 — or any language, for that matter. Reflect on your personal learning style, experiment boldly, challenge yourself regularly, and continually explore new ways to dive deeper into the rich world of this new language. Let 호기심 be your guide!

Chapter 20

Ten Things to Avoid Doing in Korea

S ocial and cultural norms are as diverse as the world itself. For instance, walking around a house with your 신발 (sheen-bahl) (*shoes*) on is totally fine in some countries, but in Korea, that's a definite no-no. While personal space is highly valued in many cultures, in Korea, closeness is often a sign of trust and friendship. It's not unusual to see friends casually holding hands or touching each other's arms — a gesture known as 스킨쉽 (seu-keen-sheep) ("*skinship*").

This chapter helps you navigate 문화 차이 (moon-hwah chah-ee) (*cultural differences*) without any stress. Don't worry if things seem a bit complex at first; the more you interact with others, the deeper your understanding of these diverse practices will become.

TIP

Let's kick off with a fun Korean term you might find handy: 꿀팁 (kkool-teep) ("*sweet advice*"), which blends 꿀 (kkool) (*honey*) for "sweet" and 팁 (teep) (*tip*) for "advice." Here goes ten 꿀팁 to help you smoothly adapt to new cultural practices in Korea.

Entering a House with Your Shoes On

First things first: In Korea, stepping into a home means stepping out of your shoes! This practice is linked to Korea's unique floor heating system, known as 온돌 (ohn-dohl) ("*heated stone*"). This ingenious system heats from beneath the floorboards, and has fostered a culture where much of life is lived on the floor, to make the most of the snug 온돌 warmth. Whether it's dining, lounging, sleeping, or binge-watching TV, many activities are enjoyed down at the floor level. While you'll often find dining tables, sofas, and beds, the floor remains a beloved gathering spot. And to keep the floor clean, wearing outdoor shoes inside is a definite no-go!

Calling Bosses or Teachers by Their First Name

In Korea, addressing your bosses or teachers by their first name is considered inappropriate, no matter how close you are to them. Instead, use their name followed by their job title, as in 박 선생님 (bahk suhn-saeng-neem) (*Teacher Park*) or 전 매니저님 (juhn mae-nee-juh-neem) (*Manager Jeon*). If needed, you can include their full name, like 박정국 선생님 (*Teacher Park, Jungkook*) or 전민지 매니저님 (*Manager Jeon, Minji*).

When the context doesn't require specifying, you can simply use their job title — for example 선생님 (*Teacher*) or 매니저님 (*Manager*). Remember, in Korean, the name always comes before the title. So it's 박 선생님, not 선생님 박, unlike how you would say it in English.

TIP

If unsure about someone's job title, simply add the respectful suffix 님 (neem) after their name, either full or first only, like 박수지 님 (bahk-soo-jee neem) (*Park, Suzie*) or 수지 님 (soo-jee neem) (*Suzie*). Alternatively, you can ask directly how they prefer to be addressed by saying: 호칭을 어떻게 할까요? (hoh-cheeng-eul uh-ttuh-keh hahl-kkah-yoh) (*How can I address you?*). For peers or juniors at work, you can add 씨 (ssee) instead of 님, like in 수지 씨 (*Ms. Suzie*). Note 씨 is not suitable when addressing higher-ups.

Using "ssee" or "neem" in Self-Reference

When you're at a checkup, the doctor or nurse might call your name followed by 님 (neem), like 피터 (스미스) 님 (pee-tuh (seu-mee-sseu) neem) (*Mr. Peter (Smith)*), as a sign of respect while maintaining professional distance. But remember, this form of address doesn't apply when you talk about yourself! Terms like 님 or 씨 are for addressing others, not for self-reference. So, you'd say 저는 피터예요 (juh-neun pee-tuh-yeh-yoh) (*I am Peter*), not 저는 피터 씨예요 or 피터 님이에요, unless you're in the mood for a joke.

Visiting Someone Empty-Handed

When visiting someone's house in Korea, people usually bring a small token of appreciation. Nothing lavish is needed. Simple fruits, beverages, or desserts are perfect. When invited to a 집들이 (jeep-tteu-ree) (*housewarming party*), practical essentials like 세제 (seh-jeh) (*detergents*), 화장지 (hwah-jahng-jee) (*toilet paper*), or 키친타올 (kee-cheen-tah-ohl) (*paper towels*) are popular choices. For a more personal touch, consider gifts like a potted plant, candles, homemade treats, or anything else you know the host will enjoy. The possibilities are endless! Forgot to bring something? Don't sweat it. Your presence is more than enough, and there's always next time!

One-Handed Exchanges

In Korea, when giving and receiving items from elders or in formal settings, it's essential to use 두 손 (doo sohn) (*two hands*). Think of it as a way to show you're giving the task your full attention (and maybe even a little extra respect). Whether it's 악수 (ahk-soo) (*shaking hands*), exchanging gifts or 명함 (myuhng-hahm) (*business cards*), or accepting or pouring a drink, lightly support your 오른손 (oh-reun-sohn) (*right hand*) with your 왼손 (waen-sohn) (*left hand*), or just use both hands.

Getting Rattled by Personal Questions

In Korea, chatting with older generations sometimes might feel like a spontaneous quiz show. You might be asked questions like 몇 살이에요? (myuht ssah-ree-eh-yoh) (*How old are you?*), 결혼했어요? (gyuhl-hohn-hae-ssuh-yoh) (*Are you *married?*), or 여자/남자 친구 있어요? (yuh-jah/nahm-jah cheen-goo ee-ssuh-yoh) (*Do you have a girl/boyfriend?*). These queries may initially seem intrusive but are typically friendly overtures. Meanwhile, the younger generations might skip straight to modern icebreakers like "MBTI가 뭐예요?" (MBTI-gah mwuh-yeh-yoh) (*What's your MBTI?*). From traditional to trendy, all these questions are just ways to forge connections, one question at a time!

Picking Up Your Rice Bowl

Many Asian cultures may cuddle their rice or soup 그릇 (geu-reut) (*bowls*) during meals. In some cultures, rice bowls are even rounded at the bottom to make holding them up easier. But Korean bowls typically come with a flatter bottom, which are designed to stay put on the table. Feel free to lift your bowl for a final polish to scoop up the last bits of soup or rice, but for the most part, let your bowl rest easy on the table.

Also, a quick tip on chopstick and spoon decorum: Avoid sticking them upright in your rice bowl. This position is traditionally associated with rituals for the deceased and is not something you do in everyday settings. (For more on table etiquette, see Chapter 9.)

Overstating: Embracing Modesty

겸손 (gyuhm-sohn) (*modesty*) is highly valued across many cultures, but in Korea, it's prized to the point where deflecting compliments might as well be a national sport. For instance, if a Korean family hosts you for dinner, they might modestly say "차린 건 없지만 많이 드세요" (chah-reen guhn uhp-jjee-mahn mah-nee deu-seh-yoh) (*We haven't prepared much, but please enjoy*), even as they present a table heaving with dishes. If you compliment a Korean with phrases like "You're so smart!" or "Your English is really good!", the likely response will be 아니에요 (ah-nee-eh-yoh), meaning "Not at all." Similarly, if you thank them, they might also say 아니에요, translating to "Oh, it's nothing." Remember, when you hear the modest 아니에요, it's not a dismissal of your praise; rather, they're just keeping it humble in the modesty league. But don't be surprised if a younger Korean flips the script with a cheerful 고맙습니다 (goh-mahp-sseum-nee-dah). They may be a bit more direct with their gratitude!

Eating Before Your Higher-Ups

In Korea, respect for elders and those in higher social ranks is a long-standing tradition. In formal settings, it's considered proper etiquette to wait to eat until after the higher-ups have begun their meal. Don't feel jealous of their seniority; checks are often their responsibility. Even in more casual settings like 가족 모임 (gah-johk moh-eem) (*family gatherings*), this etiquette also applies, although the rules are more relaxed there.

Mixing it All Up in One Bin

Respect in Korea doesn't just extend to people; it also reaches the 환경 (hwahn-gyuhng) (*environment*). Since strict waste management laws were implemented in 1995, including 분리수거 (bool-lee-soo-guh) (*"separate collection," recycling*) and 쓰레기 종량제 (sseu-reh-gee johng-nyahng-jeh) (*volume-based waste fee system*), everyone must meticulously sort their trash. Mandatory biodegradable 쓰레기 봉투 (sseu-reh-gee bohng-too) (*garbage bags*), which you purchase, are used for food waste and general garbage, while 재활용품 (jae-hwah-ryohng-poom) (*recyclables*) like paper, plastics, PET bottles, glass, and cans are sorted into color-coded bins. Slip up? You might end up paying a fine! It might seem like a lot at first, but this sorting effort really underscores your commitment to the planet, as nearly 100 percent of food waste gets recycled there. Don't worry if you're not used to it; you'll catch on quickly!

5
Appendixes

Learn basic Korean verb conjugation in verb tables.

Find essential, everyday Korean vocabulary in mini dictionaries.

Check out the answers for the Fun & Games.

Appendix A
Verb Tables

The Three Types of Conjugation

아/어	으	Consonant-Initial
-어요/아요 (Polite Present)	-을 거예요 (Polite Future)	-습니다/ㅂ니다 (Deferential Present)
았어요/었어요 (Polite Past)	-으세요 (Honorific/Polite Command)	-지요 (Seeking Agreement)
아서/어서 (Conjunction; because)	-으면 (Conjunction; if)	-고 (Conjunction; and)

아/어 Conjugation: Regular Consonant-Ending Verbs

Verb	Polite Present 아요/어요	Polite Past 았어요/었어요	because 아서/-어서
Consonant-ending Verb Stems with ㅏ/ㅗ			
알다 (to know)	알아요 (ah-rah-yoh)	알았어요 (ah-rah-ssuh-yoh)	알아서 (ah-rah-suh)
좋다 (to be good)	좋아요 (joh-ah-yoh)	좋았어요 (joh-ah-ssuh-yoh)	좋아서 (joh-ah-suh)
Consonant-ending Verb Stems with Other than ㅏ/ㅗ			
맛있다 (to be delicious)	맛있어요 (mah-shee-ssuh-yoh)	맛있었어요 (mah-shee-ssuh-ssuh-yoh)	맛있어서 (mah-shee-ssuh-suh)
먹다 (to eat)	먹어요 (muh-guh-yoh)	먹었어요 (muh-guh-ssuh-yoh)	먹어서 (muh-guh-suh)

아/어 Conjugation: Irregular Consonant-Ending Verbs

Verb	Polite Present 아요/어요	Polite Past 았어요/었어요	because 아서/어서
ㄷ-ending Verb Stems			
듣다 (to listen)	들어요 (deu-ruh-yoh)	들었어요 (del-ruh-ssuh-yoh)	들어서 (deu-ruh-suh)
걷다 (to walk)	걸어요 (guh-ruh-yoh)	걸었어요 (guh-ruh-ssuh-yoh)	걸어서 (guh-ruh-suh)
ㅂ-ending Verb Stems			
춥다 (to be cold)	추워요 (choo-wuh-yoh)	추웠어요 (choo-wuh-ssuh-yoh)	추워서 (choo-wuh-suh)
돕다 (to help)	도와요 (doh-wah-yoh)	도왔어요 (doh-wah-ssuh-yoh)	도와서 (doh-wah-suh)

ㅎ-ending Verb Stems

그렇다 (to be so)	그래요 (geu-rae-yoh)	그랬어요 (geu-rae-ssuh-yoh)	그래서 (geu-rae-suh)
하얗다 (to be white)	하얘요 (hah-yae-yoh)	하얬어요 (hah-yae-ssuh-yoh)	하얘서 (hah-yae-suh)

ㅅ-ending Verb Stems

짓다 (to make)	지어요 (jee-uh-yoh)	지었어요 (jee-uh-ssuh-yoh)	지어서 (jee-uh-suh)
낫다 (to heal)	나아요 (nah-ah-yoh)	나았어요 (nah-ah-ssuh-yoh)	나아서 (nah-ah-suh)

아/어 Conjugation: Vowel-Ending Verbs

Verb	Polite Present 아요/어요	Polite Past 았어요/었어요	because 아서/어서
ㅏ/ㅐ/ㅓ/ㅔ-ending Verb Stems			
가다 (to go)	가요 (gah-yoh)	갔어요 (gah-ssuh-yoh)	가서 (gah-suh)
지내다 (to get along)	지내요 (jee-nae-yoh)	지냈어요 (jee-nae-ssuh-yoh)	지내서 (jee-nae-suh)
건너다 (to cross)	건너요 (guhn-nuh-yoh)	건넜어요 (guhn-nuh-ssuh-yoh)	건너서 (guhn-nuh-suh)
세다 (to count)	세요 (seh-yoh)	셌어요 (seh-ssuh-yoh)	세서 (seh-suh)
ㅗ-ending Verb Stems			
오다 (to come)	와요 (wah-yoh)	왔어요 (wah-ssuh-yoh)	와서 (wah-suh)
보다 (to see)	봐요 (bwah-yoh)	봤어요 (bwah-ssuh-yoh)	봐서 (bwah-suh)
ㅜ-ending Verb Stems			
배우다 (to leran)	배워요 (be-wuh-yoh)	배웠어요 (bae-wuh-ssuh-yoh)	배워서 (bae-wuh-suh)
나누다 (to divide)	나눠요 (nah-nwuh-yoh)	나눴어요 (nah-nwuh-ssuh-yoh)	나눠서 (nah-nwuh-suh)
ㅡ-ending Verb Stems			
예쁘다 (to be pretty)	예뻐요 (yeh-ppuh-yoh)	예뻤어요 (yeh-ppuh-ssuh-yoh)	예뻐서 (yeh-ppuh-suh)
아프다 (to be sick)	아파요 (ah-pah-yoh)	아팠어요 (ah-pah-ssuh-yoh)	아파서 (ah-pah-suh)
ㅣ-ending Verb Stems			
흐리다 (to be cloudy)	흐려요 (heu-ryuh-yoh)	흐렸어요 (heu-ryuh-ssuh-yoh)	흐려서 (heu-ryuh-suh)
치다 (to hit)	쳐요 (chyuh-yoh)	쳤어요 (chyuh-ssuh-yoh)	쳐서 (chyuh-suh)

어/아 Conjugation: 하- and 르-Ending Verbs

Verb	Polite Present 아요/어요	Polite Past 았어요/었어요	because 아서/어서
하-ending Verb Stems			
일하다 (to work)	일해요 (eel-hae-yoh)	일했어요 (eel-hae-ssuh-yoh)	일해서 (eel-hae-suh)
필요하다 (to be needed)	필요해요 (pee-ryoh-hae-yoh)	필요했어요 (pee-ryoh-hae-ssuh-yoh)	필요해서 (pee-ryoh-hae-suh)
르-ending Verb Stems			
모르다 (to not know)	몰라요 (mohl-lah-yoh)	몰랐어요 (mohl-lah-ssuh-yoh)	몰라서 (mohl-lah-suh)
빠르다 (to be fast)	빨라요 (ppahl-lah-yoh)	빨랐어요 (ppahl-lah-ssuh-yoh)	빨라서 (ppahl-lah-suh)

으 Conjugation: Regular Verbs

Verb	Polite Future -을 거예요	Honorific/Polite Command -으세요	if -으면
Consonant-ending Verb Stems			
많다 (to be a lot)	많을 거예요 (mah-neul kkuh-yeh-yoh)	많으세요 (mah-neu-seh-yoh)	많으면 (mah-neu-myuhn)
씻다 (to wash)	씻을 거예요 (ssee-seul kkuh-yeh-yoh)	씻으세요 (ssee-seu-seh-yoh)	씻으면 (ssee-seu-myuhn)
Vowel-ending Verb Stems			
하다 (to do)	할 거예요 (hahl kkuh-yeh-yoh)	하세요 (hah-seh-yoh)	하면 (hah-myuhn)
쓰다 (to use)	쓸 거예요 (sseul kkuh-yeh-yoh)	쓰세요 (sseu-seh-yoh)	쓰면 (sseu-myuhn)

으 Conjugation: Irregular Verbs

Verb	Polite Future -을 거예요	Honorific/Polite Command -으세요	if -으면
ㄷ-ending Verb Stems			
듣다 (to listen)	들을 거예요 (deu-reul kkuh-yeh-yoh)	들으세요 (deu-reu-seh-yoh)	들으면 (deu-reu-myuhn)
묻다 (to ask)	물을 거예요 (moo-reul kkuh-yeh-yoh)	물으세요 (moo-reu-seh-yoh)	물으면 (moo-reu-myuhn)
ㅂ-ending Verb Stems			
덥다 (to be hot)	더울 거예요 (duh-ool kkuh-yeh-yoh)	더우세요 (duh-oo-seh-yoh)	더우면 (duh-oo-myuhn)
눕다 (to lie down)	누울 거예요 (noo-ool kkuh-yeh-yoh)	누우세요 (noo-oo-seh-yoh)	누우면 (noo-oo-myuhn)
ㅎ-ending Verb Stems			
그렇다 (to be so)	그럴 거예요 (geu-ruhl kkuh-yeh-yoh)	그러세요 (geu-ruh-seh-yoh)	그러면 (geu-ruh-myuhn)
까맣다 (to be black)	까말 거예요 (kkah-mahl guh-yeh-yoh)	까마세요 (kkah-mah-seh-yoh)	까마면 (kkah-mah-myuhn)
ㅅ-ending Verb Stems			
잇다 (to connect)	이을 거예요 (ee-eul kkuh-yeh-yoh)	이으세요 (ee-eu-seh-yoh)	이으면 (ee-eu-myuhn)
붓다 (to swell)	부을 거예요 (boo-eul kkuh-yeh-yoh)	부으세요 (boo-eu-seh-yoh)	부으면 (boo-eu-myuhn)
ㄹ-ending Verb Stems			
살다 (to live)	살 거예요 (sahl kkuh-yeh-yoh)	사세요 (sah-seh-yoh)	살면 (sahl-myuhn)
만들다 (to make)	만들 거예요 (mahn-deul kkuh-yeh-yoh)	만드세요 (mahn-deu-seh-yoh)	만들면 (mahn-deul-myuhn)

Consonant-Initial Conjugation

Verb	Deferential Present -습니다/ㅂ니다	Seeking Agreement -지요	and -고
Any Korean Verb Stems			
괜찮다 (to be alright)	괜찮습니다 (gwaen-chahn-sseum-nee-dah)	괜찮지요 (gwaen-chahn-chee-yoh)	괜찮고 (gwaen-chahn-koh)
싸다 (to be cheap)	쌉니다 (ssahm-nee-dah)	싸지요 (ssah-jee-yoh)	싸고 (ssah-goh)

Irregular Verb Conjugation Summary

Irregular Type	Verb	아/어 (아요/어요)	으 (-으세요)	Consonant-Initial (-지요)
ㄷ	듣다 걷다	들어요 걸어요	들으세요 걸으세요	듣지요 걷지요
ㅂ	덥다 쉽다	더워요 쉬워요	더우세요 쉬우세요	덥지요 쉽지요
ㅎ	그렇다 하얗다	그래요 하얘요	그러면 하야면	그렇지요 하얗지요
ㅅ	낫다 짓다	나아요 지어요	나으세요 지으세요	낫지요 짓지요
ㄹ	살다 알다	살아요 알아요	사세요 아세요	살지요 알지요
르	모르다 빠르다	몰라요 빨라요	모르세요 빠르세요	모르지요 빠르지요

Appendix B

Mini-Dictionaries

Korean-English Mini-Dictionary

ㄱ

가게: (gah-geh) store

가격/값: (gah-gyuhk/gahp) price

가구: (gah-goo) furniture

가깝다: (gah-kkahp-ttah) to be close

가끔: (gah-kkeum) sometimes

가다: (gah-dah) to go

가르치다: (gah-reu-chee-dah) to teach

가방: (gah-bahng) bag

가수: (gah-soo) singer

가을: (gah-eul) autumn

가족: (gah-johk) family

갈아타다: (gah-rah-tah-dah) to transfer (vehicle)

감기: (gahm-gee) a cold

갑자기: (gahp-jjah-gee) suddenly

강아지/개: (gahng-ah-jee/gae) puppy/dog

같다: (gaht-ttah) to be the same

같이: (gah-chee) together

거기: (guh-gee) over there

거스름돈: (guh-seu-reum-ttohn) change (money)

걱정: (guhk-jjuhng) concern, worry

건강: (guhn-gahng) health

건너편: (guhn-nuh-pyuhn) the other side

건물: (guhn-mool) building

걷다: (guht-ttah) to walk

걸리다: (guhl-lee-dah) to take [time]; to be caught

것/거: (guht/guh) thing

겨울: (gyuh-ool) winter

결제(하다): (gyuhl-jjeh[-hah-dah]) payment; to pay

결혼식: (gyuhl-hohn-sheek) wedding ceremony

경찰서: (gyuhng-chahl-ssuh) police station

경치: (gyuhng-chee) scenery

경험: (gyuhng-huhm) experience

계란/달걀: (gyeh-rahn/dahl-gyahl) egg

계산(하다): (gyeh-sahn[-hah-dah]) calculation; to calculate, to pay a bill

계시다: (gyeh-shee-dah) to stay, exist, be (for honorific person)

계약(하다): (gyeh-yahk[-hah-dah]) contract; to make a contract

계절: (gyeh-juhl) season

계획: (gyeh-hwaek) plan

고객: (goh-gaek) customer

고기: (goh-gee) meat

고속버스: (goh-sohk-buh-sseu) express bus

고장나다: (goh-jahng-nah-dah) to be out of order, broken

고치다: (goh-chee-dah) to cure, fix

고향: (goh-hyahng) hometown

곧: (goht) soon

곳: (goht) place

공부[하다]: (gohng-boo[-hah-dah]) study; to study

공원: (gohng-wuhn) park

공항: (gohng-hahng) airport

공휴일: (gohn-hyoo-eel) official holiday

과일: (gwah-eel) fruit

관광[하다]: (gwahn-gwahng[-hah-dah]) tour; to tour

관심: (gwahn-sheem) interest

괜찮다: (gwaen-chahn-tah) to be alright

교육: (gyoh-yook) education

교통: (gyoh-tohng) traffic, transportation

교환[하다]: (gyoh-hwahn[-hah-dah]) exchange; to exchange

구경[하다]: (goo-gyuhng[-hah-dah]) sightseeing; to sight see

구급차: (goo-geup-chah) ambulance

국: (gook) soup

국적: (gook-jjuhk) nationality, citizenship

국제: (gook-jjeh) international

군인: (goo-neen) soldier

그것/그거: (geu-guht/geu-guh) that thing, that one

그냥: (geu-nyahng) just

그래서: (geu-rae-suh) so, therefore

그런데/근데: (geu-ruhn-deh/geun-deh) by the way, but

그럼: (geu-ruhm) if so

그릇: (geu-reut) bowl, dish

그리고: (geu-ree-goh) and

극장: (geuk-jjahng) theater

근처: (geun-chuh) nearby, vicinity

기념품: (gee-nyuhm-poom) souvenir

기다리다: (gee-dah-ree-dah) to wait

기사: (gee-sah) driver, technician

기차: (gee-chah) train

기회: (gee-hwae) opportunity

길: (geel) road, street

ㄲ

깎다: (kkah-ttah) to cut price, peel, shave

깨끗하다: (kkae-kkeu-tah-dah) to be clean

꼭: (kkohk) surely, firmly

끝나다: (kkeun-nah-dah) to be over, to end

ㄴ

나라: (nah-rah) country
나쁘다: (nah-ppeu-dah) to be bad
나이: (nah-ee) age
나중에: (nah-joong-eh) later
날마다/매일: (nahl-mah-dah/mae-eel) everyday
날씨: (nahl-ssee) weather
날짜: (nahl-jjah) date
남편: (nahm-pyuhn) husband
내년: (nae-nyuhn) next year
내다: (nae-dah) to turn in, to submit
내리다: (nae-ree-dah) to get off, to drop
내일: (nae-eel) tomorrow
냉장고: (naeng-jahng-goh) refridgerator
너무: (nuh-moo) too, very much
노래[하다]: (noh-rae[-hah-dah]) song; to sing
놓다: (noh-tah) to put down, to let go
누구: (noo-goo) who
눈: (noon) eye; snow
늦다: (neut-ttah) to be late

ㄷ

다니다: (dah-nee-dah) to attend regularly, to work for
다르다: (dah-reu-dah) to be different
다리: (dah-ree) bridge, leg
다시: (dah-shee) again
다음: (dah-eum) next
닦다: (dahk-ttah) to wipe
다치다: (dah-chee-dah) to get hurt
단어: (dah-nuh) word, vocabulary
닫다: (daht-ttah) to close
달다: (dahl-dah) to be sweet

달력: (dahl-lyuhk) calendar
대사관: (dae-sah-gwahn) embassy
대중교통: (dae-joong-gyoh-tohng) public transportation
대화: (dae-hwah) conversation
더: (duh) more
덜: (duhl) less
덥다: (duhp-ttah) to be hot
도시: (doh-shee) city
도착(하다): (doh-chahk[-hah-dah]) arrival; to arrive
돈: (dohn) money
돌다: (dohl-dah) to turn, to spin
돕다: (dohp-ttah) to help
동료: (dohng-nyoh) colleague
동생: (dohng-saeng) younger sibling
되다: (dwae-dah) to become, to be available, to work [plans, machines]
뒤: (dwee) behind
듣다: (deut-ttah) to listen, to take [a class]
등산[하다]: (deung-sahn[-hah-dah]) hiking; to hike

ㄸ

따뜻하다: (ttah-tteu-tah-dah) to be warm
딸: (ttahl) daughter
또: (ttoh) again, also
뜻: (tteut) definition, meaning

ㅁ

마시다: (mah-shee-dah) to drink
마음: (mah-eum) heart, mind
막히다: (mah-kee-dah) to be clogged, blocked
만나다: (mahn-nah-dah) to meet
만들다: (mahn-deul-dah) to make

많다: (mahn-tah) to be many, a lot

말[하다]: (mahl[-hah-dah]) language, speech; to talk, speak

맑다: (mahk-ttah) to be clear, sunny

맛없다: (mah-duhp-ttah) to be tasteless

맛있다: (mah-dee-ttah, mah-sheet-ttah) to be tasty, delicious

매일: (mae-eel) everyday

매주: (mae-joo) every week

맵다: (maep-ttah) to be spicy

머리: (muh-ree) head, hair

먹다: (muhk-ttah) to eat

먼저: (muhn-juh) ahead, in advance, before anything else

멀다: (muhl-dah) to be far

며칠: (myuh-cheel) a few days; how many days

면접: (myuhn-juhp) interview

명함: (myuhng-hahm) business card

몇: (myuht) how many [number]

모두: (moh-doo) all

모르다: (moh-reu-dah) to not know

모자: (moh-jah) hat, cap

목마르다: (mohng-mah-reu-dah) to be thirsty

무료: (moo-ryoh) free [of charge]

무슨: (moo-seun) what [kind of]

무엇/뭐: (moo-uht/mwuh) what

문화: (moon-hwah) culture

물: (mool) water

미술관: (mee-sool-gwahn) art gallery

민속촌: (meen-sohk-chohn) folk village

ㅂ

바깥/밖: (bah-kkaht/bahk) outside

바꾸다: (bah-kkoo-dah) to change

바다: (bah-dah) sea, ocean

바쁘다: (bah-ppeu-dah) to be busy

박물관: (bahng-mool-gwahn) museum

반: (bahn) half; class

반말: (bahn-mahl) intimate speech style

반찬: (bahn-chahn) side dishes

받다: (baht-ttah) to receive

발표(하다): (bahl-pyoh[-hah-dah]) presentation; to present

밤: (bahm) night

밥: (bahp) meal, [cooked] rice

방: (bahng) room

방학: (bahng-hahk) vacation [school]

방향: (bahng-hyahng) direction

배고프다: (bae-goh-peu-dah) to be hungry

배달(하다): (bae-dahl[-hah-dah]) delivery; to deliver

배부르다: (bae-boo-reu-dah) to be full

배우다: (bae-oo-dah) to learn

백화점: (bae-kwah-juhm) department store

버스정류장: (buh-sseu-juhng-nyoo-jahng) bus stop

별로: (byuhl-loh) not really

병: (byuhng) illness, sickness

병원: (byuhng-wuhn) hospital, clinic

보내다: (boh-nae-dah) to send

보다: (boh-dah) to see, watch; than

보통: (boh-tohng) usually, normally

보험: (boh-huhm) insurance

봄: (bohm) spring

부르다: (boo-reu-dah) to call out, to sing

부모님: (boo-moh-neem) parents

부엌: (boo-uhk) kitchen

부탁(하다): (boo-tahk[-hah-dah]) request, favor; to ask a favor

불친절(하다): (bool-cheen-juhl[-hah-dah]) unkindness; to be unkind

불편(하다): (bool-pyuhn[-hah-dah]) inconvenience, discomfort; to be inconvenient, uncomfortable

비: (bee) rain

비누: (bee-noo) soap

비싸다: (bee-ssah-dah) to be expensive

비자: (bee-jah) visa

비행기: (bee-haeng-gee) airplane

ㅃ

빨래: (ppahl-lae) laundry

빨리: (ppahl-lee) quickly, hurry, fast

ㅅ

사고: (sah-goh) accident

사과: (sah-gwah) apology, apple

사다: (sah-dah) to buy

사람: (sah-rahm) person

사랑(하다): (sah-rahng[-hah-dah]) love; to love

사무실: (sah-moo-sheel) office

사이: (sah-ee) interval, distance, relationship

사진: (sah-jeen) photo

산: (sahn) mountain

산책(하다): (sahn-chaek[-hah-dah]) walk; to go for a walk

살다: (sahl-dah) to live

상사: (sahng-sah) boss, supervisor

상자: (sahng-jah) box

새: (sae) new, bird

새벽: (sae-byuhk) pre-dawn, dawn, late night

색/색깔: (saek/saek-kkahl) color

생각: (saeng-gahk) thought

생선: (saeng-suhn) fish [eatable]

생일/생신: (saeng-eel/saeng-sheen) birthday

생활: (saeng-hwahl) everyday life

서류: (suh-ryoo) documents

서점: (suh-juhm) bookstore

선물: (suhn-mool) gift

선생님: (suhn-saeng-neem) teacher

설거지: (suhl-guh-jee) dishwashing

성격: (suhng-kkyuhk) personality

성실(하다): (suhng-sheel[-hah-dah]) sincerity; to be hardworking, diligent

성인/어른: (suhng-een/uh-leun) adult

세제: (seh-jeh) detergent

세탁기: (seh-tahk-kkee) laundry machine

소개(하다): (soh-gae[-hah-dah]) introduction; to introduce

소포: (soh-poh) package, parcel

손: (sohn) hand

손님: (sohn-neem) guest

솔직히: (sohl-jjee-kee) honestly

송금(하다): (sohng-geum[-hah-dah]) wire transfer, remittance; to remit

쇼핑[하다]: (shoh-peeng[-hah-dah]) shopping; to shop

수건: (soo-guhn) towel

수업: (soo-uhp) class

수영(하다): (soo-yuhng[-hah-dah]) swimming; to swim

숙소: (sook-ssoh) accommodation

숙제(하다): (sook-jjeh[-hah-dah]) homework; to do homework

숟가락: (soot-kkah-rahk) spoon

술: (sool) alcohol, liquor

쉬다: (shwee-dah) to rest

시간: (shee-gahn) time

시계: (shee-gyeh) clock, watch

시끄럽다: (shee-kkeu-ruhp-ttah) to be noisy

시원하다: (shee-wuhn-hah-dah) to be cool, refreshing

시장: (shee-jahng) market

시차: (shee-chah) time difference, jet lag

시청: (shee-chuhng) city hall

시험: (shee-huhm) test, exam

식당: (sheek-ttahng) restaurant, eatery

식사(하다): (sheek-ssah[-hah-dah]) meal; to have a meal

신고: (sheen-goh) report

신문: (sheen-moon) newspaper

신발: (sheen-bahl) shoes

신분증: (sheen-boon-jjeung) ID card

신용카드: (shee-nyohng-kah-deu) credit card

신호등: (sheen-hoh-deung) traffic light

싫어하다: (shee-ruh-hah-dah) to dislike

심심하다: (sheem-sheem-hah-dah) to be bored

싱겁다: (sheeng-guhp-ttah) to be bland

ㅆ

싸다: (ssah-dah) to be cheap

쌀: (ssahl) rice [uncooked]

쓰다: (sseu-dah) to write, to use, to be bitter

쓰레기: (sseu-reh-gee) trash

씻다: (sseet-ttah) to wash

ㅇ

아내: (ah-nae) wife

아니다: (ah-nee-dah) to not be

아들: (ah-deul) son

아름답다: (ah-reum-dahp-ttah) to be beautiful

아버지/아빠: (ah-buh-jee/ah-ppah) father/dad

아이: (ah-ee) kid, child

아저씨: (ah-juh-ssee) middle aged man

아주: (ah-joo) very

아주머니/아줌마: (ah-joo-muh-nee/ ah-joom-mah) middle aged woman

아직: (ah-jeek) yet, still

아침: (ah-cheem) morning, breakfast

아프다: (ah-peu-dah) to be sick

악수: (ahk-ssoo) handshake

안: (ahn) in, inside; not

안내: (ahn-nae) guidance

앉다: (ahn-ttah) to sit

알다: (ahl-dah) to know

앞: (ahp) front

약: (yahk) medicine

약국: (yahk-kkook) pharmacy

약사: (yahk-ssah) pharmacist

약속: (yahk-ssohk) promise, appointment

얘기/이야기(하다): (yae-gee/ee-yah-gee[-hah-dah]) talk, story; to talk, speak

어디: (uh-dee) where

어떻게: (uh-ttuh-keh) how

어머니/엄마: (uh-muh-nee/uhm-mah) mother/mom

어서: (uh-suh) quickly, hurry, fast

어울리다: (uh-ool-lee-dah) to go well with, match

어제: (uh-jeh) yesterday

언어: (uh-nuh) language

언제: (uhn-jeh) when

얼굴: (uhl-gool) face

얼마: (uhl-mah) how much

없다: (uhp-ttah) to not have, to not exist

여권: (yuh-kkwuhn) passport

여기: (yuh-gee) here

여름: (yuh-reum) summer

여자: (yuh-jah) female

여행(하다): (yuh-haeng[-hah-dah])
trip; to travel

역: (yuhk) station

역사: (yuhk-ssah) history

연락(하다): (yuhl-lahk[-hah-dah])
contact; to get in contact, keep in
touch

연휴: (yuhn-hyoo) consecutive holiday,
long weekend

열다: (yuhl-dah) to open

열쇠/키: (yuhl-sswae/kee) key

열심히: (yuhl-sseem-hee) diligently

영수증: (yuhng-soo-jeung) receipt

영어: (yuhng-uh) English

영화: (yuhng-hwah) movie

영화관: (yuhng-hwah-gwahn) movie
theater

옆: (yuhp) side, next

예매(하다): (yeh-mae[-hah-dah])
ticketing; to purchase in advance

예약(하다): (yeh-yahk[-hah-dah])
reservation; to reserve

예절: (yeh-juhl) etiquette

오늘: (oh-neul) today

오다: (oh-dah) to come

오래: (oh-rae) a long time

오른쪽: (oh-reun-jjohk) right [side]

오전: (oh-juhn) AM

오후: (oh-hoo) PM

올해: (ohl-hae) this year

옷: (oht) clothes

왕복: (wahng-bohk) round trip

왜: (wae) why

외국: (wae-gook) foreign country

외식(하다): (wae-sheek[-hah-dah])
dine-out; to eat out

왼쪽: (waen-jjohk) left [side]

요금: (yoh-geum) fee

요리(하다): (yoh-ree[-hah-dah])
cuisine, cooking; to cook

요즘: (yoh-jeum) lately, these days

우편번호: (oo-pyuhn-buhn-hoh)
zip code

운동(하다): (oon-dohng[-hah-dah])
workout; to work out, do sport

운전면허증: (oon-juhn-myuhn-huh-
jjeung) driver's license

운전(하다): (oon-juhn[-hah-dah])
drive; to drive

유학: (yoo-hahk) studying abroad

은행: (eun-haeng) bank

음료수: (eum-nyoh-soo) beverage,
drink (non-alcohol)

음식: (eum-sheek) food

음악: (eu-mahk) music

응급실: (eung-geup-sseel)
emergency room

의사: (eui-sah) doctor

의자: (eui-jah) chair

이거/이것: (ee-guh/ee-guht) this thing,
this one

이력서: (ee-lyuhk-ssuh) resume

이름/성함: (ee-reum/suhng-
hahm) name

이미: (ee-mee) already

이번: (ee-buhn) this time

이불: (ee-bool) blanket

이쪽: (ee-jjohk) this way

인기: (een-kkee) popularity

인사(하다): (een-sah[-hah-dah])
greeting; to greet

일어나다: (ee-ruh-nah-dah)
to get up

일찍: (eel-jjeek) early

일(하다): (eel[-hah-dah]) work;
to work

일회용: (eel-hwae-yohng) disposable

읽다: (eek-ttah) to read

입구: (eep-kkoo) entrance

있다: (eet-ttah) to have, to exist

ㅈ

자녀: (jah-nyuh) children, son and daughter, offspring

자다: (jah-dah) to sleep

자동차: (jah-dohng-chah) automobile, car

자리: (jah-ree) seat

자전거: (jah-juhn-guh) bicycle

자주: (jah-joo) frequently

작년: (jahng-nyuhn) last year

작다: (jahk-ttah) to be small

잘: (jahl) well

잠깐/잠시: (jahm-kkahn/jahm-shee) for a moment, short while

재미있다: (jae-mee-eet-ttah) to be fun, interesting

저거/저것: (juh-guh/juh-guht) that thing over there

저기: (juh-gee) over there

저녁: (juh-nyuhk) evening, dinner

적다: (juhk-ttah) to be few/little, to write down

전통: (juhn-tohng) tradition

전화번호: (juhn-hwah-buhn-hoh) phone number

전화(하다): (juhn-hwah[-hah-dah]) phone call; to make a call

점심: (juhm-sheem) lunch

점원: (juh-mwuhn) clerk

젓가락: (juht-kkah-rahk) chopsticks

정말: (juhng-mahl) truth, really

정보: (juhng-boh) information

제일: (jeh-eel) most

ㅊ

친구: (cheen-goo) friend

친절(하다): (cheen-juhl[-hah-dah]) kindness; to be kind

친척: (cheen-chuhk) relative

침대: (cheem-dae) bed

칫솔: (cheet-ssohl) toothbrush

ㅋ

크다: (keu-dah) to be big

ㅌ

타다: (tah-dah) to ride, get on

택배: (taek-ppae) door-to-door delivery

통역: (tohng-yuhk) interpretation

통화(하다): (tohng-hwah[-hah-dah]) phone conversation; to talk on the phone

ㅍ

편도: (pyuhn-doh) one way

편의점: (pyuh-nee-juhm) convenience store

편하다: (pyuhn-hah-dah) to be convenient, comfortable

평일: (pyuhng-eel) weekdays

포장(하다): (poh-jahng[-hah-dah]) packing; to wrap, pack

표/티켓: (pyoh/tee-keht) ticket

피곤(하다): (pee-gohn[-hah-dah]) fatigue; to be tired

필요(하다): (pee-ryoh[-hah-dah]) necessity; to be needed, necessary

ㅎ

하다: (hah-dah) to do

하루: (hah-roo) one day

학교: (hahk-kkyoh) school

학기: (hahk-kkee) term, semester

학년: (hahng-nyuhn) school year, grade

학생: (hahk-ssaeng) student

학원: (hah-gwuhn) cram school

한국말/한국어: (hahn-goong-mahl/hahn-goo-guh) Korean language

할머니: (hahl-muh-nee) grandmother

할아버지: (hah-rah-buh-jee) grandfather

할인: (hah-reen) discount

항공권: (hahng-gohng-kkwuhn) flight ticket

항상: (hahng-sahng) always

해외: (hae-wae) overseas

핸드폰/휴대폰: (haen-deu-pohn/hyoo-dae-pohn) cell phone

행복[하다]: (haeng-bohk[-hah-dah]) happiness; to be happy

현금: (hyuhn-geum) cash

형제: (hyuhng-jeh) siblings

혹시: (hohk-ssee) by any chance

혼자: (hohn-jah) alone

화장실: (hwah-jahng-sheel) restroom

화장지: (hwah-jahng-jee) tissue paper, toilet paper

화장품: (hwah-jahng-poom) cosmetics

확인[하다]: (hwah-geen[-hah-dah]) checking, confirmation; to check, confirm

환불[하다]: (hwahn-bool[-hah-dah]) refund; to refund

환율: (hwah-nyool) exchange rate

환전[하다]: (hwahn-juhn[-hah-dah]) currency exchange; to exchange money

회사: (hwae-sah) company

회식: (hwae-sheek) company get-together

회의(하다): (hwae-ee[-hah-dah]) meeting; to have a meeting

휴가: (hyoo-gah) vacation

휴게실: (hyoo-geh-sheel) lounge

휴지통: (hyoo-jee-tohng) trash can

흐리다: (heu-ree-dah) to be cloudy, vague

힘들다: (heem-deul-dah) to be tiring, to have a hard time

English to Korean Mini-Dictionary

A

accident: 사고 (sah-goh)

accommodation: 숙소 (sook-ssoh)

adult: 성인/어른 (suhng-een/uh-reun)

again, also: 또 (ttoh)

age: 나이 (nah-ee)

airplane: 비행기 (bee-haeng-gee)

airport: 공항 (gohng-hahng)

alcohol: 술 (sool)

all: 모두 (moh-doo)

alone: 혼자 (hohn-jah)

already: 이미 (ee-mee)

alright, be (v): 괜찮다 (gwaen-chahn-tah)

always: 항상 (hahng-sahng)

AM: 오전 (oh-juhn)

ambulance: 구급차 (goo-geup-chah)

and: 그리고 (geu-ree-goh)

apology: 사과 (sah-gwah)

arrive (v): 도착하다 (doh-chah-kah-dah)

art gallery: 미술관 (mee-sool-gwahn)

ask a favor (v): 부탁하다 (boo-tah-kah-dah)

attend regularly (v): 다니다 (dah-nee-dah)

automobile: 자동차 (jah-dohng-chah)

autumn: 가을 (gah-eul)

B

bad (v): 나쁘다 (nah-ppeu-dah)

bag: 가방 (gah-bahng)

bank: 은행 (eun-haeng)

beautiful, be (v): 아름답다 (ah-reum-dahp-ttah)

become available (v): 되다 (dwae-dah)

bed: 침대 (cheem-dae)

behind: 뒤 (dwee)

beverage (non-alcohol): 음료수 (eum-nyoh-soo)

bicycle: 자전거 (jah-juhn-guh)

big, be (v): 크다 (keu-dah)

birthday: 생일/생신 (saeng-eel/saeng-sheen)

bland, be (v): 싱겁다 (sheeng-guhp-ttah)

blanket: 이불 (ee-bool)

blocked, be (v): 막히다 (mah-kee-dah)

bookstore: 서점 (suh-juhm)

bored, be (v): 심심하다 (sheem-sheem-hah-dah)

boss: 상사 (sahng-sah)

bowl: 그릇 (geu-reut)

box: 상자 (sahng-jah)

breakfast: 아침 (ah-cheem)

building: 건물 (guhn-mool)

bus stop: 버스정류장 (buh-sseu-juhng-nyoo-jahng)

business card: 명함 (myuhng-hahm)

busy, be (v): 바쁘다 (bah-ppeu-dah)

but: 그런데/근데 (geu-ruhn-deh/geun-deh)

buy (v): 사다 (sah-dah)

by any chance: 혹시 (hohk-ssee)

C

calendar: 달력 (dahl-lyuhk)

call out (v): 부르다 (boo-reu-dah)

cash: 현금 (hyuhn-geum)

caught, be (v): 걸리다 (guhl-lee-dah)

cell phone: 핸드폰/휴대폰 (haen-deu-pohn/hyoo-dae-pohn)

chair: 의자 (eui-jah)

change (money): 거스름돈 (guh-seu-reum-ttohn)

change (v): 바꾸다 (bah-kkoo-dah)

cheap, be (v): 싸다 (ssah-dah)

check (v): 확인하다 (hwah-geen-hah-dah)

chopsticks: 젓가락 (juht-kkah-rahk)

city: 도시 (doh-shee)

city hall: 시청 (shee-chuhng)

class: 수업 (soo-uhp)

clean, be (v): 깨끗하다 (kkae-kkeu-tah-dah)

clear, be (v): 맑다 (mahk-ttah)

clerk: 점원 (juh-mwuhn)

clock: 시계 (shee-gyeh)

close (v): 닫다 (daht-ttah)

close, be (v): 가깝다 (gah-kkahp-ttah)

clothes: 옷 (oht)

cloudy, be (v): 흐리다 (heu-ree-dah)

cold (illness): 감기 (gahm-gee)

colleague: 동료 (dohng-nyoh)

color: 색/색깔 (saek/saek-kkahl)

come (v): 오다 (oh-dah)

comfortable, be (v): 편하다 (pyuhn-hah-dah)

company: 회사 (hwae-sah)

company get-together: 회식 (hwae-sheek)

contact (v): 연락하다 (yuhl-lah-kah-dah)

convenience store: 편의점 (pyuh-nee-juhm)

convenient, be (v): 편하다 (pyuhn-hah-dah)

conversation: 대화 (dae-hwah)

cook (v): 요리하다 (yoh-ree-hah-dah)

cool, be (v): 시원하다 (shee-wuhn-hah-dah)

cosmetics: 화장품 (hwah-jahng-poom)

country: 나라 (nah-rah)

cram school: 학원 (hah-gwuhn)

credit card: 신용카드 (shee-nyohng-kah-deu)

culture: 문화 (moon-hwah)

customer: 고객 (goh-gaek)

cut (v): 깎다 (kkah-ttah)

D

date: 날짜 (nahl-jjah)

daughter: 딸 (ttahl)

dawn: 새벽 (sae-byuhk)

delicious, be (v): 맛있다 (mah-dee-ttah mah-sheet-ttah)

deliver (v): 배달하다 (bae-dahl-hah-dah)

department store: 백화점 (bae-kwah-juhm)

detergent: 세제 (seh-jeh)

different, be (v): 다르다 (dah-reu-dah)

diligent, be (v): 성실하다 (suhng-sheel-hah-dah)

diligently: 열심히 (yuhl-sseem-hee)

dine out (v): 외식하다 (wae-shee-kah-dah)

dinner: 저녁 (juh-nyuhk)

direction: 방향 (bahng-hyahng)

discount: 할인 (hah-reen)

dishwashing: 설거지 (suhl-guh-jee)

dislike (v): 싫어하다 (shee-ruh-hah-dah)

disposable: 일회용 (eel-hwae-yohng)

distance: 사이 (sah-ee)

do (v): 하다 (hah-dah)

do homework (v): 숙제하다 (sook-jjeh-hah-dah)

doctor: 의사 (eui-sah)

documents: 서류 (suh- ryoo)

dog: 개 (gae)

door-to-door delivery: 택배 (taek-ppae)

drink (v): 마시다 (mah-shee-dah)

drive (v): 운전하다 (oon-juhn-hah-dah)

driver: 기사 (gee-sah)

driver's license: 운전면허증 (oon-juhn-myuhn-huh-jjeung)

E

early: 일찍 (eel-jjeek)

eat (v): 먹다 (muhk-ttah)

education: 교육 (gyoh-yook)

egg: 계란/달걀 (gyeh-rahn/dahl-gyahl)

embassy: 대사관 (dae-sah-gwahn)

emergency room: 응급실 (eung-geup-sseel)

end (v): 끝나다 (kkeun-nah-dah)

English: 영어 (yuhng-uh)

entrance: 입구 (eep-kkoo)

etiquette: 예절 (yeh-juhl)

evening: 저녁 (juh-nyuhk)

every week: 매주 (mae-joo)

everyday: 날마다/매일 (nahl-mah-dah/ mae-eel)

everyday life: 생활 (saeng-hwahl)

exchange (v): 교환하다
(gyoh-hwahn-hah-dah)

exchange money (v): 환전하다
(hwahn-juhn-hah-dah)

exchange rate: 환율 (hwah-nyool)

exist (for honorific person) (v): 계시다
(gyeh-shee-dah)

exist (v): 있다 (eet-ttah)

expensive, be (v): 비싸다
(bee-ssah-dah)

experience: 경험 (gyuhng-huhm)

express bus: 고속버스
(goh-sohk-buh-sseu)

eye: 눈 (noon)

F

face: 얼굴 (uhl-gool)

family: 가족 (gah-johk)

far, be (v): 멀다 (muhl-dah)

father/dad: 아버지/아빠 (ah-buh-jee/
ah-ppah)

fee: 요금 (yoh-geum)

female: 여자 (yuh-jah)

few days (a): 며칠 (myuh-cheel)

few, be (v): 적다 (juhk-ttah)

fish (edible): 생선 (saeng-suhn)

fix (v): 고치다 (goh-chee-dah)

flight ticket: 항공권
(hahng-gohng-kkwuhn)

folk village: 민속촌
(meen-sohk-chohn)

food: 음식 (eum-sheek)

foreign country: 외국 (wae-gook)

free (of charge): 무료 (moo-ryoh)

frequently: 자주 (jah-joo)

friend: 친구 (cheen-goo)

front: 앞 (ahp)

fruit: 과일 (gwah-eel)

full, be (v): 배부르다
(bae-boo-reu-dah)

fun, be (v): 재미있다
(jae-mee-eet-ttah)

furniture: 가구 (gah-goo)

G

get hurt (v): 다치다 (dah-chee-dah)

get off (v): 내리다 (nae-ree-dah)

get up (v): 일어나다 (ee-ruh-nah-dah)

gift: 선물 (suhn-mool)

go (v): 가다 (gah-dah)

go for a walk (v): 산책하다
(sahn-chae-kah-dah)

go well with (v): 어울리다
(uh-ool-lee-dah)

grandfather: 할아버지
(hah-rah-buh-jee)

grandmother: 할머니 (hahl-muh-nee)

greet (v): 인사하다
(een-sah-hah-dah)

guest: 손님 (sohn-neem)

guidance: 안내 (ahn-nae)

H

half: 반 (bahn)

hand: 손 (sohn)

handshake: 악수 (ahk-ssoo)

happy, be (v): 행복하다
(haeng-boo-kah-dah)

hat: 모자 (moh-jah)

have a meal (v): 식사하다
(sheek-ssah-hah-dah)

have a meeting (v): 회의하다
(hwae-ee-hah-dah)

head: 머리 (muh-ree)

health: 건강 (guhn-gahng)

heart: 마음 (mah-eum)

help (v): 돕다 (dohp-ttah)

here: 여기 (yuh-gee)

hike (v): 등산하다
(deung-sahn-hah-dah)

history: 역사 (yuhk-ssah)

holiday: 공휴일 (gohn-hyoo-eel)

hometown: 고향 (goh-hyahng)

honestly: 솔직히 (sohl-jjee-kee)

hospital: 병원 (byuhng-wuhn)

hot, be (v): 덥다 (duhp-ttah)

how: 어떻게 (uh-ttuh-keh)

how many [number]: 몇 (myuht)

how much: 얼마 (uhl-mah)

hungry, be (v): 배고프다
(bae-goh-peu-dah)

hurry, fast: 어서 (uh-suh)

husband: 남편 (nahm-pyuhn)

I

ID card: 신분증 (sheen-boon-jjeung)

if so: 그럼 (geu-ruhm)

illness: 병 (byuhng)

in advance: 먼저 (muhn-juh)

inconvenient, be (v): 불편하다
(bool-pyuhn-hah-dah)

information: 정보 (juhng-boh)

inside: 안 (ahn)

insurance: 보험 (boh-huhm)

interest: 관심 (gwahn-sheem)

international: 국제 (gook-jjeh)

interview: 면접 (myuhn-juhp)

intimate speech style: 반말
(bahn-mahl)

introduce (v): 소개하다
(soh-gae-hah-dah)

J

just: 그냥 (geu-nyahng)

K

key: 열쇠/키 (yuhl-sswae/kee)

kid, child: 아이/어린이 (ah-ee/
uh-ree-nee)

kind, be (v): 친절하다
(cheen-juhl-hah-dah)

kitchen: 부엌 (boo-uhk)

know (v): 알다 (ahl-dah)

Korean language: 한국말/한국어
(hahn-goong-mahl/hahn-goo-guh)

L

language: 언어 (uh-nuh)

last year: 작년 (jahng-nyuhn)

late, be (v): 늦다 (neut-ttah)

later: 나중에 (nah-joong-eh)

laundry: 빨래 (ppahl-lae)

laundry machine: 세탁기
(seh-tahk-kkee)

learn (v): 배우다 (bae-oo-dah)

left (side): 왼쪽 (waen-jjohk)

leg: 다리 (dah-ree)

less: 덜 (duhl)

listen (v): 듣다 (deut-ttah)

live (v): 살다 (sahl-dah)

long time (a): 오래 (oh-rae)

long weekend: 연휴 (yuhn-hyoo)

lounge: 휴게실 (hyoo-geh-sheel)

love (v): 사랑하다
(sah-rahng-hah-dah)

lunch: 점심 (juhm-sheem)

M

make: 만들다 (mahn-deul-dah)

make a contract (v): 계약하다 (gyeh-yah-hah-dah)

make a phone call (v): 전화하다 (juhn-hwah-hah-dah)

many, be (v): 많다 (mahn-tah)

market: 시장 (shee-jahng)

meal: 밥 (bahp)

meaning: 뜻 (tteut)

meat: 고기 (goh-gee)

medicine: 약 (yahk)

meet: 만나다 (mahn-nah-dah)

middle-aged man: 아저씨 (ah-juh-ssee)

middle-aged woman: 아주머니/아줌마 (ah-joo-muh-nee/ah-joom-mah)

moment (for a): 잠깐/잠시 (jahm-kkahn/jahm-shee)

money: 돈 (dohn)

more: 더 (duh)

morning: 아침 (ah-cheem)

most: 제일 (jeh-eel)

mother/mom: 어머니/엄마 (uh-muh-nee/uhm-mah)

mountain: 산 (sahn)

movie: 영화 (yuhng-hwah)

movie theater: 영화관 (yuhng-hwah-gwahn)

museum: 박물관 (bahng-mool-gwahn)

music: 음악 (eu-mahk)

N

name: 이름/성함 (ee-reum/suhng-hahm)

nationality: 국적 (gook-jjuhk)

nearby: 근처 (geun-chuh)

necessary, be (v): 필요하다 (pee-ryoh-hah-dah)

new: 새 (sae)

newspaper: 신문 (sheen-moon)

next: 다음 (dah-eum)

next year: 내년 (nae-nyuhn)

night: 밤 (bahm)

noisy, be (v): 시끄럽다 (shee-kkeu-ruhp-ttah)

not: 안 (ahn)

not be (v): 아니다 (ah-nee-dah)

not exist (v): 없다 (uhp-ttah)

not know (v): 모르다 (moh-reu-dah)

not really: 별로 (byuhl-loh)

O

office: 사무실 (sah-moo-sheel)

one day: 하루 (hah-roo)

one way: 편도 (pyuhn-doh)

open (v): 열다 (yuhl-dah)

opportunity: 기회 (gee-hwae)

out of order, be (v): 고장나다 (goh-jahng-nah-dah)

outside: 바깥/밖 (bah-kkaht/bahk)

over there: 거기 (guh-gee)

over there: 저기 (juh-gee)

overseas: 해외 (hae-wae)

P

package, parcel: 소포 (soh-poh)

parents: 부모님 (boo-moh-neem)

park: 공원 (gohng-wuhn)

passport: 여권 (yuh-kkwuhn)

pay (v): 결제하다 (gyuhl-jjeh-hah-dah)

pay a bill (v): 계산하다 (gyeh-sahn-hah-dah)

person: 사람 (sah-rahm)

personality: 성격 (suhng-kkyuhk)

pharmacist: 약사 (yahk-ssah)

pharmacy: 약국 (yahk-kkook)

phone number: 전화번호
(juhn-hwah-buhn-hoh)

photo: 사진 (sah-jeen)

place: 곳 (goht)

plan: 계획 (gyeh-hwaek)

PM: 오후 (oh-hoo)

police station: 경찰서
(gyuhng-chahl-ssuh)

popularity: 인기 (een-kkee)

present (v): 발표하다
(bahl-pyoh-hah-dah)

price: 가격/값 (gah-gyuhk/gahp)

promise: 약속 (yahk-ssohk)

public transportation: 대중교통
(dae-joong-gyoh-tohng)

puppy: 강아지 (gahng-ah-jee)

purchase in advance (v): 예매하다
(yeh-mae-hah-dah)

put down (v): 놓다 (noh-tah)

Q

quickly: 빨리 (ppahl-lee)

R

read (v): 읽다 (eek-ttah)

really: 정말 (juhng-mahl)

receipt: 영수증 (yuhng-soo-jeung)

receive (v): 받다 (baht-ttah)

refrigerator: 냉장고
(naeng-jahng-goh)

refund (v): 환불하다
(hwahn-bool-hah-dah)

relative: 친척 (cheen-chuhk)

remit (v): 송금하다
(sohng-geum-hah-dah)

report: 신고 (sheen-goh)

reserve (v): 예약하다
(yeh-yah-kah-dah)

rest: 쉬다 (shee-dah)

restaurant: 식당 (sheek-ttahng)

restroom: 화장실 (hwah-jahng-sheel)

resume: 이력서 (ee-ryuhk-ssuh)

rice (uncooked): 쌀 (ssahl)

ride (v): 타다 (tah-dah)

right (side): 오른쪽 (oh-reun-jjohk)

road: 길 (geel)

room: 방 (bahng)

round trip: 왕복 (wahng-bohk)

S

same, be the (v): 같다 (gaht-ttah)

scenery: 경치 (gyuhng-chee)

school: 학교 (hahk-kkyoh)

school year: 학년 (hahng-nyuhn)

sea: 바다 (bah-dah)

season: 계절 (gyeh-juhl)

seat: 자리 (jah-ree)

see (v): 보다 (boh-dah)

semester: 학기 (hahk-kkee)

send (v): 보내다 (boh-nae-dah)

shoes: 신발 (sheen-bahl)

shop (v): 쇼핑하다
(shyoh-peeng-hah-dah)

siblings: 형제 (hyuhng-jeh)

sick, be (v): 아프다 (ah-peu-dah)

side: 옆 (yuhp)

side dishes: 반찬 (bahn-chahn)

sightsee (v): 구경하다
(goo-gyuhng-hah-dah)

sing (v): 노래하다
(noh-rae-hah-dah)

singer: 가수 (gah-soo)

sit (v): 앉다 (ahn-ttah)

sleep (v): 자다 (jah-dah)

small, be (v): 작다 (jahk-ttah)

snow: 눈 (noon)

soap: 비누 (bee-noo)

soldier: 군인 (goo-neen)

sometimes: 가끔 (gah-kkeum)

son: 아들 (ah-deul)

son and daughter: 자녀 (jah-nyuh)

soon: 곧 (goht)

soup: 국 (gook)

souvenir: 기념품 (gee-nyuhm-poom)

spicy, be (v): 맵다 (maep-ttah)

spoon: 숟가락 (soot-kkah-lahk)

spring: 봄 (bohm)

station: 역 (yuhk)

store: 가게 (gah-geh)

student: 학생 (hahk-ssaeng)

study (v): 공부하다
   (gohng-boo-hah-dah)

studying abroad: 유학 (yoo-hahk)

suddenly: 갑자기 (gahp-jjah-gee)

summer: 여름 (yuh-reum)

surely: 꼭 (kkohk)

sweet, be (v): 달다 (dahl-dah)

swim (v): 수영하다
   (soo-yuhng-hah-dah)

T

take time (v): 걸리다 (guhl-lee-dah)

talk (v): 말(하다) (mahl(-hah-dah))

talk (v): 얘기/이야기하다 (yae-gee/
   ee-yah-gee-hah-dah)

talk on the phone (v): 통화하다
   (tohng-hwah-hah-dah)

tasteless, be (v): 맛없다
   (mah-duhp-ttah)

teach (v): 가르치다 (gah-reu-chee-dah)

teacher: 선생님 (suhn-saeng-neem)

test: 시험 (shee-huhm)

than: 보다 (boh-dah)

that thing: 그거/그것 (geu-guh/
   geu-guht)

that thing over there: 저거/저것 (juh-
   guh/juh-guht)

the other side: 건너편
   (guhn-nuh-pyuhn)

theater: 극장 (geuk-jjahng)

therefore: 그래서 (geu-rae-suh)

these days: 요즘 (yoh-jeum)

thing: 것/거 (guht/guh)

thirsty, be (v): 목마르다
   (mohng-mah-reu-dah)

this thing: 이거/이것 (ee-guh/
   ee-guht)

this time: 이번 (ee-buhn)

this way: 이쪽 (ee-jjohk)

this year: 올해 (ohl-hae)

thought: 생각 (saeng-gahk)

ticket: 표/티켓 (pyoh/tee-keht) ticket

time: 시간 (shee-gahn)

time difference: 시차 (shee-chah)

tired, be (v): 피곤하다
   (pee-gohn-hah-dah)

tiring, be (v): 힘들다 (heem-deul-dah)

tissue: 화장지 (hwah-jahng-jee)

today: 오늘 (oh-neul)

together: 같이 (gah-chee)

tomorrow: 내일 (nae-eel)

toothbrush: 칫솔 (cheet-ssohl)

tour (v): 관광하다
   (gwahn-ghwang-hah-dah)

towel: 수건 (soo-guhn)

tradition: 전통 (juhn-tohng)

traffic light: 신호등
   (sheen-hoh-deung)

traffic, transportation: 교통 (gyoh-tohng)

train: 기차 (gee-chah)

transfer (vehicle) (v): 갈아타다 (gah-rah-tah-dah)

translation: 통역 (tohng-yuhk)

trash: 쓰레기 (sseu-reh-gee)

trash can: 휴지통 (hyoo-jee-tohng)

travel (v): 여행하다 (yuh-haeng-hah-dah)

turn (v): 돌다 (dohl-dah)

turn in (v): 내다 (nae-dah)

U

uncomfortable, be (v): 불편하다 (bool-pyuhn-hah-dah)

unkind, be (v): 불친절하다 (bool-cheen-juhn-hah-dah)

use (v): 쓰다 (sseu-dah)

usually: 보통 (boh-tohng)

V

vacation: 휴가 (hyoo-gah)

vacation (school): 방학 (bahng-hahk)

very: 너무 (nuh-moo)

very: 아주 (ah-joo)

visa: 비자 (bee-jah)

vocabulary: 단어 (dah-nuh)

W

wait (v): 기다리다 (gee-dah-ree-dah)

walk (v): 걷다 (guht-ttah)

warm, be (v): 따뜻하다 (ttah-tteu-tah-dah)

wash (v): 씻다 (sseet-ttah)

water: 물 (mool)

weather: 날씨 (nahl-ssee)

wedding ceremony: 결혼식 (gyuhl-hohn-sheek)

weekdays: 평일 (pyuhng-eel)

well: 잘 (jahl)

what: 무엇/뭐 (moo-uht/mwuh)

what (kind of) [noun]: 무슨 (moo-seun)

when: 언제 (uhn-jeh)

where: 어디 (uh-dee)

who: 누구 (noo-goo)

why: 왜 (wae)

wife: 아내 (ah-nae)

winter: 겨울 (gyuh-ool)

wipe (v): 닦다 (dahk-ttah)

work (v): 일하다 (eel-hah-dah)

work out (v): 운동하다 (oon-dohng-hah-dah)

worry: 걱정 (guhk-jjuhng)

wrap (v): 포장하다 (poh-jahng-hah-dah)

write (v): 쓰다 (sseu-dah)

write down (v): 적다 (juhk-ttah)

Y-Z

yesterday: 어제 (uh-jeh)

yet: 아직 (ah-jeek)

younger sibling: 동생 (dohng-saeng)

zip code: 우편번호 (oo-pyuhn-buhn-hoh)

Appendix C

Answer Key

Chapter 2:

Activity A: 1. 예 2. 쁜 3. 양 4. 말 5. 을 6. 사 7. 야 8. 돼 9. 요

Activity B: 예 쁜 양 말 을 사 야 돼 요.

Activity C: 1. internet   2. hamburger   3. coffee   4. email
5. camera   6. Starbucks   7. computer   8. Mexico
9. television   10. drama

Chapter 3:

Activity A: (Add a question mark and raise the intonation when speaking the sentence.)

Activity B: 1. 으세요   2. 세요   3. 세요   4. 세요

Activity C: 1. 뭐 먹어?   2. 어디 가?

Chapter 4: 1. g   2. f   3. e   4. h   5. c   6. b   7. a   8. i   9. d

Chapter 5: 1. c   2. e   3. d   4. b   5. a

Chapter 6: 1. e   2. d   3. c   4. a   5. b

Chapter 7: 1. f   2. b   3. c   4. a   5. d   6. e

Chapter 8: 1. 16,100 won   2. 5,610 won   3. 1,580 won   4. 21,500 won
5. 7,250 won

Chapter 9:

Activity A: 2, 4.

Activity B: 1. Chopsticks   2. Soup   3. Fish   4. Rice
           5. Spoon   6. Stew   7. Side dish

Chapter 10: 1. d   2. c   3. a   4. f   5. e   6. b   7. g

Chapter 11: 1. c   2. f   3. d   4. e   5. b   6. a   7. h   8. g

Chapter 12:

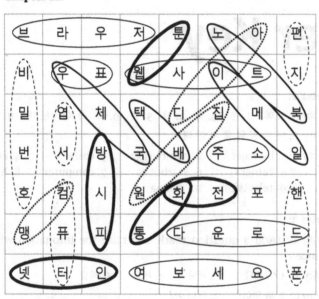

Chapter 13:

Activity A: 1. e   2. a   3. f   4. g   5. b   6. c   7. d   8. j   9. h   10. i
Activity B: 1. e   2. d   3. c   4. b   5. a

Chapter 14:

Answers vary. These are possible answers.

1. (1) 도봉산 (*Mt. Dobong*)   (2) 등산 (*hiking*)

2. (1) 이태원 (*Itaewon*)   (2) 점심 (*lunch*)

3. (1) 동대문시장 (*Dongdaemun market*)   (2) 쇼핑 (*shopping*)

4. (1) 박물관 (*museum*)   (2) 구경 (*sightseeing*)

5. (1) 한강 *(Han River)*   (2) 자전거 타기 *(biking)*

6. (1) 홍대 *(Hongdae/Hongik Univ. street)*   (2) 클럽 *(club)*

Chapter 15: 1. b 2. c   3. a 4. e 5. d

Chapter 16: 1. 지하철 (f)   2. 고속버스 (a)   3. 택시 (e)   4. 자전거 (g)
            5. 비행기 (d) 6. 기차 (c)   7. 오토바이 (b)

Chapter 17: 1. 건너편   2. 사이   3. 옆   4. 뒤   5. 안

Chapter 18: 1. ear: 귀   2. hand: 손   3. eye: 눈   4. foot: 발

Index

About the Authors

EunYoung Won, a Teaching Professor of Korean at the University of Washington, has over twenty years of teaching experience, including at Harvard and Columbia University. She brings Korean language and culture to life in the classroom, helping students reach their full potential and cultivate a passion for world languages and cultures. Beyond teaching, she's involved in national-level projects and workshops, serving on committees for distinguished professional awards and student scholarships. With her dedication to education and linguistic expertise, EunYoung enjoys making meaningful impacts both inside and outside the classroom

Jeongyi Lee, PhD, has taught Korean language and culture for over twenty years, focusing directly and indirectly on extending the foreign language paradigms. She is currently a Professor at Kennesaw State University, where she strives to raise global awareness and understanding through teaching and research. Within the purview of second language acquisition, all her research interests are part of the larger enterprise of discovering the cultural and linguistic aspects of Korean. Dr. Lee is the recipient of Kennesaw State University's 2024 Distinguished International Achievement Award.

Dedication

To our daughters.

Authors' Acknowledgments

We sincerely express our gratitude to the editorial team — Lindsay Berg, Tim Gallan, Kelly Henthorne, and Kristie Pyles — for their patience and dedication to the *Korean For Dummies* project. Special thanks to Hannah Hertzog, Jeongha Park, Maree Suhalim, Liahn, and Lijin Yoon for sharing their invaluable insights and feedback throughout this process. We are also grateful to our technical reviewer, Dr. Chan Young Park, and to Professors Zev Handel and Amy Ohta for their review and feedback on the Hangeul chapter. Our appreciation extends to the voice production team — Daeun Lee, Inchan Hwang, Sungjin Park, Hosup Won, and Vivianna Oh — and to the Department of Asian Languages & Literature at the University of Washington and the Department of World Languages & Cultures at Kennesaw State University Finally, we extend our heartfelt thanks to everyone who supported us in various ways; your prayers and encouragement have been invaluable.

Publisher's Acknowledgments

Executive Editor: Lindsay Berg
Senior Managing Editor: Kristie Pyles
Development Editor: Tim Gallan
Copy Editor: Kelly Henthorne
Technical Editor: Dr. Chan Young Park

Production Editor: Saikarthick Kumarasamy
Cover Image: © TRAVEL TAKE PHOTOS/ Shutterstock

Take dummies with you everywhere you go!

Whether you are excited about e-books, want more from the web, must have your mobile apps, or are swept up in social media, dummies makes everything easier.

Find us online!

dummies.com

dummies
A Wiley Brand

Leverage the power

Dummies is the global leader in the reference category and one of the most trusted and highly regarded brands in the world. No longer just focused on books, customers now have access to the dummies content they need in the format they want. Together we'll craft a solution that engages your customers, stands out from the competition, and helps you meet your goals.

Advertising & Sponsorships

Connect with an engaged audience on a powerful multimedia site, and position your message alongside expert how-to content. Dummies.com is a one-stop shop for free, online information and know-how curated by a team of experts.

- Targeted ads
- Video
- Email Marketing
- Microsites
- Sweepstakes sponsorship

20 MILLION PAGE VIEWS EVERY SINGLE MONTH

15 MILLION UNIQUE VISITORS PER MONTH

43% OF ALL VISITORS ACCESS THE SITE VIA THEIR MOBILE DEVICES

700,000 NEWSLETTER SUBSCRIPTIONS TO THE INBOXES OF

300,000 UNIQUE INDIVIDUALS EVERY WEEK

PERSONAL ENRICHMENT

9781119187790
USA $26.00
CAN $31.99
UK £19.99

9781119179030
USA $21.99
CAN $25.99
UK £16.99

9781119293354
USA $24.99
CAN $29.99
UK £17.99

9781119293347
USA $22.99
CAN $27.99
UK £16.99

9781119310068
USA $22.99
CAN $27.99
UK £16.99

9781119235606
USA $24.99
CAN $29.99
UK £17.99

9781119251163
USA $24.99
CAN $29.99
UK £17.99

9781119235491
USA $26.99
CAN $31.99
UK £19.99

9781119279952
USA $24.99
CAN $29.99
UK £17.99

9781119283133
USA $24.99
CAN $29.99
UK £17.99

9781119287117
USA $24.99
CAN $29.99
UK £16.99

9781119130246
USA $22.99
CAN $27.99
UK £16.99

PROFESSIONAL DEVELOPMENT

9781119311041
USA $24.99
CAN $29.99
UK £17.99

9781119255796
USA $39.99
CAN $47.99
UK £27.99

9781119293439
USA $26.99
CAN $31.99
UK £19.99

9781119281467
USA $26.99
CAN $31.99
UK £19.99

9781119280651
USA $29.99
CAN $35.99
UK £21.99

9781119251132
USA $24.99
CAN $29.99
UK £17.99

9781119310563
USA $34.00
CAN $41.99
UK £24.99

9781119181705
USA $29.99
CAN $35.99
UK £21.99

9781119263593
USA $26.99
CAN $31.99
UK £19.99

9781119257769
USA $29.99
CAN $35.99
UK £21.99

9781119293477
USA $26.99
CAN $31.99
UK £19.99

9781119265313
USA $24.99
CAN $29.99
UK £17.99

9781119239314
USA $29.99
CAN $35.99
UK £21.99

9781119293323
USA $29.99
CAN $35.99
UK £21.99

Learning Made Easy

ACADEMIC

9781119293576
USA $19.99
CAN $23.99
UK £15.99

9781119293637
USA $19.99
CAN $23.99
UK £15.99

9781119293491
USA $19.99
CAN $23.99
UK £15.99

9781119293460
USA $19.99
CAN $23.99
UK £15.99

9781119293590
USA $19.99
CAN $23.99
UK £15.99

9781119215844
USA $26.99
CAN $31.99
UK £19.99

9781119293378
USA $22.99
CAN $27.99
UK £16.99

9781119293521
USA $19.99
CAN $23.99
UK £15.99

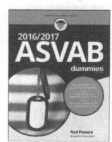

9781119239178
USA $18.99
CAN $22.99
UK £14.99

9781119263883
USA $26.99
CAN $31.99
UK £19.99

Available Everywhere Books Are Sold

Small books for big imaginations